RUSSIAN POLITICS IN TRANSITION

In the day of prosperity be joyful, but in the day of adversity consider...

Ecclesiastes.

Russian Politics in Transition

Institutional Conflict in a Nascent Democracy

NIKOLAI BIRYUKOV
and
VICTOR SERGEYEV

Routledge
Taylor & Francis Group

LONDON AND NEW YORK

First published 1997 by Ashgate Publishing

Reissued 2018 by Routledge
2 Park Square, Milton Park, Abingdon, Oxon, OX14 4RN
52 Vanderbilt Avenue, New York, NY 10017

Routledge is an imprint of the Taylor & Francis Group, an informa business

A Library of Congress record exists under LC control number: 97030129

ISBN 13: 978-1-138-35421-0 (hbk)
ISBN 13: 978-0-429-42497-7 (ebk)

Contents

PART THREE: PARLIAMENTARY BEHAVIOUR AT A FORMATIVE STAGE (THREE CASE STUDIES)

Acknowledgements

This book is an outcome of a study that would have hardly been completed without the financial support of the Russian Foundation for Fundamental Research. Chapters 7 and 8 summarise the results of a research project supported by the Economic and Social Research Council, Great Britain, (ESRC Award Reference No. R000234454, "Political Culture and Social Innovation: The Russian Supreme Soviet"). The authors are glad to express their deep gratitude to both these institutions.

They would also like to thank Dr. Sergei Filatov, former First Deputy Chairman of the Russian Supreme Soviet, for the singular opportunity to observe the workings of the Russian parliament from the inside, to Mr. Vladimir Novikov, former Chairman of the Council of Factions, and to Mr. Vladimir Pryamukhin, former Adviser to First Deputy Chairman, the Russian Supreme Soviet, for their timely assistance in obtaining the relevant material. We are likewise thankful to Dr. Leonti Byzov, in 1992-93 Chief Specialist of the Supreme Soviet Committee for Mass Media, Connections with Public Organisations, Mass Movements of Citizenry and the Study of Public Opinion, for consistent cooperation.

We thank the Analytical Centre for Scientific and Industrial Policies, the Russian Academy of Sciences, for providing facilities for their research and, in particular, its Director, Dr. Yakov Dranyov, and Dr. Andrei Belyaev for their most valuable contribution in it. We are also grateful to the Moscow State Institute of International Relations (University) and, especially, to the members of its Department of Philosophy and for their agreeable attitude and intelligent comments.

Some of the ideas that form the theoretical background of this study have originated from our previous research that resulted in *Russia's Road to Democracy* (Aldershot, Hampshire: Edward Elgar, 1993). We would like to thank Professor George W. Breslauer of the University of California, Berkeley, Professor Eric P. Hoffmann of the University of Albany, Profeesor Olof Petersson of the University of Uppsala, Professor Robert C. Tucker of Princeton University and Professor Stephen White of the University of Glasgow for their challenging criticisms of that book that encouraged us to embark on this new academic adventure.

Throughout these months of scholarly effort and civil discomfort we have been lucky to enjoy the unfailing support of the faculty and staff of the Department of Politics, the University of Leeds. We would like to thank its Head, Professor David Bell, and Professor Lionel Cliffe for the repeated opportunity to discuss our findings with learned colleagues from Great Britain, and Dr. Jeffrey Gleisner and Dr. Paul Chaisty for their competent comment. Our special thanks are due to Professor David Beetham, Director of the Centre for Democratisation, the University of Leeds, for the obliging stimulus of including this book in the series of the Centre's publications.

We are grateful to the Know-How Fund and the Westminster Foundation for Democracy for their financial support for the seminar on "Making Parliament and Its Fractions Work" (London - Leeds, January 1993) which we helped to organise and which gave us a remarkable chance to communicate with leading members of the Russian Supreme Soviet's factions and committees in an informal and friendly atmosphere.

This research might have remained a clannish endeavour, but for the friendly assistance of colleagues from various countries that enabled us to present our findings, both preliminary and final, to gatherings of professional critics. We thank Professor Walter F. Murphy and Professor Robert C. Tucker of Princeton University, for the opportunity to discuss "Problems of Russian Constitutionalism" with American students of constitutional law (Princeton, November 1993); Professor David Anderson, Director, and Professor Steffen Sachs, Deputy Director, Aspen Institute, Berlin, for the opportunity to attend the conference on "Russia's Path to an Open Society" (Aspen Institute, Berlin, April 1994); Professor Lorina Repina of the Institute of Universal History, Russian Academy of Sciences, for the invitation to participate in the international conference on "Political History on the Eve of the 21st Century: Traditions and Innovations" (Institute of Universal History, Moscow, May 1994); Professor Axel Hadenius of the University of Uppsala, for the organisation of the seminar on "Russian Political Culture" (the University of Uppsala, May 1994); Professor Dr. Gerhard Goehler of the Free University of Berlin, Professor Bhikhu Parekh of the University of Hull, as well as the Press and Information Bureau, the Federal Government, Germany, for the unique chance to meet the leading political scientists of today at the Sixteenth World Congress of the International Political Science Association (Berlin, August 1994); Professor Rei Shiratori, Director, Research Institute of Social Science, Tokai University, and Professor Fred

W. Riggs, the Committee on Viable Constitutionalism, for the obliging invitation to partake of the international symposium on "Presidential System and Parliamentary System in Crisis" (Tokai University Pacific Center, Honolulu, November 1994); Dr. Jeremy R. Azrael, Director, Russia Initiative, RAND Corporation, for the chance to debate on "Problems of Russian Federalism" with experts from the RAND Corporation (Santa Monica, California, January 1995); Professor Alexei V. Shestopal of the Moscow State Institute of International Relations (University), for the permission to address the standing seminar of the Department of Philosophy (May 1995) and Professor Bjoern Wittrock of the Swedish Collegium for Advance Study in the Social Sciences, for the opportunity to attend the seminar on "Social Revolutions" (Uppsala, June 1995).

The authors are obliged to Professor Paul Chilton, of the University of Warwick (Coventry), Professor Arthur Marwick of the Open University (Milton Keynes, Buckinghamshire), Professor William Kerby of the University of Hamburg, Dr. Dina Model of the Institute of Universal History, Russian Academy of Sciences, and Professor Rei Shiratori of the Tokai University for their help in publishing our findings in scholarly magazines.

In addition to the persons already named, we would like to thank Professor Hayward Alker of the University of Southern California (Los Angeles); Professor Roger Benjamin of the RAND Corporation; Professor G. Matthew Bohnam of the Maxwell School of Citizenship and Public Affairs (Syracuse, New York); Professor Archie Brown of St. Antony's College, University of Oxford; Professor S.N.Eisenstadt of the Hebrew University of Jerusalem; Professor George Lakoff of the University of California (Berkeley); Professor Jean Leca of the National Foundations of Political Sciences (Paris); Dr. David MacLaren McDonald of the University of Wisconsin - Madison; Dr. Michael MacFaul and Mr. Sergei Markov of the Moscow Carnegy Center; Professor Dr. Werner J. Patzelt of the Institute for Political Science, the Dresden Technological University; Dr. Eric Ringmar of London School of Economics; Professor Don Robinson of Smith College (Northampton, Massachusetts); Dr. Richard Sakwa of the University of Kent; Professor Natalia Selunskaya of the Moscow Lomonosov University and Professor Valeri Zhuravlyov for the inspiring discussion of some of our basic ideas.

Needless to say, none of the persons mentioned above can be held responsible for either the contents of this book or its possible shortcomings and inaccuracies.

The authors are particularly pleased to express their profound gratitude to Dr. Caroline Kennedy, Deputy Director, Institute for International Studies, the University of Leeds, for reviewing the full text of this book. Apart from the competent scholarly advice, her editorial skills and self-denying effort saved us much humiliation on the account of our inferior English.

Our particular thanks are due to Lesley and Peter Mansers whose friendship and hospitality made the last days of this work much more pleasant than it probably deserved. We are also indebted to Peter Manser for his valuable comment on verse translations that occur in this volume.

We do not owe this book solely to our public commitments and scholarly ambitions. Little of what follows would have been written, but for the tender sympathy and unassuming support of our wives, Svetlana Biryukova and Marina Sergeyeva.

Introduction: The Predicament of Russian Parliamentarianism

The epoch burns down as a farewell fire
And here we are watching the shade and the light
For the last autumn ...

Yu.Shevchuk, "The Last Autumn"

In October 1993 close-ups of the White House, the recent residence of the Russian parliament on Krasnopresnenskaya Embankment, were often on TV screens. The white building had grown black, running deputies looked back at the 'chirr' of submachine gun fire behind, militia guards left the building with raised hands. The shots were accompanied by a song by Yuri Shevchuk which has been quoted here in the epigraph, a song which matched the emotional impact of the event. For the second time in the course of two years (the first one, in August 1991) one could sense the rare savour of an epoch which had come to its end.

Together with this sense of an "epoch" which was over, there were other emotions - gone was also the pre-revolutionary "sweetness of life", and it must have been that feeling that was behind the dominant mood shared, in essence, by everyone, democrats as well as conservatives. Yet the changes did not produce elation, and there were few ready to celebrate the victory over "the lost time" while the state of emergency was still in effect in Moscow. Indeed the dead bodies were not yet removed from the smoking building. There were many who characterised all that had happened as a national tragedy.

Two months later, there was no longer any doubt as to the attitude of the populace. The democrats suffered a serious set-back at the new election. Only a year later, after the military intervention in Chechnya, the most radical of them found themselves in opposition to the executive that set about to restore order with an "iron hand".

All these "post-revolutionary" developments prompt a rethink of the events of 1990-93. Much appears clearer in retrospect, especially the fact

1

that the conventional dualistic picture of an apocalyptic battle between the forces of a nascent democracy and agonising communism had little relation to the reality. A more plausible explanation is that of the recovery of a traditional political culture (in its original, pre-communist, form) as the preponderant feature of the Russian political scene.

The impact of that culture on the institutional developments in the USSR during *perestroika*, and more specifically, on the fate of the representative institutions of 1989-91, was the subject of our previous book.[1] At that time the renovating effort of "institution-building" was the focal point of Soviet/Russian political life. In 1991-93, after the failure of *perestroika*, it pivoted specifically on the conflict between the representative and the executive branches of state government. But whereas centralised executive authority is a familiar feature of Russian politics, national political culture seems to resist any attempt to introduce genuine representative institutions.[2]

In fact, the issue of the survival of parliament has proved to be one of the most painful issues of the country's political history. Two recent examples are the Congress of People's Deputies of the Soviet Union, which was abolished in September 1991 (while the Supreme Soviet, the last remnant of the USSR representative authority, followed suit three months later), and its counterpart on the republican level and once its major rival - the Congress of People's Deputies of the Russian Federation, which was suspended and dissolved (together with its subordinate Supreme Soviet) in September-October 1993.

The succeeding Russian parliament (the Federal Assembly) was in a delicate situation, too. Ever since its members had been elected, it operated amid incessant talks about its likely dissolution. Due to the latest constitutional arrangements, such an outcome would have hardly been as dramatic an occasion as the events of 1991 or 1993.[3]

The democratic press which had been so eloquent in its propaganda of parliamentarianism in the early years of *perestroika* has grown (and, for the most part, still remains) very critical towards it. Indeed, the doubtful benefit of having got unexpected support from communists and nationalists served only to strengthen this suspicious attitude. In 1989, televised debates in the USSR Congress of People's Deputies signalled major political reforms; four years later the Russian parliamentarians were so unhappy about the media coverage of their activities that the most zealous of them were prepared to take Moscow TV Centre by force.

So far there have been six failures during the last ninety years. These take into account the First, Second and Fourth State Dumas in 1906, 1907 and 1917; the Constituent Assembly in 1918; the Congresses of People's Deputies and the Supreme Soviets of the USSR and the Russian Federation in 1991 and 1993. Given this, it is more than appropriate to ask why all attempts to institute representative authority in Russia seem to come to an apparently inevitable dramatic, not to say, tragic end? Since these events occurred under different historic circumstances and different regimes, it is also appropriate - in our inquiry concerning factors that prevent development of representative democracy in Russia - to turn to those features of the Russian society that undergo slow changes and remain relatively invariable under all political regimes. Political culture is, presumably, the first to be considered.

When viewed in this historic perspective, more recent events appear in a different light. All the major forces present on the Russian political scene at the time had their own good reasons for presenting the conflict between the legislative and the executive in 1992-93 in the classical dualistic manner, that is as a struggle between a "democratic president" and a "communist parliament".

Radical democrats tended to portray the events in this fashion because they believed that failure to reform, especially failure to reform the economy, would have been disastrous. Hence reforms had to continue, despite the growing discontent of the voters, presumably, unable to think of anything that went beyond their immediate needs and therefore unlikely to welcome "shock measures". If an "iron hand" were necessary, so radical democrats argued the reforms would have to be pursued by an "iron hand". This attitude made some radicals on the right[4] advocate the introducion of pro-market authoritarianism as modelled after Pinochet's Chile or Chun Doo-hwan's South Korea. However, that would mean that the parliament had to be severely restricted, perhaps, even dissolved, although such a measure would certainly go against democratic conventions. To denounce the parliament as "red" and then fight it as deserved a cardinal fiend, seemed a convenient means to overcome that obstacle.

On the other hand, the leaders of the parliament must have believed that by playing "more red", than they had originally and, perhaps, actually been, would be to their advantage. It would win them the support of all those whom the "shock reforms" had driven to the brink of survival, and who were therefore in favour of even a partial restoration of the socialist "welfare state". This strategy had additional benefits insomuch as the ramified system of local Soviets was still under control of the pro-socialist and conservative provincial elites. The parliament would thus be able to play the provinces against the central executive authority in Moscow.

Yet, if one considers the real legislative output of the Russian parliament of 1990-93, its activities do not fit in with the "red-and-white" dualistic picture. The most active among the legislators were the centrist factions, whose involvement in the struggle for power was not too strong, and their efforts usually resulted in reasonably civilised end products.[5] From the standpoint of radical reformers, these might have come too late, but parliaments are by their nature slow. They are designed to be. A couple of decrees can be passed in revolutionary fervour, but on the whole deliberation becomes a legislator, to say nothing about the slow workings necessary for consensus-building.

In short, the real problems Russian society faced at the time were not properly understood and were but inadequately discussed by the mass media entrapped in the dualistic *Weltanschauung*.

Those real problems are best presented in the following order: (1) How to secure integration of the society and of the country, when the ideology that had secured the integration of the polyethnic Soviet society was gone and the political culture that had kept the state mechanism running was in crisis? (2) How to strike a reasonable balance between the branches of government while each claimed absolute authority and sought to justify that by appealing to the peculiar understanding of the nature, functions and prerogatives of political power imbedded in the national culture? (3) How to develop a new political culture that would be able to uphold the vulnerable democratic institutions amid sharp ideological conflict?

Unfortunately, the mass media was not alone in its failure to grasp the real problems of a country caught in the calamity of transition. The same vision of the dualistic apocalypse prevailed among professional political analysts, including those in the West.

Whilst, this is hardly surprising after decades of ideological war and in absence of a satisfactory theory of society in transition, as time goes by, the dualistic mist starts to dissipate, and growing number of researchers adopt a more realistic view of the current situation.[6]

In this volume we intend to add to that debate and present our analysis of the political developments in Russia at the time of the "Second Republic" (by the "First" we refer to the period between 16 March 1917[7] and 19 January 1918[8]) in the light of the three problems outlined above. The task requires an elaboration of a conceptual framework that could be used to describe and analyse societies undergoing transformations of their traditional political cultures. This problem is dealt with in Part One.

Part Two describes and analyses the main stages of Russia's political development between January 1990 and October 1993.

Part Three comprises three empirical studies of selected aspects of parliamentary activities which are directly relevant to our three problems.

Underpinning this as the book's focal point is the story of the Russian parliament elected in 1990 and dissolved in 1993. This institution not only had throughout these three dramatic years been the principal arena of political confrontation, but had also provided the forum for an unprecedented (by Russian standards) public discussion of the most burning problems of Russian society and state.

Soviet politics had long been the exclusive domain of "sovietology", whose primary concern had always been with the Soviet political elite and - narrower still - with the relations between its top-ranking members, their struggle for power and the influence they were able to wield on various spheres of the Soviet social life. *Perestroika* changed all this: the field, as well as the discipline. Students of post-Soviet politics suddenly found themselves in an embarrassing situation: traditional skills of sovietology were rapidly becoming obsolete, new problems called for new approaches.

This book argues that in order to understand Russian society in transition one must address a broader problem of how to harmonise the need to perpetually adjust to the transient conditions of modern life with the conservatism of political mentality and social institutions that has for millenia served to absorb disintegrating tendencies and secure social stability? Understanding Russian political problems is, of course, an important task in view of the general situation observed in Eastern Europe after the collapse of communism. But we also believe that re-thinking this situation gives us yet another chance to realise the primary challenge of modernity that is addressed to the world community in general.

Our personal concern in this has been with the obvious incompatibility between our cherished political ideas and the political culture of the Russian people. But we would like to convey a message that differs substantially from that often voiced in and outside this country: rather than simply resign to the discouraging fact that Russia is not fit for democracy, we would place our hopes for a democratic future for our nation on the human capacity to understand the ways political cultures operate and transform. It was with a view to contributing to this goal that this book was conceived and written.

Notes

[1] Sergeyev and Biryukov 1993.

[2] Cf. White 1979, pp. 22-39.

[3] In April 1994 Ivan Rybkin, Speaker of the State Duma, in his public speech at the Moscow State Institute for International Relations mentioned as worthy to remember the fact that the State Duma had just attained its one-hundredth day and had in this outlived the First and Second State Dumas of 1906 and 1907.

[4] In the Russian post-perestroika political discourse some terms seem to have switched meanings. During *perestroika* "left" would normally mean an "anti-communist democrat", whereas "right" would be applied to the *apparatchiks*, representing the "old regime". That use of the words was obviously contrary to the Western conventions. It no longer is, although the peculiar Russian political set-up would occasionally cause confusion. "Left" has grown to stand for proponents of the "socialist idea", that is - in Russia - communists. Champions of liberal reforms are usually defined as "right", and since this segment of the Russian political spectrum is, by no means, lacking in radicals, "radical right" would have two different, moreover, contradictory meanings, being also applied to radical nationalists that now ally with communists.

[5] By this we mean its political and ideological tendency not its "juridical quality" *per se*. This latter question, viz. whether the Russian legislation of 1990-93 met the requirements of political and economic modernisation, is discussed in Chapter 9.

[6] See, for example, Hoffmann 1994, Lapidus (ed.) 1995, McFaul 1995.

[7] The day following the abdication of Nicholas II.

[8] The day the Constituent Assembly was dissolved after some 13 hours in session.

PART ONE

Dualism and *Sobornost'*

(A Theory)

... Reflexion suggests that it is not so easy to repudiate one's heritage.

A.J.Toynbee, "Civilization on Trial".

1 Transition to Modernity and the Problem of Social Integration

Rules alone can unite an extended order. (Common ends can do so only during a temporary emergency that creates a common danger to all. the 'moral equivalent of war' offered to evoke solidarity is but a relapse into cruder principles of coordination).
F.A. Hayek, "The Fatal Conceit".

1. Integration Mechanisms as Elements of Political Cultures

All societies are possessed of integration mechanisms - so long as they exist. These must be internal mechanisms, even if the original integrating impetus comes from outside, as in the case of an aggression or a threat of an aggression. A community that fails to develop such mechanisms and/or build them into political culture is ephemeral.

Political culture can be generally defined as basic knowledge about, or a vision of social life shared by a relatively large section of society that determines for those who belong to it their understanding of particular political situations and their behaviour in them. Knowledge of this kind can be divided into three main categories, viz. social ontology, political values and operational experience.

Social ontology is a system of basic beliefs about the nature and structure of social reality that provides a general framework for classification of social situations. Ontological categories are used to identify ("name") these situations.

The knowledge of this kind is for the most part irreflexive. This would account for the spontaneity and uniformity of the behaviour such knowledge instigates. The cognitive schemes that constitute social ontology are highly conservative and tend to persist even in the face of a presumably refuting experience - for the simple reason that they themselves are used to interpret all kinds of experience, as well as the world behind it. (Particular

9

interpretations may fail, of course, but this can always be blamed on the failure to allow for one of the apparently innumerable circumstantial factors, rather than on the limitations of the interpretation scheme itself).

Values enable one to range situations along some scale of "acceptability". Although related to social ontology, values are much more open for reflexion because they constantly reappear in public discourse and are consequently more flexible.

Operational experience is the most varied element of political culture. "Varied" here stands for "differentiated", not "changeable". This is a complex of means that have been developed within a political culture in order to deal with typical problems - a collection of standard scenarios for standard situations. Situations may change, but it would take both time and effort to acquire and interiorise new skills.[1]

As a "built-in" mechanism, the integrating mechanism is intimately linked to the kind of knowledge that constitutes a political culture. No society can exist for long, unless a critical mass of its members share beliefs that contribute to its continuation, beliefs that give sense to and justify their living together.[2]

One would expect *social ontology* to have the strongest integrating potential possible. After all, it is the political culture's least exposed, most stable element. However, for social ontology to act as an integrating factor, the people who share it must believe, among other things, that they constitute some primaeval, "natural" unity. Cultures of this kind are conceivable, but if they are to exist for a relatively long period of time, a combination of conditions is required that is rarely encountered nowadays. One has to turn to more traditional societies for examples.

First and foremost among these conditions is absence of structural conflicts *within* the body politic that the community would accept as legitimate. In Russian political jargon such a state of affairs and the respective frame of mind would be called *sobornost'*.

The Culture and Politics of Sobornost'

Though this term in its present meaning is an invention of Russian philosophers of the 19th century, they were obviously inspired by the traditions of medieval Eastern Christianity.[3] When applied to political life, *sobornost'* is basically a demand to make decisions and act "all in common". The demand implies the community in question is an intrinsically integral entity. It is also a legitimate (perhaps, the *only* legitimate) political agency. Autonomous actions of any other agency within the community are seen as violation of unity and an outrage against *sobornost'*. When seen in this perspective, the society does not appear a product of human interaction (whether of individuals or groups) and its internal structure is not a result of their efforts and conventions. The whole is a primary reality and within that primary unity the constituent parts are legitimate only inasmuch as they contribute to the general goal.

There is no reason to believe that societies that adhere to this creed are in themselves any more homogeneous than any other. However, the ontology of *sobornost'* implies a tacit "restriction" on any speculation concerning social structure and social stratification.[4] The priority of the whole is so pronounced that all internal distinctions appear irrelevant, which creates a specific "egalitarian" attitude that, after it has been incorporated in the value system, affects both political decision-making and political behaviour.

But this is an "egalitarianism" of a peculiar, totalitarian kind: while presuming that all individuals and groups that constitute a society are equal *vis-a-vis* the "social whole", it does not infer that they must therefore enjoy the status of free political agencies. The pluralism implied by that inference would obviously contradict the ideal of *sobornost'*. It is not surprising under the circumstances that this pseudo-egalitarian system of values proves a weak barrier when it comes to establishing elitist political institutions and promulgating the corresponding operational experience.

Moreover, this model of hypertrophied holism depicts society as so amorphous a unity that within it no single structure may legitimately claim an independent status, at least on a lasting basis. Ideally, even such vital functions as social security and social control are presumably spontaneous and require no specific institutions. Naturally enough, reality and ideal are at odds on this, but it is precisely because the social ontology of *sobornost'* is anti-institutional in principle, that the institutions created to perform these functions in a society that professes the ideals of *sobornost'* have the paradoxical mark of permanent extraordinariness: they are established as if *ad hoc* and retain this character for decades.[5] This is best illustrated by the pledge concerning a near and inevitable "withering of state" which one of the most *statist* regimes in human history entertained its commoners with.

No less paradoxical, though by no means any less unnatural, a consequence of this attitude is the hypertrophy of institutions of power. Their anti-institutionally minded subjects can neither think of a reasonable alternative, nor bring them under effective control. Contrary to the initial anti-institutionalism and egalitarianism of its prevailing ideology, a society of the *sobornost'* type quickly develops oligarchic bureaucratic structures and invests them with extraordinary powers. These oligarchies excel in behind-the-scene decision-making: like pluralism, openness and *glasnost'* would immediately destroy the illusion of *sobornost'*. The result of this is the duality (or duplicity) of political life: the politics of *sobornost'* splits into a *sobornost'*-flavoured political show performed for the benefit of the masses, in contrast with the *Realpolitik* practised by the power elite behind the Kremlin or similar walls.[6]

Sobornost' power is extraordinary and unrestricted. Russian political thinkers have suggested various explanations (justifications) for this. Explanations varied from the sinful nature of all politics and all power (whence the Slavophils inferred autocratic monarchy as a means to minimise the number of persons involved in this evil, albeit indispensable job[7]) to Lenin's doctrine of "the revolutionary vanguard" (meaning the Bolshevik Party) that, having mastered the only true science of social development, is entitled to supervise that development, i.e. to rule.[8]

Acts of government are thus identified with those of the community. Indeed, a community that exalts its own shapelessness as a realisation of an ideal is virtually unable to act otherwise than through its one legitimate institution, i.e. the Government. The mythology of *sobornost'*, it has been argued, knows of only one political agency, "the Community" as a whole. The reality of *sobornost'* identifies the former as "the Government". The apparent inconsistency is overcome by presuming a fundamental innate affinity between the two agencies: as numerous posters once displayed throughout the Soviet Union used to claim, "The People and the Party are one!". The lack of conflicts this presumed affinity implies, is by no means sheer illusion: a community that is denied a capacity to act on its own cannot enter a conflict with those in power, even if to an external observer such conflict appeared long overdue.

Values as the Integrating Force

The holistic vision of society outlined in the preceding section is by no means a unique Russian phenomenon. To some extent it can be considered as a feature common to all traditional cultures. It was certainly to be observed in medieval Europe where its "termination" would fall some time between the 15th and the 17th centuries.

The process of modernisation and the perpetual structural adjustments characteristic of it undermine the capacity of social ontology to serve as an integrating force. This means that political culture must be readjusted to fit the new situation; the crux of this structural transformation is that the function of integration is originally transferred onto *the system of values*. This transformation does not necessarily affect the contents of the socio-ontological patterns: the community may continue to believe in its innate unity, even if it no longer relies on this belief as the main, or the sole, mechanism of integration.

For a community that has set off on the process of social stratification and needs a new basis for integration, the values' primary attraction consists in forming a *hierarchy*. On the cognitive level this would support a sufficiently differentiated, but on the whole coherent world view; on the pragmatic level, to integrate activities of people with different, moreover, incompatible operational background. It goes without saying, that the hierarchy of values "matches" the complex of ontological attitudes.

This discussion requires a brief but relevant diversion. Ontology-based integration does not in itself preclude hierarchy, which naturally has to be accommodated by the system of values. The difference is that this system of values is not expected to secure social integration.

A good, but by no means the only, example of this kind of culture is provided by patriarchy. A patriarchal society is perceived by its members as a kind of family or organism. Both are characterised by differentiation of functions and ontological statuses of individual members who/that, nevertheless, form an organic unity. Within this world view what is required of the head, for example, is different from what is required of a hand; the criteria of performance assessment differ accordingly. The same stands true for family heads and family members (mark the etymology!).[9] However, integration of and cooperation within such a community are secured by the literary "reading" of this metaphor of organism, not by the imperatives of patriarchal ethics, the sphere of which does not extend beyond interpersonal relations.[10]

To return to the main subject of this discussion, the "organismic" understanding of society is necessarily teleological, for it is only by reference to a goal common to all its members that one can justify coercion to cooperation. This ontological subtlety is of no trivial importance, if one is to understand the transition to the value-based integration. For cultures integrated on the ontological level a common goal appears as natural, as the unity is spontaneous. If belief in this unity persists, but is no longer relevant as far as social integration is concerned, the integration function can only be transferred onto a system of values that would "fit" the organismic (teleological) pattern, i.e. would be eschatological or chiliastic in character.

Social bonds of this kind presuppose the existence of an *organisation*, of which the mission is to lead the community to a state realising the professed values. After these new institutions have been created, the society can no longer rely exclusively on the "natural", spontaneous cooperation of its members, for all the "naturalism" of the organismic ontology. This is because a culture that is to be integrated through a system of values must abide by the specific logic of value thinking and hence adopt the appropriate mode of functioning. Values have to be realised (otherwise they would not be values), realisation requires effort (moreover, effort that is collective, as collective is the legitimating goal), collective effort is impossible without some organising activity. The fact that the goal that is eschatological or chiliastic is also transcendent, and therefore, not actually attainable proves of minor importance, unless, of course, one insists on viewing it all from the long-term perspective. So, an organisation created to achieve it will find something to justify its existence.

The make-up of such an organisation is determined by the following two factors. In the first place, in its capacity as the sole legitimate intermediary between this profane world of daily existence and the transcendent realm of realised values, it functions as a kind of "grace-distributing" administration. From the standpoint of a rationalist critic, the function is mythical, even fraudulent, but it would make sense from the standpoint of securing social cooperation within a community soldered by a common adherence to transcendent values.

Secondly, in the true spirit of the society within which it operates and in accordance with the nature of its mission, such an organisation takes the form of a hierarchy - a highly centralised one. Within this hierarchy the status of an individual member depends on how close or how far he/she happens to stand *vis-a-vis* the transcendent "source of grace". This structural principle helps to assure congruence of the actual *status* and its public *appraisal*. The criterion of evaluation is precisely the proximity to, or remoteness from, the realm of realised values. This legitimates the idea of the hierarchy and the hierarchy itself.

Organisations that provide for this value-based integration are exemplified by the Catholic Church at the time of its war against heresies (from the 12th to the 16th century) and, more recently, by the communist parties of socialist countries.

The system of values' integrating potential is, however, limited to specific socio-cultural conditions. Since the immediate fibre of value thinking is comprised of value judgements, the congruence of the former depends on the availability of an authoritative body that could be appealed to in case of a disagreement between the latter. This appears to be the only way to avoid relativism, as well as the sacramental question: "Who are our judges?"[11] Value thinking is therefore characteristically authoritarian. This is true of the traditional patriarchal cultures, which are thoroughly and unequivocally authoritarian. It also stands true of the modern democratic societies insofar as they have institutions of which the primary function is to make value judgements (e.g. courts of law).

Pluralism of values, inasmuch as it extends beyond the diversity permissible within a hierarchy of values and implies plurality of authorities or even their absence, undermines the values' capacity to integrate. For a value-integrated culture ideological dogmatism is simply a means of survival, and tolerance can only exist as a kind of "indulgence" towards the "miserable"; otherwise dissent must be crushed in the bud. Even the relative plurality of values that goes with a diversified system is permitted so long as those "remote" from the source of grace unequivocally accept the privilege and authority of those "closer" to it.

But hence it follows that this mechanism of social integration is only possible (effective) in a relatively unchanging environment in which one could safely rely on what operational experience is transmitted through and sanctified by tradition. A substantial change in the community's living conditions may render the tradition irrelevant, but its rigidity will naturally limit the community's capacity to adapt to the new, "irregular" situation. What follows is that a community integrated by values always runs the risk to fail to withstand the shock of change. Where changing social environment is a rule rather than an exception, value-based integration appears as obsolete as the ontological integration it has come to replace.

2. Value-Based Integration: From Mystic Unity to Dualism

The Socio-psychological Dynamics of Schism

How then does it happen that this changes-allergic integration mechanism develops in the first place? After all, what, apart from significant social changes, can cause one (new) cultural type of integration to come up to take the place of another (old) one? The answer lies in the character of the political culture in question and the dynamics of cultural transformation.

Abrupt social differentiation characteristic of the initial stages of modernisation debilitates the integrating potential of the traditional social ontology. *Schism* emerges as the society in transition's characteristic feature and this manifests itself as *dualism*.

The sequence is not surprising. Belief in the ontological unity of the body politic implies marginality of those who do not belong to it. This belief must therefore be shared by the absolute majority of the community members, and not only as far as they themselves are concerned, but also in respect of all their fellow-members. If this condition is not fulfilled, e.g. if a considerable number of the community members dissociate themselves (or are dissociated by others) from the identifying unity, an acute psychological conflict is unavoidable. This conflict is resolved by means of a process that threatens either the ontological unity as a mental fact or the integrity of the community as a fact of politics.

Dualism is the ideological core of this process. If belief in ontological unity is preserved, but the unity itself is no longer there, a psychological climate sets in of which the dominant is a sense of *antagonism*. Moreover, in accord with the prevailing cultural attitude, the antagonism is granted the highest ontological status. It turns out to be something more that an ordinary fact of life, a commonplace collision of opposing interests. The latter can be observed in any society, but if a society practises explanation schemes that are based on the ontology of organic unity, what causes such conflicts can only be considered as something trivial and circumstantial. The dualistic conflict is, on the contrary, recognised as the most fundamental fact of being. It is ascribed a higher, transcendent meaning.

However, one should not mistake the dualistic conflict for a manifestation of a genuine ontological difference. Its dynamics have nothing in common with the dynamics of an antagonism that arises out of a natural opposition.[12]

A dualistic creed, therefore, does not necessarily generate dualism in politics. *Political dualism* develops only if "membership" of a mystic unity becomes a meaningful social marker, and this implies a specific mechanism of integration, one based on values. The core of such a mechanism is the "grace-distributing" organisation described in the preceding section. In societies that are integrated by social ontology, *political* dualism based on values is inconceivable. In political cultures of this type there is no room for value judgements as to the membership of a mystic unity. You either belong to it or not. It is a matter of fact, not a matter of judgement. Even on those rare occasions when the question assumes practical importance, e.g. in case of a contact with those outside the unity, no dualism develops, because emphasising ontology as the integrating factor makes the very fact of "membership" a mystery. Being outside the mystic unity is equally not an occasion to pass a sentence. For a Buddhist, for example, to blame a person for having not yet attained "enlightenment" is as meaningless as for an Orthodox Christian to credit oneself for the descent of the Holy Spirit: grace is no human concern!

It is not dualism of the universe (be it real or imaginary) that a political dualistic myth reveals, but a conflict *inside* a culture, and not just *any* culture, but only one that asserts, on the ontological level, the mystic unity of its proponents. This conflict develops as a result of a fundamental change in the world outlook of a considerable segment of the society in question that, having left unaffected the socio-ontological layer of the political culture, destroys the integrity of its value patterns by causing certain key institutions and key aspects of the social life to be appraised differently. From the institutional standpoint, this means that integration based on social ontology must be replaced by integration based on values, because continuation of the society depends henceforth on its capability to re-integrate its system of values.

In so far as the ontological axiom of unity remains (despite value conflict) valid for all community members, "orthodoxes" as well as "dissidents", congruence of the political consciousness can only be preserved by a kind of ontological "divorce" of the proponents of different values. Those adhering to "wrong" values are cast aside, "expelled" from the mystic unity and, with it, from "normal", "positive" existence. They are no longer just "alien", they are antipodes; they are real only inasmuch as they counterpose "us",[13] for to accept proponents of *different* values as "normal" members of *this* community would invalidate the dogma of the community's intrinsic unity. At the same time, if their presence in the community is an empirical fact that can neither be denied nor belittled, there seems to be only one way to resolve the apparent contradiction that would be logically and psychologically possible, viz. to assert that their participation in the community is strictly *negative*. And once again this assertion happens to be not an *appraisal* of the actual state of affairs, but just another ontological axiom. On the other hand, the opposition "kindred - alien" becomes value-laden, and "membership" of this or that comm*unity* is henceforth a matter of value judgement.

With this transformation the idea of mystic unity is not dismissed, it simply assumes a different form. But in one respect, at least, the change is consequential: operationally the "unity" is defined in a different manner. It is henceforth construed from outside, through opposition, rather than from inside, through belonging. *Omnis determinatio est negatio.* Good is not devoid of a positive meaning, of course, but this content is forced into the background. From the practical standpoint (instrumentally), it is now defined by its contrast to Evil. But as Evil is never defined otherwise than by it being the opposite to Good and can be possessed of no meaning of its own (to attribute one to it would again lead to pluralism and destroy the ontological unity), the meaning of "Good" itself, when defined in this manner, is lost in infinite reflexion, growing vaguer with each subsequent iteration: what is good is not simply good because it is good in itself, but it is good because it fights evil which is evil because it opposes good, etc. The meaning of Good bifurcates, the above operational definition neighbouring upon the original conceptual one,[14] and there is no reason to believe in a "pre-established harmony" between the two (though one can believe without reason, of course). Since it is the practical point about opposition and not the theoretical "intrinsic" properties that matters, Good may now have the superficial appearance of Evil; Evil can also disguise itself as Good. To give an objective appraisal becomes extremely difficult; in fact, judgements are for the most part irrational, based on *ritual*, rather than analysis.

In a community of this type adherence to values appears to be the most important instrument of social and cultural identification. At the previous, pre-dualistic, phase of its existence congruence between social status and value appraisal was taken for granted. Now community members are expected to *profess* their ideals. The demand cannot help affecting the structure of social interaction and the psychological atmosphere within the community. Values emerge as the community's basic concern, and all its active members come under close surveillance.

But this is precisely why such value-oriented cultures would not allow of any rational procedure of value judgement. When values are "ontolosied", they turn into something transcendental. The function of value judgements is henceforth not *to regulate* everyday behaviour, but *to separate* "the sheep from the goats". A profession of values is evidence not of their genuine interiorisation, but of the person's willingness to symbolically identify with the *community*. But then appraisal is no longer a matter of *a value judgement*; it becomes *a ritual sacrosanct performance*, of which the mundane (profane) meaning is no longer relevant to the appraisal as such. We would not enlarge on the purely religious performances (e.g. ritual prayers or the Eucharist), but one cannot help noticing that the value-laden rituals practised in the secularised Soviet society (entry into the party, voting at a meeting, participation in a *subbotnik*[15], a visit to the Lenin Mausoleum) fulfilled essentially the same function. The same stands true of the actions (or even the circumstances) that deserved "negative" appraisal: having been taken "prisoner of war", having lived on "an occupied territory", having "relatives abroad"[16] were not seen as facts of life (regrettable, perhaps), but as evidence of identification with the Enemy. And since the ontology of dualism demands that such cases be treated on "the presumption of malevolence", a person thus stigmatised is automatically considered as an apostate.

Integration through Antagonism?

The result is important from the standpoint of cultural continuity: the ontological axiom of the intrinsic unity of the body politic is not invalidated despite all evidence to the contrary, because all actual or potential "trespassers" acquire special ontological status that "relegates" them beyond the mystic unity.

This "relegation" is, of course, ideal: in actual life "apostates" have nowhere to go. But they are treated in the most hostile of manners. Strong permanent pressure is exerted on all members of the community to make them assume (immediately and unequivocally) a negative attitude towards these people: this type of conflict allows for no neutrality. As a result, the style of social intercourse undergoes a dramatic change: it becomes confrontational and paranoid.

Dualistic heresies of medieval Europe and the reaction of the established church provide an illustration. While Christianity remained a dominant creed and had no feasible ideological rival, it secured the (ontology-based) integration of Western Europe that, for all its political divisions, was still seen by the overwhelming majority of its inhabitants as a distinct cultural unity.[17]

The heretics challenged the all-European value consensus that had been reached by the end of the 10th century. This challenge marked an abrupt shift towards dualism which henceforth characterised both the Albigensian theory and the inquisitorial practice. There had been no need for an inquisition, while there had been no conflict. The inquisitors came after the Albigensians, in both senses of the word. As in more recent times, terror on so grand a scale could only be practised in an atmosphere of dualism and confrontation.

On the one hand, therefore, a social ontology that asserts the respective community's mystic unity (*sobornost'*, to take the Russian example) proves not incompatible with confrontational environment, nor with confrontational practice. On the other hand, a community that has passed through this dualistic mutation lives in a political and socio-psychological atmosphere that is totally devoid of the state of *goodness* that becomes an *ideal sobornost'*.

This oscillation between *sobornost'* and dualism poses a question: how often does the ontology of *sobornost'* appear in the dualistic disguise and isn't this "deviant" variant more common than the original, "pure" variety? The answer seems to depend on the type of integration. If this function is performed by social ontology, dualism is impossible in principle, for it would contradict the fundamental ontological beliefs of the community members and could only gain a foothold after the collapse of the respective political culture and at its expense.

The situation changes if the integrating function is transferred onto values. In that case dualism appears as the most powerful socio-psychological instrument for the preservation and re-assertion of the ontology of mystic unity. It can be considered as a kind of protective reaction on the part of a political culture that has found itself in a situation of crisis in which its conflict-managing skills and behaviour patterns (the operational experience) have proved inadequate to the new circumstances and provoked a conflict of values. The mystic unity sort of "contracts": it no longer extends to include all the members of the community, but is professed with increased zeal and pugnacity within the narrowed circle. It develops and revels in the psychological atmosphere of a "besieged fortress": the Enemy is everywhere on the outside; its spies and agents penetrate everywhere on the inside.[18]

Once formed, a political culture of this sort develops its own mechanism of self-perpetuation. The core of this mechanism is the relentless "search for Enemy". The process is self-contradictory. On the one hand, the Enemy must be uncovered and destroyed, because he is the Enemy; on the other hand, the Enemy must persist, because in his absence this type of political culture becomes meaningless and cannot function. It is obvious that whatever political force occupies "the niche" at the moment, it cannot be treated in a purely empirical manner, but must be "reconsidered" from the standpoint of ontological dualism. "The Enemy" is mystified out of all proportions and stripped of practically all meaningful sociological characteristics: it may now be called "The World Imperialism", or "The Judeo-Masonry", or "The Islamic Threat", or "The Empire of Evil".

Under these circumstances any "outside" candidate for the role of the Enemy quickly fades into a mere symbol and becomes almost anonymous. On the contrary, "internal" enemies (symbolic by definition, for the body politic is still considered a mystic unity) concretise and multiply. Dualistic mentality generates the abhorrent reality of mass terror.

The entire dynamics if, of course, self-extinguishing. Like revolution, of which it forms the psychological background, dualism devours its own children. The political practice it generates and nurtures cannot be durable, for the most natural of reasons: the community must either end it or cease to exist. The inherent incongruity between the functional goal of integration and the conceptual/psychological basis of its mechanism, the outward-bound and inward-reflected dualism, will slowly but surely corrupt the integrating mechanism. Political cultures cannot integrate and disintegrate concurrently: integration implies toleration, dualism breeds intolerance.

Dualism can be overcome in one of two ways: either by restoring *sobornost'* in its original pre-dualistic form or by restructuring the ontological foundation of the political culture and abandoning the paradigm of *sobornost'*. The feasibility of the former depends on the society's capability to resolve the value conflict that caused the initial dualistic rupture. This implies a new consensus about the basic values of the political culture as a precondition for the re-consolidation of the deranged mechanism of social integration. If, however, the original discord was prompted by some substantial shifts in the social structure, for the above re-consolidation to materialise, the relevant processes would have to be "frozen". If the primary impulse that triggered the cultural crisis was related, for example, to an attempt at modernisation, restoration of the traditional regime may well be the price the society and its political elite would have to pay for the re-consolidation, with all the consequences for the prospects for future development.

The second way out of dualism does not imply an all-embracing consensus about values: inasmuch as it involves renunciation of the ontology of mystic unity, it is quite compatible with pluralism of values. But it requires instead an alternative mechanism of integration, based neither on ontology nor on values, since none of these can perform the function under the new circumstances.

3. From Dualism to Institutional Democracy

Pressing our historical argument somewhat further, one might say that Protestantism must be given credit for having solved the above contradiction between the function and the mechanism of integration in a society afflicted by dualism. The unity of the body politic, that could no longer be secured by compulsory identification with a system of values without annihilating the society's "human matter", was restored by discarding both the claim to the ultimate excellence and the respective ontological beliefs. The function of integration was shifted onto *operational experience*. After the initial dualistic ardour of the earlier years of Reformation gave way to religious tolerance and the Catholic Church succeeded in restoring consensus with respect to values within what remained of its domain, Inquisition became an anachronism. The North and the South of Europe presented two ways out of the impasse of dualism.

Developing the kind of operational experience that *could per se form a basis for social integration* is thus a pre-condition for re-consolidating society, if the polity opts for the second approach. Since operational experience varies within any culture, this would imply its "hierarchisation" and a consensus about *a special status* for certain kinds of political behaviour and certain political procedures. In practice that would mean establishing (or singling out) political institutions, whose procedures would take on special value and become the point of a new consensus that would secure the integration of the body politic.

Not any institution would suit the purpose. In our previous book we have already examined the difference, both in structure and procedures, between two types of representative institutions: parliaments and *sobors*.

That difference was traced to the difference in the social ontologies sustained within the West European and the traditional Russian political cultures.[19] Whatever the character and the functions of the earlier parliaments, they entered modernity as institutions generally expected to represent *different* social and group interests and, as far as that was possible, to co-ordinate (integrate) them. Accordingly, the parliaments were divided into estate groups; later they saw the birth of political parties.

One point is of particular importance here. What is called "the modern democratic theory" was originally developed by thinkers who were, for the most part, empiricists and/or sceptics. They were not taken in by human wisdom and did not trust the would-be legislators to always find "true" solutions to their problems; consequently, they did not ask for them. They rather thought - in the true spirit of nominalism - that the very word "truth" did not make much sense when applied to parliamentary agenda. Members of parliament did not study nature, they were not called to pass judgement on philosophical or theological issues. Their activities lay almost entirely in a sphere where everything riveted on human preferences.

When a person makes a decision that is to shape his life and destiny, he has a perfect right to be "mistaken". Even if the "fallacy" of this or that of his decisions appears obvious to an outside observer, this is not in itself a reason to deny him his "sovereign" right to dispose of himself and his life (except, perhaps, in a limited number of special cases). For, contrary to what is often claimed, this right is not based on the assumption, whether true or false, that every person is the best judge of his own needs and his own interests. Come to think of it, many people, perhaps, most people, often do not know what they want and have but vague ideas about what they would, least so should, do. Their inalienable and unconditional right to make responsible decisions is based on the principle of *freedom*, not on the principle of *competence*. There is no will above the will of a free person in the matters of his personal concern, and there must not be any. Of value here is not so much the substance of his decision, as the *autonomy* of the will that underlies it.[20]

If this principle is extended to a community of individuals and established as the principle of *popular sovereignty*, the key question to be asked about the performance of political institutions is whether their decisions conform to the sovereign's *actual will*. Just as an individual can be deceived or forced to do something against his interests and even against his own better judgement, a collective agency, whether the electorate or a representative assembly, can become subject to threats, manipulations and fraud. If practised systematically, such abuse of the sovereign's will makes a spontaneous social consensus impossible; it paralyses political activities within the community and eventually destroys its political culture.

Special *rules of procedure* have to be introduced to prevent this uninspiring outcome. Their primary function is to secure the authenticity of the will of both the electors and the elected. This is achieved by means of free elections, parliamentary immunity and parliamentary procedures.

Unlike populism that, under the indigenous name of *narodnichestvo*, has been an important feature of Russian politics for the last thirteen decades and is characterised by an inexplicable belief in popular (grass-roots) wisdom, parliamentary democracy emphasises popular sovereignty, but not because "the people are always right".[21] Parliaments do not presume therefore to always pass the best possible decisions, "best" that is from some abstract, objective point of view. Instead, they are expected and, indeed, obliged to find decisions that could be implemented without regular, systematic coercion. If observing rules of procedure secures this outcome, the rules themselves can no longer be viewed as mere formality. Rather they rise to become the nucleus of the political culture: parliaments owe them their ability to perform their social functions and hence their political viability.

From the standpoint of the understanding of political culture which is developed in this volume, procedures come under operational experience. With the parliament-type representative bodies emerging as the principle policy-makers in the respective political cultures, the operational experience that maintains them acquires special status. It becomes the primary pre-condition of social consensus and political integration of the community.

Notes

[1] For a more detailed analysis of the three basic components of political culture, see Sergeyev and Biryukov 1993, pp. 10-6.

[2] As R.Tucker puts it (Tucker 1987, p. 22):

> A human society is something beyond the total complex of ideal and real culture patterns constituting a community's way of life and thought, even when allowance has been made for the existence of subcultures. There is always a core belief, a central motif, in which the ideal culture patterns are

imbedded, and I propose to call this the society's *sustaining myth*. The term *myth* is not being used here in the frequently encountered derogatory sense in which it means an untruth. Such myths are the sources in which people find meaning in membership in their society; thus in a matter of speaking, the myths *are* the society as a mental fact. A sustaining myth is a notion or concept of that society as a common enterprise. It represents what is distinctively valuable about the society from the standpoint of its members. [Original italics]

[3] The word *sobornost'* has no English equivalent. As R.M.French (translator of N.Berdyaev's *Slavery and Freedom*) writes (see Berdyaev 1944, p. 4):

> Sobornost, is the despair of all translators from Russian. 'Altogetherness' would come near to its meaning. It is the dynamic life of the collective body.

The word is a derivative of the Russian *sobor*, which means both "cathedral" and "[ecclesiastical] council"; representative institutions of medieval Muscovy were also called *sobory* (*Sobors*). (For the latest survey of historic data on these, see Cherepnin 1978). In the Russian philosophical jargon the notion of *sobornost'* (in its present abstract form) is used to express a vision of some mystic unity that presumably characterises the Church and, by analogy, the body social and the entire mankind. In this the idea of *sobornost'* has had a profound impact on the Russian political mentality. For its cultural implications and especially for the way it affected the understanding of political representation, see Biryukov and Sergeyev 1993; Sergeyev and Biryukov 1993.

[4] There is a striking contradiction between the Marxist theory that accentuates social stratification and class differences and the specific Marxist "eschatology" that envisages the birth of a homogeneous, "classless" society. The blend of Western Marxism and the traditional Russian mentality of *sobornost'* has produced the grotesque phenomenon of Soviet "social science" with its ridiculous mystification of the social structure of the Soviet society. For example, from the standpoint of Marxist definition of a social class, "the working class" and "the kolkhoz peasantry" were absolutely indistinguishable, for the difference between them was *not* related to the type of ownership for the means of production (the "cooperative" property of kolkhozes being pure fiction). Nevertheless, they were persistently portrayed by the official propaganda as "the basic (though, of course, not antagonistic) classes of the socialist

society". On the other hand, the really meaningful distinctions (as, for instance, between Party members and non-Party citizens) were presented as purely ideological.

5 The Extraordinary Commission for the Struggle against Counter-revolution and Sabotage (the notorious Cheka) was established in December 1917 and carried on, under different names, for 35 years, if one counts till the deaths of Stalin and Beria; for 74 years, if one opts for the failure of the August coup; or even for 76 years - till December 1993, when it was "eventually" abolished once again. Will it be for long?

6 On the sociopolitical functions of this duality, see Sergeyev and Biryukov 1993, pp. 75-8.

7 On the Slavophils' attitude toward tsarist autocracy, see Berdyaev 1947a, pp. 145-7.

8 See Lenin 1961. On the cultural impact of this attitude, see Tucker 1987 pp. 33-50. On the institutional consequences thereof, see Sergeyev and Biryukov 1993, pp. 57-75.

9 An early example of the use of the metaphor of organism in political reasoning is Menenius Agrippa's address to the rebellious plebeians to be found in Livy's History of Rome (II:32:8-12, see Livy 1965, pp. 125-6):

10 For the analysis of the type of value reasoning practised in societies modelled after a patriarchal family, see Titarenko 1974, pp. 38-76.

11 A quotation from Alexander Griboyedov's The Mischief of Being Clever (see Griboyedov [no date], p. 24).

12 When dogs fight cats and cats kill mice, they do not exercise in dualism. If we followed the fabulist in assuming the animal world to be a parable of the human one, we could say that the war of dogs against cats exemplifies a collision of cultures, not a conflict inside a culture. The "dualism" that separates dogs from cats is absolute, but this is precisely the reason why the "cultural life" of cats and dogs does not pivot on the conflict between them as the fundamental principle of being. The existence of cats presents no "ideological" problems for dogs, and *vice versa*.

13 To use Hegel's jargon, their ontological status is fixed at the level of "Being for Other" and never reaches the level of "Being for Itself" (for the exposition of the above categories, see Hegel 1966, Vol. 1, pp. 129-41, 170-3). The latter is psychologically impossible, unless at

least the ontological layer of the culture in question undergoes substantial transformation.

[14] The function of a conceptual definition is to explicate the term; of an operational, to identify the class members.

[15] The term is derived from *subbota* (Saturday) and refers to labour freely given to the state on Saturdays (or other days off) or overtime.

[16] The quoted expressions are taken from a standard Soviet "questionnaire" to be filled in when applying for a job, for instance, or a permission to travel abroad.

[17] As a medieval Latin poet put it, writing in the name of Rome (Hildebert of Lavardin, "De Roma", see Hildebert 1969, p. 26; translated by N.Biryukov):

> Thriving and lordly erstwhile I commanded the bodies of earthlings -
> Humbly reduced to the dust, souls nowadays I command.

On the idea of the European unity during the Middle Ages, see also Averintsev 1982.

[18] The description and analysis of this mode of existence by means of literary fiction constitute the core, as well as the secret of success, of the famous anti-utopias of the 20th century: Evgeni Zamyatin's *We* (with its prophetic metaphor of "The Green Wall", brought to life in the absurd reality of the Cold War) and George Orwell's *1984* (with its "Two Minutes Hate" and the ubiquitous poster "Big Brother Is Watching You").

[19] See Sergeyev and Biryukov 1993, pp. 24-28, 32-34, 146-47 or Biryukov and Sergeyev 1993.

[20] Cf. to Kant's distinction between the *autonomy* and the *heteronomy* of will and the third formulation of categorical imperative.

[21] Little can be said to defend this presumption against the critical arguments repeatedly put forward since the time of classical antiquity (Socrates, Plato, etc.).

2 Pluralism and Integration

*We have now to consider what and what kind of government is
suitable to what and what kind of men.*

Aristotle, "Politics".

1. The Stability of Democracy

The advance towards democracy, that has arguably in the course of the last
few decades become a global phenomenon, brings up a serious question
about the institutional forms that make democracy viable. The problem is
of particular significance for those "divided" societies that are characterised
by a deep cleft between the elites and the masses in income and influence;
but also for societies in "transition" that experience major changes of
economic and social systems.

The principal conclusion to be drawn from the above discussion of the
integration mechanisms within different political cultures is that political
institutions of a society are not "indifferent" towards the society's political
culture and that these institutions' success or failure in securing social
stability depend on whether they agree with the character of the integration
mechanisms maintained by the culture in question. Changes in political
culture are likely to affect the institutions' performance and probably their
very existence.

The institution of monarchy may be said to agree well with political
cultures that rely on social ontology for integration. A monarch personifies
the unity of a body politic, especially if his authority is legitimated by
reference to divine grace, as exemplified by the case of medieval Europe.
Nevertheless, even within a tradition such as this the role of a monarch can
be interpreted in different ways.[1]

In the earlier stages of modernisation, societies that have already parted
with the traditional notions of social life and the respective ontology-based
integration mechanisms, but have not yet developed cultural patterns that
allow of operational integration, tend to integrate on the basis of values.
They soon find themselves in the circumstances that favour a specific type
of political power institutions: *caudillo*, to use a Latin American term;

28

Bonapartism or *Stalinism*, to remain within the European tradition. In a sense, the Italian Renaissance tyrannies, so audaciously described and analysed by Machiavelli, come under the same category.[2]

The power of these populist leaders is based on their presumed capacity to "embody" certain values, usually the values of the masses as opposed to the values of the elites,[3] and on their genuine capability to exploit the ideas and techniques of political dualism. The type is exemplified by figures such as Maximilien Robespierre (*the Incorruptible*) and Juan Rosas.

A phenomenon that deserves special mention is rapid bureaucratisation of populist regimes founded on political dualism. The phenomenon appears natural in the light of the "dualistic" society's tendency (analysed in the preceding chapter) to structure itself as a hierarchy "descending" from a "source of grace". There can be different beliefs about the intrinsic nature of this "grace", but it usually functions in "this world" as some kind of "true (superior) knowledge": either the "popular wisdom", or a new doctrine (the "expert mastery" of which would determine a person's hierarchical status in a dualistic society), or else the leader's "foresight" (personal charisma).

It is also important to note that this "hierarchy" is not "organic". It is not based on ancestry or valour, as was typical for the traditional medieval societies of Europe and Japan for example. It is instrumental and manipulative in character; its maxim might sound (to twist a Russian proverb) as follows: "It is not the man that adorns the place, but the place that adorns the man".

The third type of integration, operational integration, requires a complex system of representative institutions. Strictly speaking, this would not be "democracy" in the classical, literal sense of the word, but rather something like Robert Dahl's "polyarchy"[4] or Arend Lijphart's "consociational society".[5] Both models emphasise fixed procedures as a prerequisite for a lasting distribution of power between different social groups and different elites.

It was this type of integration that could be observed in the initially "divided" societies that yet managed to preserve some balance of power between their various communities: for example, the Netherlands (that had to gap the breach between Protestants and Catholics), Lebanon (divided between Christians, Sunni Muslims and Druzes) and India (with its multiethnic population).

Societies such as these do not impress one as particularly stable during the initial period, while the procedures and institutions of power are still novel and relatively unperfect, but their stability grows with time, if they manage to avoid a "dualistic disaster".

What is decisive in this is the ability to correctly "design" the procedures and institutions of power. One of the key aspects of this problem is usually seen as the choice between two alternatives: a parliamentary republic and a presidential republic. ("Modern" monarchies, like those of Sweden or the Netherlands, are, for all that matters, parliamentary republics in a traditional disguise).

2. Presidentialism versus Parliamentarianism

We now turn to the textbook problem of democratic theory and it is worthwhile to recall a recent debate in the *Journal of Democracy*. In 1990, the magazine published a series of articles by a number of leading political scientists who attempted to compare and assess the effectiveness of the two principal models of democratic government, the presidentialist and the parliamentary. The debate was initiated by an article titled "The Perils of Presidentialism"[6] which was written by Juan J. Linz, of the Yale University. The response came in the form of two articles: one by Donald Horowitz, of the Duke University,[7] and one by Seymour M. Lipset, of the George Mason University and the Hoover Institution.[8] Linz replied to his opponents in an essay titled "The Virtues of Parliamentarianism" that concluded the series.[9] Here we intend to review this debate from a special standpoint, viz. the congruity of political institutions and political cultures.

Linz's principal arguments in favour of the parliamentary government can be summarised as follows. A divided society would be correct to prefer presidentialism to a parliamentary system because:

(1) Inasmuch as it is based on the principle of "the winner takes all", presidentialism is likely to cause additional conflicts in polities that already suffer, above all, from lack or inadequacy of conciliatory mechanisms. A candidate for the presidency will either win or lose, whereas the parliamentary system allows of a variety of outcomes. Moreover, a president who has passed through a direct election may conclude that he has got the mandate of all the people even if he was in fact supported by a marginal majority (sometimes 40 percent or even less would suffice). In case of the presidency, incumbents tend to believe their authority to be far

more legitimate than it actually is; the delusion may well lead to confrontation where a less arrogant attitude might help smooth the matters out.

(2) Further, it is argued conflicts arise from the separation of powers that estranges presidents from legislatures. Separate elections and fixed terms of incumbency make the system rigid. Unlike presidentialist systems, parliamentary systems allow of a change of leadership at any time, as a means of conflict resolution.

(3) Separate nation-wide elections make politics a harsher game than it would otherwise be and create an atmosphere that instigates divisions and gives additional chances to extremists.

Elections in two rounds create additional problems. On the one hand, the necessity to regroup for the second round may encourage moderates to join forces. On the other hand, when the "field of confrontation" is narrowed to the two candidates who have achieved a relative majority in the first round, the risk of polarising the society is increased.

(4) Since presidents may appoint officials and enjoy the rights of legislative initiative and of veto and a fixed term of office, they may retain power despite virtual loss of party support. With fixed incumbency *an ordinary cabinet crisis becomes an institutional and a constitutional crisis*, because there is no legitimate way to get rid of a bad president before his term expires.

On the contrary, a parliamentary government that no longer has a majority in the assembly must go, whether it is time to hold a new election or not. The conflict is solved by routine measures and is not allowed to develop into a national crisis.

Linz's arguments have been challenged on three grounds. The first objection is that parliamentary government is also known to have failed in solving the problems of divided societies. The political history of post-colonial Africa provides sufficient proof that a parliamentary majority, having gained control of the state, is quite capable of pursuing remarkably authoritarian policies.

On the other hand, there are counter-examples of successful presidential democracy. First and foremost among them is the example of the United States. One more, although less convincing example, is provided by Nigeria. The separation of powers was instrumental in averting (for a time, at least) the threat of particular ethnic groups monopolising the government of that country.

The third objection to Linz is that the presidentialist model can be improved by introducing election procedures that would preclude the direst consequences of the "winner-takes-all" formula. For example, rules about territorial distribution of electoral support, encourage centrist forces to consolidate and can help repair the damaged tissue of a divided society. Again, if we look at Nigeria, it practised this system of presidential election at the time of the Second Republic.

One could also conceive of other electoral procedures that might serve the same purpose, i.e. prevent a consolidated minority from monopolising power through presidential elections. In Sri Lanka, for example, voters are asked to rank presidential candidates in the order of preference, so that the second and the third choices are taken into account when tallying votes.

Indeed, some of the arguments offered by proponents of the parliamentary model can actually be turned against it. Majoritarian systems, for example, result in the majority parties, i.e. the parties that have got most, but *not all*, of the votes becoming *sole* power holders. In this system substantial groups of population are thus denied *their* share of power. To this, one might add that those who emphasise public (popular) control over power holders as a definitive aspect of democracy[10] should not forget that a leader of a majority party in a parliamentary system is, in fact, far less restricted in his or her daily exercise of power than even a U.S. president. In other words, what critics of the presidentialist model seem to object to, is a particular electoral system rather than the presidentialist model as such.

The fact that presidents and presidential administrations do not depend on legislative vote for their terms of office is, indeed, not conducive to organisation of well disciplined political parties. Lipset maintains, however, that the amorphous parties that operate in presidentialist regimes prove more effective in absorbing waves of discontent than the classical parliamentary parties.

In our opinion, the entire debate is pointless if political culture is left outside the scope of inquiry. Lipset is certainly right in asserting that the model of government is, by no means, the only factor of significance as far as the stability of democratic regimes is concerned. One can cite numerous examples of failing parliamentary democracies (Spain, Portugal, Greece, Italy, Austria, Germany, most East European countries of the 1920s and 1930s), on the one hand, and of successful and stable democratic presidencies (France of the Fifth Republic, Chile before Allende, Costa Rica and Uruguay for the most part of this century), on the other hand.

It is our firm conviction that traditions of political culture are much more important, as far as prospects for democracy are concerned, than a certain model of government. As Lipset correctly indicates, it is relevant that most stable democracies happen to be rich Protestant countries. The record of poor and Catholic countries has been far less impressive. According to Lipset, serious cultural obstacles to Western-type democracy are presented by Islam. Most "new" countries with stable parliamentary regimes are former British colonies that managed to transplant the rules and institutions of British democracy onto their native soils.[11]

The importance of political culture is best appreciated, if one considers the fact that electoral systems and other constitutional arrangements are relatively easy to manipulate, whereas political cultures are long-term factors. Any political culture changes slowly, and even when it does, the change is likely to go hand in hand with social catastrophes.

Advocates of parliamentary model recognise that not every presidentialist regime must eventually choose between authoritarianism and instability. Even imperfect democracies stand good chances of survival, if all the salient actors find non-democratic alternatives even less acceptable.

What is most important about the relative merits and demerits of the presidentialist and parliamentary models is the apparent danger of a conflictful rivalry between the branches of power built into the presidentialist system. (It is hardly necessary to stress the significance of this aspect from the standpoint of present-day Russian politics). The critics of presidentialism are fully aware of this. In an analysis of Horowitz's so-called "American argument", Linz points out the predicament of the presidentialist "divided government". This is when the president represents a party that does not enjoy a congressional majority. Under the circumstances, Linz argues, both parties are likely to resort to mutual "blame-laying" in an attempt to restore undivided government. If the United States have been a stable democracy, Linz argues that it has been despite presidentialism, not because of it. The system has owed its stability to three (compensating) factors: the lack of ideological rigidity, the availability of public sinecures and the politics of (centred on) local concerns.

Moving from the issue of a "divided government", it now is appropriate to turn to the issue of consociational democracy, i.e. a system of shared power practised in some "divided societies". The model has recently been subject of careful examination and some lively debate within the framework of "viable constitutionalism" which has a special interest in the problems of polyethnic and polyconfessional societies.[12]

The fiasco of consociational democracy in Lebanon in the 1970s has been the cause of much doubt as to the viability of its "semi-presidential" system. Distribution of offices between various ethnic (confessional) groups did not prevent them from coming into armed conflict. A similar conclusion may be drawn from the Cypriot experience. Recent political developments in the USSR, Georgia, Azerbaijan and Yugoslavia suggest that autonomous national units are likely to become a serious factor of destabilisation at times of cardinal socio-political changes: whereas inequalities between regions in levels of development and life standards, though hardly surprising, arouse much resentment, ethnic (confessional) identities provide regional elites with an easy but powerful means of consolidation/mobilisation in political and economic bargaining.

From this standpoint the *pillar model*, that allows for considerable cultural autonomy, but without strict territorial demarcation between ethnic groups and confessions, seems to promise greater stability.

An examination, as indeed the very existence, of the consociational approach attest to the complexity - and the relevancy - of the interplay between the two factors: political institutions and political culture.

3. Institutional Alternatives and Cultural Constraints

In this section we compare the two models, presidentialist and parliamentary, from a standpoint of integration mechanisms that characterise different political cultures.

Let us consider first the prospects for parliamentarianism in an ontologically integrated polity. As indicated above, the monarchical form of government is typical for such a society. The combination of authoritative monarchy with parliamentarianism is institutionally unstable. Since the parliament and the monarch are possessed of different legitimations, political disagreements between the executive and the parliamentary majority easily acquire an institutional dimension. In an attempt to assert the parliament's authority, rival factions tend to vote together on all relevant issues, and the deputy corps eventually unites against the monarch for institutional, rather than for immediate political reasons.

The chief executive, for his part, would have to take a distinctly anti-parliamentary stand and try to protect *his* legitimacy that he owes to no assembly.

There are numerous examples of this type of conflicts in the course of transition from monarchical to parliamentary regimes. The classic one is the English Civil War which took place in the mid-seventeenth century. The rivalry between the parliament and the king unfolded as a conflict of legitimacies within an ontology-integrated culture. The king appealed his "Divine Right", while the parliament referred to the idea of popular sovereignty. (It would be worthwhile to note here that Northern Europe managed, on the whole, to escape the phase of value-based integration that Spain and Italy had to pass in the course of their transition from Middle Ages to modernity).

A similar conflict was to be observed in France at the earlier stages of the Great Revolution. Both conflicts were characteristically resolved by executions of the kings, thus marking the victory of a new ontological principle over the old one.

The Westminster model evolved in the course of a gradual transfer of the executive functions from the king to a head of a parliamentary committee; in this the Divine Power of the monarch was superseded by the power of the sovereign nation. Concurrently, a new, operational, mechanism of integration evolved that was based on the consensus about the procedures of power.

As mentioned above, England and the Netherlands achieved the transition, skipping the value phase. The phase is characterised by populist leadership. Though William of Orange and Oliver Cromwell could be called "populist" in a sense, their "populism" did not match the populism of, for example, the French revolutionary leaders.

In France the value phase of integration was represented by Bonapartism whose triumph was preceded by a severe dualistic conflict. Napoleon skilfully manipulated the revolutionary values, as well as the values of nationalism, to re-integrate the French society. It was his use of these mechanisms of value (populist) integration that allowed him to mobilise the society in almost no time and raise and inspire an army that proved able to wage wars against virtually all Europe for twenty years.

(The nationalist idea, by the way, was behind many institutions of European modernity, such as universal military service for instance).

Value-based integration, being fraught with dualism, is not likely to produce stable parliamentary governments for it incites conflicts that tend to be resolved on barricades rather than on the floors of parliaments.[13] Nor is it conducive to stable democratic presidentialism: the ever growing ideologisation and politicisation of institutions aggravates the institutional conflicts already built into the presidentialist system and stimulates emergence of authoritarian regimes of the Latin American type.

If the executive and the legislative are legitimated independently of each other (as happens to be the case with the presidentialist model), neither ontology-based nor value-based integration mechanisms are likely to prevent conflicts between the branches of power. Consensus about procedures is, therefore, the only remedy for this type of institutional confrontation.

It seems to be this feature of the American society, viz. consensus about procedures, that accounts for the unique stability of the U.S. presidentialist regime. From this standpoint, it appears unwise for "new" states to rely on the U.S. experience. Innocent desire to reproduce this experience has already led astray many a country in Latin America. There can be no consensus about procedures in divided societies that lack its basic pre-requisite, common operational experience. Under the circumstances, presidentialism can produce nothing but perpetual conflicts between the branches of government that periodically relapse into authoritarianism of varying degrees of ferocity (a conclusion attested by the seventeen decades of the Latin American history).

Borrowing the presidentialist model, as many of the most post-Soviet states have done, has had similar results. It is sufficient to enumerate the more serious cases: Armenia, Azerbaijan, Belorussia, Chechnya, the Crimea, Georgia, Moldova, Russia, Ukraine. Four of these countries conflicts have already seen armed conflicts and harsh forms of reprisal, namely Azerbaijan, Chechnya, Georgia and Russia.

Even in countries, such as Poland and Lithuania, where the breach in operational experience between various social strata is not as deep as in Russia or Georgia, the relations between presidents and parliaments have sometimes been tense.

It would be interesting to observe in this respect that the presidentialist idea has been subject to growing criticism in the former Soviet states in recent times. Salambek Khadzhiev, for example, said (soon after he had been appointed head of the government of national revival of the Chechen Republic) that a presidential republic does not suit the Chechen people, because it contradicts its national traditions. Yet in 1991, when Chechnya held its first, and hitherto only, presidential election, the idea did not seem as alien as it would later be claimed to be.

In this respect, what is of special interest is the debate about the optimal form of government for Russia that took place at the Third and Fourth Congresses of People's Deputies of the Russian Republic in the aftermath of the March 1991 referendum on establishing presidency.[14]

It seems that the choice between presidentialism and parliamentarianism becomes meaningful (from the standpoint of democratisation) only after the value phase of integration has been or is about to be passed. If it is true, as has been argued above, that independent legitimation of the executive and the legislative requires a preliminary consensus about procedures to manage the ensuing institutional conflict and prevent it from destroying the state, the two branches are supposed to govern, one may venture to formulate the following theorem of transitology. *An institutional model that,* like presidentialism, *allows of rival legitimacies of the principal power institutions is unfit for the transitory stage of democratisation because it implies the kind of integration mechanism that has yet to be created.*[15] If played by democratic rules, the politics of dualism generate mobilisation patterns that are characterised by high level of participation and militant attitude, and this populism threatens to invalidate the tacit foundations of democratic presidentialism.[16] Once it has been replaced by or has degenerated into authoritarianism, the regime of presidential power can easily do away with what will yet remain of representative democracy.

To judge the stability of the new democratic regimes and the prospects for this or that form of democratic government, therefore, students of democratisation must pay special attention to political cultures of the countries in question. Otherwise disputes about the relative advantages and disadvantages of presidentialism and parliamentarianism are of little practical value. If we cannot identify the relevant cultural factors, especially the type and character of the integration mechanisms, our knowledge will remain lamentably inadequate.

Notes

[1] The *Bible* can be used to substantiate, at least, two different theories of kingly power. The one of the *New Testament* is best stated in Paul's *Epistles*. It maintains that people are to be governed by monarchs responsible to no one but God. The other, to be found in the *Old Testament*, e.g. in *Psalms*, sees God as a kind of judge who presides the case of the subjects vs. the monarch. By containing two different ontological models, the Holy Scripture could provide arguments for different parties in case of an ideological conflict in a culture that belonged to the Christian tradition.

A good example of such a conflict is the correspondence between Ivan the Terrible and Prince Andrei Kurbsky. Kurbsky, as becomes an intellectual with some relation to the *nestyazhateli* ("non-grabbers"), a group of religious activists in the first half of the 16th century who objected to accumulation of wealth by religious institutions and therefore supported secularisation of Church estates but put spiritual authority above secular power, defends the second version of the monarch-to-subject relations, the idea of God's Trial; Ivan draws on the authority of St. Paul to claim unlimited power over his subjects (see Fennel (ed.) 1955). For a detailed analysis of this aspect of the debate between the two antagonists, see Sergeyev 1989b.

[2] See Machiavelli 1979.

[3] Cf. ibid, pp. 107-10.

[4] See Dahl 1971.

[5] See Lijphart 1977; see also Lijphart 1984, Lijphart 1990, Lijphart 1994 (preprint), Riggs 1994 (preprint).

[6] Linz 1990a.

[7] Horowitz 1990.

[8] Lipset 1990.

[9] Linz 1990b.

[10] See, for example, Beetham 1994, p. 28.

[11] See also Blais and Dion 1990, Hadenius 1994, pp. 80-2.

[12] See Riggs 1994 (preprint).

[13] See Chapter 1.

[14] See Sub-sections on "The Third Congress" and "The Fourth Congress" in Section 4, Chapter 4.

[15] See also Sub-section on "The Rival Legitimacies" in Section 1 and Sub-section on "Lessons of Another October" in Section 4, Chapter 6.

[16] As Fred Riggs puts it (Riggs 1994, p. 124):

> ... the more 'undemocratic' a presidentialist system (with low turnout), the more viable it will be. The more 'democratic' a presidentialist regime (with high turnout), the more likely it is to be overthrown and replaced by authoritarianism.

3 *Perestroika* and the Crisis of *Sobornost'*

> At the moment when God created the world the movement of
> chaos must have made chaos more disorderly than when it was
> lying in peaceful disorder. So in our case, the disturbance of a
> society that is reorganizing itself must seem like an excess of
> disorder.
>
> *Chamfort, "Maxims and Thoughts".*

1. The Crisis of the Socialist Idea and the Disintegration of the USSR

Sobornost' as a Model of Political Representation

The striking institutional changes in the USSR and Russia after 1985 cannot be properly understood, unless one views them against the background of traditional political culture and, specifically, in light of the earlier experiences of political representation in Russian society.

The Russian *Zemskie Sobors* of the 16th and 17th centuries borrowed their organisational forms and their operational experience from the local ecclesiastical councils (*sobors* in Russian). The fact was not surprising and would only be of historical interest, had not the borrowed model happened to fit perfectly with the mentality of both Russian society and its political elite. From a cognitive standpoint, the primary feature of that frame of mind was *realism*, in the sense implied by medieval scholastic philosophy.

Realism is a philosophical theory that asserts the reality of universals, i.e. generalised properties of ordinary, observed things. A realist philosopher maintains that objects of true thought are no less real than objects perceived by senses. The practical attitude that follows from this ontological belief is that an "objectively true" answer can (and, therefore, must) be found to any question. What consequences this attitude may have for scientific investigation is beyond the scope of this inquiry. However, if applied to politics, the realistic stand undermines the very idea of

40

representation as an institution of a pluralist society: looking for a compromise that would suit all the principal participants in the discourse must appear, from this standpoint, absolutely foolish. Truth does not depend on human choice and cannot be a subject of compromise. Indeed, it would be absurd to negotiate to accept something as "grey" because one party argues that it is white, whereas another insists that it is black. It would be more sensible to trust an expert to suggest a solution. Philosophical realism can thus serve as a theoretical justification for a regime that the 20th century would name a technocratic utopia.

But if a representative assembly is not to represent particular positions and particular interests, why call it "representative"? Why convene it? To answer this question, one has to turn to the East Christian notion of authority. Who is the best expert and the best judge in the field of dogmatics? The Catholic Church would say "the Pope", the head of the church hierarchy and the heir to the apostolic seat of St. Peter. The Eastern Church asserts the priority of the Church which is understood as the totality of all true believers.

At first glance, the stand of the Eastern Church appears far more "democratic" than the elitist (technocratic) attitude of the West. Yet how then has the West turned out to be the birthplace of the classical democratic institutions, while the East is still perceived as the bogey of absolutism and totalitarianism? It is because the Church, in its capacity as the repository of ultimate truth, is seen as a kind of mystic unity, which makes it impossible to operationalise the procedures that could be used to arrive at the same end, i.e. the truth it possesses as a mystic whole, in an independent, non-mystic way.[1] In other words, however noble and beneficial the relations within the mystic unity, they cannot be institutionalised in principle. If we agree that stable democracy is an efficient system of problem-solving institutions, the democratic potential of the ontology of *sobornost'* remains wholly in the sphere of the transcendent and cannot provide a conceptual basis for institutional democracy.

A *sobor* is a symbolic representative of the Church as a whole and, like it, is seen and expected to act as a mystically united entity. Its members do not represent different parts of the community, an arrangement that would allow the represented groups to remain constantly in touch with each other and work out a joint (i.e. commonly approved of and therefore mutually obliging) policy. Their function is to "represent" the *entire* community. The natural question is "represent in relation to whom"? If a representative assembly is viewed as the representative of the entire community, its only conceivable counterpart within that community would be alienated *authority*. A representative institution of this type would have no *raison d'être* unless the ontological picture of the body politic included an agent of power that were set apart and above the community,[2] and even then only in a situation of crisis, when this agent of power needs to have his legitimacy reconfirmed. Under the circumstances individual members of a *sobor* are not independent politicians that represent recognised social interests. Consequently, they need no specific rights to fulfil their functions; and in the absence of rights there is no need for rules and procedures to protect those rights.

Representative institutions of *sobornost'* are modelled after the same pattern of totalitarian holism that forms the bed-rock of the culture of *sobornost'*. This culture reduces all functions of political representation to a single one: the representative body is expected to "represent" the community as a whole in its intercourse with the Authority. Naturally, the body must be a replica of the society it "represents" - not of the *actual* society, but of its ideal model, of what its members believe it to be. In true accord with the prevalent understanding of the community, the representative body is also seen as a kind of unstructured unity that permits no internal divisions. If these appear, they are treated as temporary flaws soon to be removed.

Strictly speaking, no representative institutions are necessary, if the idea of an intrinsic affinity that unites all the members within the community and ties the latter with the Government is taken seriously. Under "normal" conditions the administration (the only legitimate decision-making body and the only real political agency) has no use for them, and even if they exist, they operate in a "demonstration mode". Crises of legitimacy alone can make them influential politically, but even at times of crises their sole task is to provide new legitimation for new (or old) institutions of power. (Was it by chance alone that truly powerful, i.e. responsible, representative bodies only appeared in Russian history at "times of troubles" and revolutions? Is it surprising under the circumstances that a common mind instinctively associates the very idea of representative power with a major crisis, not to say with a national catastrophe?)

One of the most striking features of representative institutions of the *sobornost'* type is their anti-procedural bias. The obligation to abide by "the rules of the game" is invariably renounced in favour of political expediency. This fits the pattern: a mind that believes in intrinsic unity between the rulers and the ruled sees no sense in trying to restrict the former with "rules" (whatever these may be). Such restriction must, moreover, be regarded as an attempt on the government's *raison d'etre*, potency. In an atmosphere like this, even raising a point of procedure would normally bring one under suspicion as to one's real (presumably dubious) motives.[3]

The model's other idiosyncrasy is intolerance toward factions or, to put it in broader terms, toward any particularistic stand that dares to manifest itself within the representative institution.[4] In an institution modelled after the pattern of *sobornost'*, all internal differences must appear abnormal. The *sobor* members belong to some groups (classes, estates, strata, "factions" or "parties"), but the *sobor* is, by no means, considered an "appropriate" place for voicing and defending their particular interests. In its capacity as the representative of the society in general, of the "entire land" the *sobor* can be an arena of debate, but not of negotiations and voting. What has to be done in that respect, must be done elsewhere, and if not elsewhere, then at least "behind the scene".

A good and recent example of this type of representative institution is provided by the pre-*perestroika* Supreme Soviet. It seems inconceivable at first glance how the body might have managed to earn its reputation of a "rubber stamp". Although political publicists, both home and abroad, pictured the Supreme Soviet as an assemblage of helpless puppets,[5] the picture was far from the reality. In actual fact the deputy corps consisted almost exclusively of representatives of the national elite (the *nomenklatura*): high-level party functionaries, cabinet members and other top-ranking officials, including those responsible for the national economy, generals, well-known and highly esteemed representatives of free professions. It would be ridiculous to believe that all these people were always of the same opinion on all matters, without ever having a reason or an occasion or will to disagree. However, if they argued and quarrelled, it was always outside the Supreme Soviet. Within the Soviet itself, full and pathetic accord reigned, as if the deputies had no other wish but to show to the entire world and perhaps mostly to themselves that fundamentally they were at one with each other. Even those who were *contra* would unfailingly vote *pro*.[6]

In our opinion, this pattern behaviour has to be explained not by reference to unique servility of the Supreme Soviet deputies (which, given their real political weight in the society, would in turn call for an explanation), but by the character of the national political culture within which a representative body could not be conceived to behave in any other manner. Disagreement does not agree with the idea of mystic unity and if such unity is considered a primary political value, it must be shown to exist, even if it does not.

It must be obvious by now that no rational procedures designed to secure elaboration of mutually acceptable decisions are likely to exist within such an institution. It is not meant to make decisions: if by decision-making we mean the entire process, not the formal act alone,[7] these are worked out and made elsewhere. The proponents of *sobornost'*, for all their populist rhetoric,[8] are careful to maintain the distinction between the public sphere of representatives' activity and the actual process of political decision-making in which profane laymen must have no share.

The Institutional Innovations of Perestroika

The crisis of the Soviet political culture and the breakdown of the Soviet state cannot be analysed separately from the history of the institutional reforms in the USSR during *perestroika*. The most important object of this inquiry are the Congresses of People's Deputies of the USSR.

From the standpoint of political culture, the history of the Union Congresses can be described as a collision between the institutionally oriented operational experience, basically borrowed from the political culture of Western democracies, and the ontology of mystic unity characteristic of the native political culture.

Orientation to the Western models was part of the modernisation drive; its basic proponents were scholarly and artistic *intelligentsia* whose educational and cultural background was predominantly European. Modernisation has for decades been the catchword of the technocratic Soviet elite. But the deeper the crisis of "real socialism" and the less dynamic the basic institutions of the Soviet society, the more favourable the attitude of, at least, a part of the power elite to the *modus vivendi* and *modus operandi* of the political and ideological adversary. In the situation of prolonged confrontation when all plans and decisions had to be made with reference to the enemy's supposed response, the enemy was gradually (and unconsciously) emerging as a major reference point. On the other hand, permanent (for that was after all "peaceful co-existence") contacts with it contributed to the dissemination not only of its ideological values, but also of some knowledge about its operational political experience.

The influence, however, did not affect the deepest and the most stable layer of the political culture - social ontology. Its main guardians were the rank and file citizens, who were least exposed to Western cultural influences, although prepared, after the obvious failure of the communist "project", to discard its ideological (value) objectives. *Glasnost'* dealt basically with the ideological aspects of the political discourse, and so long as participation in it remained the privilege of the intellectual elite, the breech with Soviet political culture appeared decisive and irrevocable. After the constitutional reforms of 1988, however, broad masses of voters entered the game of politics and traditional attitudes were instantly revoked. The reformers' modernisation formulae, defined in terms of Western political culture and justified by reference to its political values, collided with the political culture of the overwhelming part of the populace.

The consequences have been dealt with in *Russia's Road to Democracy*. The central argument in that book is that the traditional Russian political culture - with its presumption of an inherent consensus between all participants in a political process and by its aspiration to political decisions that would be objectively true and, therefore, same for all and binding on all - has effectively deterred representation of specific interests in the would-be parliament and has prevented it from becoming an arena where a genuine social consensus based on compromise between diverse interests and competing visions of the country's future might have been worked out. The attempts, on the part of the leadership, to impose what they saw as "objectively correct" decisions proved, under conditions of apparent social discord, disastrous to both the parliament and the entire country.

The reformers themselves often acted in the traditional manner, whether because they, too, sought unconsciously to reproduce the traditional models or because they could not resist the temptation to capitalise on the real or imaginary advantages application of those models promised to political manipulators.[9] These tactics proved self-defeating. They alienated the voters by bringing the manipulatory techniques they practised inside their party into a modern electoral process.[10] They alienated the democratic minority of the Congress by trying to manipulate the deputy corps through party discipline. They also alienated the conservative majority of deputies by their hesitant but unmistakable reformism.

They managed to produce a queer institutional hybrid. The new representative body combined the agenda of modernisation with the behavioural patterns of a Party Congress and the thought-patterns of *sobornost'*. Ostensibly it was claimed (or at least expected at some point in future) to imitate the Western institutional models. In fact it operated in a traditional Soviet fashion and proved inadequate to the tasks faced by the nation and suffered a humiliating fiasco. The "Soviet parliament", that had been enthusiastically welcomed by the "foremen" of *perestroika* less than three years earlier[11] and had inspired great hopes among the broader masses of the electorate, left the political arena in the most miserable of ways. The state it had been called on to rule and modernise was lying in ruin.

Admittedly, the Russian deputies took some pain to bring the Union legislature and its members to that uninspiring end. In a sense, the story of the Russian parliament, at least its first chapters, is the story of the disintegration of the Soviet Union. But when a state falls to pieces, a logical question to ask is what kept it intact up to that moment and what made the integration mechanisms fail eventually?

There are answers to this question in store to suit any taste and any ideological bias. One may say that the Soviet Union, that heir to the czarist "prison of peoples", was an artificial political entity created and maintained by military force alone. It came to its natural end, as soon as the force ceased to be strong enough. In short, *tout empire périra* - "every empire shall perish".[12] Alternatively, one may say that the USSR was simply betrayed by ambitious upstarts who served the interests of world imperialism and will yet be called to account for this. The event was, however, of proportions too grand and of consequences too grave for these cliched platitudes to be taken seriously.

It may be true that "every empire will perish". But this does not mean that while they exist, empires are sustained by violence alone. It goes without saying that empires engage in violence, and not only for immediate practical reasons. They sometimes do it to demonstrate how strong they are. The cult of military strength is one of the most important elements of imperial political cultures. Yet force cannot be resorted to always and everywhere.[13] An imperial nation that does nothing but fight its subject states is soon left without resources. The Soviet Union could, by strained effort, suppress resistance in the Baltics, Western Ukraine and Northern Caucasus, as was the case in the 1940s - during and after the Second World War. Yet, it is difficult to conceive of an empire that was able to maintain that level of mobilisation permanently for several decades. On the other hand, great powers are not destroyed by mere treacheries, save perhaps in epos. (The curious thing is that the discourse of many a critic of "the

Belovezh conspiracy" is indeed modelled after epic tales: a small group of traitors, a foreign enemy, the cheated people that will eventually shake the delusion, punish the renegades and, last but no least, restore what has been so treacherously destroyed).

We have already mentioned that integration mechanisms are built around some core belief that provides explanation and justification for the members of a community living together and is shared by a sufficiently large number of these members.[14] A belief of this sort cannot arise out of nothing. To disentangle the mess of conditions and influences that produce, augment and perpetuate such beliefs is one of a social scientist's most rewarding tasks. On the other hand, no "objective" conditions and no reasoning that appeals to "objective" needs would in themselves secure the integrity of a body politic, if its members do not will it to continue. The downfall of the USSR is the best evidence for this. In vain did political and cultural leaders argue that history had tied the republics of the USSR with thousands of strings together, that any attempt to sever them would have catastrophic consequences, that everything, from the geopolitical situation and the level of economic integration to the mixed population of virtually any territory within the country, committed us to living together. These arguments failed to convince the majority and prevent the disintegration of the Union - but not because they were mistaken or insincere. They just did not elicit the intended response because their reasoning did not fit in the cultural patterns of the peoples (the Russian people included) that lived in what was quickly ceasing to be a "country" and turning into mere "space"; their arguments did not appeal to any meaningful elements of that culture. On the other hand, there are many instances known of communities surviving under the most unfavourable of circumstances without losing their identities.

The Soviet Union collapsed because the mechanisms of social integration that had hitherto secured the predominance of the centripetal over the centrifugal tendencies stopped working, indicating, to be sure, a deep crisis of the Soviet political culture.

The unity of the Soviet body politic rested not so much on its military strength and the economic ties between its constituent parts (which does not mean that the economic ties were irrelevant and the military force had never been used) but rather on a belief in the peculiar Soviet social project.[15] It was this belief that gave meaning and value to that *particular* system of economic ties (not always and, as the future was soon to show, by no means indisputably advisable from the standpoint of disinterested economic science) and supported that *particular* power structure. After it became clear that the project had failed, *a re-evaluation of values* commenced. That painful process determined the emotional atmosphere of that period of Soviet history that would be later referred to as *the period of stagnation.* The basic institutions of Soviet society were quickly losing prestige and the Soviet way of life, its appeal. Communism figured less and less as a programme goal and ever more often as a character in spiteful jokes.[16]

However, that "re-evaluation of values" did not imply discarding the values of the preceding generations. They were discarded, indeed, but not by everyone. Public opinion polls prove that beyond doubt. We have every reason to believe that the majority of Russians, as probably the majority of people in all other countries that emerged on the ruins of the USSR, still appreciate much of what the Soviet propaganda called "the achievements of socialism", viz. relative equality in wealth, social security for the disabled, state-sponsored education and health programmes etc.[17] A curious confirmation of this is provided by the unexpectedly positive response to the somewhat paradoxical statement that such strongholds of capitalism as the U.S., the U.K. and Germany display a higher level of "socialism" than the Soviet Union and other recently "Socialist" countries.[18] The statement was taken in, because people believed that a "reasonably organised" society could not fail to implement so obvious an ideal.

The crisis' main point was not that the old Soviet social and political values were discarded, but that the hierarchy of values was upset. The first elements of the hierarchy to be "amputated" were those that were immediately related to practical politics: the authority of the governing party and its domestic and foreign policies. In other words, values were not overthrown, but their visible embodiments, "the idols" were.

But a system of values that is not crowned by an organisation of which the function is to realise the values in question and does not encompass the policies of such an organisation[19] would not do as the integrating factor. Traditional values were still believed widely, but even the believers no longer alleged that their implementation required them living together. How could they if it turned out that their cherished ideals were in fact realised more thoroughly and with greater success in the countries long regarded antipodes of socialism?

Suffice it to say that the Soviet regime relied on the system of political values as it integration mechanism. The pattern is a typical one for a culture that combines the ontology of mystic unity (*sobornost'*) with the operational experience of a violent internal conflict (the Civil War and the Great Terror). Whether this function can be transferred onto other elements of the *Russian* political culture and what the consequences are likely to be, both institutionally and politically, is the subject of the subsequent research.

2. The Game and the Failure of *Perestroika*

The political situation in Russia in the early nineties differed substantially from the political situation in the USSR in the late 1980s - during the period of *perestroika*. The political scene looked different and was full of newcomers.[20]

The question was whether the changes went beyond the situational politics to encompass the type and style of policy-making? Were they as deep as sweeping? Can we say that they amount, or promise to amount, to that shift in political culture that makes operational experience the basis for integration, as was suggested by Chapter 1? To put it otherwise, did a new leadership actually mean a new political regime?

The collapse of the Soviet Union marked the failure of the attempt at institutional innovation made by previous leaders. But what are we to think of the attempt itself? What was the outcome supposed to be, if it had been crowned with success? We argue that the whole enterprise was actually an exercise in *elitist* politics. Indeed, the authors seem to have known perfectly well what it was they wanted when they chose the name of *perestroika* ("re-construction") for the policy they were about to initiate. What they had in mind was a balanced system of Western-type political institutions intended to push forward the aborted process of modernisation. The plan originated with the political elite, and its only chance of success lay in the whole affair remaining the private concern of the establishment. The establishment was institutionalised, it possessed corporate ethics and corporate experience, it recognised and cultivated rules of the game - and in that it differed substantially from the counterelite that was soon to take its place.

The old elite sought a normal Western-style institutionalisation. Those people cherished operational experience, although what experience they had had been gained from Soviet political institutions. They were not obsessed by revolutionary zeal. Whatever they planned to do, they intended to do all by themselves. They did not want outside interference and would not allow outsiders in, although the difference between "ourselves" and "aliens" was not ontologised and the distinction remained purely corporate in character. Political pluralism, as seen by the initiators of *perestroika*, implied a renunciation of imposed conformity of opinion within the power elite, not political freedom for alternative political forces. As to the rank and file, they were to comply and to applaud the leadership - in a traditional manner. To obtain your own part in the oratorio of *perestroika* you had to be "one of us". The entire campaign was directed, or was at least meant to be directed, by the ideological department of the CPSU Central Committee. The "nightingales" and "foremen" of *perestroika* were no dissidents (the exceptions were few and, by no means, accidental), but veteran soldiers of the "ideological struggle". This does not mean they did not believe in the idea of *perestroika* and did not want it to succeed. A considerable part of the Soviet political, administrative and cultural elite (including officers of the KGB, functionaries of the Central Committee, officials of the Foreign Ministry and various departments involved in foreign trade, the *nomenklatura* of the Academy of Sciences) had already "tasted the West" and did not mind indulging that kind of life at home. Yet they had no desire to part with their power and privileges.

The attitudes and ideas of these people differed sharply from those of the middle stratum of the bureaucracy. If the two echelons of the bureaucratic elite were not divided by a cultural abyss, they were divided by mutual estrangement. Both were westernised, but in different ways. The first-rank elite had long since "appropriated" the state and was accustomed to disposing of the national resources as if these had been their own property; those of "the second sort" had to content themselves with the precarious control over commercial structures and corruption as the primary means of "utilising" that control. An official at the Foreign Ministry would live or travel abroad and enjoy the pleasures of "the Western way of life" and the privileges of legal income in hard currency. He would not accept bribes and would despise those who did. The two castes had different operational experience. The "second-rate" elite would also be looking, or believed to be looking, West. They would worship entrepreneurship, market and power given by money. But what they knew of the West was mainly hearsay and they seemed never to understand properly the difference between their social position and that of the Western business elite.

The breakdown of *perestroika* can be seen then as a political fiasco of the "cream" elite, or rather of the part of it that espoused the cause of modernisation. These people started reforms and failed. The re-organised Soviet party elite was disoriented. It lacked the operational experience that conformed to the reformers' institutional designs and could not rely on what experience it had. Attempts to administer the Congress of People's Deputies and the Supreme Soviet in the customary fashion, through party channels and territorial deputy groups most of which were still under effective Party control, aroused vehement opposition on the part of outsiders (whose support was vital for the reforms to succeed). This presence of legal organised opposition, although it did not amount to genuine multipartyism, made traditional skills obsolete, whereas faction politics required skills the "Old Guard" had never had. This state of confusion was redoubled by the fact that behind the variety of social, economic and political problems - that had emerged as a devil from the box and, with the customary methods of problem-managing suspended, allowed for no immediate solutions - there was a Gordian knot of potential political alliances which they could not hope to untie for want of almost everything: experience, desire, ideological guidance.

Incompetent tactics in the field of institution-building predetermined the failure of the policy the new institutions were meant to realise. Both personal motives and external stimuli that had prompted the Soviet elite to embark on the course of reforms were still there, but confidence and mass support were gone. As it turned out, the existing operational experience could not be overcome in an hour, or ignored. Under the circumstances alternative mechanisms of policy-making were in demand that would combine the traditional social ontology and the traditional operational experience with a new set of values.

3. The Conflict of Elites

The "re-evaluation of values" that unfolded amid the social crisis of the 1970s and 1980s and consummated in renunciation of the communist ideology paved the road for the reforms: mass support was secured, the rest depended on leadership. In 1990-91 the counter-elite consolidated around the movement *Democratic Russia*. Initially this united virtually all opponents to the regime and promised to become (although it never did) the nucleus of a nation-wide democratic party. In what was a rather strange alliance of liberals and populists the former were easily pushed aside. Through its appeal to new values and its invocation of the traditional ontology and operational skills, populism offered fantastic opportunities for political mobilisation.

The majority of the USSR Congress of People's Deputies used to reproach its political opponents for indulging in "idle talk" and for inability (and, presumably, unwillingness) to do "real work".[21] As used against members of a legislative assembly, the complaint meant simply that the bulk of the Soviet political elite did not understand the nature and meaning of parliamentary "work". But after the new representative body was discredited and the epicentre of political discord moved from the parliament floor into city squares, the worst fears, whether sincere or assumed, of the orators of the First Congress suddenly came true: there was, indeed, no work to be done at a mass rally, except to talk, better still to chant.

The new counterelite was thus given a unique chance. Instead of wresting power from political rivals in the legal framework of new political institutions (a tedious endeavour with uncertain prospects) they would have rather used rallies and other forms of mass politics to ram the gates of authority and force their way to power positions. August 1991 seemed to have made that chance a reality, but it also made it clear that the political skills of the new elite were limited to their ability to capitalise on mass discontent and that they had no programme of institution-building because, like their defeated rivals, they were possessed neither of an operational experience adequate to the situation, nor of definite ideas as how to deal with it. In retrospect, Gorbachev appears to have been far more a "parliamentary" politician than Yeltsin.

The immediate difference between the new post-communist and post-*perestroika* elite and the old elite lay in the methods of recruitment. The traditional Soviet political elite was enrolled from "the select circles" of the *nomenklatura*: membership of the *nomenklatura* and corporate solidarity were decisive factors in political career. Both were carefully regulated and monitored. Everything depended on how close you were to those in power: either directly, through party offices, or indirectly, through the *nomenklatura* positions in "civil" institutions and "public organisations" (ministries, academic institutions, trade unions, etc.). The same stands true of the *perestroika* elite: despite the peripeteia of reforms and the inner-party fight triggered by them, it preserved the traditional pattern of intraelite relations and its corporate ethics.

The new people distinguished themselves at mass rallies (including those during the two run-ups). All of a sudden a cohort of activists managed to penetrate into the sphere of politics, the sort of customers who would not have been allowed within gunshot of it had they had to pass the filters of party committees. For them, as well as for the society at large, that was a radically new type and new level of vertical social mobility: 1989, 1990 and 1991 saw stupendous careers. But natural as it was to be expected for that level of vertical mobility, the influx of "fresh blood" was not the only effect: the dull progress of the *nomenklatura* careers was replaced by giddying rises and falls characteristic of political favouritism. Patronage flourished: in a sense the nucleus of the new Kremlin elite was picked from Yeltsin's personal favourites, and that team was soon to learn the vicissitudes of that kind of fortune.[22]

In 1991 Russia underwent a radical change in the type and style of social development: tentative institutional innovations introduced and monitored by the establishment culminated in the collapse of old institutions and the ascent of a counter-elite. If the vocabulary of political science is to consist of words with reasonably fixed meanings, the event can only be termed a revolution. The spectacular change in the conditions and span of vertical social mobility characteristic of a revolution paved the way to positions of power for people with the mentality of marginal outsiders, politicians who not only lacked a definite and stable social basis but demonstrated a tendency to break away from whatever links that connected them to their society.

Yet what looks so gloomy in retrospect, was almost indiscernible at the beginning. At face value, the representative institutions of the Russian Federation did not seem to fit the model of *sobornost'* as this has been described above. The anti-procedural philippics, once so successful at the USSR Congresses of People's Deputies, aroused little sympathy on the newly elected republican forum. The Russian political elite was now looking to the West in an attempt, more or less conscious, to imitate the classic patterns of Western parliamentarianism. Naturally enough, the superficial forms, including procedures, were the first to be borrowed, and this could not help but change the attitude towards this aspect of parliamentary activities. New Rules were soon adopted, and a special Order Group was established to supervise their implementation and help resolve procedural conflicts.

The old antifactional sentiments were of little avail. If the election campaigns of 1990 did not take place under conditions of genuine multipartyism,[23] they were at least conducted in an atmosphere of unprecedented political freedom. Under the circumstances the existence of factions was taken for granted, and no objections were raised as to their official status at the Congress and in the Supreme Soviet.[24]

Patterns of political behaviour were also undergoing change. Public discussion of vital political issues and the new practice of televising parliamentary debates promised to reduce to the minimum the divorce between the overt and esoteric aspects of politics typical of the *sobornost'* model.

The difference between the new republican legislature and the representative institutions of the USSR was obvious. This was strengthened by the rivalry between them and the frustration resulting from the subordinate status of the republican assembly that initially dominated over all other considerations. To distance themselves from their Union fellow-deputies was a sign of style, whereas any comparison with them was intended as either a reproach or an insult.[25] The rivalry between the Union and the Russian legislatures was not enough to eliminate political disagreements within the latter, but for the time being it served to push them into the background and even to appease them to some extent.

For all their ideological differences, the two major political forces, *Democratic Russia* and *Communists of Russia*, displayed not only touching, albeit superficial, accord on the issues that directly involved the powers of the republican institutions, but also a mutual desire to abide by the rules of chivalry.[26]

However, subsequent developments were yet to show that the contrast was mainly due to short-term situational factors and the changes did not go so far as to affect the deep-most layers of the political culture. While the newly elected republican Congress and Supreme Soviet, which at that moment possessed but a semblance of power, practised rhetoric rather than politics, the illusion they produced of a major break with the old culture was almost absolute. But after the fiasco of the August coup and the subsequent collapse of the USSR changed the entire political landscape, the republican organs were boosted to the pinnacle of state power or, to put it otherwise, after the political warming-up was over and the real game began, the traditional patterns of political behaviour re-emerged, apparently superseding the fashionable innovations of the latter days.[27]

4. Political Dualism and the Fate of *Sobornost'*

Yet this should not be taken to mean that the traditional culture had undergone no changes whatsoever. Under the impact of the general social crisis and the institutional innovations of *perestroika* it entered a specific phase of which the distinctive feature was a high level of political and ideological confrontation. Under the circumstances the idea of *sobornost'* as a "natural" and "normal" state of affairs could not remain unchanged. Taken together these changes would amount to what can be called a crisis of the culture of *sobornost'*.

We have already mentioned that at the initial stage of *perestroika* the culture of *sobornost'* remained latent, even anonymous. Under the communist rule the term was never used, due to its obvious religious connotations,[28] although the ontological and value attitudes it stood for remained paramount in the Soviet political culture. The collapse of the communist regime drew *sobornost'* out of a cultural underground. Appeals to revive "the lost *sobornost'*" and restore the society's "spiritual unity" were soon to be heard more often and sound ever louder.[29]

On the other hand, the broad masses and the political elite were apparently beginning to think in the opposite fashion. Both political life and political rhetoric were growing ever more confrontational. If not bygone, the fear, perhaps affected, of a split within the society was pushed in the background.

In the first years of the dramatic social experiment known as *perestroika* the Soviet society appeared as united and quiet as before. Whether we see that project as an attempt to "realise the potential advantages of socialism" or as the dismantling of the socialist system disguised as "socialism with a human face", *perestroika* and *glasnost'* had revealed latent social conflicts and polarised the country's political life. It split the ostensibly monolithic Soviet society and made social integration - an issue long believed to have been solved once and for ever - the primary point of the political agenda. After the six years of *perestroika* the Soviet (and later Russian) territorial identity was called into question. Moreover, the rupture affected the basic structures and institutions *inside* Russian society.

By the time the would-be Russian deputies entered the election campaign in spring 1990, little had been left of "the moral and political unity of the Soviet people" that the official propaganda still occasionally strove to evoke. Russian society was stirred up.

Despite a conscientious effort to observe what was believed to be the rules of parliamentary propriety, the Russian Congress of People's Deputies and the Russian Supreme Soviet exhibited the level of confrontation that surpassed by far the harshest conflicts of the Gorbachev period. From the first clash over the election of the Chairman of the Supreme Soviet[30] and up to the tragic finale of 4 October 1993, the Russian parliament displayed anything but the serene accord within itself and with the Government, first that of the USSR and then of Russia proper, that became a true monolithic *sobor.*

Dualism emerged as the psychological dominant of the time. Political activists (regardless of their ideological orientations and political preferences) became firmly convinced that a bitter and uncompromising contest between two opposing forces was the distinctive feature of the present stage of development. Yet if we asked what forces, the answer would vary from group to group. Some would define them as "partocrats" and "democrats"; others, as the imperialistic "Centre" and the oppressed peoples of "the colonies"; others still, as "Judeo-Masons" and "genuine Russian patriots". But the confrontational attitude and political intolerance was common for all.

In that situation proponents of extreme views arose as the salient or, at least, the most noticeable characters on the Russian political scene. On the contrary, invocations of centrism as an influential political force proved of no avail and the central segment of the political spectrum tended to shrink. Although migration of political activists from one flank to the other produced an illusion of a multitudinous and influential political centre, the "delay" at the centre would normally be a short one: political forces gravitated towards the flanks, the centre eroded and lost both its political and ideological identity. This was despite the fact that "centrism" as a political stand enjoyed a very high rating and a considerable part of the Russian political elite (including many parliamentary politicians) consciously sought to identify with it.[31]

This circumstance alone indicates that the dualistic outlook was not so much a description of the respective state of affairs, but rather the cause of it. The vision of a society as an arena of struggle between two irreconcilable forces expressed an ontological attitude that required no empirical confirmation. It was not by chance that the participants in the political discourse began to speak in that characteristically mythologised language of which the terms are not operationalised and allow of no verification: cliches like "the Destructive Forces", "the Centre", "the

Apparatus", "the Mafia", "the Partocracy", "the Agents of Imperialism", "the Red-browns" and "the Judeo-Masons". The peculiar feature of this type of labels is that they are not used to characterise social and political forces, but to be "fastened" on them. The would-be "label-bearers" need not even exist as real political groups: they can always be "cut out" of the available political material.[32]

Disintegration of Sobornost':
Individual Emancipation versus Institutional Innovations

To properly assess the recent political developments in Russia, including the emergence of a new political elite, one has to view them in the context of cultural transformation. Two alternatives appear plausible when one considers the possible disintegration of the culture of *sobornost'*. One is individual's emancipation from the totality of the community. When pressed to its extreme, this is likely to bring about utter decomposition of the society and transform it into a chaotic aggregate of egoistic individuals, thus reproducing Hobbes' classical metaphor of a "war of all against all".

It must be noted here that disintegration of the "organic whole" postulated by the mentality of *sobornost'* ("the moral and political unity of the Soviet people" in the communist jargon) started long before *perestroika*. It suffered its first blows in the years of Khrushchev's thaw. True, that celebrated "moral and political unity" had, by no means, precluded the existence of all sorts of "renegades" and "turncoats", who were seen as the people's adversary in the desperate war it fought against its apostates in the spirit of classical dualism.

However, the 1960s seemed to indicate an alternative course for transformation of the traditional culture, viz. emergence of social institutions of a new (non-*sobornost'*) type, particularly in the field of the so called "shadowy economy". It would be interesting to observe here that the institutions of the "shadowy economy" ("*tsekhoviki*"[33]) acted at that time, unlike their more recent twins, primarily as producers, not as intermediaries. It was the period when economic cooperation with the West seemed more and more attractive, a characteristic change that would eventually pave the way for the "joint ventures" of the early *perestroika* years.

An alternative to the individualistic emancipation with its characteristic relativisation of values and the ensuing debilitation of the value-centred integration mechanisms is the development of modern procedure-oriented institutions within the traditional *sobornost'*. Their subsequent emancipation *qua* institutions, accompanied by dissemination of the relevant operational experience, may help evade the double danger of complete disintegration of society and restoration of the old regime as the only means to re-integrate it.

It is worthwhile to reiterate at this point that these alternatives were also made manifest in Western Europe at the time when European medieval society and its political culture (both resembling, indeed, the society and culture of *sobornost'* in a number of important ways) were approaching their end. The two alternatives appeared then as the difference between Renaissance and Reformation. Whereas the emancipation of personality that the Renaissance exalted as the ultimate goal of cultural transformation failed to guarantee the realisation of the relevant ideals of political freedom and proved, moreover, instrumental in the emergence of tyrannical regimes that indulged in all sorts of atrocities,[34] the countries that embarked on Reformation (England, the Netherlands, etc.) witnessed the growing role of parliaments and the flourishing of institutions that were to shape the economic life of modernity. Moreover, they proved able to introduce a fundamental cultural innovation by inventing an entirely novel mechanism of social integration, one that invoked operational experience and procedures rather than ontological beliefs and values.

The Renaissance Model and the Allure of Authoritarianism

This was the dilemma that Russia faced in 1990. The initial period of *perestroika*, before 1989, was characterised by manifest attempts at institution-building (constitutional amendments, the new representative assembly, legislation on the cooperatives), but then different tendencies prevailed. In our opinion, the turning point was the Second Congress of People's Deputies of the USSR and, by coincidence, the death of Academician Andrei Sakharov (December 1989). The democratic movement has since shifted toward populism, rallied round the charismatic figure of Boris Yeltsin, and sought power as its primary objective, a precondition for the future reforms. The program of these it never cared to elaborate in advance.

Democratic Russia was basically forged as a movement *contra*. In this capacity it managed to unite all those who rejected the values and institutions of the Soviet society. However, it failed to provide a consolidating idea *pro*. The result was inevitable: immediately after its impressive success in the elections of 1990, the movement split, and some of its former candidates, like Ilya Konstantinov and Sergei Baburin, rapidly shifted toward extreme "patriotism". The electoral campaign staged and won in a spirit of populism produced a deputy corps, whose members felt more at ease at mass rallies than in parliamentary committees.

On the other hand, proclamation of "radical" bourgeois values, such as absolute freedom of economic activity, the obvious tendency, on the part of the official state structures, to shirk responsibility for maintaining social stability under the pretext of opening a new chapter in the relations between the state and the civil society (all quite remote, indeed, from the actual values and activities of the renowned Western prototypes) served to create a peculiarly nihilistic social atmosphere - nihilistic towards new social institutions, that is. This closely resembled the social atmosphere in tiny Italian states of the Renaissance period.

It was not, perhaps, too surprising that in such an atmosphere distinguished democrats began to advocate authoritarianism, and former champions of social justice and fighters against immoral privileges turned blind eyes to the growing corruption. The political culture of *sobornost'* was obviously in crisis, but it has been supplanted by the culture of dualism, of which the focal point is relentless struggle between Good and Evil, whether the latter is identified as the gloomy heritage of communism or the anti-national, "occupationist" regime of pro-Western reformers.

This uninspiring outcome is a natural consequence of the elite's refusal (or inability) to embark on the course of institutional innovations. This is not to say that the country was to see no activity in the field of institution-building. It would, perhaps, see too much of it, but those would be mainly unsystematic improvisations that tended to produce helpless and ephemeral mongrels. These managed to combine the incompatible: most obsolete features of the old regime with stunning elements of a radically new social order. The nation naturally gained very little from those fanciful monsters. Both parliamentary acts and presidential decrees often proved to be out of touch with realities, and were consequently seldom realised. It was customary for bills of law to be passed unsupported by secondary administrative acts and even regardless of their economic cost, that is without due consideration of their practical feasibility.[35] Democratic and reformist rhetoric proved insufficient even to justify itself. The result was a dramatic loss of confidence in democracy and its leaders.

Notes

[1] Cf. Berdyaev 1939, p. 186:

> The Pope is infallible when inspired by the Holy Spirit. But there is no
> criterion to decide when he is so inspired. An even more complicated
> situation arises when infallible authority is claimed by a council [*sobor*] or
> a synod. A council is infallible only when it is inspired by the Holy Spirit
> and gives utterance to truth. But there is, again, no criterion for judging
> when a council is so inspired. Nor is there any criterion of the Holy Spirit.
> And in any case the Holy Spirit is not a criterion, always a rational and
> legal concept, but is rather grace, freedom and love. It is independent of
> any kind of determinism. Khomyakov grasped the fact very well in his
> doctrine of *Sobornost* which repudiates any external authority . The agency
> of the Holy Spirit is manifest in *Sobornost*, in the Church as an integral
> whole, in the Church community. But there are no criteria to establish the
> fact. We have on the one hand truth, the utterance of a council, and we
> have on the other the council in which truth is uttered. The Holy Spirit is
> not revealed in the council, but the council is implied in the revelation of
> the Holy Spirit.

[2] See Sub-section on "The Culture and Politics of *Sobornost'*" in Section 1,
Chapter 1.

[3] See Sergeyev and Biryukov 1993, pp. 112-8 for recent examples.

[4] On recent manifestations of this attitude, see ibid, pp. 147-51.

[5] "A juridical Potemkin village", as Peter Vanneman put it contrasting the
prevalent "non-Soviet characterisations" to "Soviet exaltations of the
body as the supreme manifestation of democratic-representative
government" (see Vanneman 1977, p. 3).

[6] We cannot resist the temptation to quote here a.Russian pre-*perestroika*
joke enumerating "the six dialectical contradictions of developed
socialism": (1) We do not have unemployment, but no one is working.
(2) No one is working, but all production plans are fulfilled. (3) All
production plans are fulfilled, but there is nothing on sale. (4) There is
nothing on sale, but everyone manages to get everything he wants.
(5) Everyone gets everything he wants, but everyone is discontented.
(6) Everyone is discontented, but when it comes to voting, everyone
votes *pro*.

[7] On the stages of the decision-making process, see e.g. Agger *et al.* 1972, p. 24.

[8] On the populist rhetoric at the Congress of People's Deputies of Russia, see Chapter 8.

[9] For a detailed analysis of the 1988 constitutional reform and the institutional innovations envisaged by it, see Sergeyev and Biryukov 1993, pp. 90-101.

[10] See Sub-section on "Boris Yeltsin and the Idea of Russian Sovereignty" in Section 1, Chapter 4 for an example.

[11] See, for example, Burlatski 1988.

[12] The title of a book by J.-B.Duroselle (see Duroselle 1981).

[13] Cf. to Hume [no year], p. 24:

> No man would have any reason to *fear* the fury of a tyrant, if he had no authority over any but from fear; since, as a single man, his bodily force can reach but a small way, and all the farther power he possesses must be founded either on our own opinion, or on the presumed opinion of others.

[14] See Section 1 "Integration Mechanisms as Elements of Political Cultures" in Chapter 1.

[15] The memo of that project, "The Programme of the CPSU", caught but the last remnants of the one-time enthusiasm; still, even this much-mocked document enjoyed some popularity for a while.

[16] To give but one example. Capitalism, Socialism and Communism have set off on a drinking-bout. Capitalism and Communism have procured a bottle of vodka and are waiting for Socialism who is late. "Where on earth have you been?", they ask when he eventually turns up. "Queueing for sausage". "What's 'queueing'?", asks Capitalism. "What's 'sausage'?", asks Communism.

[17] See Grushin 93.

[18] Following is a typical example borrowed from the field of this study (Yu.Gekht's speech at the First Congress of People's Deputies of Russia; see *First Congress RSFSR* 1992, Vol. 1, p. 513):

> [My] trips to the West have confirmed that the ideas of socialism are
> correct. By what means has the West achieved its [present] level? By
> developing social forms of ownership of the means of production.

[19] On the role of such "grace-distributing organisation" in this type of
political cultures, see Sub-section on "Values as the Integrating Force" in
Section 1, Chapter 1.

[20] Recent research indicates, however, that the personal changes have not
been as far-going as it is sometimes believed (see Kryshtanovskaya
1995).

[21] See Sergeyev and Biryukov 1993, pp. 112-8.

[22] Sergei Stankevich spent several months as Vice Premier to end as a rank-
and-file deputy. Yegor Gaidar, only recently head of a department in a
journal (incidentally, *Kommunist*), unexpectedly promoted to the
headship of the first non-communist government of Russia, grew to
become the symbol of reform but was dismissed as a result of an abstruse
political manoeuvre (see Section 2 "The Seventh Congress" in Chapter 6
for details). Sergei Shakhrai passed through a number of career
revolutions in the short span of a few months. And, last but not least,
Gennadi Burbulis, Yeltsin's chief strategist and presumably the second
person in the post-August hierarchy, had soon to content himself with
membership of the State Duma and directorship of an obscure "research
centre".

[23] See Section 2 "The 1990 Republican Election" in Chapter 4.

[24] This does not mean that the political culture at large does no longer have
any problems accommodating political pluralism. Following is striking
evidence of the revived hostility towards factionalism (Vasilyev 1994):

> There must be no parties, blocs or factions in the new body [the proposed
> Legislative Assembly - N.B. & V.S.]. Everyone in the Assembly lives by
> his own mind, behaves and votes as his conscience and his knowledge
> suggest.

This is an excerpt from a letter sent (of all the newspapers) to the liberal
daily *Nezavisimaya gazeta*.

[25] See, e.g., A.Zakharov's speech on 13 December 1990 (*Second Congress
RSFSR*, 1992, Vol. 5, p. 113):

Till the present moment we have never resembled the Union parliament as closely as today.

[26] See, for example, speeches by A.Tikhomirov on 7 June 1990 and S.Akhmetkhanov on 20 June 1990 (*First Congress RSFSR*, 1992, Vol. 3, p. 432 and Vol. 5, p. 122, respectively).

[27] See below Sub-section on "The Third Congress" in Section 4, Chapter 4 and especially Section 1 "At a Turning-Point" in Chapter 5.

[28] Its objectionable semantics were made even less agreeable by the fact that *sobornost'* became the catchword of the exiled idealistic philosophers: Nikolai Berdyaev, Sergei Bulgakov, Semyon Frank, Nikolai Lossky and others. Like Jewish priests in the Babylonian captivity, these thinkers set to conceptualise the type of mentality that had evolved in the pre-revolutionary Russia and is the subject of the present analysis (see Berdyaev 1944, pp. 102-17, 200-22; Berdyaev 1951, pp. 103-12; Bulgakov 1971, pp. 401-8; Lossky 1953, pp. 380-3; Lossky 1994, pp. 322-9; Vysheslavtsev 1955, pp. 55-8; Frank 1926, pp. 21-6; and especially Frank 1930, pp. 97-120, 182-202, 265-314). The emigre philosophers naturally opposed their ideal of *sobornost'* to the Soviet reality, as sacred to profane and as spiritual to material (see Berdyaev 1944, pp. 68-9, 201-2; Berdyaev 1947b, pp. 144), but although they regarded the revolution as a national catastrophe, they did not deny the obvious continuity between the pre-revolutionary and post-revolutionary cultures.

[29] See, e.g., an apologia by one of Russia's most "politicised" ecclesiastics, Ioann, the late Metropolitan of St.Petersburg and Ladoga (Ioann [Snychev] 1994-95). Of the more learned writings see Gulyga 1995 (the following excerpt is on p. 305):

> What form of government must we choose? There are among us proponents of monarchical rule, the advantages of which have been considered in the beginning of the book. There are proponents of socialist choice convinced that the course of violence chosen after 1917 was mistaken, but the direction was shown right. There are proponents of popular rule, supporters of democracy. *Let us not waste our strength in argument, the important point now is national consolidation* in the spirit of that *sobornost'* that was nursed by the theorists of the Russian idea. After all *the essence of a state does not depend on its external forms.* The

former shows itself in the way the state guard national interests, whether it acts for the benefit or to the detriment of the people. [Italics added]

Noteworthy here is not only the explicit message, but the pattern of reasoning (see italicised passages) which is in full accord with the message, as becomes a professional philosopher of Gulyga's calibre, of course.

[30] See below Sub-section on "The Balance of Political Forces and the First Parliamentary Encounters" in Section 3, Chapter 4.

[31] Centrism on the Russian soil must be distinguished from its Western namesake: it should be regarded as a kind of traditional establishment party that withstands marginal radicals of all kinds, rather than a position in the centre of the political spectrum. Significant in this respect are Victor Chernomyrdin's repeated claims that he does not engage in politics and prefers to do a real job (of governing the country). We have demonstrated elsewhere, that this technocratic attitude, for all its modern jargon and apparent rationalism, is easily married to the belief in the existence of an objectively "correct" social order that constitutes the ontological background to the political mentality of *sobornost'* (see Sergeyev and Biryukov, 1993, pp. 67-8).

[32] On the use of "pseudo-agencies" in the Russian parliamentary discourse, see Section 1 "The Problem of Political Agency: Methodology Considerations" in Chapter 8.

[33] The word is derived from *tsekh* ("[factory] shop") and alludes to the illegal practice of manufacturing consumer goods "outside the plan", i.e. without entering them in account books. The products would then be sold through a network of retail shops, likewise evading official control.

[34] Cf. to Pipes 1974, p. 51:

> ... Liberty not grounded in law is incapable of evolution and tends to turn upon itself; it is an act of bare negation which implicitly denies any mutual obligation or even a lasting relationship between human beings.

[35] On the analysis of the legislation enacted by the Russian parliament in 1990-93, see Chapter 9.

PART TWO

The Rise and Fall of the First Russian Parliament

(A History)

No wonder that, young as I was, I cherished the belief that they would lead the city from an unjust life, as it were, to habits of justice and really administer it; so that I was intensely interested to see what would come of it. Of course, I saw in a short time that these men made the former government look in comparison like an age of gold.

Plato, "Epistle VII"

4   From a Regional Assembly to the National Legislature

The House of Han took everything it could from the Land under the Sky, but the means ran short and the strength was exhausted. For the point is how to avail of each man and only this, and not how numerous they are.

Li Hua, "Lament on an Ancient Battlefield".

1. The Prelude

Boris Yeltsin and the Idea of Russian Sovereignty

The early months of 1990 passed in anticipation of the approaching republican election. This new round of political competition was due to climax on 17 March. Democrats hoped to succeed. Their trump card was Boris Yeltsin, a former member of the top party leadership, dismissed from his post of Moscow party boss in November 1987. The expulsion had been preceded by his attack on Gorbachev and a demand for more radical reforms. His bold criticism of the "first person" and especially his subsequent fall from favour won Yeltsin the love of all those who detested "the powers that be". These were many, and every subsequent move against Yeltsin on the part of the authorities only added to his popularity. That popularity made him the favourite of the first Soviet free election in 1989. It also opened the doors of the parliament to many of those who had openly sided with Yeltsin. Yeltsin's success was all the more impressive as he had declared his candidature, in quite a challenging manner, in the key national-territorial constituency of Moscow and had won more than 5,000,000 votes. Gorbachev, by contrast, rather than undergo the ordeal by competitive election, had resigned to a second-rate but secure mandate and had been voted into the parliament by 629 Central Committee members against 12 within the CPSU quota of 100 seats.[1]

Under the circumstances Yeltsin's defeat at the election to the USSR Supreme Soviet was scandalous, moreover as the procedure was absolutely unfit for a political representative body. Members of the Supreme Soviet (numbering 542) were to be elected by the Congress from among its own deputies. As the number of constituencies was far greater than that (1,500, to say nothing about the additional 750 deputies elected from "public organisations") and they could not all be represented in the Supreme Soviet, even with due regard for partial rotation, equal representation of, at least, larger regions was bound to become a sensitive issue. Regional quotas appeared to be the obvious solution, but the quota principle did not easily agree with the constitutional rule that provided for secret ballot by deputies *in pleno*. From the practical standpoint that meant that after the quotas for particular regions had been agreed upon, somebody had to compile lists of candidates to the Supreme Soviet (a prerogative naturally to belong to the deputies representing the respective regions) which would then be presented to the Congress for secret ballot. With quotas fixed, election from "lists" would in turn mean that to lose the election one did not have to get more than 50 percent of votes against oneself (although one had to get 50 percent of votes for oneself to win): suffice it to get one vote less than the other contestants. As most of the names entered in the ballot papers would be totally meaningless to most of the voters (i.e. other deputies), this unfortunate adaptation of the first-past-the-post system was to the obvious disadvantage of candidates of renown: it would be unlikely they did not receive at least a few "no" votes, whereas the electors would have no reason to vote against perfect strangers.

This "predestined" outcome was Punchinello's secret, of course: the procedure was standard in Soviet times for forming party, Komsomol, trade union and other presumably elected bodies. Since the direct election of top officials was never practised in the Soviet Union, multistage election providing far better opportunities for manipulation, claimants to top offices (by definition, persons of prominence) had to be guaranteed against losing the very first, least controlled, round. This could be achieved by one of two tricks. The first one was to change the quota after the voting results were known. (This naturally required the quota to be the prerogative of the voters, so that they could change it at will). In that case, if the number of those elected exceeded the initial quota, the voters would be faced with a dilemma: either to enter a new round of nomination and voting or to vote to fix the quota at the level equal to the number of contestants who had passed the 50-percent-plus-one-vote barrier. The latter would be much easier, of course, and there was usually little doubt as to the assembly's choice. In practice that would mean that, with the exception of absolutely notorious customers, to get on the list of candidates amounted to being elected. If, for some reason, re-considering the initial quota were deemed impossible or inadvisable, one could resort to the other stratagem, viz. an assurance that the number of contestants be exactly the same as the number of seats (mandates). But the device was only available to those able to manipulate the process of nomination and registration of candidates. In 1989 it was used to elect the people's deputies within the Communist Party quota of 100 seats which were "contested" by precisely 100 candidates. (But for that ruse, incidentally, Mikhail Gorbachev was more than likely to lose the election even at the plenary session of his own party's Central Committee[2]).

A few months later, at the First Congress of People's Deputies of the USSR, all regional groups followed suit, except for the Russian Federation. For their 11 seats at the Supreme Soviet's Council of Nationalities Russia nominated 12 candidates. The one to have lost was none other than Yeltsin.[3] However, he did become Member of the Supreme Soviet, for one of his more successful rivals ceded his seat to Yeltsin, although doubts were raised as to the legitimacy of this settlement.[4]

The scandal only accentuated Yeltsin's unique position in the deputy corps. In July 1989 he was elected one of the leaders of the Interregional Deputy Group that functioned in fact as a faction of democratic opposition. The IDG was soon to become the embryo of a powerful mass movement, *Democratic Russia* (organised early next year).

The Russian parliamentary election was also conducted under the motto of *pro* or *contra* Yeltsin. Leaders of *Democratic Russia* were confident for some reason that in Yeltsin they had not just a sure winner, but a staunch democrat as well. A team of bright and ambitious politicians and experts was soon to gather around him, of which the leading person was Gennadi Burbulis, known to Yeltsin since Sverdlovsk (Ekaterinburg) where he used to teach "scientific communism" at a local university.

One more crucial issue of the election campaign was Russia's role in the USSR. Leaders of the democratic movement viewed the coming election as a chance to get control of the Russian government institutions and turn the republic into a "territory free of communism". This did not seem impossible as, formally speaking, the Constitution endowed republics with sovereign powers.[5] Moreover, one could invoke the recently recovered "Leninist" principle of the sovereignty of the Soviets (meaning each Soviet) over the territories under their jurisdiction. The principle was sometimes stretched to absurdity. In Moscow, for example, the new democratic administration of one such "liberated" district conducted formal registration of nation-wide political organisations; another district proclaimed its sovereignty over "its" air space, etc.

Ironically enough, the democrats campaigned under the slogan of their archetypal enemies, the Bolsheviks, viz. "All Power to the Soviets".[6] The idea was that, having won the local election in a particular district, they would then appeal to the principle of the Soviets' sovereignty to safely ignore any objectionable decision of any superior body. The weapon would be double-edged, since the superior Soviets would also be "sovereign". It was that contradiction that had once undermined the Soviets' capacity to exercise state power effectively and had turned them into puppet institutions behind which a truly powerful, albeit not exactly "sovereign", hierarchy had operated, viz. the Communist Party.[7]

Nevertheless, democrats welcomed this chance to come closer to power through "the back door". Russia's unique position in the Soviet Union made the plan all the more alluring. By asserting the constitutional principle of republican sovereignty and proclaiming the priority of Russian laws over the legislation of the USSR (as had already been done by the Baltic republics) democrats would in fact get control over the greater and most important part of the Soviet territory.

The idea of Russian sovereignty was first articulated at the opposite end of the political spectrum, however. Its author, Valentin Rasputin, a famous writer of "patriotic" orientation, had something different in mind when he suggested - at the peak of *perestroika* - that Russia, too, might secede from the USSR as other republics had threatened to do. His concern was ostensibly for the welfare of Russia, presumably "plundered" by other republics, and over the future of the Russian people faced with dissolution in the ever growing mass of "aliens" and with a loss of its national identity.

All of a sudden, the idea was borrowed by democrats. The reason was pure expediency: a chance to win the election; the motive, sheer impatience. They did not want to wait for the next all-Union election and, in a curiously Bolshevik fashion, sought power with little regard for the consequences; for *Democratic Russia* had neither a clear, definite programme of reforms, nor cadres of trained statesmen to carry it out. But the future "dealing out" of power promised instead enlistment of the support of the lower bureaucracy, ever resentful and jealous of the central administration. And, last but not least, the fear that reforms might be "reversed" was also of no minor importance.

Experts and Advisers

An important, perhaps the most important, feature of *Democratic Russia* as a broad movement, as well as of its lesser, constituent "parties", was the entrance into politics of new men and women who had no political record and no political experience,[8] but who obviously believed themselves to be intellectually superior to the party *apparatchiks* and ministerial bureaucrats.

Here, we are not referring to the dissidents of the 1960s and 1970s. Most of those who did not end their lives in labour camps were in exile. Their role in *Democratic Russia* was, in fact, modest. Of the prominent human rights activists one could name Sergei Kovalyov, Fr Gleb Yakunin and, perhaps, a dozen other less well known persons. The movement's intellectual resource were the staff, predominantly the younger members, of the academic institutions and universities. Most active among them were those who stood little chance of a successful scholarly career and were consequently ready to welcome a possibility of a breakthrough in some other, in this case political, field. It would be from among these people that the nascent democratic parties recruited their political experts and advisers.

The first step towards this informal network had been made in January 1989, after the Presidium of the Academy of Sciences had refused to register Academician Andrei Sakharov, as well as some other renowned nominees, as candidates for the forthcoming election of People's Deputies of the USSR within the Academy's quota of 25 seats.[9] The indignation aroused by this decision had taken the form of a mass rally in front of the Presidium headquarters attended by thousands of the Academy staff.

As a result a Club of Voters had been established within the Academy of Sciences that soon became an influential political organisation. Another organisation established in the aftermath of the conflict was the Union of Scientists of the USSR. The fate of the latter had anticipated that of the Soviet Union: all conflicts that had aggravated the relations between the Centre and the republics, the differences in the republics' attitude towards the Union, the growing tendency towards "autonomisation". In short, all that had been latent then on the political agenda, was to be observed at the meetings of the Union of Scientists. Even before it was properly instituted, the organisation split into separate republican unions and, even within Russia, into those of Moscow, Leningrad and Novosibirsk. The entire enterprise did not survive August 1991.

However, both initiatives proved important catalysts for *Democratic Russia*; the Club of Voters, at any rate, remained one of the movement's most influential intellectual centres till autumn 1991, i.e. the beginning of the radical economic reform. Many experts and advisers who turned up at the Russian Supreme Soviet in 1990 and 1991, came from the Unions of Scientists and the Academy's Club of Voters. They formed the nucleus of the radical "RF-Politics" Centre, that wielded considerable influence on Yeltsin's immediate following.

In 1989-91 a "community" of experts of democratic orientation was taking shape that provided advice to the principal democratic political organisations connected with Yeltsin and dominated the political columns of such mass media organs as *Kuranty* ("The Chime"), *Stolitsa* ("The Capital") and the numerous newspapers of small circulation published by the new political parties. The community operated as the "brain centre" of the democratic movement and was actively involved in planning all major political actions of *Democratic Russia* and of Yeltsin's coterie in 1990 and 1991, that is during their struggle for power against the central Union authorities.

United by little but common values, this community was split by the beginning of reform. However while it existed, it was a living embodiment of value-based integration. It had also inherited the operational experience of the Soviet period, not, of course, the experience of "grand politics" (which could only be acquired in the Kremlin offices or on the international arena), but the experience that the masses would have derived from their daily contacts with the Soviet bureaucrats. Hence, those freshmen's common belief, expressed both in private and in press, that politics is a dirty trade in which ends justify means, etc.

The reform exposed latent tensions within the community of "advisers". Respectable experts from the "think tanks" of the Soviet period, with their long-standing foreign contacts and international reputation, would have nothing to do with "upstarts"; hence the insulting allusions to "test-tube washers" in politics and "lab chiefs at power". This does not mean that the academic establishment sided with conservative communists like Ligachev. However, the establishment looked with suspicion and, perhaps, aversion at former junior research workers and doubted their roots and expertise. These doubts were fed by the incompatibility of operational experience of the two groups. The establishment has long since intuited that consensus about procedures is *conditio sine qua non* of modern-type social integration. Their attitude was predominantly liberal and differed sharply from the populism of "radical democrats" as represented by members of the numerous Voters' Clubs and the younger staff of the natural science institutes of the Academy.

The distinction thus drawn between the dualistic outlook of "radical democrats", who would see nothing in Russian politics but the apocalypse of communism, and those who realised that Russia's only chance after the collapse of the USSR lay in some new consensus about how the game of politics had to be played, i.e. in a genuine multipartyism (as different from the total and "final" annihilation of political adversaries) and a sound legislation (as different from the "revolutionary law" of the transition period) was to become pivotal in the future conflict between the parliament and the president.

2. The 1990 Republican Election

The year 1989, the beginning of which had been marked with the first free parliamentary election of the Soviet period, ended on a tragic note: the death of Academician Andrei Sakharov. The patriarch of the Soviet human rights movement died on 14 December, at the height of the Second Congress of People's Deputies of the USSR. For Soviet democrats, the loss proved irreparable. Sakharov's death divided the history of the democratic movement into two distinctly different stages.

On the eve of the Second Congress Sakharov issued an appeal for mass actions in support of the demand to annul Article 6 of the Constitution of the USSR. Article 6 guaranteed the Communist Party its monopoly of state power and was the principal, in essence the only, constitutional basis of the Soviet regime. The Congress then voted against putting the issue of Article 6 on its agenda. Three months later, on 13 March 1990, the Third Congress passed the appropriate constitutional amendment without much ado.

This "weathercock" behaviour naturally did not add to the Congress's prestige. But the "gain in time" thus achieved allowed, at least, for the pre-election campaign and the first round of the republican and local elections to be conducted under conditions of the still valid, albeit not too effective monopartyism. The fairly delayed "constitutional reform" fell precisely on the fortnight between the first and the second rounds (4 and 18 March, respectively).

The second round, therefore, took place in a "multiparty" state. To be sure, that "multipartyism" was purely nominal: five days were obviously too short a time for new parties to appear. The only organisation then active on the political scene and calling itself a "party" (except, of course, the CPSU) was *Democratic Union*, but it was not registered and had no legal status. (As later publications indicate, there was a party that managed to convene its constituent congress right in March 1990.[10] That was the Liberal Democratic Party, the future favourite of the December 1993 election. However, the public had heard nothing of it at the time).

This constitutional incertitude determined the character of the election campaign. The previous election (that of 1989) was accompanied by unscrupulous manipulation on the part of those responsible for its organisation. Registration of candidates was subject to approval by the so called *district pre-election meetings*. The meetings were to be convened by the district election commissions, and their status as representative assemblies was more than dubious. The meetings had a right to reject any candidate without giving their reasons.

As a result of their activities there were only two competitors or less in most districts in 1989.[11] By March 1990 the "screening" mechanism was already removed, and all candidates nominated by authorised agencies were allowed to run in the election. As the right of nomination belonged, among others, to "workers' collectives",[12] the number of nominees was unprecedented, at least for the Soviet Union.[13]

However, the situation was also unique from the standpoint of established democracies, too. The Soviet voter of 1990 was denied the guide-lines available to voters in countries of long-standing democratic tradition. Under the Soviet regime elections had been pure fakes. There would be only one candidate in every district, all candidates in all districts representing only one party (nominally one electoral bloc, "the inviolate bloc of Communists and non-Party citizens"). Recruitment of political elite had in fact been impervious; politicians had been, for the most part, unknown to the common voter and, frankly speaking, of little interest to him. This time, too, with the exception of the salient functionaries of the governing party (from its upper echelons or local leadership) and, perhaps, a few public figures who owed their popularity to hits of *glasnost'* (and most of whom had already held seats at the USSR parliament) the candidates were perfect strangers.[14] Nor would party symbols do as signs of political identity, because the candidates were not nominees of parties or other political organisations (with the exception - again - of the Communist Party there could have been none of these before 14 March).

As a result of all this, a common voter could only judge candidates by their programmes and the scanty biographical data they cared to publish about themselves - in short by their own words, and, perhaps, by their demeanour during the run-up. The information was pathetically inadequate to make a conscious choice, especially as the programmes basically repeated each other and were wholly declarative in character. Everyone pledged to defend democracy, contribute to the revival of the national economy and improve everything that could be improved. Variations were mainly due to some candidates emphasising issues that were within the sphere of their professional interests; to point out the candidates' respective skills was a means to explain to the voters why they should vote for them rather than for their rivals. In the majority of cases the tactics only served to add a tint of professional or provincial bigotry to the candidates' agendas. Thus, an epidemiologist accentuated the urgency to improve the sanitary conditions; a headmaster, to perfect education. None of this sounded particularly convincing. After all, if one was worried about epidemics, he had better remain a doctor, not become a legislator!

Since the candidates did not represent definite political forces, the voters could do nothing but take (or refuse to take) their words that they would indeed serve the causes they pleaded. The voters had no means to ascertain whether the candidates meant what they said, least so if they were possessed of the skills required to fulfil their promises. In short, this was a time for demagoguery.

The latter was all the more important as behaviour at pre-election meetings and rallies was, in effect, the candidates' only means to distinguish themselves. Under the circumstances, the more modest of the candidates invariably lost to those who were ready to denounce all without exception and promise the earth. Since both the candidates and the voters would be, for the most part, in opposition to the old Soviet regime, it was not easy to tell a constructive critic from a clamorous crook.

It was not surprising therefore that in this atmosphere of almost universal euphoria success would often be enjoyed by people unfit for the walk of life they sought. The adverse affects were felt almost instantly, especially in local councils, i.e. representative bodies that were least of all in need of people with ready tongues and no administrative skills.

On the republican level this political incompetence had different manifestations, but just as dismal consequences.

The matter was not just the "demagogic temptation" (already mentioned above) to which representatives of all political trends succumbed equally: radical democrats as well as conservative communists, nationalist separatists as well as *derzhavniki*.[15] After all, it is not that bad if aspirants to offices of importance care for the feelings of the populace and are ready to adjust their behaviour to the voters' interests.

The critical point lay elsewhere, namely in the tragic split in the minds of the future democratic elite. For all their demagogueries and coquetries (shared, in fact, by their political opponents), there could be little doubt about the sincerity of their beliefs. They were highly critical of the Soviet regime, and their criticism was no mere expediency. The Soviet regime had long since lost popularity, and one did not have to be a time-server to act as its forthright opponent.

But sincerity does not necessarily imply profundity. As the future behaviour of many a distinguished democrat was yet to show, some of them were mistaken (*bona fide*, one would like to think) about the democratic nature of their beliefs. In an earlier work we have sought to demonstrate that populism (*narodnichestvo*) is not equivalent to democracy, at least in the contemporary sense of the word.[16] Although on the level of rhetoric, incidentally the principal aspect of election campaigns, the two political attitudes appear close enough, the underlying cognitive structures, especially the social ontologies, are better viewed as mutually exclusive.

Social ontologies are implicit, of course, and therefore subconscious. People are usually unaware of having them. Conscious and enlightened protagonists of political causes are not necessarily exceptions. Russian democratic leaders were, for the most part, educated persons, well versed in democratic theory. Although the knowledge was bookish, it was not their fault: the Russian realities left them no chance to try their professed principles in practice.

On the other hand, bookish beliefs were no guarantee that the democratic shibboleths of "popular rule", "political pluralism" and "separation of powers" were backed by genuine understanding of the nature and functioning of the respective political institutions and the social practice they support.

The foible was of little importance while the goal was to break down. It came in the foreground, when it was time to build up. The majority of the new democratic elite proved incapable of positive political activity - not only because they lacked the relevant political skills and civic experience, but mainly because their socio-ontological attitudes were incongruous with their conscious beliefs and hence with the type of activity these beliefs would solicit.

Members of the democratic movement sincerely believed that by subscribing to the classical democratic values they came to possess an authentic democratic mentality. We have argued above, however, that unlike social ontology, political values constitute the most superficial (though it is also the most conspicuous) layer of political consciousness. It would be stretching the argument too far if we said that the socio-ontological attitudes of the Russian political elite were left untouched by the recent political and cultural developments (although they were in many cases and in many respects). However, what changes had taken place did not amount to the ontological patterns of *sobornost'* being supplanted by the institutionalist paradigms of the modern democratic thinking. *Sobornost'* did not succumb to democratic institutionalism, but to the type of mentality that was born of (and in its turn served to reproduce) the dualistic *Weltanschauung*.[17]

3. The First Congress and the Sovereignty of Russia

The Structure of the Russian Parliament

In spring 1990 the prospects for Russian parliamentarianism seemed rosy enough, despite the fact Russia was the only Soviet republic that had reproduced the constitutional absurdity of the two-level (clumsy and ineffectual) Union legislature.

The top governing body of Russia was the Congress of People's Deputies. Its 1,068 members were elected directly by the voters in two types of constituencies. The entire territory of Russia was divided into 900 territorial constituencies of approximately equal number of voters. Besides, 168 deputies were elected in the so called national-territorial constituencies (a novelty that imitated the Union pattern). Of these, half were to represent the various autonomous territories (four from each of the 16 autonomous republics; two from each of the 5 autonomous regions and one from each of the 10 autonomous districts); the other half, the remaining 55 ("non-autonomous") regions and territories and 2 major cities (Moscow and Leningrad/Saint Petersburg).[18] The Congress was to meet once a year for a short period of time (or more often, should need arise).[19] As the growing number of mandates became vacant and most of these vacancies were never filled,[20] the Congresses were in effect attended by 900 to 1,000 deputies.

The Constitution invested the Congress of People's Deputies with sovereign powers. It could amend the Constitution by a majority of two thirds,[21] ratify or repeal legislation enacted by the Supreme Soviet, and, after the presidency was instituted in 1991, impeach the president. The majority of the Congress members were not professional parliamentarians: they had other jobs and would only be convened two or three times a year for about a fortnight.

The Supreme Soviet was formed by the Congress from among its deputies. As mentioned above,[22] that was a complicated and frustrating procedure, totally unfit for multiparty politics. On the one hand, the members were to be voted in, which implied political choice on the part of the voters. On the other hand, the voters had to maintain a precarious and asymmetrical balance between regions, types of constituencies (territorial and national-territorial), chambers, professional groups and, as long as common political sense was not lacking, parties or whatever stood for them. The task was not made easier by the fact that the Constitution provided for equal membership of the two chambers, even though the number of territorial and national-territorial constituencies (and hence the number of deputies elected from them) were far from equal. It was not surprising, under the circumstances, that there were many who would view the entire system of electing the Supreme Soviet as "monstrous".[23]

The Supreme Soviet consisted of two chambers: the Council (Soviet) of the Republic and the Council (Soviet) of Nationalities (of 126 members each) that worked on a permanent basis. Their functions were current legislation. Laws passed by the Supreme Soviet could be repealed by the Congress.

The obligation to preserve the numerical equality of the chambers prevented the Congress from increasing the membership of the Supreme Soviet beyond the constitutional figure of 252 deputies, even though that threatened to leave the various committees and commissions grossly undermanned. It was envisaged at the time that there would be more than 20 of them.[24] On the one hand, the Council of Nationalities could, by no means, consist of more than 168 members (the number of national-territorial constituencies); in fact, far less than that, since many regional bosses who had found it expedient to run for election in that type of constituencies would not trade their posts for a seat in the republican parliament. On the other hand, representatives of the non-Russian territories bluntly refused to agree to a Council of Nationalities smaller in membership than the other chamber. They argued it would be an infringement on their rights, even if the two houses had equal status and equal powers. The compromise was eventually achieved by allowing the deputies who had not been elected to the Supreme Soviet to join the committees and commissions with a deciding vote (they would also have a deliberative vote in the appropriate chamber of the Supreme Soviet) and thus become professional legislators, albeit of a non-conventional status.

The work of both the Congress and the Supreme Soviet was to be organised by the Presidium of the Supreme Soviet. This body consisted of the Chair of the Supreme Soviet, his deputies, chairs of the two houses and chairs of the standing commissions and committees. The Presidium wielded considerable power, even though there were no formal provisions for that in the Constitution.

This two-level structure, already known for its poor performance at the Union level, had been subject to harsh criticism from the very beginning. Even 100 percent annual rotation would not suffice to secure each of the presumably equal People's deputies his/her term in the Supreme Soviet. True, not all of them wanted it, but the democratically minded deputies would generally view the non-professional mass of the Congress members as a potential object and instrument of manipulation by the Union authorities and conservative forces - all the more so as *Democratic Russia* and its supporters held but a slim and precarious majority.

It was suggested - already at the First Congress, and the motion would be repeated regularly afterwards - to constitute the Congress as a professional legislature that would work on a permanent basis.[25] (Apart from other considerations, that would have relieved the deputies of the maddening task of forming the Supreme Soviet). The proposal would be rejected with the same regularity as it would be made, mainly by the votes of the provincial and Moscow *nomenklatura* whose members would have had to resign from their administrative posts if they were to become professional parliamentarians. The only other alternative would have been to give up their seats altogether - and the privileges that went with it, of which immunity from legal persecution was but one. (It might have been one of the Congress's initial attractions, indeed, that it provided one with a kind of cushy job that, while not too demanding in terms of time and effort, meant considerable advantages in terms of status and influence).

This stubborn refusal was to prove fatal in the long run, for it was precisely the Russian parliament's non-conventional structure, totally unknown to other parliamentary democracies, that was constantly brought up to justify its dissolution. Still, although it was clear that the argument would be rendered groundless and the parliament's chances for survival greatly increased, should all the deputies be given equal status and the parliament itself become a fully professional body, the bid was invariably rejected.

The Balance of Political Forces and the First Parliamentary Encounters

For all that, expectations inspired by the election of the new Russian legislature and especially with the majority, albeit a marginal one, of democrats were high enough.[26] These expectations were naturally shared by the bulk of the newly elected deputy corps. For them to be realised, however, the status of the Russian representative body had to undergo a fundamental change.

The First Congress of People's Deputies of the RSFSR opened in Moscow in the Grand Kremlin Palace[27] on 16 May 1990 and sat in session till 22 June. It was to remain the longest forum in the entire history of the institution.[28] Its agenda included 15 issues, of which the most important were elections of the Chair and Deputy Chairs of the Supreme Soviet, elections of the Supreme Soviet's chambers and Russian sovereignty. Besides, the Congress was to hear the report of the Chair of the Council of Ministers, appoint his successor, pass Temporary Rules and Temporary Provisions regulating the deputies' activities.

The Congress's political countenance was multifold. Although the two major political forces, associated with the Russian Communist Party, on the one hand, and *Democratic Russia*, on the other, assumed confrontational attitudes at once, the majority of deputies consciously sought to evade identifying definitely with either of them. As registered at the First Congress, the deputy group called *"Democratic Russia"* (subsequently transformed into a faction of the same name) numbered 66 members.[29] Many deputies who had waged their election campaigns on behalf of *Democratic Russia* did not join the group, though it could, as a rule, reasonably count on their support in case of an open encounter with communists. As to *Communists of Russia*, that group (later also re-instituted as a faction) was originally the most numerous of all: 355 members at the First Congress,[30] but tended to decrease in numbers ever since - up to 67 deputies at the Ninth Congress.[31] On the whole the

First Congress carried as a classical two-party assembly: the amorphous "Centre" failed to put forward a leader of its own and could do little to counterbalance the two "flanks".

The first test of strength was election of the Chairman of the Supreme Soviet. Though democrats managed to have their nominee, Boris Yeltsin, elected, the victory was more than marginal: *precisely 50 percent plus one vote* from the constitutional membership of 1,068 deputies (or 50 percent plus five from their actual number).[32] One could argue, indeed, that Yeltsin and the democrats owed their victory not so much to their own popularity with the newly elected deputy corps as to the self-defeating tactics of *Communists of Russia* and the latter's failure to put forward a tenable alternative: the uninspiring figure of Ivan Polozkov served only to rally almost all parliamentary "swamp" around *Democratic Russia*. Besides, Yeltsin's undeniable success with the electorate could not help affecting the deputies' voting behaviour.

It was not long though before the democrats were given to understand how weak their influence in fact was. Having won the chairmanship of the Supreme Soviet for their candidate, they were utterly defeated at the election of his deputies. The idea of a "coalition" presidium, though praised on both sides, proved difficult to realise: everyone, identified with *Democratic Russia*, was blackballed, and even the compromise figure of Ruslan Khasbulatov had to be nominated twice before he was eventually elected First Deputy Chair.

Russia Proclaims Sovereignty

There was a point on which the two irreconcilable enemies, democrats and communists, managed to find common language without too much effort. For all the overt attributes of sovereignty (their own constitutions, Supreme Soviets, national flags and, for Ukraine and Belorussia, even membership of the United Nations), the powers of the republican bodies were nominal rather than real. Not only would all significant political decisions be made by the Union authorities, the bulk of industry was also under the Union control and was administered from Moscow.

Russia was no exception. Moreover, its formal position seemed even inferior to that of the other Soviet republics, for the republican bureaucracy in Russia was denied those limited privileges that were granted to their provincial counterparts as a "concession" to national minorities. What other nations would see as an embodiment of Russia's imperial status (e.g. absence of many institutions taken for granted elsewhere, such as the republican Communist Party or the Russian Academy of Sciences), many a Russian resented as deplorable inequality and infringement of rights.

On the issue of Russian sovereignty, therefore, democrats and communists acted as one. The proposal to put it on the agenda was made by the Presidium of the Supreme Soviet (of the previous convocation) and the report was delivered by its Chairman Vitali Vorotnikov.[33] Having asserted that

> The Russian Federation can nowadays develop itself and contribute to the development of the entire Soviet Union only as an independent and sovereign state[34]

and that

> Policy aimed at attaining such sovereignty is in full accord with the ever more insistent demands of the public that reflect the growing self-consciousness of Russians,[35]

the speaker went on to itemise the basic means by which such sovereignty might be secured, namely through the signing of a new Union Treaty (that was to replace the old one signed in 1922), the reform of the republican political institutions, the re-distribution of national property in favour of the republics, and the republican control over some part of media. Though stated delicately, the demands were essentially the same as those of the radical democrats. Vorotnikov concluded his speech with the following noteworthy statement:

> I see no implacable enemies among the deputies. ... And it seems to me we are united enough to adopt a document that would express the will of the peoples of Russia towards independence and sovereignty clearly and definitely.[36]

The only point of discord was the priority of the republican legislation over that of the Soviet Union. It was a key question, of course: the provision of Article 74 of the Constitution of the USSR, viz. that in case of a disagreement between a law of a constituent republic and a law of the Soviet Union, the law of the USSR was to have precedence,[37] made the republican "sovereignty" proclaimed by Article 76 of that very Constitution a mere fiction and obviously contradicted Article 72 according to which the Union republics had the right to secede from the USSR. Clearly, if a republic could resolve any constitutional conflict in its favour by the ultimate means of secession, to insist on the priority of the legislation of the

Union over that of the republics would be to provoke the republican leaderships into secessionist blackmail, which certainly was dysfunctional from the standpoint of preserving the integrity of the Union.

In the meantime, none of the opponents questioned the need of preserving it. In that respect democrats did not dissent from communists. It was simply that "sovereignty" meant for democrats a chance to "intercept" the power without having to wait for the next all-Union election (which at that moment lay still far ahead); for conservatives, a possibility to use the republican power institutions as strongholds of the old regime.

The entire conflict over sovereignty was thus *institutional*, not ideological. To safeguard sovereignty meant to secure the right of a social elite, located in a particular institutional milieu, to exercise unchallenged control over the social and political life within its domain.[38]

Under the circumstances the issue was decided in advance. The priority of the republican legislation over the legislation of the USSR was endorsed by 544 deputies against 271 with 30 abstentions.[39] On 12 June 1990 the First Congress of People's Deputies of the RSFSR passed Declaration "On State Sovereignty of the Russian Soviet Federal Socialist Republic" by the overwhelming majority of 907 votes against 13 with 9 abstentions.[40]

The democrats' plan was fulfilled. The Declaration marked the beginning of a major institutional conflict between the Union and the republican authorities, a conflict on which the entire Soviet politics was soon to pivot.

4. The Presidency

The Crisis of the Union Authority

The Second Congress of People's Deputies of the RSFSR opened on 27 November 1990. The Congress was convened out of order and was to work out a new agrarian policy. Everyone was ready to admit the situation in the "agro-industrial complex" was desperate, but there was little consensus about what was to be done to improve it. The kolkhoz bosses called for state protectionism, the democrats demanded privatisation of land. The resolution was a compromise: the peasants were promised 15 percent of Russia's national income every year for "the development of the social sphere"; kolkhozes and other agricultural enterprises were to be pardoned debts worth 23,000,000 roubles; private property was no longer outlawed, but sale of land was not allowed except to the state as represented by the local Soviets.[41] The Congress passed the appropriate constitutional amendment, together with a few others, and "exchanged ideas"[42] on the principles of the forthcoming Union Treaty.

It was still in session when the Fourth Congress of People's Deputies of the USSR met in Moscow. The political situation was growing more and more complicated. It was determined by two basic factors: the acute economic crisis brought about by the obvious failure of the hesitant, inconsistent economic reforms of Ryzhkov's government, and the growing tension between the new republican authorities and the so-called "Centre". This opposition was accompanied by "a parade of sovereignties", with republics one after another claiming precedence for their laws over the laws of the Union. This threatened to paralyse the already not particularly successful activity of the Union legislature and plunge the country into a state of legal and political havoc.

In this situation President Gorbachev proposed a new constitutional reform that would greatly enhance the role of the republics. Apart from re-organisation of the government (the Council of Ministers was to be replaced by a Cabinet of Ministers, presumably under closer presidential control), Gorbachev's plan envisaged establishment of the Council of Federation. That organ, with somewhat vague prerogatives, was to consist of the leaders of the republics.

Gorbachev presented this draft programme to the USSR Supreme Soviet in November 1990 as his preemptive response to the severe criticism he expected to be levelled at him and his policies by the deputies frightened by the rapidly worsening economic situation .

Another essential element of the "new wave" of *perestroika* was to be the Union Treaty. The idea of a new treaty that was to replace the old one signed in 1922 had originated with the republics controlled by the democratic opposition, but it waned somewhat after "the parade of sovereignties" reached its peak in the summer.[43]

However, the attempt to strike a balance between the Centre and the republics, rather than between the democrats and the party conservatives, as before, marked by the establishment of the Council of Federation, failed, too. The manoeuvre was aimed at neutralising Gorbachev's critics on both sides: the democrats' *protegé* Boris Yeltsin would be "promoted" to the membership of the new Council, but on the whole that Council would still be dominated by moderate and conservative republican leaders;[44] the conservative critics of Gorbachev's reforms would be allowed to gain premiership of the new Cabinet, but the Cabinet itself would henceforth come under direct presidential control.

That policy might have succeeded, but only if general political trends had been in its favour: that is, if the various republican political elites, content with more power in the provinces and a greater role in the Union, had supported "the Centre", and if the conservative *Soyuz* ("Union") group in the Soviet parliament had recognized Gorbachev's patronage.

But the republican elites, that had formed as far back as the times of "stagnation", found themselves under growing pressure from democratic and nationalist movements and felt that their only chance of survival lay in "hi-jacking" the nationalist slogans and promoting "sovereignisation". In independent states they might still hope to retain their power by endeavouring to draw on the conservative political culture of the bulk of the population.

In Russia itself regional political elites, especially those of the former "autonomous units", faced a similar situation. In the circumstances the "central" (Union) leadership was tempted to try to play them against the federal Russian authorities, reducing the latter to the position they themselves had already experienced. That was bound to encourage radicalism on the part of the Russian leaders and to foster their unyielding opposition to Gorbachev's policy. Gorbachev's attempt to "dissolve" Yeltsin amid republican leaders failed, therefore. Moreover, the leaders themselves proved less prone to support the "Centre" than Gorbachev had hoped.

Nor did negotiations about the new Union Treaty promise Gorbachev great political award: the republics' claims were growing from day to day, while no definite text of the treaty was likely to be framed in the near future.

In a hope to get some trump card for the game he was playing with the republican leaders Gorbachev suggested a referendum on the future of the Soviet Union, but the ambiguity of the wording[45] and the intended uncertainty of legal consequences[46] served merely to pour fuel on the flames. The Baltic republics simply refused to hold the referendum on their territories and conducted their own "polls" instead. Although, from the legal standpoint, those straw polls were no more binding than the all-Union referendum, their results were interpreted as the popular mandate to secede from the Union. The referendum was also boycotted by Armenia, Georgia and Moldavia. As to Russia and Ukraine, the fact that the majority voted to "preserve the renewed Union"[47] did not substantially affect the official position of these republics: the leaders of both still insisted on downgrading the "Centre".

On the same day, when the all-Union referendum was held, Russia had its own republican referendum on the institution of presidency. 69.8 percent of the participants voted for the presidency. The Third (Extraordinary) Congress of People's Deputies of the RSFSR, assembled eleven days later, commissioned the Supreme Soviet to amend the Constitution accordingly and appoint the presidential election.

The Third Congress

The Congress (Extraordinary again) was convened at the demand of *Communists of Russia*. Its opening was marked by a clamorous political scandal. Shortly before a group of members of the Presidium of the Supreme Soviet, including some Deputy Chairs, issued a "political statement" that sharply criticised Boris Yeltsin and called for his resignation from chairmanship of the Supreme Soviet. Yeltsin's critics also appealed to the USSR authorities to "protect them from external pressure". Under that pretext, the Soviet government banned mass actions in Moscow for the time of the Congress. Strictly speaking, the matter was under the jurisdiction of the Moscow City Council in which democrats were in majority after the election of March 1990, but the government, quoting Moscow's special status as the capital of the Union state, persisted in its decision. On 28 March 1991, the day the Congress was to open, soldiers blocked the approaches to the Kremlin. Despite the governmental ban and the cordons of troops and riot police rallies in support of Yeltsin took place and assembled masses of people. The political and institutional conflict acquired distinctive features of a dualistic confrontation.

The situation was further aggravated by the strike of Kuzbass miners that began on the eve of the Congress. In addition to economic, the miners made political demands including resignation of the Union government headed by Valentin Pavlov and resignation of President Gorbachev himself.

The same dualistic attitude prevailed while the Congress sat in session. Its verbatim records are full of expressions like "sabbat of the kind any parliament would feel ashamed of",[48] "we flog each other here and rejoice",[49] "our Congress resembles a battlefield",[50] "an adversary is wanted urgently",[51] "some people find it to their advantage to start an attack against the decisions of the extraordinary Congress of People's Deputies of the RSFSR right from the beginning".[52]

As usual, the aggravation of the situation was blamed on the opponents:

Honourable Boris Nikolaevich [*Yeltsin*]! I would like to draw your attention to the fact that the charge of unfriendliness, hostility, and malice we saw in full measure yesterday is initiated by you in the first place through your statements about enemies, about the need to form battle ranks and the like, as well as through participation in rallies where one hears words it would be simply improper to quote here.[53]

How are we to appraise our yesterday's work at the Congress? I received five telegrams from [my] voters yesterday with a demand for constructive work. Would you, please, tell me what I can do in this situation if you [*the speaker addresses Yeltsin*] and Ruslan Imranovich [*Khasbulatov*] purposely do everything to stir up passions, sow implacability?[54]

And now we see that some comrades, and not perhaps just some, but many comrades from Staraya Square[55] set course not just for confrontation, but for war against the legitimately elected state power as represented by the Supreme Soviet of the USSR.[56]

Interethnic conflicts in Russia are the result of the policies of the party that rules our country and the Union power structures that lately profess the principle "divide and rule". ... Russia will not make a single step forward either in economy, or in interethnic relation until it removes from its path the formidable obstacle against which Khrushchev's thaw broke in its time, and Kosygin's reforms, and our *perestroika*. Russia, I repeat, will not move forward until it eliminates the destructive force that opposes the authorities elected by the people, sets nations onto each other, village onto city, conservative regions onto democratic [ones], whose representatives, being at the head of enterprises, kolkhozes and sovkhozes, administrative structures, have driven the people to poverty and famine. I am speaking of the CPSU.[57]

On both sides voices were raised calling for an ultimate break-off:

I would like to draw your attention once again, comrades deputies, to the fact that an idea of a "round table" is insistently suggested to us now. I remind you that this idea was successfully tested, was one-time devised in special brain centres, realised in practice in Poland, Romania. What consequences it lead to is known. ... I call for vigilance, against uniting at this "round table" with those who destroy the state and the constitutional order, being ashamed of nothing, call for disorder and a breakdown of the foundations that be of both the state and the society.[58]

> I propose to discontinue the work of this Congress until we answer the following question: what people do we represent? If we represent the people of Russia, then I do not understand why we do not implement its will. I mean the resolute "yes" the Russian people said at the referendum. If we represent some other people, then I do not understand why our Congress is called the Congress of People's Deputies of Russia. [*Applause*]. And in this connection I think we must somehow make official, organisationally and juridically, such a sad fact that our Congress has split in two and hold two separate Congresses. One Congress will be the Congress of People's Deputies of Russia, and it will be attended by those deputies who are going to implement the will of the people of Russia; the other Congress will be the Congress of People's Deputies of some unknown people which will apparently be attended by *Communists of Russia*. [*Noise in the hall*].[59]

After the referendum and the mass rallies in Moscow, the deputies could hardly doubt as to the voters' real preferences - regardless of their own political views. Everyone understood perfectly well that Yeltsin was the obvious candidate for the presidency and that the referendum was universally regarded as the voting for Yeltsin. In this situation the attempt to have him removed from his office as Chairman of the Supreme Soviet was bound to fail and it did. The effect of this anti-Yeltsin manoeuvre proved, as usual, opposite to what had been expected. The faction of *Communists of Russia*, the democrats' principal opponent, split: on 2 March 179 deputies led by Alexander Rutskoi expressed their support for Yeltsin, quit the faction and formed their own group originally called *Communists for Democracy* (subsequently *Free Russia*). Giving the results of the republican referendum and the need to consolidate the executive in the present tense situation[60] as their reasons, Yeltsin's supporters managed to obtain for him "special powers" for the period up until the presidential election.

The outcome needs some discussion. For the second time in the recent history of the country, the parliament dissatisfied with the government's activities showered the chief executive with reprimand and threats, but rather than have him fired or, at least, brought under stricter control, ended by voting him additional powers! The Supreme Soviet of the USSR had done this the previous November: Gorbachev had been told first that he had had but a few weeks to improve the situation and then invested with extra powers presumably required "to overcome the crisis". A month later the Fourth Congress of People's Deputies of the USSR had followed suit: although a motion to put the vote of no confidence for the President on the agenda had been rejected, Gorbachev had heard little flattery of himself, even from his own lieutenants,[61] but despite this, the right of direct control over the reformed Cabinet of Ministers he had sought had been granted.

Now the story was going to be repeated. After having found "all the work - from the top government body of the republic to the local executive committees and Soviets" unsatisfactory, a deputy would suggest - in obvious contradiction to what he had just said:

> Summing up this sharp debate we must, as a matter of principle, give our appraisal of the activities of both the Supreme Soviet leadership and the government leadership and *make them work, command them to roll up their sleeves and work, work, work!*[62]

This amazing behaviour on the part of the political elite can only be explained by a very special understanding of the role and functions of the executive. We have argued above, that within the culture of *sobornost'* "the Government" turns up invariably as the sole (monopolistic) political agency. A mystic *community* is unable to act: it lacks the appropriate organs and cannot acquire or create them because that would mean acquiring differentiated structures and must, therefore, be rejected as manifestly contradicting the idea and ideal of *sobornost'*. And since some actions have to be taken, the task must be turned over to the executive as the only available agency and the only conceivable branch of power.[63]

We may conclude, therefore, that for all their rhetoric exercises on the subject of separation of powers and the splendours of representative democracy, the deputy corps of both Russia and the Soviet Union had not left the ground of *sobornost'*. Consolidation of the executive was considered the only means to solve problems, indeed as a panacea for all complaints. In itself, it did not mean, of course, that individual incumbents of administrative posts could not be displaced; but if they were, it would be a matter of personal rather than institutional change. In the long run the idea that in its present predicament Russia required new institutional decisions, new *mechanisms* of problem-solving proved alien not just to the broad masses of citizenry, but even to that very political elite that had verbalised it.

The resolution "On Redistribution of Powers between the Top State Bodies of the RSFSR for the Implementation of Anti-crisis Measures and Realisation of the Congress's Decisions" was eventually passed by the majority of 607 against 228 with 100 abstentions.[64]

The Fourth Congress

In the short period between the Third and the Fourth Congresses the Russian Supreme Soviet passed (although it exceeded its commission in that[65]) laws "On the President of the RSFSR" and "On the Election of the President of the RSFSR" and drafted the appropriate constitutional amendments. The acts were then presented to the Fourth Congress of People's Deputies of Russia for authorisation. The Congress, convened on 21 May 1991, was also to deliberate on the reform of the local self-government and the Constitutional Court.

The presentation of the laws "On the President of the RSFSR" and "On Amendments and Supplements to the Constitution (Fundamental Law) of the RSFSR" was made by Sergei Shakhrai, then Chair of the Supreme Soviet's Committee on Legislation.[66] As delineated by Shakhrai, Russia' constitutional regime was to be a presidential republic with "a strong parliament". The President was to become the chief state official of the republic and the head of the executive. The office of the Chair of the Council of Ministers was to be preserved, by the appointments were to be made by the President, "subject to the consent of the Supreme Soviet", and the Council of Ministers itself was to become a body accountable to the President. All other cabinet ministers, including deputy chairs, were to be appointed by the President on the Chair's proposals. In Shakhrai's opinion, the arrangement would not infringe on the parliament's powers of control as the parliament would always be able to dismiss the head of the government.[67] The speaker insisted that the provision to have cabinet members approved by the parliament would, on the contrary, reduce the latter's control "to zero" as it would be illogical to hold a Chair of the Council of Ministers responsible for the performance of the staff "imposed" on him. (Strangely enough, the principle was not applied to the relations between the head of the government and the President; for either the Chair of the Council of Ministers could not be held responsible to the President for the performance of his cabinet, as it would be the President who would appoint its members, or the like appointments on the same terms, i.e. "on the proposal of the Chair of the Council of Ministers", might be made by the Supreme Soviet, as well).

The procedure proposed by the Chair of the Legislation Committee for the formation of the government raised doubts in the minds of many a deputy. Among others, Oleg Rumyantsev, Executive Secretary of the Constitutional Commission, rejoined:

I would like to draw your attention to the need for serious checks and balances for the President. For instance, I disagree and the arguments of Sergei Mikhailovich Shakhrai that the President should appoint members of the government himself, have proved unconvincing to me. The Supreme Soviet must not be deprived of so important a lever of the legislative control over the head of the executive. Otherwise, our Russian presidency will become a strange mixture of the French and Latin American systems.[68]

The draft law laid a foundation for the future conflicts over personal appointments to the government. In fact, the Supreme Soviet could not influence the composition of the cabinet, even if it fired its head, for there would be nothing to prevent the President from assigning the portfolios to the same persons after nominating a new Chair of the Council of Ministers. The President might even keep the dismissed Chair by providing him with some other office. Furthermore, the President would have at his disposal a manoeuvre overlooked by the legislators and, strictly speaking, of dubious constitutionality. The President could assume the chairmanship of the Council of Ministers himself, intrusting a Deputy Chair or an "Acting" Chair with the daily control of the cabinet. To dismiss a President in his capacity as Chairman of the Council of Ministers would be problematic, while the letter of the amended Article 123 of the Constitution would not require the Supreme Soviet's approval for a Deputy Chair (as to the "Acting" Chair, the office would not even be mentioned).[69] It was this manoeuvre that later allowed President Yeltsin to keep Yegor Gaidar as virtual head of the government for more than a year despite the fact that the latter lacked the necessary parliamentary support.

The President's other chance (and one more source of potential confrontation) lay in the fact that the structure and powers of the government were not defined, as were not its relations *vis-a-vis* other state bodies. The issues were to be settled by a special law on the Council of Ministers, but that was still a matter of future legislation. Until then, the President could dispense with the cadres of the executive as he pleased: abolishing, instituting or simply renaming offices; and the opportunity would not be missed!

One more source of conflict was the President's legislative powers as envisaged by the proposed constitutional reform. Apart from the right of legislative initiative[70] and the right of suspensive veto,[71] the President was to be endowed with the right to enact decrees that would be "mandatory on the entire territory of the RSFSR".[72] This latter right, or rather the parliament's right to rescind the President's decrees, was a matter of a bitter controversy. Yeltsin's political opponents insisted that the Congress of People's Deputies and likewise the Supreme Soviet should be entitled to annul any presidential decree. Yeltsin's supporters would only assent to the parliament retaining a right to revoke decrees that were found to contradict the law. That standpoint they sought to substantiate by reference to the separation of powers:

> The conception that was presented to the Supreme Soviet was that if we were to establish the powers - legislative, executive and judicial - as responsible and independent, the Supreme Soviet was not to have the right to rescind the President's decrees. That might be done, if they violated the Constitution, by the Constitutional Court. However, this approach, this conception was rejected in the Supreme Soviet and it was proposed that the Supreme Soviet and the Congress be also endowed with the right to rescind the decrees of the President. ... When we discussed this amendment at the Committee on Legislation on the eve of the voting [in the Supreme Soviet], we proceeded from the assumption that the balance of the three powers had to be secured in that respect. Yes, the parliament would be endowed with the right to rescind the President's decrees. But let us put some restrictions in order there be no arbitrariness, there be no pressure of the legislative on the executive. What restrictions? A decree of the President may be repealed only if it violates the Constitution or the law. Who will judge whether the Constitution or the law are violated? The very body we institute - the Constitutional Court. This balance of the three powers is a guarantee against the arbitrariness of any one of them.[73]

> If we endow the Supreme Soviet with the right to overrule any decision of the President, that will not be the executive, that will be I do not know at all what. Let legislators engage in legislation, and the executive, I beg your pardon, will operate within its commission, the commission of the executive.[74]

The main objection against this distribution of powers would fit the classical parliamentary model:

> ... it is well known that there may be decisions that are quite legitimate from the standpoint of law, but essentially wrong. ... In that case the mistake can be corrected neither by the Supreme Soviet nor by the Congress of People's Deputies. It is necessary to supplement the article [*Article 8 of the Law on the President of the RSFSR*] [to the effect] that the Supreme Soviet can also repeal President's decisions, orders and decrees upon [*as the text goes; the meaning is "without"*] the ruling of the Constitutional Court.[75]

A similar debate was held on the President's right to suspend decisions of local government bodies and dismiss their officials. Shakhrai would stress in his speech that the right could only be exercised in case the decision or the official in question violated the Constitution or the law:

> The President has no right to dismiss, to release from his duties an official if he does not like... the colour of his eyes, the size of his shoes or something else.[76]

"The colour of eyes" and "the size of shoes" had nothing to do with the issue, of course. However, "the violations of the Constitution and of the law" referred to in the above passage did not mirror similar demands on the President. The issue at stake was in fact legal possibility to dismiss any official who might refuse to obey a President's decree, since the provision of Article 121[8] of the Constitution, viz. that presidential decrees were to be "mandatory on the entire territory of the RSFSR", would automatically rank such a refusal as a violation of the Constitution. The right would "consolidate", as the protagonists of the presidentialist model would put it, "the vertical of the executive".

Their opponents emphasised the danger of relapsing into "dictatorship" that lay in so dramatic expansion of presidential power:

> I think the President must be endowed with a right to bring in a motion at the respective government bodies of the republics, provinces [*krai*] and regions [*oblast'*] suggesting that the acts of the executive/administrative bodies be repealed or the officials of these executive/administrative bodies be dismissed. But [we must] by no means endow him with a right to dismiss them himself, as this would only indicate institution of a dictatorship.[77]

Rhetoric exercises on the subject of "dictatorship" that formed the background to the debate at the Congress were not new, of course: the issue had been raised every now and then since the beginning of *perestroika*. The only new element was that the opponents seemed to have switched sides. The stands of the parties depended largely on their predictions of the outcome of the forthcoming presidential election. With Yeltsin all but elected, his political opponents, communists and *derzhavniki*, resorted to the classical arguments of parliamentary democracy, invoking the condemned recent past:

> It seems to me that with our *gensec*[78] traditions to remove control over the executive is very dangerous, we can easily get a new version of authoritarian regime.[79]

Democrats, on the contrary, confident of their candidate's electoral success, seemed to have forgotten of what they had stood for only a year or two ago and strove to secure the would-be President as vast powers as possible - and were not ashamed to appeal to the need for "order" and a "tough hand":

> ... every democracy requires tough state, social and working discipline. The distinguished orator speaking before me has sought to terrify us with totalitarianism and dictatorship. He has apparently forgotten that we need strong, I would even say, tough power. And in my opinion, Boris Nikolaevich Yeltsin could be a guarantor of such strong power. I shall give no other reason. You all know them well.[80]

The unnaturalness of both these positions was realised by everyone, but nobody seemed confounded or embarrassed. On the contrary, both parties were quite outspoken in linking their "theoretical" preferences to their immediate political perspectives. In this respect the question of time acquired special importance: the date of the election and the duration of the election campaign. The Congress began on 21 May, the election was scheduled to take place on 12 June. Yeltsin's opponents claimed - not without reason - that it would be ridiculous to try to squeeze a presidential campaign in three weeks:

> We are laughed at and told that it took us two months to elect even district Soviets. And nowadays we, having more than 70 territories, of which a candidate cannot visit even a half in the span of time that remains, we say that to adjourn the election is absurd.[81]

Democrats insisted that the election could not be postponed and that whatever was said to substantiate the motion was in fact meant to prevent Yeltsin's victory:

> About the time. To adjourn from June 12. I see it as a tactical move - perhaps, everything will fail after that, because the situation in the republic is of a kind that the principal adversary, the principal rival for all our Presidents, all our candidates - and they are all worthy people - is the sharply worsening situation. The hope is that already in July-August it would come to no election. But the question is that in this brief span of time we have a legal, constitutional, legislative chance to introduce the [executive] vertical, introduce the executive power and to attempt to get out of the crisis by legal, rather than dictatorial means.[82]

The issue of time was related to another delicate issue. Though procedural, it touched on the constitutional prerogatives of the Congress and the Supreme Soviet. As mentioned above, the Supreme Soviet, striving to set the mechanism of presidential election in motion as soon as possible, had enacted the relevant laws on the presidency and presidential election even though that had not been within its constitutional powers. Both laws providing for substantial changes of the constitutional regime, they could have been passed only by the Congress and only by a majority of two thirds of the People's Deputies.[83] They had in fact been passed and promulgated by a simple ("unqualified") majority of the Supreme Soviet members. To justify the action, Shakhrai referred to the previous, Third, Congress's resolution on redistribution of powers between the top state bodies of the RSFSR for the implementation of anti-crisis measures. The resolution had, indeed, intrusted the Supreme Soviet with adopting a number of laws, but the laws on the presidency and presidential election had not been among these: the Supreme Soviet had only been commissioned to "work them out". It was true, the Supreme Soviet had exceeded its commission, but "the train was gone": the laws were passed and promulgated and, what was most important, the outcome of the March 17 referendum made any objection essentially meaningless.

As a result, the Congress ratified the law "On the President of the RSFSR" (against protestations of communists and *derzhavniki* by a simple, "unqualified" majority[84]) and amended the republican Constitution respectively[85] - this time by the required majority of two thirds. The decisions were a political compromise with a pronounced advantage for the presidency. Presidents gained personal control over the personnel and the activities of the government; their sole obligation to the parliament would be a need to seek the latter's approval for their nominees for the chairmanship of the Council of Ministers.

The parliament lost its control over the executive. The latter's responsibility to the legislative (collective, for the Council of Ministers; and personal, for the President, as Shakhrai would put it[86]) would be purely nominal: the parliament would have no legal means of "pressing" the President and the government, at least, in everyday matters. It would have but three levers at its disposal: the budget, the re-structuring of the government and the governmental powers by means of legislation, and the vote of confidence - all the three of "extraordinary" effect.

The parliament's reward was fivefold. In the first place, the President would not be entitled to dissolve the Congress and the Supreme Soviet or, for that matter, any other "legitimately elected" body of power.[87] Although a motion to invest the President with the power to dissolve parliament - to balance the latter's right to reject presidential nominees for the premiership - was made, the presidential side judged it unrealistic. As Shakhrai commented,

... will the Law "On the President of the RSFSR" be adopted, if it contains a right to dissolve the Congress and the Supreme Soviet? The answer is more than predetermined.[88]

Secondly, the President would have no right of veto: he would only be entitled within 14 days after a law is passed to return it to the parliament for re-consideration. The right would apparently be of little avail, as the same (simple) majority would be needed to re-enact the law as was required to pass it originally.[89]

Thirdly, the question of the parliament's right to rescind presidential decrees was settled to the satisfaction of the former, though the decision was a compromise: the Supreme Soviet would only be able to do it on a ruling by the Constitutional Court;[90] the proviso did not stand for the Congress.[91]

Fourthly, the President was denied the right to dismiss officials as the advocates of "strong executive vertical" had sought. He would only be allowed "to suspend decisions of executive bodies" provided they contradicted the Constitution and the law of the RSFSR.[92]

Finally, the Congress of People's Deputies would be endowed with a right to impeach the President by a majority of two thirds in case he violated the Constitution, the law or the presidential oath. But the fact would have to be ascertained by a ruling of the Constitution Court.[93]

For all the importance of the above restrictions on the presidency, one has to admit that of Shakhrai's formula, viz. "a strong parliament and a strong executive headed by a President",[94] only the second part was to be fully realised. The system of mutual checks and balances was not itself balanced. In this respect, of decisive importance was the fact that the list of presidential powers was not "closed": "has *other* powers bestowed on him by the Constitution of the RSFSR and by laws of the RSFSR".[95] Whereas the parliament was to lose a considerable share of its constitutional prerogatives, legislative restrictions on the executive were largely "framing" in character[96] and were poorly elaborated from the standpoint of procedure: the parliament would find it hard to exercise its control except by resorting to radical and extraordinary means and "crisis-style" behaviour.

On the other hand, despite the apparent shift towards presidentialism, the Constitution retained the principal relic of the original parliamentary model, viz. the sovereignty of the Congress. The Congress was "authorised to take into its consideration and resolve any issue to fall within the jurisdiction of the RSFSR".[97] Thus the field for the looming mortal fight between the two branches of power lay waiting for the combatants.

On the Eve of the Breakdown

The first Russian presidential election took place on 12 June, the first anniversary of the Declaration of Russian sovereignty. Yeltsin won in the first round with 57.3 percent of the vote, having left other candidates far behind.[98] At the Fifth (Extraordinary) Congress of People's Deputies of the RSFSR in July he was sworn in as President. His former office, chairmanship of the Supreme Soviet, became the object of intense rivalry. Having failed to elect Yeltsin's successor, the Congress was adjourned.

The direct presidential election in Russia and Yeltsin's clear-cut victory changed the political set-up both in the biggest republic and in the Soviet Union in general. Yeltsin's prestige was boosted beyond comparison, whereas that of Gorbachev bordered on zero. Unlike Yeltsin, Gorbachev had never ventured direct election. In 1989 he obtained his seat as People's Deputy of the USSR from within the CPSU share of the public organisations' quota. But even there, at the Plenary session of the Central Committee of his own party, he did not risk competitive election: as it were, there was no "election", since the 100 seats were contested by exactly 100 candidates. This precaution proved not unnecessary.[99] A year later he was elected President of the USSR by the Third Congress of People's Deputies - by way of exception and in deviation from the constitutional amendments just ratified by that very Congress and providing for the direct election by the populace,[100] and once again on the non-competitive basis.

Gorbachev's might have been a wise choice, if one considers the initially negative attitude of the masses of voters to him personally and the strong opposition to his policies within the party leadership. Still, the fact was there: he had been no match for Yeltsin in terms of popularity, now his legitimacy was also shown to be inferior to Yeltsin's.

Yeltsin's opponents needed some other leader. In June, Prime Minister Pavlov attempted to play the role and demanded additional powers for his Cabinet. He by-passed the President, but secured the support of the top figures in the army and the law enforcement agencies. However, to grant him what he requested meant in effect a state of emergency. The Supreme Soviet refused to comply.

Gorbachev, who hardly wished to see Pavlov and the *Soyuz* group behind him still more powerful, swung towards Yeltsin and other republican leaders. In July the text of the Union Treaty, containing numerous, far-reaching concessions to the republics, was finally agreed, and the signing was scheduled for 20 August 1991.

The Union Treaty drafted in Novo-Ogaryovo bore little resemblance to a legal document. It was a pure political agreement, and not a particularly impressive one at that. The leviathan it envisaged was incredible: the old Union was not to be disbanded; state relations between the Centre and the republics that refused to sign the new Treaty were to continue; they would still be subject to the old Treaty of 1922, whereas relations between the others would henceforth be based on the new Treaty. The result would be two totally different states on the same territory at the same time: with different bodies of law and even different boundaries. Whoever devised that plan did not seem to be concerned about the apparent absurdity of the arrangement.

No less absurd was the procedure envisaged for the election of the head of the would-be state. The election was to be direct and general, but the votes were to be counted separately for each of the republics. To win a candidate for the presidency of the proposed Union would have to meet two sufficiently contradictory criteria: on the one hand, to get not less than fifty percent of the vote over the whole Union; on the other, not less than fifty percent in most of the constituent republics. The populations of the republics being far from equal, there might easily prove to be not a single candidate able to meet both requirements at the same time; one of the candidates might be in the majority if that were counted one way; the other, if the majority were counted in a different way. The possibility was ignored: the draft treaty provided for no way out of the plausible stalemate.

The Soviet political elite demonstrated again its fundamental anti-institutionalism. It designed and proposed a political mechanism that obviously would not work. The envisaged procedure would allow the election of a president in one of two cases only. Either his functions had to be reduced to mere ceremonies; an easy consensus would then be made possible by taking the competition for the downgraded office out of the realm of power politics. (But would not a direct nation-wide election of a rather unimportant official be too expensive a procedure? And, of course, the issue of power would remain and would have to be solved in some other way). Or the successful outcome of the election would have to be somehow secured regardless of the voters' actual attitudes, rendering the entire procedure symbolic. In that case the real decisions about who would head the state would have to be elaborated and made elsewhere and in a different way, too, as had been the case with the Soviets.[101] In other words, a "renewed Union" simply meant a "renewed" facade of the Union, and behind that facade the traditional segregation of the operational experience of *sobornost'* into acted reality and real action was to be preserved.

It is difficult to say what the consequences would have been, had the Union Treaty been signed on 20 August as intended. The course of history proved to be different.

5. The August Coup

In the early morning of 19 August, one day before the scheduled Treaty-signing ceremony, a state of emergency was imposed in "some" regions of the USSR. Vice-President Gennadi Yanayev announced that in connection with Gorbachev's "inability to carry out his duties of President of the USSR due to reasons of ill health" he assumed all presidential powers. State power was transferred to the newly established State Emergency Committee (*GKChP* in its harsh-sounding Russian abbreviation) organised by some key figures in the government and the military. Apart from Yanayev, the Committee included Prime Minister Valentin Pavlov, KGB Chairman Vladimir Kryuchkov, Minister of Defence Dmitri Yazov, Minister of the Interior Boris Pugo, and representatives of the party, agrarian and industrial elites Oleg Baklanov, Vasili Starodubtsev and Alexander Tizyakov. Army units entered Moscow, newspapers were suspended (except *Pravda* and some other official organs), on T.V. channels Tchaikovsky's *Swan Lake* would alternate with the few documents, so far issued by the State Emergency Committee, repeated again and again.

The reaction of the republican and foreign leaders was prompt. Despite the fact that the state of emergency was not approved by the parliament (then on vacation) and that its speaker, Anatoli Lukyanov, issued a somewhat vague "Statement" in which he, though subscribing to the GKChP's assessment of the situation as "serious", did not side with it directly, the majority of the republican leaders withheld their protests, and the most radical of them, Zviad Gamsakhurdia, recently elected President of Georgia, even ordered the republican military units still in the process of formation to disband.

Early that day Boris Yeltsin was blocked in his *dacha* outside Moscow. To judge from the memoirs and recollections of the staff and members of the Russian Supreme Soviet, there were no attempts to co-ordinate the democratic response from the White House in the morning of 19 August.
Everything changed when President Yeltsin and a number of Russian deputies suddenly appeared in the White House about 11 a.m. The President promulgated a decree that outlawed the State Emergency Committee and its members and called on the Moscovites to come defend the White House. Yeltsin was supported by the Moscow authorities: Mayor Popov and Vice-Mayor Luzhkov; their open sabotage of the GKChP's orders played an important role in thwarting the plans of the plotters. Xeroxed copies of Yeltsin's decree appeared on street walls and in Metro (Underground) trains. People began to gather around the White House, barricades were set up. Journalists of the major democratic organs combined to publish a common newspaper, *Obshchaya gazeta*. The GKChP failed to prevent the *Echo of Moscow*, an independent radio station, from broadcasting Yeltsin's decrees and appeals.

At the same time neither the Congress of People's Deputies of the USSR, nor the Supreme Soviet were convened. Its Chairman Lukyanov was obviously playing for time and followed a wait-and-see policy.

In Moscow mass demonstrations began protesting the coup. Moscow businessmen delivered a huge cloth of the Russian tricolours to the White House. Troops positioned in Moscow streets were in dismay: soldiers were subjected to intense propaganda by activists of *Democratic Russia* and simply objecting Moscovites. As a result a small tank unit, under command of Major Yemelyanov, switched sides and raised the Russian flag. Later that day journalists at the Central Television, working on the evening newsreel, managed to cut in a piece that showed Boris Yeltsin addressing a mass of demonstrators around the White House from an armoured vehicle. The press conference of the GKChP members broadcast the same evening seemed far less convincing: they failed to provide an intelligible answer to the question about Gorbachev's state of health, looked obviously nervous and proved unable to formulate any reasonable political programme. Thorny questions from the audience would clearly nonpluss them, thus showing to the entire country that they were not in control of the situation. In St. Petersburg Mayor Sobchak managed, upon his return from the morning conference with Yeltsin, to reaffirm his control and reached an agreement with the commanding officer of the Leningrad military district that the army would not enter the city. A formidable demonstration was held in support of Yeltsin and democracy in Dvortsovaya Square in front of the Winter Palace.

Russian provinces reacted differently. Many local leaders were in no hurry to pledge their allegiance to either side and obviously waited for one of the parties to win before joining it.

Indecision was to be observed on the international scene as well. The governments of the UK and the USA pledged support for the Russian authorities. The latter's resistance to the coup was made known to public all over the world by foreign TV and radio correspondents broadcasting from the White House. Of these the most informative proved correspondents of Radio Liberty and BBC to whom the Russian audience owed its chance to hear a non-official part of the story.

By the night of August 20 the White House was already encircled by a "live ring", a defence technique tested in January 1991 in Vilnius when such a "ring" of defenders around the Lithuanian parliament had prevented the Soviet authorities from using military force to dissolve it.

By the next morning the balance seemed to begin to tilt in favour of the Russian leadership. Demonstrations in Moscow became more multitudinous; some Russian provinces pledged support for the White House, the Soviet Air Force refused to obey orders from the State Emergency Committee. As telephones in the White House were not disconnected, the Russian deputies, especially servicemen, used personal ties to influence their middle-ranking contacts in the power agencies. A few hundred men from private security agencies were assembled in the White House; the recently established Russian Security Agency, headed by Colonel Ivanenko, would issue telephone messages to KGB local offices ordering them to disobey the GKChP.

At their meeting held on the night of August 20 most Cabinet members supported the State Emergency Committee, but the support was far from universal. Some influential politicians, among them Vadim Bakatin and Arkadi Vol'ski, tried to contact President Gorbachev personally. By the afternoon of August 20 the coup leaders began to realise that victory was slipping from their hands and undertook some impetuous actions. A curfew was imposed in Moscow, but even the Moscow commandant had to recognise the task was hard to fulfil because it involved a great number of supplementary measures: new time-tables for enterprises and transport, places for detention of curfew violators, etc. An assault on the White House was contemplated, too. On the basis of sources available to us it is difficult to decide if the order to attack the residence of the Russian parliament and the Russian government was actually issued or not. Some officers from the elite unit "Alpha" would subsequently assert that the order was given, but was not carried out. On the other hand, persons involved in the decision-making process would deny such an order ever existed.

However that may have been, something was done. There were troop movements in the Leningradskoye Chaussee in the direction of the White House. Later the movements would be explained by the need to replace the units that had been found unreliable after their contacts with the populace. Nevertheless, in the White House they were taken to indicate a near assault. About 5 p.m. the White House was put on alert. One after another deputies would address the people over the *Echo of Moscow*. They would bid farewell and ask to forgive them for having failed to defend Russian democracy. The guard of the White House that consisted of militia officers, people from private security agencies and President Yeltsin's personal guards was quite pessimistic. When interviewed by journalists, they would say they hoped to hold out for half an hour. A group of deputies was busy preparing evacuation of the Russian leaders outside the country. The Russian Prime Minister Ivan Silayev left for Sverdlovsk region where a reserve communication post was organised.

The democrats viewed the situation with a sense of tragedy and foreboding. In the White House, arms would be given out not only to the guards, but also to the deputies and cabinet members. Close-ups (often to be repeated afterwards) showing the White House corridors filled with armed men sleeping right on the floor, the Russian Vice-President Rutskoi with a sub-machine gun, surrounded by bodyguards, a crowd in front of the White House, in what would soon be called the Square of Free Russia, and shields in the guards' hands to protect Yeltsin and Rutskoi addressing the crowd from the White House balcony. It all looked so much like those outlandish Latin American coups familiar from TV reports and reminded one of Allende's last hours. To see it here in Moscow, so close at hand proved a terrible shock to many of its inhabitants.

In the evening of August 20, the *Echo of Moscow* warned that they expected the station to be closed and the staff arrested, this time once and for all (the KGB officers had already stopped them broadcasting for a while the previous morning). In the meantime distinguished artists turned up at the station on their own initiative to address the public, curse the GKChP and express their hopes that the democratic cause was not lost for ever. They voiced their hope that Russia's progress towards democracy could not be thwarted and that any victory of its enemies would only be a temporary one. About 10 p.m. the operator said good-bye to the audience and played an old song by Vertinski[102] "Madame, the leaves are falling already". At that moment the broadcast was interrupted.

By the night of August 20, reports started to arrive from the White House about the imminent assault. Shooting was heard from the direction of Sadovoye Kol'tso ("Garden Ring"), about 400 meters away from the White House. For two days already the parliament had been surrounded by a tight crowd of people determined to protect the building and prevent the assault. However, what the reporters thought was the beginning of an assault was in fact an encounter between a patrol of a few armoured vehicles and the demonstrators. The patrol was caught in a trap on the intersection of New Arbat and Sadovoye Kol'tso, close to the US Embassy and not far from the White House. At this place the Ring road dives into a short tunnel, the exit from which was then blocked by a line of trolleybuses forming a barricade. One of the vehicles attempted to ram their way through the barricade, when a few demonstrators jumped down and tried to blind the driver by covering the observation slots with a piece of cloth. The soldiers inside the vehicle opened fire; three demonstrators were killed. The incident was brought to an end by the interference of Moscow Soviet deputies who persuaded the patrol men to cease fire.

But by the next morning, 21 August, the situation changed completely. A number of prominent functionaries of the CPSU, including Bakatin and Vol'ski, called a press conference at the Central Committee headquarters and informed it of the flight of the GKChP members. As turned out later, they went to the Crimea to meet President Gorbachev. The session of the Russian Supreme Soviet, that opened the same day, decided to send there Vice-President Rutskoi accompanied by a group of armed officers to arrest the GKChP members and set Gorbachev free. That was done by the evening. The coup failed.

The next day a grandiose funeral ceremony was held at which President Yeltsin, perhaps for the first time in Russian history, publicly asked the people and the relatives of the three killed young men to forgive him for having failed to save their lives. It was as if all the three had been specially selected by the old Soviet staff department, always anxious about the right representation: they were a young businessman, a veteran of the Afghan war and a Jewish architect. It was also the first time when Soviet TV showed a Jewish funeral. Later that day a gala concert was held in the square in front of the White House. Traditional Russian round dance would alternate with classic ballet pieces and rock groups. A popular rock singer

Igor' Tal'kov, known for his anti-communist feelings, sang: "The devil is tired of the carouse, the candles are out, the ball is over".[103]

Yeltsin issued a decree banning, or rather suspending the activities of the CPSU on the territory of Russia.[104] He signed it in a rather dramatic manner, in the presence of Gorbachev who tried feebly to intervene, and before the eyes of millions TV viewers watching the Supreme Soviet session broadcast live. A few days later some Central Committee functionaries responsible for the party funds would jump from the windows and balconies of their homes.

In the meantime, a crowd of demonstrators rushed towards Lubyanka Square to demolish the KGB, the symbol of the communist dictatorship, but demolished instead the statue of Dzerzhinski[105] that stood in front of the KGB headquarters. Two more statues were removed, those of Sverdlov[106] and Kalinin.[107] Though there were no other signs of mass violence, the party *nomenklatura* was downright frightened by what seemed to be the beginning of a revolution. The fear was soon shown to be groundless: nothing whatever happened, President Yeltsin took his leave and went away.

Any event on a scale of a coup d'etat or a revolution would probably leave some questions unanswered. It seems, however, that the events of 19-21 August 1991 in the USSR beat all records in this respect.

One group of questions concerns the plotters' professional skills. What was the sense of sending troops to Moscow if they were not to be used? The army units did not take control of the salient points: communication centres, main roads and road junctions, government buildings. They were simply stationed, frightening, or rather irritating, the population. If the White House was to be stormed, how did it happened that even the telephones inside the building were not disconnected? And what plan of assault against the seat of the parliament and the President of Russia might have been contemplated or was, indeed, needed, if in the morning of August 19 the mission could have been accomplished by a platoon-strong task force which, however, had never been sent?[108]

All these follies can be explained away, of course, as mere incompetence. However, some of the coup leaders, at least, had not seemed *that* incompetent when they had been called to do that kind of job before, as for example in Budapest in 1956, in Prague in 1968 or in Kabul in 1979.

Another group of questions centres round two problems, that of the "nuclear button" and that of Yeltsin's "sudden arrival" in the White House. The problem of the "nuclear button" can be stated as follows. Is it that easy to "isolate" a president, who is also the commander-in-chief of the armed forces of a nuclear super-power, and deprive him of all control of the armed forces he is supposed to command? It was "isolation" of that kind that Gorbachev would talk about upon his return to Moscow from his Crimean captivity. We do not know, of course, details of the system that was used in the USSR to maintain the control of the strategic forces; we know of no description and/or analysis of it in the open press. However, it is highly unlikely that the system would have differed much from the one used in the USA, and this latter was described and discussed both in press and in professional literature that is publicly available.[109] In the USA, at least, the "nuclear button" is, of course, not a button, but a system of communications with the relevant commanding officers. A successful attempt to deprive the President of this system of communications would undermine the country's capacity to strike back in case of a nuclear attack. From what we know of the mentality of Soviet generals, we cannot conceive them going *that* far. That the government's communications network could have been disabled from Simferopol sounds naive. Is it really true that, the President of the USSR being on vacation in the Crimea, a group of commandos of the potential enemy could have destroyed his strategic communications system by simply seizing a switchboard in Simferopol? Or would the chief of the President's personal guard "isolate" the head of state on an order from his superior officer instead of arresting that officer for high treason?

No less enigmatic was Yeltsin's appearance in Moscow in the morning of August 19. How was he allowed, being "blocked" in his *dacha*, to escape to Moscow and set the mechanism of democratic consolidation in motion? Did he manage to convince the security officers responsible for his detention to let him go? Or had he reached some understanding with their bosses, having promised, perhaps, to bring to Moscow and make public something different from what he brought and made public in real life?

The official story provides no answers to these questions. Nor do we have them. Moreover, we doubt the answers will ever be known. What is surprising, however, is the fact that, for all the analyses of the August 1991 events made by journalists and professional political scientists, no one seems to be willing to ask the questions?

It is, probably, in the nature of things when analysing events of this sort to suspect the influence of concealed factors. They may be difficult to identify, but even if lacunae cannot be filled, it does not become a scholar to pretend they do not exist. The absence of a coherent account of the events, which surprisingly no one found disturbing, is noteworthy. In itself, this sheds light both on the character of the events and on the political culture of the actors and the audience, especially if they all take it for granted that the "mise-en-scene" on this side of the political coulisse has nothing to do with what is going on behind it. If so, we must distinguish between two essentially different processes: on the one hand, the mass resistance to an attempt to restore the communist regime; on the other, a political intrigue of which the winners and losers are known, but in which the course of the struggle remains a sealed book. Thus, both the "heroic" and the "cynical" versions would get their respective correlates.

It may also be, that the situation, as it existed on the eve of and during the coup, was simply due to the Russian habit of doing everything in a manner so disorderly that the impossible is made possible; or due, perhaps, to that peculiar "Russian soul" that seems never to abide by "rules" or "instructions" in *genuinely* serious cases, but would proceed by inspiration, as if really guided by "the Holy Spirit".

A few days before the coup one of the authors had a chance to discuss with an adviser to Premier Pavlov the government's possible actions with respect to the new Union Treaty. The impression was that of utter confusion: the Cabinet's primary concern, it seemed, was themselves. It is thus conceivable that in that extraordinary situation no one would have cared about planning the coup "according to rules" and that, therefore, the actions of both the GKChP and Gorbachev were just a convulsive response of a group of politicians who had lost their foothold in the past and had failed to gain a new one in the future. After all politicians are human beings, like the rest of us.

Notes

1 See "The Results of the Election of the USSR People's Deputies from the Communist Party of the Soviet Union: Information of the Election Commission for Election of USSR People's Deputies from the CPSU, 15 March 1989", in *Party Worker* 1991 pp. 17-24.

2 As was already noted, Gorbachev received 12 "no" votes; his result was the eighty-sixth. Now, the public organisations at that election had 912 registered candidates for 750 seats (see "The Report of the Credentials Commission" in *First Congress USSR* 1989, Vol. 1, p. 41), which gives an average of 1.2, compared to 1.9 (in the first round in

March) and 6.1 (in the second round in May) in the territorial constituencies. If, therefore, the ratio of candidates to seats in the Communist Party had been equal even to the average for the public organisations only, there would have been 20 candidates who would have lost. The voting results being what they were, none of those who got more than 8 "no" votes (out of 641!) would have been elected. Beside Gorbachev and his Prime Minister Nikolai Ryzhkov (10 votes against), these would have been the remaining eight members and candidate members of the Politburo, including all Central Committee's Secretaries.

[3] Yeltsin got 1,185 votes against 964 (see *First Congress USSR* 1989, Vol. 1, p. 211).

[4] The deputy's name was Alexei Kazannik (see *First Congress USSR* 1989, Vol. 1, pp. 424-433). Kazannik was later a member of the Presidential Council. After the autumn crisis of 1993 Yeltsin appointed him Prosecutor General instead of Valentin Stepankov. Kazannik soon resigned, however, unwilling to conflict with the newly elected State Duma over the proposed amnesty for participants of the September-October events.

[5] Article 76 of the Constitution (see *Constitution USSR* 1985, p. 44).

[6] On the intricacies of the Bolsheviks' tactics with regard to the Soviets in 1917, see Sergeyev and Biryukov 1993, pp. 57-60.

[7] The developments are analysed in Sergeyev and Biryukov 1993, pp. 61-75.

[8] Compare to Cotler 1995.

[9] For details, see Davydov 1990.

[10] A striking (not to say, suspicious) promptness.

[11] In March 1989 the 1,500 seats (the readers will remember that only two thirds of the 2,250 People's Deputies were to be elected directly by the populace; 750 seats were reserved for "public organisations") were contested by 2,895 candidates. In 384 districts (25.6 percent) there were no alternative candidates (in 399 districts if one adds the second round). In 953 districts there were but two registered contestants, and districts with more than two candidates numbered only 163 (10.9 percent). (See Sergeyev and Biryukov 1993, p. 104).

[12] Article 10 of the Law "On Elections of People's Deputies of the RSFSR" (see *Law on Elections* 1989, p. 5).

[13] The 1,068 seats were contested by 6,705 candidates (i.e. 6.3 per district on the average). There were only 33 districts (3.1 percent) without alternative candidates; in 300 districts (28.1 percent) the number of candidates was more than four; in 24, more than twenty (see *First Congress RSFSR* 1992, Vol. 1, p. 4).

[14] The Russian deputy corps elected in March 1990 consisted for the most part (93.9 percent) of people who had never held elected office before (see *First Congress RSFSR* 1992, Vol. 1, p. 5).

[15] The term is difficult to translate, but easy to explain. Thanks to the Soviet propaganda that has for decades used the word "imperialism" to denote (and denounce) political adversaries to the Soviet Union, the word "empire" has strong negative connotations in present-day Russian. This use of the word can be traced to Lenin's definition of imperialism as a stage (the highest and, presumably, the last) in the development of capitalism (see Lenin 1964). As, according to Lenin, this stage is characterised, apart from other features, by the establishment of colonial empires (ibid., pp. 254-65), the adjective has eventually become part of the definition. The Roman state would still be called an "empire" (as, for that matter, would the Chinese or the pre-revolutionary Russian state), but this is merely historic slang. That is why the majority of those who regret the disintegration of the Soviet Union would vehemently object to it being called an "empire". From their point of view, this makes sense, for the colonial element was certainly marginal to the Soviet political system. On the other hand, contemporary Russian has a word that is an exact synonym for "empire" (in the traditional sense, obviously implied by the founders of the Russian Empire in their time), but free of the negative connotations of the Soviet newspeak. This word is *"derzhava"* (from *derzhat'* - "to hold"). Defined as a high-style synonym for "state", *derzhava* is not applied to modest-size and/or ethnically homogeneous countries, but usually suggests a political entity of which integrity and the very existence depend on centralism, i.e. subordination of provinces to the "Centre".

[16] Sergeyev and Biryukov 1993, pp. 22-8; see also Biryukov and Sergeyev 1994. For a summary exposition of the difference between the *populist* and the *pluralist* interpretations of democracy as seen from the Russian cultural perspective, see Biryukov and Sergeyev 1995.

17 Cf. the following quotation (Vishnevskaya 1993):

> "DemRussia *[a common abbreviation for* Democratic Russia] and the CPSU are twin brothers. The psychological attitudes are the same for both. And the nearly first of these is the attitude that a group of people be discovered and rendered powerless that is the embodiment and the principal source of universal evil: be it the "Judeo-Masons", the "Landlords-and-Capitalists", the "Kulak Saboteurs", or finally the "*Nomenklatura*". And this is, of course, not the kind of concept that forms the basis of genuine democracies.

18 Article 105 of the Constitution (see *Constitution RF* 1992, p. 43).

19 Article 106 of the Constitution (ibid.).

20 There were 1,059 elected deputies at the time of the First; 1,063, at the Second and the Third; 1,061, at the Fourth; 1,051, at the Fifth; 1,049, at the Sixth; 1,040, at the Seventh Congress; 1,033, at the Eighth and the Ninth Congresses; (see *First Congress RSFSR* 1992, Vol. 1, p. 5 and the roll calls for the other Congresses).

21 Articles 104 and 185 of the Constitution (see *Constitution RF* 1992, pp. 41 and 78, respectively).

22 See Sub-section on "Boris Yeltsin and the Idea of Russian Sovereignty" in Section 1 of this chapter.

23 S.Kovalyov's speech on 8 June 1990 (see *First Congress* 1992, Vol. 3, p. 456).

24 In fact, in January 1993 the number of only standing commissions and committees, including the two operating under the Presidium, equalled 30.

25 A similar motion had been made earlier with respect to the Congress of People's Deputies of the USSR, though the strength of its deputy corps (2,250 members) had made its feasibility doubtful. As far as the Russian Congress was concerned, the motion to constitute the Supreme Soviet so as to consist of all People's deputies had the highest rating of all the proposals about the numerical composition of the two houses voted on 5 June 1990: it got 603 votes against 317 with 46 abstentions, leaving the alternative suggestions far behind (see *First Congress RSFSR* 1992, Vol. 3, p. 199).

[26] This is attested, in particular, by the high turnout: 77 percent (see *First Congress RSFSR* 1992, Vol. 1, p. 4).

[27] The Grand Kremlin Palace had hitherto been the seat of the Supreme Soviets of the USSR and the RSFSR. The Congresses of People's Deputies of the USSR were held in the Kremlin Palace of Congresses built originally to accommodate party forums.

[28] 51 sittings were held. By comparison, the Second Congress sat in session between 27 November and 15 December 1990 (30 sittings); the Third, between 28 March and 5 April 1991 (17 sittings); the Fourth, between 21 and 25 May 1991 (9 sittings); the Fifth, between 10 and 17 July and then, after an interval, between 28 October and 2 November 1991 (23 sittings); the Sixth, between 6 and 21 April 1992 (29 sittings); the Seventh, between 1 and 14 December 1992 (24 sittings); the Eighth, between 10 and 13 March 1993 (7 sittings); the Ninth, between 26 and 29 March 1993 (8 sittings). As to the Tenth Congress, convened on 23 September 1993 after President Yeltsin's controversial decree on "the step-by-step constitutional reform" and the official dissolution of the legislature, it remained in session till the White House was stormed on 4 October 1993; its verbatim records for the first five days (23 to 27 September) have been published in excerpts; no records were taken after that, as the electricity supply in the White House was cut off.

[29] See *First Congress RSFSR* 1992, Vol. 2, p. 267.

[30] Ibid.

[31] Other sources give the number as 55 (see Note 45 to Chapter 5).

[32] On the day of the voting the Congress consisted of 1,060 deputies, 8 seats being vacant. However, not all of the deputies took part in the voting (the word "total" in the following sentences refers to the number of valid ballot-papers). On 25 May 1990 Boris Yeltsin got 497 votes out of the total of 1,032 (535 *contra*); his principal rival Ivan Polozkov, First Secretary of the Krasnodar Regional Party Committee, 473 (559 *contra*); 32 votes went to the third candidate. Though Yeltsin was slightly more successful in the second round the next day (he got 503 votes; Polozkov, only 458), the victory went to no one, and that meant new election. It was held on 29 May. That time Yeltsin's main rival was Alexander Vlasov, Chairman of the Council of Ministers of the Russian Republic. Yeltsin got 535 votes out of 1,037; Vlasov lost with 467 *pro* and 570 *contra*; the

third candidate got 11 votes. (See *First Congress RSFSR* 1992, Vol. 2, pp. 343, 347, 445-446).

[33] See *First Congress RSFSR* 1992, Vol. 1, pp. 554-63.

[34] Ibid., p. 555.

[35] Ibid., p. 556.

[36] Ibid., p. 563.

[37] See *Constitution USSR* 1985 p. 43.

[38] For the analysis of the cognitive structure of the discourse of sovereignty, see Sergeyev and Biryukov 1993, pp. 121-6.

[39] The voting on the respective article of the draft Declaration of State Sovereignty of the RSFSR was held on 8 June 1990 (see *First Congress RSFSR* 1992, Vol. 3, p. 512).

[40] See *First Congress RSFSR* 1992, Vol. 4, p. 251.

[41] *Second Congress RSFSR* 1992, Vol. 2, p. 328-30; for the appropriate constitutional amendment, see Vol. 6, pp. 246-7.

[42] That was the official wording of the agenda.

[43] Lithuania was the first to declare independence on 11 March 1990. It was followed by Estonia on 30 March and Latvia on 4 May. The process acquired new impetus after Russia proclaimed sovereignty (as distinguished from independence) on 12 June. Other republics followed suit: Uzbekistan, on 20 June; Moldavia, on 24 June; Ukraine, on 16 July; Belorussia, on 27 July; Armenia and Turkmenia, on 23 August; Tajikistan, on 24 August; Kazakhstan, on 25 October. Kirghizia was the last of the Union republics to declare sovereignty and did it precisely on the day, the Fourth Congress opened: 12 December (see Balzer (ed.), 1991 pp. 236-238).

[44] It was only leaders of Russia, Armenia and Moldavia that could be counted on to support radical reforms at the moment; as to the Baltic leaders, it was doubtful, if they could be convinced to participate at all.

[45] "Do you consider necessary the preservation of the Union of Soviet Socialist Republics as a renewed federation of equal sovereign republics, in which the rights and freedom of the individual of any nationality will be fully guaranteed?" Would voting "against" have to be understood as

voting against *preservation* or against *renewal* of the Union? This was sheer casuistry, of course, but it added to the emptiness of the undertaking.

[46] The referendum was conceived as an all-Union venture, but the votes were to be counted for individual republics. The natural question was, what would happen if in some republic the majority voted against "the preservation of the renewed Union"? Was voting "against" preservation of the Union to be considered as voting "for" secession from the Union? This interpretation was officially rejected: secession was subject to a special law enacted a few months earlier in the aftermath of Lithuania's declaration of its independence. But in that case why hold a referendum at all? If a "no" vote was not binding, neither would a "yes" vote be (as the future was soon to show)! Such a referendum could solve no real problems that the preservation or the transformation of the Union, or both, might pose, but it was bound to cause widespread irritation by the very intention to impose the will of the Slavic majority on all other nations, for instance, on the Baltic peoples.

[47] The referendum was held on 17 March 1991. 147,000,000 voted (80 percent of the electorate), of whom 112,000,000 (76.4 percent of the turnout) voted for the preservation of the Union.

[48] B.Tarasov's speech on 31 March 1991 (*Third Congress RSFSR* 1991, Bulletin 6, p. 5).

[49] E.Tsibikzhapov's speech on 31 March 1991 (ibid., p. 6).

[50] S.Filatov's speech on 31 March 1991 (ibid., p. 31).

[51] A.Sokolov's speech on 31 March 1991 (ibid, p. 32).

[52] V.Agafonov's speech on 2 April 1991 (ibid., Bulletin 10, p. 7).

[53] B.Tarasov's speech on 31 March 1991 (ibid., Bulletin 6, p. 5).

[54] A.Nazarchuk's speech on 2 April 1991 (ibid., Bulletin 10, p. 7).

[55] An allusion to the Communist Party Central Committee situated in Staraya (Old) Square.

[56] The speech of R.Khasbulatov, Deputy Chairman of the Supreme Soviet, on 1 April 1991 (*Third Congress RSFSR* 1991, Bulletin 9, p. 11).

[57] A.Krivchenko's speech on 4 April 1991 (ibid, Bulletin 15, pp. 17-8).

58 B.Tarasov's speech on 1 April 1991 (ibid, Bulletin 8, p. 4).

59 A.Klimenok's speech on 1 April 1991 (ibid, Bulletin 9, p. 3).

60 We have already mentioned the strike of the Kuzbass miners and the resolute stand they took towards the government of the USSR. The situation was aggravated further by the centralised "price reform" carried out by Pavlov's Cabinet early in April 1991, i.e. when the Congress was already in session. The reform's practical effect did not extend beyond the three-fold (on the average) rise in prices for consumption goods.

61 See N.Nazarbaev's speech on 17 December 1990 (*Fourth Congress USSR* 1991, Vol. 1, pp. 103-7) and E.Shevardnadze's speech on 20 December 1990 (ibid., pp. 407-10).

62 Yu.Makarov's speech on 1 April 1991 (see *Third Congress RSFSR* 1991, Bulletin 8, p. 10). [Italics added]

63 For a more detailed discussion of the subject, see Sergeyev and Biryukov, 1993, pp. 70-2.

64 See *Third Congress RSFSR* 1991, Bulletin 16, p. 11.

65 The question will be discussed somewhat later.

66 See *Fourth Congress RSFSR* 1991, Vol. 1, pp. 54-63.

67 See also Shakhrai's concluding remarks on 22 May 1991 (ibid, pp. 132-4).

68 O.Rumyantsev's speech on 22 May 1991 (ibid, p. 124).

69 See Item 13 of the Law of the Russian Soviet Federal Socialist Republic "On Amendments and Supplements to the Constitution (Fundamental Law) of the RSFSR" (ibid, Vol. 3, p. 138); see also *Constitution RF* 1992, pp. 60-1.

70 Article 110 and Section 1 of Article 121^5 of the amended version of the Constitution (ibid, pp. 48 and 56); Items 6 and 11 of the law on constitutional amendments (*Fourth Congress RSFSR* 1991, Vol. 3, pp. 134 and 136).

71 Article 110 and Part 1 of Article 121^5 of the amended version of the Constitution (*Constitution RF* 1992, pp. 53 and 56); Items 9 and 11 of the law on constitutional amendments (*Fourth Congress RSFSR* 1991, Vol. 3, pp. 134 and 136).

[72] Item 11 of the law on constitutional amendments (ibid., p. 137).

[73] S.Shakhrai's presentation of the laws "On the President of the RSFSR" and "On Amendments and Supplements to the Constitution (Fundamental Law) of the RSFSR" (ibid., Vol. 1, pp. 58-9).

[74] I.Muravyov's speech on 21 May 1991 (ibid., p. 92).

[75] O.Smolin's speech on 21 May 1991 (ibid., p. 81).

[76] S.Shakhrai's presentation (ibid., p. 59).

[77] Yu.Slobodkin's speech on 22 May 1991 (ibid., p. 110).

[78] A common abbreviation for "General Secretary [of the CPSU Central Committee]".

[79] O.Smolin's speech on 21 May 1991 (ibid., p. 81).

[80] V.Rasskazov's speech on 22 May 1991 (ibid., p. 115).

[81] N.Pavlov' speech on 22 May 1991 (ibid., p. 113).

[82] S.Shakhrai's presentation (ibid., p. 62).

[83] Articles 104 and 185 of the Constitution (see *Constitution RF* 1992, pp. 41 and 78).

[84] The decision was passed by the majority of 609 votes against 121 with 87 abstentions; a simple majority required 531 votes; "qualified", 708 (see *Fourth Congress RSFSR* 1991, Vol. 1, pp. 137 and 223).

[85] Ibid., pp. 132-42.

[86] Ibid., Vol. 1, p. 57.

[87] Article 121^6 of the Constitution (see *Constitution RF* 1992, p. 58); Item 11 of the law on constitutional amendments (*Fourth Congress RSFSR* 1991, Vol. 3, p. 137).

[88] Ibid., Vol. 1, p. 71).

[89] See Note 71 to this Chapter.

[90] Item 19 of Article 109 of the Constitution (see *Constitution RF* 1992, pp. 47); Item 5 of the law on constitutional amendments (see *Fourth Congress RSFSR* 1991, Vol. 3, p. 133).

[91] Item 14, Part Three, Article 104 of the Constitution (see *Constitution RF* 1992, p. 42); Item 2 of the law on constitutional amendments (see *Fourth Congress RSFSR* 1991, Vol. 3, p. 133).

[92] Item 11 of the law on constitutional amendments (ibid., p. 137).

[93] Item 13 of Part Three, Article 104 and Article 121^{10} of the amended version of the Constitution (*Constitution RF* 1992, pp. 42, 59); Items 2 and 11 of the law on constitutional amendments (*Fourth Congress RSFSR* 1991, Vol. 3, pp. 133 and 138).

[94] Ibid., Vol. 1, p. 61).

[95] Item 16 of Article 121^{5} of the amended version of the Constitution (see Item 11 of the law on constitutional amendments in *Fourth Congress RSFSR* 1991, Vol. 3, p. 137). [Italics added]

[96] On the "framing" character of Russian legislation, see Chapter 9.

[97] Part 2 of Article 104 of the Constitution (*Constitution RF* 1992, pp. 41); Item 2 of the law on constitutional amendments (*Fourth Congress RSFSR* 1991, Vol. 3, p. 132).

[98] The second was Nikolai Ryzhkov, former Chairman of the Soviet Council of Ministers, with 16.8 percent; the third, Vladimir Zhirinovski, leader of the Liberal Democratic Party, with 7.8 percent; the fourth, Aman Tuleyev, Chairman of the Kemerovo Regional Council, with 6.8 percent; the fifth, General Albert Makashov, Commander of the Volga-Urals military district, with 3.7 percent; the sixth, Vadim Bakatin, the former Minister of Interior in Ryzhkov's government, with 3.4 percent (see "Information of the Central Election Commission for the Election of the President of the RSFSR"; in Russian; *Izvestiya*, 20 June 1991).

[99] See Note 2 to this chapter.

[100] Article 127^{1} of the Constitution of the USSR (see *Third Congress USSR* 1990, Vol. 3, p. 195).

[101] See Sub-section on "*Sobornost'* as a Model of Political Representation" in Section 1, Chapter 3.

[102] A Russian pre-revolutionary and emigré chansonnier.

[103] It turned out soon that his own ball was over, indeed: a few weeks later Tal'kov was killed in St. Petersburg under unclear circumstances.

[104] On 29 August the USSR Supreme Soviet followed suit and on 6 November, on the eve of the 74th anniversary of the October revolution, the Communist Party was formally banned.

[105] The first Chairman of the Cheka (see Note 5 to Chapter 1).

[106] The first Chairman of the Central Executive Committee of the Congress of the Soviets, i.e. the titular head of the Soviet state from November 1917 to March 1919.

[107] Succeeded to Sverdlov's office upon the latter's death in March 1919 and continued in it till shortly before his own death in 1946.

[108] Even later, when the situation around the White House changed and an attempt to take the parliament building by force was fraught with innumerable casualties among its civil defenders, it was still possible to find "propitious" moments for attack. As eye-witnesses to the events, the authors can testify that in the morning of August 20, after the Moscow metro was opened, the majority of those who had spent the night around the White House were gone and by 9 a.m. but a few hundred people remained to man the barricades. A similar picture could be observed the next morning, on 21 August, although on a much grander scale: throughout the coup's second night the White House was surrounded by a few dozen, perhaps a few hundred thousand men and women; however, only a few thousand were still there by the next morning.

[109] See Blair 1985; Carter *et al.* (eds.) 1987.

5 The Parliament and the Reform

Whoever having undertaken to speak or write on Medicine, have first laid down for themselves some hypothesis to their argument, such as hot, or cold, or moist, or dry, or whatever else they choose (thus reducing their subject within a narrow compass, and supposing only one or two original causes of diseases or of death among mankind), are all clearly mistaken in much that they say; and this is the more reprehensible as relating to an art which all men avail themselves of on the most important occasions, and the good operators and practitioners in which they hold in especial honour.

Hippocrates, "On Ancient Medicine".

1. At a Turning-Point

The first few weeks after the failure of the coup passed in anticipation of major changes. With the Communist Party suspended, a radical re-structuring of the political system and new elections were expected to consolidate the victory of democracy over communism. Yet, none of these took place.

Throughout the first two months of autumn Yeltsin initiated nothing of significance and even left for a vacation. The task of forming the new Russian government was carried out primarily by Gennadi Burbulis. When after a three-months break the Fifth Congress of People's Deputies of Russia resumed its sessions, the main issue was the new cabinet. Suddenly Yeltsin announced his decision to head the government himself, with Burbulis as his First Vice-Premier and Gaidar as Vice-Premier in charge of economic reform. The latter brought with him a team of relatively young "radical" economists who had never held important political posts before. The new government presented no concrete programme of reforms, but the mass media soon nicknamed them "Chicago boys" - by analogy with the team of Chicago economists invited by Pinochet after the September 1973 coup in Chile.

The analogy was hardly flattering, since, rather than allude to the collapse of the totalitarian regime, it invoked something quite different, viz. the idea of authoritarian *perestroika*, which had been widely discussed already before August.[1] In that context the "Chilean analogy" appeared natural enough, but it was difficult to see how it would fit into the general democratic atmosphere of 1989-91 and be reconciled with the slogans of *Democratic Russia*.

In the preceding chapter, however, we have already had an occasion to dwell on the populist aspects of *Democratic Russia's* political countenance and comment on the inadequate understanding of the institutional nature of democracy that characterised many its activists. To judge from what happened, the leaders of *Democratic Russia* had decided - even before their victory in August 1991 - to join forces with "progressive bureaucracy". This concord had in fact been realised. It was best exemplified by Gavriil Popov and Yuri Luzhkov running together for mayor and vice-mayor of Moscow. Through this alliance the activists of *Democratic Russia*, heretofore as far removed from positions of power as heaven from earth, had gained access to many an important post. This was most obvious in Moscow and St. Petersburg, and it may well have been the reason why *Democratic Russia* did not insist on holding new elections. Had the election taken place in October-November 1991, the majoritarian election law then in force would have secured *Democratic Russia* an overwhelming majority in the new parliament.[2]

The policy adopted by *Democratic Russia* in autumn 1991 proved a fatal mistake. By the time of the Sixth Congress (April 1992) its deputies found themselves hostages to the executive and after the parliament's dissolution in October 1993 *Democratic Russia* lost the last vestige of influence on the course of events. This refusal to hold new elections, the unconditional support for Yeltsin (who, for his part, did not show a great desire to reciprocate), as well as the unwillingness to formulate a clear programme of reforms can only be properly understood if seen against the background that was determined by two major factors: the political culture of *sobornost'* and the continued rivalry between Russia and the USSR.

The latter circumstance shaped the entire political set-up in the country by transforming the political strife between "democrats" and "communists" into an institutional conflict between the parliament and the President of Russia, on the one hand, and the parliament and the President of the USSR, on the other. It seems interesting to note that at the time of the August coup "communists" and "democrats" in the Russian Supreme Soviet voted together, substantiating the hypothesis (never properly considered) that the silent support for the GKChP on the other side, in the Supreme Soviet of the USSR, for which the Union deputies were soon to pay by what had been left of their prestige and power,[3] had in fact arisen out of the same institutional conflict that threatened - after Russia had proclaimed its sovereignty and set its legislation above that of the Soviet Union the other year - to turn the Union parliament into a mere "talking-shop", the mock of the conventional anti-parliamentary rhetoric.

It seems that amid strictly confidential preparations for the Belovezh agreement, Yeltsin did not want to hold a new election. In the course of the election campaign it would have been virtually impossible to avoid discussing the main political problems, of which the future of the USSR was, perhaps, the most important. However, a proposal to simply denounce the 1922 Union Treaty, rather than have it replaced by a new one, stood little chance, in case it had been made public, of being welcomed by the electorate.

With the signing of the Belovezh agreement and its subsequent ratification by the Supreme Soviet the public was confronted with a *fait accompli*. The widespread resentment about the fact would later be fully exploited by various nationalist groups and, indeed, become one of the major factors behind Zhirinovski's electoral success in December 1993. It is worthwhile to note in this connection that the Russian policy of 1990-91 with respect to the dissolution of the USSR set a questionable precedent in the field of international relations. The routine transformation of borderlines between the Soviet republics, i.e. administrative boundaries *within* a state, into internationally recognised borders *between* independent states was in apparent contradiction with the 1972 Helsinki agreements, of which the most important provision was the inviolability of borders between European states. According to those agreements, no borders could be changed without negotiations.

In the case of the USSR this provision was not fulfilled. The Russian-Ukrainian treaty on the unalterability of common borders, which had been signed at the time when both republics had been parts of the USSR, stipulated that no revision of borders take place *within* the Soviet Union. This, combined with the Russian Supreme Soviet's subsequent ruling that the transfer of the Crimea from Russia to Ukraine in 1954 had been unlawful,[4] aggravated, and indeed continues to aggravate, the situation around the Crimea. From the standpoint of law, the issue is still unsettled and can, in principle, be brought up, depending on the kind of government Russia has and the balance of power between Russia and Ukraine. It thus presents a potential threat to peace in Eastern Europe. The dire consequences of leaving the status of a territory unregulated have been recently demonstrated by the conflict in Chechnya.

Formally speaking, after the Soviet Union was dissolved the parliament and the President of Russia had to resign and a Constituent Assembly (or some such body) had to be convened to draw up and adopt a new Russian Constitution, which would then allow to hold new elections under provisions of a new Fundamental Law. Both the parliament and the President had been elected while Russia had yet been a republic within the Soviet Union and could therefore have no legitimacy apart from what had been conferred on them by the Constitution of the USSR. However, the rupture with that legitimacy had begun already at the First Russian Congress in May-June 1990 when Russia had proclaimed its sovereignty. The absence of an immediate and appropriate reaction on the part of the Union authorities had amounted to a *de facto* recognition of Russia's sovereignty, which could only have consummated in the eventual disintegration of the USSR.

Russian sovereignty proclaimed in 1990 was quoted as the main argument against immediately promulgating a new constitution (that would fit the new political realities to have ensued from the fall of the Soviet Union) and against holding new elections. The logic, or rather the motif behind this argument was simple: why abide by "mere formalities", if one's powers could be extended by one's own decision?

Such a decision, however, presented a serious rupture with the idea of legitimacy - a more serious issue, indeed, than the proclamation of sovereignty eighteen months earlier. It made the quarrel about whose legitimacy was "greater", the parliament's or the President's, unavoidable. The illegitimacy of the parliament, that had arbitrarily prolonged its powers beyond the existence of the USSR, was repeatedly emphasised by the President's supporters, whereas the fact that "the President of the all-nation choice" had also been elected under the "old regime" and was, therefore, no more legitimate after the Belovezh agreement than the parliament would hardly be mentioned by either party. In practice that would have again amounted to a *de facto* recognition by the parliament of its own illegitimacy.

From the standpoint of public opinion, the parliament's position was inferior by far to that of the President. Yeltsin's high reputation was throughout 1989, 1990 and 1991 beyond doubt. As to the parliament, it had been elected in 1990 as a regional assembly. Unlike the electorate of the other republics, striving for independence, the Russian voters had not expected their legislature to set about some major national problem. Its seats had been contested, indeed, by "second best" politicians, whereas "the cream" of the nation had aimed for the Union parliament.[5] The Russian parliament became the nation's top government body overnight and under circumstances that were no occasion for celebration. Whereas the President's party did not hesitate to bring up the issue of legitimacy and call for a referendum (that was eventually held in April 1993 and indeed demonstrated the majority's support for Yeltsin and his policies), the parliament was made into an object of faultfinding and a communist scapegoat. It was repeatedly depicted the ultimate culprit responsible for all the failures of the government's policy of reforms. Its popularity was unvaryingly on the decline.

Under the circumstances the decisions soon to be made by the parliament, viz. "additional" powers for Yeltsin's government (including priority for presidential decrees, subordination of the local authorities and a temporary right to re-organise the system of the government institutions and)[6] and suspension of the constitution-making process, were bound to prove suicidal in the long run. We shall discuss the problem of parliamentary control over the executive in 1990-93 later in this chapter, in connection with the Sixth Congress, but one remark must be made right away. November 1991 was not the first time for the parliament to consciously cede its powers to the executive. The Union parliament did it a year before, when, following an impressive mass rally in Moscow, the Supreme Soviet, rather than sack the extremely unpopular government of Nikolai Ryzhkov, voted to grant President Gorbachev extra powers (subsequently to be confirmed, albeit in a different form, by the Fourth Congress of People's Deputies of the USSR).[7] We have also noted a similar behaviour of the Russian deputies at their Third Congress in March 1991.[8] The Union parliament had failed to respond to the state of emergency in August 1991, which, coupled with its Chairman's barely concealed solidarity with the coup leaders, had put it in an embarrassing situation and had eventually led to its dissolution and - with it - to the disintegration of the state it had been supposed to rule. It was actually amazing to see the Russian parliament embark on a similar course with presumably a similar end.

Meanwhile, this unwillingness to assume responsibility for the future of the country at a critical moment of its history and the readiness, moreover the haste, with which this responsibility was shifted off onto the executive, were in full accord with the traditional culture of *sobornost'*. In a situation of crisis the parliament simply regressed to the primeval patterns of behaviour. It confined itself to the only function the traditional culture would ascribe to it, viz. legitimation of the executive - in much the same fashion as that had been done by the *Zemskie Sobors* of the 16th and 17th centuries and the Soviets of the revolutionary and post-revolutionary era.

This attitude indicated in essence an open retreat from the attempt to re-integrate the society by means of an operational consensus, a true foundation of parliamentarianism, and transformation of the parliament into a representative assembly of the *sobornost'* type. Its members however had no idea about the dynamics of the socio-integrative processes. It was unrealistic in fact in that transitional period to expect social integration to be secured on the ontological level of political culture, which constitutes the proper meaning of *sobornost'* and the basis of the respective pattern of political representation. As to the value-based integration, that was impeded by the institutional conflict, bound (if the mechanism were set in motion) to unfold as a conflict of values. This is a battlefield on which the parliament can hardly hope to win. It stands a fairly good chance in a purely institutional struggle if it offers the society what it needs, a procedural consensus; although even in this case a "non-party" parliament - with an underdeveloped factional structure, incapable, in the absence of mass political parties, of mobilising popular support in defence of itself as a sovereign representative assembly - would be no match for the executive. But if an institutional conflict is fought as a conflict of values (like when a question is asked about whose legitimacy is "better"), an institution intended to represent plural interests and plural values can hardly hope to surpass the executive in the competition for the salient role of the integrating "grace-distributing" organisation, unless, perhaps, the rival proves exceptionally bad.

2. The Ideology of Reform and the Economic Realities

The major factor to shape the Russian politics in the period between the failure of the August 1991 coup and the dissolution of the parliament in October 1993 was the economic reform process begun in January 1992.

Already in November, right after the government was formed, a number of influential deputies demanded that Gaidar, the would-be supervisor of the reform, present its programme to the parliament. There was no response, either from Gaidar or from any other member of the new cabinet. The "additional" powers just bestowed on the executive, according to which presidential decrees on matters related to economic reform ought to have precedence over laws of the RSFSR and were to come into force automatically unless repealed by the Supreme Soviet within a week,[9] allowed the government to disregard the demand and embark on the reform without presenting it to the parliament for deliberation and approval.

The ideology of the reform, worked out in a great hurry in October-December 1991, envisaged (rather unexpectedly for both the electorate and the legislators) "shock" liberalisation of prices preceding privatisation of business and accompanied by tough monetary and fiscal policies of which the core was to be extraordinarily heavy taxation: enterprises would have to part with up to 90 percent of the profits.

The approach, advocated by a number of prominent Western economists, was straightforward enough - to prevent excessive price increase by "compressing" the mass of money and confiscating the superprofits of the monopolies. The government forecast a three to fivefold price increase against the end of 1991. However, that forecast was obviously hollow, as was demonstrated by the first three months of the reform. This period saw an unprecedented economic crisis (with price increase rates counted in dozens over the first few months only) and a crisis of mutual non-payments between enterprises that had been stripped almost overnight of virtually all their current assets by the landslide depreciation of rouble. In the course of a few weeks inflation "wiped out" all of people's savings, ruling out the very possibility of privatisation in the interests of the bulk of the citizenry and depriving the national economy of any internal sources of investment.

Economic reform was accompanied by reductions in government support for education, science and culture, on so grand a scale that they were immediately driven to the verge of survival. No less drastic was the decline in social security and medical care, which resulted in mortality rate and life expectancy dropping back to the level of the 1950s.

The Russian economic institutions responded in a way that differed from what the reformers had expected. This meant, of course, lack of foresight on the part of the reformers, not "perverted" behaviour on the part of Russia's economic agencies. The former failed to take into consideration the most simple of all facts: the Soviet economic institutions were not market institutions and could not, therefore, respond to "market" stimuli, such as restricted emission, taxation etc., as market economic institutions normally would.

Instead of reduced prices, the crisis of sales caused a crisis of payments: deliveries continued but enterprises got nothing for the despatched goods.

In order to fully comprehend the situation in Russia after the beginning of these reforms one must properly understand two points: the real structure of the Soviet economy during the last years of the Soviet regime and the cultural attitudes that shaped the reformers' vision of market economy. The latter seem to have been rooted, surprisingly perhaps, in a kind of holistic understanding of society that must by now be all too familiar to the reader of this volume.

The Soviet had been an amazingly spendthrift economy. In the 1970s and 1980s investments in agriculture had exceeded 600 billion roubles. The return had been infinitesimal. After the energy crisis of 1974 the Soviet Union had received hundreds of billions of US dollars from its oil exports. 30 billion dollars had been borrowed by Gorbachev during *perestroika*. Gaidar's government counted on additional $ 24 billion of Western financial aid (though these would have to be paid back sometime in future). But why expect these "aid" billions to prove more efficacious than the Gorby billions or the "petrodollars"? No significant structural changes in the field of national economy had been achieved yet: on the macroeconomic level the decision-making had remained essentially the same as under Ryzhkov and Pavlov. The economic policies of the Soviet and Russian governments after 1989 displayed remarkable continuity, too. They were all based on the same general approach: first financial stabilisation, then structural reforms. Only, frankly speaking, the Yeltsin/Gaidar government proved "tougher" in this respect than the cabinets of Ryzhkov and Pavlov.

Whatever general considerations may be offered in defence of this policy, it made no sense in the case of Russia. For there can be no financial stabilisation when billions after billions disappear in economic "black holes". Nevertheless, this remarkable persistence in an admittedly doomed economic policy deserves special attention, and not just from the standpoint of economics, but as a cultural, social and political phenomenon, too. To account for this phenomenon we need to review briefly the monetarist economic theory.

Freedom to Produce or Freedom to Sell?

Strange as it may sound, debate about market reforms in the Russian political discourse of 1992-93, for all the outlandish egghead slang that was poured into the innocent everyman's ear, did not go beyond the ontological assumptions of the traditional Soviet culture. Participants to the discourse proceeded from, or should one rather say, built their case, on the premise that there can be only one "scientific truth"; and that "economics", as distinct from the discredited "political economy" of Marxism, was a "science" was taken for granted. But even if we leave aside for the moment the thorny question of whether a purely "market" approach to economic problems, insofar as it excludes political and social variables relevant to economic development, can be considered viable from the standpoint of social science, one has to admit that it is not marked with the kind of unanimity of opinion that is ordinarily associated with "science". Contrary to the widespread belief, Milton Friedman and Friedrich von Hayek, two Nobel prize-winners for economics and the principal promoters of the "market approach", do not wholly agree on what constitutes "market economy". Friedman's basic model is a community of free property holders engaged in free exchange of their products. Within this model a "market" is a flow of rational decisions by economic agents striving to maximise their profits.

This vision of market is best presented in *Capitalism and Freedom* in which Friedman compares a market society to a community of Robinsons. For all his reservations about the role of government,[10] *ontologically* Friedman's market is an economy of "a community of Robinsons":

> Fundamentally, there are only two ways of co-ordinating the economic activities of millions. One is central direction involving the use of coercion - the technique of the army and of the modern totalitarian state. The other is voluntary co-operation of individuals - the technique of market place.[11]

No matter how much we sympathise with the author's intention, with his desire to demonstrate that a body social can be managed in a non-totalitarian way by means of market, his failure to appreciate the role of social institutions seems a strange aberration, for it leaves outside the picture the vital problem of maintaining the (presumably) spontaneous order or, to put it otherwise, the problem of contracts guarantees. Meanwhile, the importance of this problem is fully recognised, for example, by students of international relations, i.e. the group of scholars who deal with an assemblage of sovereign states. (This is decidedly a better application of Friedman's model of "the community of Robinsons" than the economists' far more institutionalised field.)

The latter is precisely what "market" means for Hayek, viz. a social institution supporting social innovations. In "Competition as a Discovery Procedure"[12] Hayek demonstrates beyond doubt that the very existence of market as an effective social mechanism is related to the principal deficiency of starting knowledge about the state of affairs and that market mechanisms and competition are, therefore, perpetual striving for new facts. Hayek insists that, unlike science which

> aims at the discovery of what are sometimes called 'general facts', which are regulations of events,

competition is

> a method of discovering particular facts relevant to the achievement of specific, temporary purposes.[13]

Although Hayek does not dwell on the nature of facts "discovered" by competition, it seems obvious that the most important of all discoveries in this field must be discoveries of new procedures of operation, *modi operandi*, that would allow to produce at lower costs. If this is true, competition is institutional by nature.

To sum up, the freedom of market is for Friedman a freedom of choice; for Hayek, a freedom of socially meaningful creative work. For Friedman market rivets on the freedom to set prices; for Hayek, on the freedom to set up enterprises. Friedman understands, of course, that monopoly is a threat to free market, but offers no solution; he would at best argue that private monopoly is a lesser evil than state monopoly or state regulation. Hayek views monopoly as an intellectual challenge to other economic agents; and monopoly's inevitable failure lies in *the freedom to initiate new kinds of economic activity*.

With a re-consideration of the reform policies of the Russian government from this standpoint, it appears obvious that to liberalise prices for state-owned manufacturers and hamper private entrepreneurship by the tax press means to construct market after Friedman, not after Hayek.

Monopoly as Freedom to Whirl up Prices

It seems appropriate at this junction to remind the reader about certain elementary tenets relating to the way market economies operate that have been forgotten (for reasons best known to themselves) not just by the Russian "Chicago boys", but by the Western advisers to the Russian government as well.

Suppose marketers believe the price for a commodity will increase in future. In that case those possessed of money will try to buy it straightaway; whereas those possessed of the commodity, to hold it back. The dynamics may well end up with prices far higher than those originally anticipated. If the market is closed to new manufacturers, the price spiral will speed up, while production will slow down, until the resources the market is able to allocate for buying this particular commodity are exhausted. In other words prices on a market with a limited number of participants are unstable and tend to increase, whereas production tends to decrease. Freedom to set up new enterprises (safeguarded legally, but also financially) is crucial, therefore, for the market to operate towards economic equilibrium.

That is why Friedman's non-institutional definition of market is absolutely inadequate for the Russian conditions. Roughly speaking, the difference between a market and non-market, as seen "from the Russian bell-tower" (to use a Russian idiom), is that in the USA or Great Britain it would take a few hours and a sum of money worth a few days work to register a company, whereas in Russia one will have to spend several months paying bribes right and left to have it done. The situation is further aggravated by the fact that to find money to invest in a good idea in the West, with its well-developed financial infrastructure, is relatively easy and, money procured, it is still easier by rent or buy office space, whereas money and office space were a head-aching puzzle for a neophyte entrepreneur about to launch a business in Russia in 1991-92.

Hence it follows that no market can appear in Russia until *social barriers* to establishing enterprises are removed; or, to put it otherwise, all market reform projects are mere word games while the power of both the central and local bureaucracy can still be used to extort what looks suspiciously like feudal rent.

"Black Holes" of the Russian Economy: Social Roots

The "economic reform" of 1992 was accompanied by a number of mysterious phenomena that have not been adequately discussed either in the press or by analysts.

Let us take for example the state budget. How can it be that a state that runs virtually all business in the country fails to make ends meet after having raised prices twentifold and permitted wages and salaries to rise only three to fourfold? The only viable explanation would be for the output to have decreased by four to five times. This is hard to believe , of course. Even if the production had indeed fallen by half, it would have been difficult to explain how the increase in state earnings might have failed to surpass the increase in state expenses by, at least, two times. The difference seems to have disappeared.

The explanation is however simple enough. As mentioned above, the economy of the Brezhnev era already was marked by unbelievable wastefulness at the levels of both individual enterprises and central bureaucracies. The country possessed of a colossal engineering industry of its own had billions-worth imported machinery rusting in its backyards.

The following explanation why most enterprises and ministries would want to buy abroad and spend as much "hard currency" as possible may sound absurd, but it is certainly not sophisticated. The key to the riddle lay in the peculiar mechanism of corruption. The main stimulus was the process of negotiations *per se*, because it meant trips abroad. In the long run the country (and not just the "state", but people as well) was made to pay an exorbitant price for its closed borders and restrictions on normal tourism. Business trips of its officials were in fact a kind of "tourism" at public expense; and that expense, it must be noted, exceeded by far the nominal travelling allowances. To buy equipment and machinery that the nation did not really need was foolish waste of its hard-earned petrodollars. During the economic crisis of 1992-93 the level of consumption by technocratic elite increased incredibly: purchases (for hard currency and, to be sure, at the companies' expense) of luxury cars and even aircraft became conventional. (The additional gain was, of course, saving on taxes: such expenses would be included in the "cost of production".) This mechanism of "privatisation through administrative consumption", set in motion in Brezhnev's time, was fully developed in "the period of reforms".

In other words, the mysterious "black holes" of the Russian economy of 1992-93 were not as mysterious as they seemed to be; in fact their social nature was all but obvious - the need to maintain "unofficially" the high level of consumption for the technocratic elite.

Rouble Exchange Rates: Social Roots

Another riddle of the post-Soviet economy is the ridiculously low rouble. The exchange rate of 100 roubles for one US dollar (1992) corresponded with nothing whatsoever: it was virtually impossible to find a commodity that would have been profitable to import at that rate. Nevertheless, it persisted and was even higher for "non-cash" rouble (money kept in bank accounts).

Let us review briefly the history of this exchange rate. In the 1960s and 1970s the black market exchange rate was about 3 roubles for one US dollar, roughly four times higher than the official rate of 0.68 rouble per US dollar. The black market rate depended mainly on the market for fashionable goods not manufactured in the USSR (mainly clothes and home radio-electronics), unlike the official rate that was fixed by administrative decisions but with certain respect to the ratio of official ("state") prices on the internal market and the prices for similar goods on the world market.

Not just the level, but the very existence of the black market exchange rate was a result of the government's unwillingness to import in sufficient quantities consumer goods deemed "ideologically harmful": at first, jeans and tape recorders; later, in the 1980s, videos and computers. Prices for these commodities were set on the basis of "private import": due to tourism, business trips and contraband.

The state imported high quality consumer goods, e.g. British and Italian footwear, but refuse at the same time to allow import of cars, despite the fact that they were in great demand which the underdeveloped native car industry obviously failed to meet. The motive behind this bizarre policy was concern about *nomenklatura* privileges: under conditions of Soviet pseudo-egalitarianism and low differentiation of nominal incomes it was precisely access to luxury goods through restricted "distributor shops" that distinguished the *nomenklatura* elite from the rank and file; meanwhile, the prospect of buying the same goods from "normal", i.e. non-restricted, shops at "normal", i.e. non-prohibitive, market prices would have reduced to nothing some of the most cherished advantages of the *nomenklatura* life style.

In addition to the *nomenklatura* distribution network another exclusive system of distribution emerged and functioned in the 1970s and 1980s that served the *nouveaux riches*: the staff of commercial structures and *tsekhoviki*[14] profiteering from deficit. By the late 1980s, imported consumption goods had virtually disappeared from ordinary shops: the two distribution systems, *nomenklatura* and "shadowy", became predominant.

The fewer goods on "open" sale, the lower the rouble. The Russian currency was utterly ruined by the so called trade "at enterprises", sporadically practised for some time already but fully realised and legalised in 1988. The idea to deliver consumer goods right to places of work to be sold there to employees extended the principle of restricted trade beyond the *nomenklatura* "distributor shops", making it sort of universal (though not, of course, at the same level as far as supply and quality were concerned); but it also all but legalised abuse. Trade degenerated into "exchange of favours" between enterprises and shop directors. It was then that the black market rate sank to 10 roubles per US dollar. The coup de grace was delivered by the emergence of the computer market towards the end of 1980s. The ratio of prices for personal computers on the external and internal markets in 1988-89 corresponded approximately to the exchange rate of 25 roubles for a US dollar. The state bureaucracy, rather than derive benefit from increased import of computers and ease the deplorable pressure of "free" money, chose to impose stupendous import tariffs; the effect was not difficult to guess: rouble fell still lower to cost but one twentieth of the US dollar by the end of 1990.

The final stage in the disintegration of the home market began when the official exchange rate was abolished in the end of 1991. An exchange rate more or less justified on the limited market of selected import goods was accepted as standard. The results were instantaneous fantastic, absolutely unwarranted rise in prices for all imports and a powerful stimulus to dumping exports.

In 1992-93 the rouble was so cheap as to make sales of Russian goods to foreign customers at prices three or five times below the world level still profitable. Under the circumstances even low-quality products from Russia proved competitive on the world market. Coupled with the desire to escape from "confiscatory" taxes, it stimulated massive exports of capital from

Russia (worth tens of billions of US dollars per year according to some estimates).

It seems to be clear that under conditions of open economy a country possessed of modern industry, high scientific and technological potential and rich natural resources could not go on with the average monthly income of $ 20-30 per capita. That would immediately result in outflow of skilled labour, destruction of industrial potential and total sale of national wealth for all but nothing. Giving deficit of budget money as the excuse for so low wages and salaries does not sound convincing. What must one think of the Soviet era budgets then? The latter had provided for salaries and wages three times higher on the average than the post-reform level, and these despite the enormous military expenditure that was, after all, cut substantially after the disintegration of the USSR.

Whose Interests did the Government Represent?

Why then, amid incessant talks of privatisation, independent farms, exchanges and stock markets (to be heard since, at least, 1988 - throughout the later years of *perestroika* and well after the beginning of the 1992 reform), nothing has been really done to establish conventional market institutions? One can hardly hope to explain it away by simple lack of political will or incompetence of the consecutive governments. As it were, the situation served perfectly the interests of the economic *nomenklatura*: managers of state-owned enterprises, officials of central administrative boards and ministries or, to speak the fashionable "new" slang, "restricted" joint-stock companies, concerns and holding companies. With political parties all but absent, technocratic elite remains the only organised social force in present-day Russia and the only social interest group for a Russian government to represent.

The situation created a dire paradox. In the conditions of government-sponsored economic reforms managers of state-owned enterprises found themselves personally interested in destroying national economy. In their capacity as managers, they could not help being concerned about their business, and there must have been many to suffer seeing their life-work go to ruin. But, on the other hand, the prospects for their personal enrichment had increased beyond comparison. Members of the Russian technocratic elite were provided with a unique chance to "grow capitalist" by means of "privatising" a share of goods produced by enterprises entrusted to their control, and the Russian government all but undertook to secure the necessary conditions.[15]

The scheme was not, of course, the reformers' invention. It was but further development (should we say, to the extreme?) of Brezhnev's "economical economics". But the above considerations prompt one to re-assess, indeed, the results of "the August revolution". The political history of the Soviet era can be conceived as the rivalries of two kinds of elites: partocrats and technocrats, on the one hand, the "Centre" and the "provinces", on the other. From this standpoint, the era of Khrushchev marked the victory of the Party over the technocratic elite; the era of Brezhnev, the technocrats' revenge[16]; "the August revolution", the final triumph of the technocratic elite over the Party; of regional elites, over the "Centre".

The sad irony of the 1992-93 situation was that at that critical phase of the economic reform the policy of one (perhaps, the principal one) of its supposed sponsors, the International Monetary Fund, immersed in the intricacies of neo-classic theory, hampered the emergence of a modern market economy in Russia. The IMF experts admitted they had had no experience of supervising the transformation of a command economy into a market one. Nevertheless, they insisted on the introduction of certain recommendations, even while realising they might not be appropriate. This served only to provide ammunition for Russian nationalistic propaganda that claimed this whole affair was but a grand "imperialist conspiracy" and that the West was in fact set on de-industrialising Russia.

3. *Sobornost'* and the Reform

Green Light to "Natural" Forces:
Scientific Determinism, Democratic Freedom and Civil Responsibility

Russian economic reform provides a good starting point for the analysis of mental patterns of both the technocratic elite that gained power in Russia in 1991 and the "neo-classic" economists of the West.

The ideologues of reform considered the development of market within the metaphorical framework of organism, as a natural, spontaneous growth. Their basic assumption was that market would emerge all by itself as soon as a minimum of social conditions was secured for its operation, or rather as soon as the repressive measures against market activities were lifted. It is in the light of this belief that the famous Yeltsin's decree of 29 January 1992 on freedom of trade[17] should be viewed. It took Moscow but a few days to turn into a huge oriental bazaar on which people, deprived of all accustomed means of subsistence by the price shock, tried desperately to meet ends meet trading in anything right in the snowy streets.

It may be possible to attribute this extreme anti-institutionalism which characterised the understanding of market economy by the Russian reformers to the traditional thought patterns rooted in the organismic ontology of *sobornost'*. For all their Western or westernised education, national cultural tradition could not help shaping or at least affecting their minds. It is however much more difficult to account for the similar anti-institutionalist attitude towards the reform, that was, by definition, *a transformation of the pattern of social institutions*, on the part of their Western economic advisers. It may appear strange, on the face of it, for the Western economists not to have realised that the difference between a modern market economy and a village fair lies in the tremendous complexity of institutional procedures that regulate the operations on modern market; that no banking system, no commodity or stock exchange, no joint-stock company, no audit can exist in the absence of sophisticated legislation that embodies the institutionalised reason of a community of people united by common economic activities - embodies, in other words, the "procedural consensus".

The "organic" - not to say, *sobornost'*-type - attitude towards market displayed by the monetarist-minded foreign advisers to the Russian government of 1991-92 sheds light on the political nature of the neo-classic trends in the Western economics, too.

As the analysis of political rhetoric of British Tories of late (Margaret Thatcher, for instance) seems to suggest, political conservatism and monetarism rest on a kind of social ontology that shares the organismic and holistic assumptions of the Russian *sobornost'*. The vital difference between the two political cultures is that the social institutions of democracy and market *already exist* in Western countries and that in the framework of these institutions of welfare state (conceived and created by anyone but the Conservatives) monetarist recipes can, indeed, be used to improve the performance of the *already existing* institutions.

Monetarism is essentially a means to optimise economic behaviour within a short range from the point of equilibrium. No *serious* monetarist has ever claimed to have developed an economic theory of a society in transition. Making babies and nursing them are different labours!

In Russia however, monetarism was welcomed as precisely a theory of transition economy - an interpretation facilitated, perhaps, by the close resemblance of ontological assumptions of the two cultural traditions, but one that must have struck any educated economist as singularly unfit to the situation in question. For is it conceivable, after all, for the kind of elaborate rules that regulate economic behaviour in developed market economies to "emerge" spontaneously in the conditions of unlimited freedom granted to agents of the market?

Parliament must clearly play a decisive role at this incipient stage of market economy. Only through open debate about *procedures* for market activities can one hope to achieve the necessary social consensus in this respect. By forfeiting this function in November 1991, the Russian parliament allowed itself to be expelled from the decision-making that concerned a major national issue. In fact, it sealed its own fate.

What is also interesting about the Russian reformers' mode of thinking that profoundly influenced the course of reforms was their belief in the absence of alternatives, also related to the mentality of *sobornost'*. This attitude was already manifest in the honeymoon of *glasnost'*, when the expression "no other is given" (*inogo ne dano*) was made into a title of a best-selling collection of essays by *perestroika* "foremen"[18] and became a popular political catchword. Not one of those renowned critics of Communist ideology and Soviet regime seemed to realise that the denial of viable alternatives implied by their catching expression became "scientific communists", with their claim to superior understanding of social development and knowledge of objective mechanisms of historic determination, rather than their liberal-minded opponents.

The same idea, however questionable, of the absence of genuine alternatives in history that had one-time been used by the Soviet propaganda in its defense of "real socialism" was now, after August 1991, revoked by Gaidar and Chubais for their no less "scientific" justification of the monetarist version of reforms. Its propagandist appeal especially for intelligentsia, consisted, in our opinion, in its conformity with the organismic think-patterns of *sobornost'*. Organic development is a development along the lines prescribed by "the laws of nature": lions do not issue from hares! If an economic theory exists that prescribes the "correct" course for the reform, the theory must be obeyed and the reform carried out according to these "scientific" recipes.

Reasoning of this kind was quite common among Russian intellectuals, though it was odd to overlook the apparent contradiction between the kind of ontology it implied - deterministic, holistic and realistic (in the scholastic sense of the word) - and the liberal values explicitly professed by these champions of pluralism. But after all we have all been to the primary classes of Hegelian dialectics and were all taught that "freedom is cognised necessity", even if only few of us have passed to the next form. On the one hand, Russian liberals had rather vague ideas about the state of affairs in the contemporary economic science and did not suspect how little it was prepared to discuss, let alone to judge on, the unprecedented situation that had arisen out of collapse of a planned economy. On the other hand, they did not realise and, indeed, were unlikely to believe that in institutional democracies, political decisions about the future course of development were a matter of human choice and social practice, not of social science, and that politics was a field in which the prescriptive role of scientific theories was limited, whereas the right of men and women to choose their own destiny undeniable and inalienable.

To support our position, it may be useful to turn to the interrelation between the theory and practice of reforms as seen by two scholars who have initiated a new era in economic theory. While discussing the status of economic theory and the question of how it is to be applied, John von Neumann and Oscar Morgenstern wrote that:

> The sound procedure is to obtain first utmost precision and mastery in a limited field, and then to proceed to another, somewhat wider one, and so on. This would also do away with the unhealthy practice of applying so called theories to economic or social reform where they are in no way useful.[19]

The democratic idea of man's innate rights and citizen's inviolable freedoms collided in liberal minds with the technocratic idea of "scientific control of society" and, in some of them at least, was defeated. Many saw the science of economics as a kind of social magic working miracles by spells and rites, a sad but, perhaps, natural outcome of the perverted, anti-intellectual understanding of science cultivated by the Soviet regime.

"Shock Therapy": Pro et Contra

Foreign experts were not that credulous, of course. One of the leading advisers to Gaidar's government, Anders Aslund, has recently published his analysis of market reforms in Eastern Europe.[20] Aslund gives a number of reasons why he believes shock therapy to have been an appropriate policy for Russia despite many objections (including some of those made above). He offers nine arguments to substantiate his point. Let us review them briefly.

His first argument is as follows:

Radical change is necessary to inspire confidence in people and overcome their inflationary expectations. ... The budget cannot usually be balanced by rigourous reduction of expenses alone, because the system of collecting taxes is, as a rule, in a mess. The budget's basic expenditure items that cannot be curtailed quickly are subsidies, and their abolition implies liberalisation of prices, because with high inflation any price control leads to new large-scale subsidies.[21]

The second argument is:

The command economy and the market economy are altogether alien to each other. ... Since the old price system has been utterly incoherent and arbitrary, it cannot be improved in a piecemeal fashion. Little can be done about it, except full-scale liberalisation.[22]

The third argument is central:

Before stabilisation and normal operation of market become possible, enterprises must face sufficiently hard budget restrictions. ...

An argument for quick transition is the fact that enterprises will continue stockpile finished products until they meet with shortage of money.[23]

The remaining arguments are summarised as follows: (4) outside competition is necessary to establish a genuine market;[24] (5) corruption becomes excessive at this period ("The only step that can be taken is large-scale reduction in state regulation"[25]).

Aslund's concluding argument invokes a lack of information:

If exact data are scarce, it is risky to suggest anything that goes beyond the limits of standard economic policies.[26] (sic!)

Although it would take a small dissertation to examine the above "advice" in detail, a brief hermeneutic analysis of Aslund's recommendations may help elicit some tacit beliefs about transition from the traditional to modern economic practice that is characteristic of a certain trend in the contemporary Western economic thought.

Let us consider first the general structure of Aslund's argumentation. Points 2, 4 and 9 appear to have nothing to do with "the pace" of transition. Granted, for instance, that prices in the USSR were unbalanced (Aslund's second argument). However, four years after the "full-scale liberalisation" the system of prices seems on the whole to retain the original proportions but for two notable exceptions: prices for home electronics have decreased tenfold and labour is now three times cheaper than it used to be. We have already referred to the exceptional circumstances that accounted for the overpricing of electronic goods on the Soviet market in the preceding period. The reform has set it straight, but the achievement can hardly be held to characterise the general state of Russian economy. As to the price for labour, this is certainly not an occasion to celebrate: labour was grossly underpaid already by the Soviet regime; after the beginning of the reform its price has dropped to the level that threatens its reproduction, and with it the entire economic future of Russia. Anyway, price adjustments are a continuous process depending on many variables and it seems naive to hope this king can be mated in one move.

It is likewise difficult to understand why foreign competition should be "introduced" by shock methods. But the strangest of all is the ninth argument which sounds suspiciously like confession to incompetence: no one understands what is going on, so let us follow a tried method. Aslund fails to explain, however, where and when shock therapy has succeeded in becoming a "tried", "standard" way of tackling economic problems.

Imagine a doctor (to press the "therapeutic" metaphor) saying something like "I do not understand what is wrong with this patient, but aspirin is a tried medicine, so let him take aspirin." We guess the outcome is best described by Chernomyrdin's winged words: "We meant the best, but it turned out as usual".

The rest of Aslund's reasoning is indeed relevant to the "swiftness" of transition. These arguments can be subdivided into two groups: "psychological" and "political". "Psychological" arguments stress the need for an instantaneous breakthrough to "a new reality" in order to secure the irreversibility of the reforms and inspire confidence in their supporters.

This is a sound argument. We can only add that "the packet of laws" must be thought over as best as possible and compiled with the utmost carefulness in order to avoid having to "amend" it in future, for such "corrections" would eliminate the shock effect. If the original packet falls short of perfection, there is little chance the shock will be a "short" one. It is here that the lack of information Aslund cites in his staggering ninth argument emerges as the crucial factor. If information is, indeed, inadequate, one cannot hope to devise a packet of legislation that would not require subsequent modifications. Nevertheless, we are offered a cure for an unknown malady, and the offer comes as an imperative.

In fact Aslund's ninth argument argues *against* shock therapy and does so strongly. It is how to avoid difficulties invoked by this argument that we have to learn from the "Chinese experience", not *festina lente*. The core of the "Chinese way" is not "slow progress"; it consists in building a parallel economic system that is separated from the old one not only by territorial, but also by financial barriers, a particular object of Aslund's criticism. As a result, there exists, at least, one sector of economical life (admittedly, narrow at first) that is free of uncertainty and lack of information, precisely because it has been constructed "from naught".

Russia could hardly follow the Chinese example after the Soviet political system had fallen apart, and this addresses us to the "political" group of Aslund's arguments. Let us concentrate on item 5, the threat of corruption, and item 8, the need to change the intellectual atmosphere. It seems obvious that, contrary to what Aslund asserts, the situation created by a "quick" transition is more favourable to corruption than otherwise, because "transitional" legislation leaves too many opportunities for "grey" economic activity, i.e. the kind of activity that is not subject to any law.

This is, indeed, a standard argument *against* rapid transition; that is why privatisation in Great Britain, for instance, proceeds so slowly. "Shock therapists" suggest the nation accept increased criminality (a social vice not easily extirpated) as the price for the "politically justified" swiftness of transition. The approach is hardly in the interests of people who are to live in the "patient" countries. It sounds very much like the proposal to oust the relatively civilised Party mafia in order to clear the way for "hard-boiled" gangsters.

Aslund's eighth argument is also levelled at the old elite: quick transformation of the intellectual climate is a means to "invalidate former skills". This is in fact a very strange argument, for the people are not going to disappear (Aslund does not suggest, of course, the old elite with its "obsolete skills" be exterminated). But as it is easy to learn new rhetoric, as it is difficult to acquire new operational experience. This kind of advice can only incite populism that would strip the new notions of their operational meanings and use them as "values", or rather "markers", to separate "the sheep from the goats", "our (good) guys" from "their (bad) guys". How many "new" people, i.e. people able to understand the real meanings and the real workings of the new notions, will eventually be found among "our (good) people" is difficult to say; as likely as not not too many. Anyway, the society is prompted to integrate by means of values, rather than by operational experience; this may be a way to market, but it also a direct way towards new authoritarianism, witch-hunt and other excesses of the kind described in Part 1 of this volume.

If we look at what happened in Russia after the beginning of "the radical economic reform" from this standpoint, we behold the kind of outcome that was to be expected. The old elite had not been removed.[27] It simply learnt the trick of giving the name of "reform" to anything that served its interests. As a result, the very notion of reform, as well as a number of related notions, such as "stabilisation", "liberalisation", privatisation, etc., lost their original meanings and function in the contemporary Russian political discourse as a confession of faith intended to re-integrate the society on the basis of an obscure, moreover covert, political platform.

The application of the technical terms of Western economy to Russian economic realities has produced nothing but economic monsters, usually funny, sometimes frightening. A wholesale store that trades in anything has been renamed an "exchange"; an exchange and remitment bureau with ownership capital worth $ 10,000, a bank; a group of crooks seeking to realise a financial pyramid by means of a frantic advertisement campaign and self-quotation of papers of a dubious status and suspicious origin, an investment company.

The "shock" has created a phantom reality, a kind of "dream about capitalism" in which everything appears to be, or at least is called, as in the West, but has in fact remained as it was, if not worse. Still, as the old saying goes, one person can be deceived for a lifetime; some people, for some time; everyone, for a very short time only. Many people in Russia were quick to grasp the true nature of this phantom reality.

4. The Star Hour

The problems that had accumulated after the "Cabinet of Reforms" had been appointed in November 1991 looked even more serious in April 1992, when it became clear that the economic reform had all but failed. Earlier in the year Gaidar announced that he did not expect the "liberated" prices to increase more than threefold or fourfold. By March the assertion sounded a mockery. Nevertheless, the team of reformers remained optimistic.

In late February Andrei Nechayev, Minister of Economics, pledged that the exchange rate would not fall below 300 roubles per U.S. dollar.[28] However, Russia's economic institutions responded to the shock therapy in a way that left little doubt about its imminent failure. Mutual non-payments reached an astronomical level and, coupled with enterprises' financial losses due to inflation, suggested a landslide drop in industrial output and the ensuing collapse of the economy.

Against this background a number of formerly "democratic" groups began to drift towards the Centre, while some politicians (Victor Aksyuchits, Mikhail Astafiev) moved further, towards "conservative patriots". Boris Yeltsin and Vice-President Alexander Rutskoi were in conflict. As a result Rutskoi was commissioned to supervise the agricultural sector.

Street demonstrations changed the colours of allegiances. Democrats, whose activity had reached an apogee in August 1991, withdrew, leaving the arena to communists and their new "patriotic" allies. One such demonstration was dispersed on 23 February 1992, the Soviet Army Day. On that occasion, police used clubs and other anti-riot means for the first time on so mass a scale, coming in for criticism from a number of leading human rights activists, including Elena Bonner.

In this situation the Sixth Congress of People's Deputies had to play the decisive part in setting the future political course for Russia. The Congress was faced with two major problems: it was to appraise the government's economic policies and adopt a new Russian constitution. It failed in both. A compromise resolution on the progress of economic reform proposed no viable alternative to the policy of Yegor Gaidar; once again the executive was allowed the final say. Boris Yeltsin was not stripped of his "additional powers" granted to him in November 1991. The Parliament persisted in its reluctance to assume responsibility for the political situation in the country and was quickly losing its sovereign status.

However, the most tragic mistake was that the Congress, involved in endless debate about economic matters, failed to adopt a new constitution. The failure left the existing power institutions in a state of dubious legitimacy fraught with the most dour of consequences.

The Sixth Congress turned out to be an ambivalent occasion. On the one hand, it can be considered as the high point of Russian parliamentarianism. It saw an attempt, nearly successful, to organise a parliamentary majority that would support, but also supervise, the reforms and the government that carried them out. If contrasted with the dazzling variety of small groups and factions at the earlier Congresses, the system of three blocs that emerged at the Sixth Congress was an undeniable success. On the other hand, the Congress proved unable to overcome the basic stereotypes of *sobornost'*, especially its characteristic indifference towards institution-building, and confined itself to defining "the general line" (right in the spirit of the resolutions of party congresses of old), having left all institutional problems to the discretion of the executive.

Political Situation as seen by Radical Analysts

Let us review briefly the political developments before and during the Congress. The mood of the radical wing of democrats was best reflected in a paper published by a group of analysts who called themselves Centre "RF-Politics".[29] The paper titled "The *Nomenklatura*'s Revenge: Behind the Facade of the Anti-*Nomenklatura* Revolution" contained an analysis of the post-August developments and the relevant recommendations addressed to the democratic leadership. The authors warned that the reforms were in serious danger:

> In Russia and around it a process is unfolding of an all-embracing, large-scale, deeply deployed and extremely aggressive party-*nomenklatura* revenge.[30]

The principal theses of the document are particularly interesting from the standpoint of studying the frame of mind of the Russian radical democrats. How their understanding of the events affected future developments will be analysed in detail in the next chapter.

The authors' principal thesis runs as follows:

> "Democrats" are losing [their] support and authority *first of all because they have not got the better of the nomenklatura* - have not conquered corruption as [they] had promised during the election, have not carried through the [legal] actions against the "Kremlin mafia", continue to form the power structures out of former *nomenklatura* "professionals".[31]

Of the utmost interest is the authors' understanding of the meaning and nature of social processes. They do not see the democrats' goal as transformation of the nation's social institutions, but rather as elimination of a social stratum, the *nomenklatura*, defined in very broad terms (including "professionals"[32]). On the whole this looks suspiciously like the

Bolsheviks' belief in the "decisive" role of "cadres". The main force to thwart the "*nomenklatura* revenge" is the people that have "overcome the dictate of ideological dogmas and learnt the taste of freedom".[33] However, in the worst-case scenario

> The de-ideologisation, de-partisation, de-centralisation of power ... lead ... to the totalitarian-communist nomenklatura state being transformed into a state [that will be] totalitarian-corporatist, that is by definition fascist.[34]

The essay is not devoid of insights. *Perestroika* is seen as a process in which the interests of the people, as represented by the various reformist movements, coincided temporarily with the interests of the second and third echelons of the *nomenklatura*. In the authors' opinion, by spring 1992 these interests were already divorced, the "democratic scenario" pointing towards economic freedom, private property, democracy and separation of powers, political and personal freedoms, de-criminalisation of society through elimination of the social basis for corruption; the "*nomenklatura* scenario", towards transfer of power from "the military-ideological complex" directly to the administrative-managerial elite, "economic gangsterism of uncontrolled departmental and other managerial-mafioso structures",[35] legalisation of corruption.

What had begun as a perspicacious analysis based on sound value judgements ended in rather naive operational recommendations. The authors had little to say about the complete absence of institutional transformations in the economy and emphasise sabotage on the part of the *nomenklatura* as the principal cause for the "misreform". Their think-patterns reveal the kind of dualistic ontology that is characteristic of the value stage of integration analysed in Part 1 of this book:

> The principal contradiction of the existing situation emerges as a contradiction between the results of undermining the ideological bases of the *nomenklatura* epoch and the preservation of the social-political domineering of the *nomenklatura* minority over the society.[36]

The proposed remedy was to expel representatives of the *nomenklatura* from their dominant positions in the government and business structures. The approach clearly called for radical revolutionary measures of a kind incompatible with the rule of law. In what way can the elite be removed from and/or deprived of its "position in business structures" within the bounds of law, i.e. without coercion and *violation of property rights*? The authors suggested establishing a mass political organisation:

... an alliance of creative workers, producers and entrepreneurs, directed against the interests of the repressive-distributing nomenklatura, must become the social basis of the new democratic organisation, of the entire democratic process.[37]

The authors' attitude towards parliament and the situation in it was also revealing:

In the course of the unfolding [*nomenklatura*] revenge the principal, as of today, lever of the *nomenklatura, the Russian deputy corps* infected with the spirit of democratic procedure, will be eliminated *in the first turn*, upon attaining first successes, and the deputies' attempts to reverse the [course of] events will be of no avail.[38]

This prophecy, worthy of Cassandra, deserves special attention. In one respect, at least, it is particularly interesting. The deputy corps was seen as the "lever of *nomenklatura*", an assertion supported by the high percentage of communists and the growing influence of Ruslan Khasbulatov; the latter is accused having openly converted "to the *nomenklatura* camp".[39] Yet, the same deputy corps appeared "infected with the spirit of democratic procedure", although this did not prevent it from serving as a "lever of *nomenklatura*". Everything in this passage reveals patterns of thinking typical of *sobornost'*: the presumed need to "purge" the deputy corps and the epithet used to characterise it - "infected with the spirit of procedure". It is not easy, indeed, to conceive of a better illustration to our earlier account of the type of mentality that prevails in the period of transition from the ontological to operational integration.

We have ventured this extended discussion because the quoted text is representative of the kind of reasoning that was practised by the "democratic" "experts and advisers" mentioned in the preceding chapter.[40] These people, it will be recalled, formed the main intellectual resource of the democratic movement in the brief period between 1990 and 1993. The style and rhetoric of this document resemble strikingly the style and rhetoric of the French Revolution[41] and exhibit the same fundamental discrepancy between political values, presumably new, and the operational experience - quite traditional both in its ontological foundations (the familiar holistic understanding of the nature of social life) and its practical precepts (the dualistic segregation of political agents as villains or heroes). From the philosophical standpoint, the attitude is quite Rousseauist, presenting the peculiar combination of anti-institutionalism and moralisation that almost inevitably resulted in "excesses of execution" (a formula borrowed from the Constitutional Court's ruling on "the Chechen affair"). Tongues of flame in the White House windows, dead bodies of its defenders, even the burned Chechen towns, in short all that was to become real in October 1993 and in the winter of 1994/95, might be discerned in a text published in February 1992. All of these were but manifestations and consequences of the tragic rupture between the new values and the old operational experience, a rupture, to be sure, that depreciated the "new values" and deprived them of their true humanitarian meaning.

The Sixth Congress

The political situation on the eve of the Sixth Congress was characterised by the emergence of three major parliamentary blocs: the oppositional *Russian Unity* consisting of four factions: *Agrarian Union, Communists of Russia, Fatherland,* and *Russia* (the bloc numbered 310 members at the time of the Sixth Congress); the centrist *Constructive Forces* that united three factions: *Industrial Union, New Generation (New Politics)* and *Workers' Union* (164 members); and *Coalition in Support of Reforms* initially uniting *Democratic Russia, Free Russia* (formerly *Communists for Democracy*), *Left Centre, Radical Democrats* and the united faction of *the Social Democratic* and *Republican Parties,* (about 300 members).[42] It was an attempt, unfortunately abortive, to give the parliament a more or less stable three-party structure. Whereas the opposition was successfully united (and the unity would only be strengthened in the future), the government supporters failed to consolidate. The fault lay, first and foremost, with the government and the President who did not seem particularly keen to have strong parliamentary support, probably because they were already contemplating dissolution of the parliament. Parliamentary support implied some forms of control over the government's activities, at least on the part of the supporting deputies. That was precisely what the government did not want; on the contrary, it wanted to have its hands free - right in the spirit of "the *nomenklatura* revenge" that worried the analysts of the RF-Politics so much. The danger, however, lay not where the radicals would see it, as the future was soon to prove: not with the parliament, but with the administration.

   The fears about the future of reforms and the growing influence and consolidation of communists and "patriots" in the parliament were not unwarranted, of course. But parliament as an institution is generally ill adapted to violating human rights and civil freedoms, not as good, at least, as the executive. On those occasions when legislatures did in fact exercise dictatorial rule, as was the case in France in 1793-94, they could only do it because their members were not protected from the executive by parliamentary immunity.

Interests of corrupted bureaucracy, misunderstanding of the role of parliamentary institutions and procedures on the part of radical democrats and a desire to push the reforms as far and as quick as possible in order to prevent the probable revenge of the *nomenklatura* combined to encourage authoritarian tendencies in the Russian power elite and provoked an acute conflict between the executive and the parliament that broke out at the Sixth Congress and was never properly resolved ever since, until the parliament ceased to exist.

All this is best illustrated by the story of the new constitution. The new version was originally drafted in the parliament's Constitutional Commission chaired by President Yeltsin, though its everyday work was in fact organised by its Executive Secretary Oleg Rumyantsev. By the opening of the Sixth Congress the Commission had had the draft constitution ready, but all of a sudden it became known that Gavriil Popov and Anatoli Sobchak, Mayors of Moscow and St. Petersburg, had drafted an alternative version that provided for far wider powers for the President as compared to the draft of the Constitutional Commission. It was also rumoured that Sergei Shakhrai was working on still another version - under direct supervision of the President.

Many deputies suspected "the Mayors' draft" was but an attempt to prevent adoption of the new constitution. As to the alternative "President's draft", that seemed an even stranger undertaking if one considered the fact that the President was also Chair of the Constitutional Commission that authored the main draft. It is worth mentioning however that "the Rumyantsev's draft" was formally endorsed on 28 March 1992 in Yeltsin's absence - at the Commission's sitting presided by Khasbulatov.

New constitution seemed the most urgent single legislative endeavour on the parliament's current agenda since the acting Constitution assumed the Russian Federation was as a part of the already non-existent Soviet Union. But even apart from that comparatively easily recoverable problem, "the Basic Law" was highly unsatisfactory in a number of other respects, especially as far as the relations between the autonomous units and the Federation's "Centre" and the legislature's own "two-storey" structure (the Congress - the Supreme Soviet) were concerned.

Another important problem was the interrelation between the Constitution and the Federal Treaty scheduled to be signed on 31 March 1992. It did not look reasonable to postpone that latter ceremony, especially as the sad story of the never-signed Union Treaty was still fresh in memory. This tangle of problems - federalism, presidential powers, the structure of the legislature, attitude towards and relations within the Commonwealth of Independent States - left little space for consensus as it was. The sudden appearance of a number of alternative drafts in a situation that seemed still to allow for the "simplest" of all solutions, viz. to contend once again with a series of constitutional amendments (although the Constitution had already been changed and "corrected" so many times and so thoroughly that little had been left of the original 1978 text), threatened to undermine the entire constitutional process by making it both too complicated and too vulnerable. It threatened moreover to upset the fragile balance of forces at the most unsuitable of all moments - amid severe economic crisis and in the face of the looming failure of a reckless economic reform.

This order of events, therefore (first the reforms, then the Constitution), left little other prospect except piling a political crisis onto the economic one. It was at this junction that the recent unwillingness, on the part of the Russian democrats, to hold new election straight after August 1991 (when that could have given the country a sufficiently homogeneous legislature) bore its sour fruit. But in the present situation of a rough (and delicate) balance between democrats and conservatives in the parliament any attempt to decide on the structure of power institutions once and for all was likely, no to say bound, to fail. Both parties would immediately produce the irrefutable argument about the need to "consult with the people" before making a final decision, although it was clear enough that to solve such a problem - i.e. adopt a document in which every word and every comma were meaningful and about which the active political forces disagreed so profoundly, in other words to adopt a constitution at a popular plebiscite - would not be possible until one of the parties achieved a final "victory" over its opponents, be it by means of election or in the course of an open violent conflict such as civil war or a coup d'etat. The entire problem of a constitutional referendum riveted on who had the right to draft the text to be presented to the voters, in other words, who was the true power-holder.

These considerations appeared convincing enough and one might reasonably expect the deputies to prefer to adopt the new constitution themselves, rather than refer it to a referendum. Nor could they possibly fail to understand that further delay in this matter endangered the very existence of parliamentary democracy in Russia.

There was, however, a counter-consideration that seemingly outweighed everything else: a new constitution meant new election to new institutions according to new rules. The bulk of the deputy corps proved unprepared to face such an ordeal.

After the economic reform began in January 1992, the political activity of the democratic part of the electorate was on the decline; the newborn political parties were still weak and, moreover, losing what influence they had initially gained. Under the circumstances few of the Congress deputies could hope to retain their seats after new election. Those who estimated their chances to come back as virtually non-existent proved sufficiently numerous to impede the constitutional process.

The three major blocs differed sharply in their appraisals of the situation and their plans for the future. *Russian Unity* was mainly united by their strong disapproval of the economic reform. At a press-conference given by the bloc on 6 April 1992 Mikhail Astafiev, a former activist of *Democratic Russia*, said:

> What made us unite with the leftist forces? ... Now the country is on the verge of a catastrophe, hence the task is to save it, leaving disagreement for the aftertime.[43]

The impeachment was also mentioned (by Nikolai Pavlov):

> Pay attention that no one from among the opposition has brought up the question of confidence for the President. In the meantime legal grounds for his impeachment are more than sufficient.[44]

Another point of accord within *Russian Unity* was resentment about the disintegration of the Soviet Union ascribed to "the Belovezh conspirators". At a press-conference on 15 April Vladimir Isakov stated:

> In order to re-constitute the USSR it is necessary (1) to recognise null and void the Belovezh deal, (2) to revive the USSR coordinating bodies, (3) to restore the united juridical space of the USSR, (4) to re-commence the USSR membership [*sub'ektnost'*] in the international relations and organisations, (5) to resume the negotiations on a new Union Treaty, (6) to preserve the united economic, currency/financial, informational and cultural space within the boundaries of the Union of SSR.[45]

At the Congress itself *Russian Unity* stood for resignation of the cabinet.

The pro-government bloc *Coalition in Support of Reforms* united the supporters of the cabinet and the President. At a press-conference given on 10 April Victor Sheinis, one of the bloc's leading members, whereas emphasising his disagreement with Lev Ponomaryov's appraisal of the "Rumyantsev's Constitution", stated nevertheless:

> There is however something that unites us, viz. under the present circumstances it is inadmissible to deprive the President of additional powers, [we] ought not to tie the hands of "the government of reform".[46]

Many members of the bloc were quite outspoken in their anti-parliamentary attitude. Lev Ponomaryov, for example, repudiated the "Rumyantsev's version" of the constitution because it did "not create conditions for establishment of a presidential republic",[47] while Pyotr Filippov alleged:

> The legislative seeks to rule not with the help of laws, but by appointing whom it pleases to government posts. As a matter of fact, the fragile balance between the legislative and the executive is already threatened.[48]

This attitude, although obviously diverting from standard democratic practice and theoretical assumptions about the separation of powers, was shared by many radical democrats and would later be embodied in the "presidential" (1993) Constitution. Such peculiar understanding of the separation of powers created problems already in 1992, but its consequences would be felt most acutely after "the restoration of constitutional order" began in Chechnya in late 1994.

This anti-parliamentary bias of some deputies, as well as many cabinet members, prevented *Coalition in Support of Reforms* from becoming a genuine governing majority. What the relations were between the reform-minded deputies and the pro-government radicals was partially revealed by Sergei Filatov, at that time First Deputy Chair of the Supreme Soviet, at a press-conference on 13 April 1992:

> The Congress is characterised by the absence of parliamentary majority within its deputy corps. The process is going on (it will be continued after the Congress is over) of forming a majority coalition that would be able to assume responsibility for the decisions taken. We have already been about to take a normal working course. Unfortunately, several imprudent statements have ruined it all.[49]

This resentment is easier to understand if one goes through Gaidar's statements made right after the Congress passed its highly critical resolution on the course of economic reform (11 April 1992):

> *Question:* Will you suggest B.N.Yeltsin dissolve the Congress and the Supreme Soviet? *Ye.Gaidar:* In view of the new situation the government must think everything over thoroughly. We are to meet the President, and for the time being I would not like to answer this question.[50]

In the meantime, the Congress's attitude towards the reform was far from simple. Neither its open enemies (*Russian Unity*), nor its outright supporters (*Coalition in Support of Reforms*) had a majority. The 11 April resolution "On the Course of the Economic Reform" was in fact a compromise in which important roles were played by Ruslan Khasbulatov, Chairman of the Supreme Soviet, and the centrist bloc of *Constructive Forces*. *Constructive Forces* sought not termination of the reforms, but their "correction": they advocated a change in the government's investments policy, more active social security efforts and objected to extending the extra powers granted to Yeltsin by the Fifth Congress beyond the period of three months within which the Supreme Soviet was to fulfil its commission and pass the law on government.[51]

Ruslan Khasbulatov presented his opinion about the course of reforms to the joint meeting of the Supreme Soviet's two chambers on 2 April 1992, four days before the Congress. He actually accused the government of incompetence:

> Analysis shows that the principal reason behind the reform's failures is not resistance of the workers or some political forces, still less of "*nomenklatura* underground". ... The question is purely subjective, it is that the instruments of control begin to work practically against the people, the industry, the economy itself. ... The mistake seems to be related primarily to the fact that it has not been practical work to create a market environment and organisational economic efforts as a precondition for transition to market that have been made the centre of the reform, but only measures in purely financial sphere.[52]

The next day the Chairman of the Supreme Soviet was even more explicit in his negative appraisal of the government. He said in reference to his just quoted speech:

> The question then was not some new ideology of the reform, but the level of competence of the persons who carry it out, their professionalism, the need to join efforts by the legislative and the executive.[53]

Khasbulatov's appraisal of the reforms was based, as he himself indicated, on the opinions of renowned Soviet economists: Academicians Arbatov, Petrakov, Shatalin. The latter were highly critical of the style in which the reform was carried out and made their opinion public just a few days before the Congress. It must be admitted, however, that Khasbulatov's attitude towards "the team of reformers" was overburdened with personal considerations, and the fact was not without consequences as far as the work of the Congress was concerned. On 11 April a heated discussion resulted in a resolution "On the Course of Economic Reform in the Russian Federation" that condemned the methods used by the reformers. It ran as follows:

> The standards of living have decreased sharply, social tension increases, partly due to shortage of cash money. Marked is the unsatisfactory work of the Central Bank of the Russian Federation whose activities have not been brought under effective control by the Supreme Soviet of Russia.[54]

In addition to the important general directive "to confirm the need to pursue the course of transition to market economy in the Russian Federation", the document suggested the President submit before 20 May a list of measures to forestall "a critical drop in production", achieve "financial stabilisation", relieve "the burden of taxation", implement "a real addressed social protection of the populace" and prevent "decrease in the level of consumption".[55]

On the whole the document resembled in style the resolutions of the CPSU Central Committee erstwhile addressed to the government. It was full of abstract directives ("to present", "to improve co-ordination", "to commission the government to prepare" etc.) and was, in fact, an exemplary specimen of the processual mode of thinking characteristic of the Soviet political mentality. Within this pattern of reasoning political situations are typically presented not as fields of interaction procedurally (i.e. step by step) controlled by the relevant political actors, but rather as sets of interrelated processes that can only be manipulated by changing the relative intensities of the constituent processes.[56] By its very character this mode of thinking precluded the possibility of enumerating concrete steps that could be made to improve the situation. The critics of the resolution were basically right in asserting that it was nothing else but a piece of wishful thinking full of good recommendations that could hardly be realised simultaneously. The resolution contained no serious analysis of the situation and consequently suggested nothing in the field of economy. But it strongly condemned the government's activities and made what in the Soviet times would have been called "organisational conclusions":

> To recognise as unsatisfactory the course of the economic reform in the field of social protection of the populace, fiscal, financial/credit, investments, industrial and agrarian policy, elimination of monopolism of state structures in the spheres of production and distribution, as well as complexity of the measures taken[57]

and then (in Item 3):

> [To commission] the Supreme Soviet of the Russian Federation to pass in a three-month time laws "On the Council of Ministers (the Government) of the Russian Federation", "On State Service", "On the Responsibility of Officials of the Top State Bodies for Failure to Fulfil the Constitution of the RSFSR and the Legislative Acts of the Russian Federation.[58]

The President's additional powers concerning the structure of government were *de facto* extended, but only for the period of three months, after the expiry of which the new laws enumerated in the resolution were to be promulgated. Although the additional powers were not explicitly mentioned, the government was dealt a severe blow, for hitherto it had operated practically without control.

Rumours instantly spread of the imminent resignation of the cabinet. Indeed, on 13 April Gaidar stated in public that the government would resign. Sergei Filatov said later that day, addressing the Congress, that the statement had been "premature", for it "left behind" the settlement reached by the Presidium and the government the day before.[59] In a gawky attempt to smooth the matters Khasbulatov remarked casually: "The boys have been confused".[60] This piece of tactlessness on the part of the Chairman of the Supreme Soviet poured oil on the flame: having heard themselves being called "boys", cabinet ministers left the assembly hall at once.

Curiously enough the resignation was handed in by Gaidar to the President who was himself head of the government, but who showed no intention to resign. In other words, it was not resignation of the Cabinet, as mass media would present it and as the Congress was told, but resignation of a group of Cabinet members submitted to the head of the Cabinet (Yeltsin at the time). Nevertheless, at a press-conference given on 13 April Gaidar characterised the situation as follows:

> Being aware of the impossibility to fulfil the Congress's decisions, expressing our disagreement with the actual renunciation of the radical reforms, we are compelled to ask the President to accept resignation of the government.[61]

This statement deviated from plain truth on two points. In the first place, the text of the resolution did not warrant its interpretation as "renunciation of the reforms": the vague, "processual" wording of the resolution did not stipulate, least so necessitate, any concrete measures that would mean a change in the economic policy. As shown by the verbatim records of the Congress and the subsequent statements of the government members, spokesmen for various factions and individual deputies, the entire conflict riveted not on the amorphous "wishes" about the course and objectives of the reform, but on item 3 of the resolution, i.e the problem of parliamentary control over the government's activities. The second falsity was the statement about the government's resignation handed in to the President. As mentioned above, such a paper could only be written by Yeltsin in his capacity as Prime Minister and addressed to himself in his capacity as President. Yeltsin did nothing of the kind which allowed the opposition to appraise the demarche of "the Gaidar team" as political blackmail.

The manoeuvre was followed by a series of behind-the-scene negotiations and the eventual revision of the Congress's earlier decision concerning the government's economic policies. On 15 April the Congress passed a new resolution titled this time "On the Support for Economic Reform in the Russian Federation". The declaration began as follows:

> Declaring its determination to continue the present course of economic reform consistently and steadfastly the Congress of People's Deputies of the Russian Federation supports the activities of the President of the Russian Federation, the Supreme Soviet of the Russian Federation and the Government of the Russian Federation aimed at principal transformations of the economy.[62]

Otherwise it was a languid text that contained nothing of importance except the following passage:

> The Congress deems it necessary to provide for the adoption of the law "On the Council of Ministers of the Russian Federation" and its promulgation in accordance with the Resolution of the Congress of People's Deputies of the RSFSR "On Organisation of the Executive for the Period of the Radical Economic Reform" of 1 November 1991 [the one that had granted additional powers to the President] and the Resolutions of the Congress of People's Deputies of the Russian Federation "On the Course of Economic Reform in the Russian Federation" of 11 April 1992.[63]

The declaration added up to confusion. The government was to continue and its activities, although found unsatisfactory on 11 April, were endorsed on 15 April. A series of laws were to be passed and promulgated, that were meant to restore the proper balance between the legislative and the executive, including parliamentary control over the government (item 3 of the resolution of 11 April), but the legislator was to abide by the resolution (of 1 November 1991) that had upset the balance in the first place and endowed the executive with prerogatives of the legislative. The legal situation created by these mutually excluding, but simultaneously valid resolutions allowed for all sort of arbitrary interpretations and was fraught with grave conflict between the parliament, on the one hand, and the president and the government, on the other.

Amid these peripeties, the constitution was all but forgotten. As a result, the Congress opted for the "reserve variant" proposed by Mikhail Mityukov. The 1977 Constitution was "amended" once again, although by this time hardly anything had survived from its original version. The notable exception was the Russian Federation's membership in the USSR that the Congress stubbornly refused to strike out, although it agreed to substitute a new official name of the state for the old one: "The Russian Soviet Federal Socialist Republic" was henceforth to be called "the Russian Federation" or simply "Russia" - one more ambivalent compromise between *"derzhavniki"* and "democrats".

The Voucherisation

The damage to the parliament's prestige was great. The deputy corps demonstrated once again that it was capable of nothing but meaningless manoeuvres and unproductive compromises. It was not long before the parliament was publicly humiliated about one of the most painful questions of the government's economic policy, viz. privatisation.

The entire issue was a good example of the lack of coordination and confrontation between the executive and the legislative. The Supreme Soviet had passed a law in due course that provided for "personal privatisation accounts" to be opened for each Russian citizen in the state-owned Savings Bank. The account was to certify a citizen's right to a share in the state and municipal property that was to be distributed free according to a State Privatisation Programme. The amounts to be transferred by the state onto these accounts could not be withdrawn as cash, but could only be used to buy a portion of the state property.[64]

The government proposed a different approach. It suggested to issue impersonal "privatisation cheques" (vouchers) that could be sold on the market. Anatoli Chubais, Chair of the State Committee on Property (responsible for privatisation), advocated "impersonal" vouchers and argued that, although vouchers were to be issued at the nominal value of 10,000 roubles, their real price would be much higher and exceed, indeed, $ 10,000 because enterprises were to be privatised at their pre-reform book cost. In August 1992 President Yeltsin used his "additional" legislative powers to embark on voucher privatisation. According to his decree, starting from 1 October 1992 all Russian citizens were to receive privatisation cheques of equal nominal value. The cheques, intended solely for future auctions of state and municipal property, might not be used as an ordinary means of payment, although one might sell and buy them freely.[65] The decree obviously contradicted the law passed by the Supreme Soviet, in fact annulled it. The Supreme Soviet, however, failed to rescind the decree in the stipulated seven days period, although the majority of the deputies resented it strongly. Some of them would later blame it on Khasbulatov who was said to have "pigeon-holed" the decree.

Whether the accusation was justified or not, the voucher privatisation was carried out according to the presidential decree, not the Supreme Soviet's law, and became in effect another stage in the grand-scale looting, following the inflation shock of 2 January 1992 that had invalidated the bank savings of the bulk of the populace. The market price of vouchers was initially about 7,000 roubles (about $ 35 at the exchange rate as it was at the time), although it soon dropped to about 4,000. Towards the end of the voucher privatisation campaign the price figures sounded more impressive, about 30,000 to 40,000 roubles, but that was the effect of inflation: the real price fell even lower than before, to about $ 20-25. So much for the Chubais' mythical 10,000 dollars. It would be ridiculous, not to say outrageous, to consider such a voucher a true equivalent of an individual citizen's share in the Russian state property. The total market cost of all the vouchers issued in Russia would hardly exceed the audit valuation of one such plant as the KAMAZ (about a dozen billion U.S. dollars).

That was hardly surprising. Chubais clearly did not mean it when he was telling fables about future voucher rates. His argument about the enterprises' book cost would have only been valid, if "privatisation cheques" had been the only means of payment when purchasing them. In that case the price of a voucher would have been equal, indeed, to the total cost of the enterprises to be auctioned (provided, of course, somebody wanted to buy them) divided by the total number of vouchers to be offered in payment. Since, however, it was known from the very beginning that one might pay in money, as well as in vouchers; since vouchers were to be accepted at nominal value; since, last but not least, sellers decidedly preferred money (that could buy anything) to "privatisation cheques" (that could only buy things of one sort, and even then during a limited period of time), numerous holders of vouchers were at an obvious disadvantage if compared to holders of big money. No one would purchase vouchers at a price higher than their nominal value if he could simply buy what was offered in exchange for vouchers directly for money. By the very nature of things, the voucher rate could not exceed its nominal value until most vouchers were realised: either invested or accumulated in great quantities in the so called "investment foundations". And that was the end of the story: owners of vouchers had not become owners of enterprises, but had, for the most part, simply sold their "privatisation cheques" for next to nothing to those who were in a position to buy them up in order to purchase state and municipal enterprises at the deliberately understated, pre-reform book cost.

Notes

[1] Cf. to Mandel 1992, p. 279:

> Though the Western media and politicians persist in regarding democracy and 'market reform' (a euphemism for capitalism) as virtually synonymous, many of their Soviet counterparts have long since concluded that the transformation of their economy along liberal lines requires a 'strong independent executive regime' capable of imposing 'harsh and unpopular measures'. The tendency today is increasingly towards the reintroduction of authoritarian political structures and practices that the 'democrats' now at the helm of the state vigorously condemned when the 'communists' occupied the halls of power and they stood on the outside looking in.

See also a characteristic newspaper article, published in November 1991 (Parfyonov 1991). On the cultural context of this attitude, see Subsection on "The Renaissance Model and the Allure of Authoritarianism" in Section 4, Chapter 3.

[2] Opinion poll taken in April 1991 by the Supreme Soviet sociological service showed the movement to enjoy the support of 41.4 percent of the

respondents (see Biryukov *et al.*, forthcoming, Table 1). The data are, however, contradictory (see, e.g., White 1992, p. 17).

[3] According to the decision of the Fifth Congress of People's Deputies of the USSR made right after the failure of the coup, the Congress, hitherto the supreme body of state power in the Soviet Union, ceased to exist and the Supreme Soviet, pending the signing of the new Union Treaty and new election, was to be formed by the republican bodies of power (see Sergeyev and Biryukov 1993, pp. 189-196, for details).

[4] The transfer was accomplished by a decree of the Presidium of the USSR Supreme Soviet (of 19 February 1954). No formal consent was obtained from the RSFSR Supreme Soviet as required by Article 18 of the 1936 Soviet Constitution (see *Constitution USSR* 1947, p. 24 and Article 16 of the Constitution of the RSFSR then in force (see *Constitution RSFSR* 1973, p. 472), though the deal was *de facto* recognised.

[5] Many prominent democratic deputies had not even run for the republican parliament, having either preferred local elections or confined themselves to their seats in the Union assembly.

[6] See resolutions of the Fifth Congress of People's Deputies "On Organisation of the Executive in the Period of Radical Economic Reform" of 1 November 1991 and "On Legal Support for the Economic Reform" of the same date (*VSNDiVS* 1991, No. 44, pp. 1722 and 1723). The special rules established by these resolutions were to be valid till 1 December 1992.

[7] See Sub-section on "The Third Congress" in Section 4, Chapter 4.

[8] Ibid.

[9] Clause I, Item 3 of the resolution "On Legal Support for Economic Reform" (*VSNDiVS* 1991, No. 44, p. 1723).

[10] "The existence of a free market doesn't of course eliminate the need for government" (Friedman 1963, p. 15).

[11] Ibid., p. 13.

[12] Published in English as Chapter 12 of Hayek 1978.

[13] Ibid., p. 181; see also Hayek 1989, p. 19.

[14] See Note 33 to Chapter 3.

[15] See Sub-section on "The Voucherisation" in Section 4 of this Chapter.

[16] For a brief summary of the conflict, see Sergeyev and Biryukov 1993, pp. 79-81.

[17] See *VSNDiVS* 1992, No. 6, pp. 356-7.

[18] See Afanasiev (ed.) 1988.

[19] Neumann and Morgenstern 1947, p. 7.

[20] Aslund 1994.

[21] Ibid., pp. 50-1. (This and the following quotations have been translated from the revised Russian edition).

[22] Ibid., pp. 51-2.

[23] Ibid., pp. 52-3.

[24] Ibid., p. 54.

[25] Ibid., p. 57.

[26] Ibid.

[27] See Note 20 to Chapter 3.

[28] *Moskovskaya pravda*, 25 February 1992.

[29] See *Parlamentskaya nedelya*, 1992, No. 7, p. 15-23. The paper was presented by V.Varov, A.Sobyanin and D.Yuriev at a press-conference on 21 February 1992.

[30] Ibid., p. 15.

[31] Ibid. [Original italics]

[32] Elsewhere in the paper the notion is deciphered to stand for government experts, Gosplan (the state planning committee) economists etc.

[33] *Parlamentskaya nedelya*, 1992, No. 7, p. 15.

[34] Ibid. [Original italics]

[35] Ibid.

[36] Ibid., p. 21.

[37] Ibid., p. 22. [Original italics]

[38] Ibid, p. 19. [Original italics]

[39] Ibid., p. 23.

[40] See Sub-section on "Experts and Advisers" in Section 1, Chapter 4.

[41] For the analysis of the French revolutionary rhetoric, see Sergeyev 1988 and Sergeyev 1989a.

[42] For the blocs' membership, see *Parlamentskaya nedelya*, 1992, No. 14, p. 10. It should be noted that these data differ somewhat from those received by the authors from Vladimir Novikov, Chairman of the Council of Factions. The figures are approximate anyway: deputies would move between factions, about 250 to 270 of them belonged to no faction (see below Sub-section on "Internal Homogeneity of Factions" in Section 2, Chapter 7, for details).

[43] *Parlamentskaya nedelya*, 1992, No. 13, p. 28.

[44] Ibid.

[45] Ibid., No. 14, p. 40.

[46] Ibid., No. 14, p. 18.

[47] Ibid.

[48] Ibid.

[49] Ibid., p. 30.

[50] Ibid., p. 22.

[51] O.Plotnikov's speech at the *Constructive Forces*' press-conference on 10 April 1992 (ibid., p. 20-1).

[52] Ibid., No. 12, p. 6.

[53] Ibid., No. 13, p. 10.

[54] *Sixth Congress RF* 1992, Vol. 2, p. 290.

[55] Ibid., p. 291.

[56] This mode of thinking is analysed in detail in Sergeyev 1987, Bohnam *et al.* (forthcoming); see also Section 1 "The Problem of Political Agency: Methodological Considerations" in Chapter 8 and Section 1 "Processual Thinking and Framing Legislation: Methods of Analysis" in Chapter 9 of the present volume.

[57] *Sixth Congress RF* 1992, Vol. 2, pp. 290-1.

[58] Ibid., p. 293.

[59] Ibid., Vol. 3, p. 106.

[60] Ibid., Vol. 3, p. 111.

[61] *Parlamentskaya nedelya*, 1992, No. 14, p. 23.

[62] *Sixth Congress RF* 1992, Vol. 4, p. 327.

[63] Ibid.

[64] See Law of the Russian Soviet Federal Socialist Republic "On Personal Privatisation Accounts and Deposits in the RSFSR" of 3 July 1991 (*VSNDiVS* 1991, No. 27, pp. 1033-5); see also Law "On Privatisation of State-Owned and Municipal Enterprises in the RSFSR" of 3 July 1991 (ibid., pp. 1036-54).

[65] See Decree of the President of the Russian Federation "On Implementation of the System of Privatisation Cheques in the Russian Federation" of 14 August 1992 (with an appendix; ibid., 1992, No. 35, pp. 572-576).

6   The Fall of the Parliament

*Telemachus, my son, The Trojan War is over. Who has won, I
don't remember. It must have been the Greeks, for only Greeks
can leave so many dead away from home ...*
                              J.Brodsky, *"Odysseus to Telemachus"*.

1. The Interlude

The Rival Legitimacies

The Sixth Congress left the two branches of power in a state of strange
balance. After one more abortive attempt to organise parliamentary support
for the President and the cabinet in a form of another coalition (named The
Reform) the centrists and the institutionally minded democrats within the
deputy corps realised at last that neither the President, nor the government
sought that support, because parliamentary support implied the executive
would have to count with the parliament, settle differences (sometimes
considerable) between the supporting factions, etc. After Yegor Gaidar was
appointed Acting Prime Minister in May 1992 the country found itself in a
state of dual power. The legislative and the executive acted henceforth on
their own, paying little or no attention to each other. The government
would ignore laws passed by the parliament; the latter, rescind presidential
decrees. Advocates of the Soviet model that theoretically invested the
representative bodies with administrative and executive power were
becoming ever more influential among the deputies.
    Within the parliament itself, the role of the Presidium of the Supreme
Soviet and its Chairman was strengthened substantially after Khasbulatov
concentrated all parliamentary finances hitherto decentralised (committees
had independent budgets) in his own hands by his decision of 18 July 1992.
He was henceforth able to interfere in the committees' affairs (even if their
members were his political opponents) and exert pressure on individual
deputies. The Council of Factions failed to get an official status and its
influence was on the decline. Its Chairman, Vladimir Novikov, although
holding the rank of a committee's deputy chair, had to work practically

without staff. Khasbulatov gradually emerged as the informal leader of the substantial group of non-faction deputies (these numbered 200 to 300 at different times) which allowed him to manipulate the entire deputy corps. His strategy was to engage the old "Soviet vertical", i.e. the hierarchy of the district, regional and republican Soviets of People's Deputies that was in conflict with the executive almost everywhere and on all levels. The relations between the Moscow City Soviet and the mayor of Moscow resembled closely those between the parliament and the President, both parties issuing incompatible documents and seeking to monopolise local power, and this despite the fact that the Moscow Soviet was dominated by democrats and the mayor (Gavriil Popov) was one of democrats' most acclaimed leaders. A similar situation existed in St. Petersburg, another stronghold of democrats, whose mayor, Anatoli Sobchak, was in a state of almost open war against the City Soviet. The example of the capitals was followed by the provinces. In many autonomous republics, their newly elected presidents were already in conflict with the respective Soviets.

The story of "voucherisation" highlighted the unhappy relations between the President and the government, on the one hand, and the parliament, on the other. The possibility for both parties to defy each other and use the fact of their having been elected by popular vote as an argument in the struggle for monopoly of power was the logical consequence of separate legitimation of the two branches of government, the legislative and the executive. The elections of 1990 and 1991 provided independent and presumably self-sufficient legitimacies for the parliament and the President, and neither hesitated to speak "in the name of the people", even though it was clear enough that the President had been elected by a direct but by no means unanimous vote,[1] whereas individual deputies, strictly speaking, could only claim to represent their constituencies, not "the people as a whole".

In the absence of clear procedures to regulate the interrelations between the branches of power, each sought to gain at the expense of the other and showed no intention to abide by strict constitutional provisions. The parliament referred to the sovereign powers the constitution granted to the Congress of People's Deputies. The principle was admittedly in full accord with the traditions of established democracies. In Great Britain, for example, the House of Commons is a sovereign representative body, but it occurs to no one to speak of "the dictatorship of the legislature" as the Russian democratic mass media used to do throughout 1992 and 1993. On the other hand, in the context of the national political culture the fact that the President had been elected by a direct universal vote could be interpreted (and many were those to seize the opportunity) as a privilege to do anything "in the name of the people". In other words, the presidency could be understood as popular will embodied in an individual person. This interpretation would preclude, if course, any institutional restrictions on the presidential power.

The collision between the parliament and the President was thus a collision between two different embodiments of "the popular will". A conflict of this sort seems unavoidable and total elimination of one of the parties appears the only way out of the deadlock unless the society reaches *a procedural consensus* about the character and delimitation of prerogatives of these two incarnations of "the will of the people".

We thus come back to the problems that were the subject of debate between proponents of the parliamentary and the presidentialist models of democratic government. It is our opinion - and it seems to be supported by the recent developments not only in the post-Soviet Russia but also in a number of other states that have emerged on the ruins of the USSR - that it is imprudent, to put it mildly, to introduce artificially an institutional conflict into a democracy that has not yet been firmly established. And since representative institutions cannot be sacrificed, for no political regime can be properly called democratic if representative power is absent or impotent, whereas the institution of presidency with incumbents elected by direct universal vote is sure to instigate just this type of institutional conflict between the legislative and the executive, establishing this office in young democracies may endanger the stability of the regime and is therefore inadvisable.[2] This does not mean that a constitution like that of the United States, for example, is generally unacceptable. It means only that it is unsuitable for "nascent democracies" that lack a nation-wide consensus about operational experience, i.e. for societies integrated by social ontology or values.

The Beginnings of Multipartyism

What kind of integration the Russian society strove to achieve in 1992-93 is easy to discern from the structure and ideologies of what stood for the Russian parliamentary parties, viz. the three major blocs.

Multipartyism in its classical form is alien to the Russian political culture. Nor were periods of mass involvement in politics long, and when endured, they were usually times of chaos and civil war. More characteristic of the Russian tradition were various forms of semi-covert political life, such as rivalry between different factions within the political establishment. No party that appeared on the Russian soil between 1990 and 1993 has evolved into a mass party. On the contrary, the reverse trend has been manifest: movements of all kinds ("Popular Fronts", for instance) have been degenerating quickly until they turned into little more than coteries around one of the institutional centres of political power (the President or the Chair of the Supreme Soviet).

Despite the obvious changes in the expectations of the populace, all attempts on the part of political "parties", whether the market-oriented *Democratic Russia* or the "patriotic" *Front for National Salvation*, to mobilise the "revolutionary" masses were complete failures. Had the Russian parliament been an institution in which and through which clearly defined social interests were represented, interests related, moreover, to specific segments of the electorate sufficiently large to influence the political behaviour of the relevant parliamentary factions, one might have reasonably expected the idea of parliamentary control to come to some form of institutional realisation.

In real life, however, what was called "the Russian parliament" deviated substantially from the classical model of parliamentary institutions. On the one hand, the factions were too heterogeneous politically and parliamentary discipline too low for them to function in any fashion other than as deputy clubs.[3] On the other hand, the existing political parties were not directly related to factions. It was customary for members of the same party to belong to different factions, and vice versa.[4]

All this motley diversity was organised into a more or less distinct structure only by April 1992 after three blocs had been formed on the eve of the Sixth Congress: *Coalition in Support of Reforms*, *Constructive Forces*, and *Russian Unity*.

It would be interesting to compare the three blocs from the standpoint of integrative orientations. *Russian Unity* was rallied round the idea of restoring the Soviet Union and obviously considered the Soviet society and the Soviet state as an indivisible whole. This holistic approach revealed a drive to re-integrate the society on the socio-ontological level. Allusions to "the Russian people", "the national traditions", "the Russian culture", as well as the obvious dislike for everything "alien", were prominent in the political rhetoric of this group of parties and factions.

No less obvious was the *Coalition in Support of Reforms*' orientation towards value-based integration. For the adherents of that bloc "the reform" had grown to be a value in itself; and though the parties and factions that constituted the bloc differed substantially as to the proper course of the reforms, they all maintained that the "Reform" was absolutely indispensable, making it their catchword. As was to be expected, the bloc turned out to be the most fleeting of all: its supporters were constantly in quarrel about what was to be and had already been done. Whereas *Russian Unity* survived safely till the dissolution of the parliament, growing ever stronger, the factions united into *Coalition in Support of Reforms* were afflicted by incessant splits and conflicts.

The unaccommodating behaviour of the democrats, their ambitions and conflicts were repeatedly criticised by the democratic press. From time to time calls were made for all democratic forces to re-consolidate, and some democratic leaders consciously sought the laurels of the would-be unifiers. The customary tactics was to find a common enemy. It was not long before the latter was discovered in "the red-browns". The unsurprising result was that the "democratic" propaganda of the Gaidar government assumed the form of "either we or the communo-fascism", which resembled strikingly the dilemmatic patterns of the communist propaganda of the late 1920s - with the appropriate adjustment in emphasis.

Another peculiar feature of democratic rhetoric of the period in question was perpetual complaints about the absence of a unifying democratic ideology and appeals for its urgent elaboration. The solicitation revealed the populist cultural orientation characteristic of the transition from the ontological to the operational type of social integration.

Finally, the bloc of Constructive Forces, at face value an unnatural alliance of labour (The Workers' Union) and Soviet-style employers, the "red directors" (Industrial Union), represented an attempt to reach an operational consensus, provide for clear delimitation and cooperation of the branches of government, transform "the spontaneous monetarism" of the cabinet into conscientious economic policy, amend fiscal legislation, etc. One of the bloc's factions, *New Generation - New Politics* that united comparatively young deputies openly seeking the status of the nation's future political elite, was notable for its unfailing concern for institution-building, parliamentary procedures and competent legislative activity.

Despite their considerable success at the Sixth Congress, when *Constructive Forces* played a major role in working out the compromise between the parliament and the government about the course and the future of reforms, the bloc lost much of its influence later in the year, after aggravation of the conflict between the branches of power brought extremists on both sides in the foreground again. At that time, when the growing number of democrats, aware of losing their stand in the parliament, sought employment in the quickly expanding presidential structures (further weakening what had been left of their factions), Khasbulatov was consolidating his control over "the swamp".

2. The Seventh Congress

In summer the abortive attempts at "shock" stabilisation gave way to a cancelling of mutual defaults carried out by Victor Gerashchenko, the new Chairman of the Central Bank, who was instantly accused by democrats of diverting from the course of reforms. The industry was saved from total collapse at the expense of accelerated inflation. In autumn the rouble dropped almost two-fold.

In this situation the confrontation between the President and the parliament entered a new round and on the eve of the Seventh Congress the economic problems were pushed to the background by the more immediate issue of power. The Supreme Soviet had fulfilled the commission of the Sixth Congress and adopted a law on the Council of Ministers, but the President had vetoed it. (The law had indeed contradicted the Constitution on a number of points.) It was now up to the Congress either to revoke the law or amend the Constitution.

The principal points of controversy between the parliament and the President were the extent of parliamentary control over cabinet appointments (ministers and deputy ministers) and the President's right to institute new departments and alter the structure of the government. The Supreme Soviet insisted such alterations be subject to its approval, a provision strongly objected by the President.

Another important issue was the premiership. Gaidar's appointment had not been confirmed and he was still Acting Prime Minister.

The third problem was the government's economic policy. That had undergone considerable change since May and had deviated perceptibly from strict monetarist standards, especially after Gerashchenko had replaced Georgi Matyukhin as Chairman of the Central Bank in July.

The Congress opened on 1 December 1992. In his introductory speech Khasbulatov outlined the main problems faced by the society and the Congress:

First. Why have we not succeeded in fulfilling the promise given to our people?

Second. Is the state power capable of proposing to the society a realistic programme of riding out of the crisis?

Third. What government can realise this programme?

Fourth. What are the outlines of the society we are striving after?

And fifth. Will the representative and the executive powers be able to organise constructive cooperation on all levels after all?[5]

Despite attempts to question the constitutionality of the President's actions[6] the Congress started peacefully enough.

The deputies were addressed by President Yeltsin who delivered a long speech delineating his assessment of the current political situation.[7] Yeltsin's "additional" powers expired on the Congress's opening day and one of his major tasks was to secure in some form his decisive influence on the political and economic development of the country. With that goal in mind he proposed a substantial re-distribution of political functions between Russia's governing institutions. Yeltsin suggested that:

First. For the period of stabilisation the Congress of People's Deputies of Russia must concentrate in its legislative activity exclusively on amending and supplementing the Constitution of the Russian Federation. Other legislative acts must be entrusted wholly to the Supreme Soviet of Russia. ...

Second. All executive and administrative activity on the federal level, including control of the federal property, must be entrusted to the Government. The Government is to be accountable to the President and the Congress. ...

Third. The President takes and is responsible for the most important decisions in the economic sphere within the competence of the executive.

Fourth. The President forgoes prolongation of [his] additional powers in the sphere of legislative regulation of the economic reform, if the preceding items are accepted. ...

Fifth. For the period of stabilisation the order envisaged by the Constitution for the formation of the Government is to be preserved... The law on the Government is to be suspended till the new Constitution is adopted.[8]

The programme was obviously conceived as a kind of compromise proposed to the Congress with intent to retain full control over the membership of the cabinet.

Soon after that the floor was taken by the Chairman of the Supreme Soviet. Khasbulatov's speech was as long as the President's and full of biting criticism of the government's economic policies.[9] He offered no definite answer to the President's proposal but made an important remark:

> Like many of you I have already talked more than once of the need to depart from the practice of "extraordinariness". [*Applause*]. All reforms, economic as well as political, must be carried out on the basis of laws, respect for the existing Constitution.[10]

The Congress then listened to Valeri Zor'kin, Chairman of the Constitutional Court, who disapproved of the mounting tension between the branches of power.[11] The floor was also given to Yegor Gaidar, whose speech, devoted mainly to economic problems, gave a fairly cheerful picture of the current situation, albeit with a grain of self-criticism,[12] and to Vladimir Ispravnikov, Chairman of the Supreme Economic Council (a body subordinate to the Presidium of the Supreme Soviet), who presented a kind of anti-Gaidar version of a plausible economic policy.[13] Ispravnikov criticised the fundamentals of fiscal system and the confiscatory character of liberalisation of prices. He also emphasised that the course of marketisation pursued by Gaidar's government was by no means the only alternative to the economic system that had existed prior to the reforms.

The discussion of the government's economic policy that followed was on the whole tolerant enough. The usually aggressive Chubais, for example, said when expounding the government's stand on the issue of property:

> To conclude my speech I would like to say: the Government is ready for compromises. By the way, everyone of you has a document before his eyes. This is the Government's programme that has been worked out on a compromise basis together with the Civic Union, in which account has been taken of the proposals of the Supreme Economic Council, People's deputies, the Central Bank.[14]

Vice-President Rutskoi also talked much of compromise:

> Let us do the most important thing: reach a national civic consensus on the issue of tactics (I emphasise, the tactics) of reforms. I would like to call on the Government: it is time to stop using the slogan "Either we reform or return to communism". This is a false premise. The society does not wish to go back, and there is a wide spectrum of political reformist forces in the Russian society

that can [constitute] and, I emphasise, are capable of constituting a wide platform for reforming the Russian society.[15]

One might have reasonably expected the Congress to pass a sufficiently peaceful resolution on the issue of economic policy, but the Congress had two more matters to attend to, viz. constitutional amendments and election of the Premier. The first "bang" happened on 3 December when the deputies were discussing constitutional amendments. Radical democrats demanded to select the amendments related to the issue of government (i.e. those implied by the Supreme Soviet's vetoed law on the Council of Ministers) and treat them as a separate bloc. A heated argument broke out over the voting procedure. The proposal to vote by secret ballot in voting cabins, defended by a number of deputies on the ground that the electronic system did not guarantee confidentiality even if the Congress decide on secret ballot, was vehemently opposed by radical democrats. The argument over the voting procedure and over the proper procedure of deciding on the voting procedure ended up in fist fighting between deputies. The deputies voted twice to decide on the procedure for voting constitutional amendments: first by secret, then by open ballot. The secret ballot resulted in 673 deputies supporting the motion to vote in cabins; the open ballot, only 630. As the two-thirds majority required for constitutional amendments constituted at the moment 694 votes, one could easily estimate the probability of the Congress adopting anti-presidential amendments: it was not high.

The debate on the constitutional amendments themselves showed that the deputies had learned from their thirty-month experience in the parliament: the importance of procedures had won universal recognition. Chairman of the Council of Factions Vladimir Novikov said on the day following the fight:

> In olden times people would say: we'll die for a single "ahz".[16] One letter was worth a life, and here whole articles of the Rules are violated at times and [there is] no reaction.[17]

It would be highly interesting, from the standpoint of general state of affairs, to find out when exactly intense conflicts would occur at the Congress. The scrutiny of its fourteen days shows that they would break out as soon as the issue of parliamentary control over the executive was brought up. In less important cases the position of the presidential party would usually be represented by Vladimir Varov; in more important, by

Vladimir Shumeiko or Sergei Shakhrai; in the most important, by President Yeltsin in person.

After the first clash over the amendments the situation was obviously judged important enough. Yeltsin took the floor to warn that he considered some of the amendments "unacceptable":

> In case they are adopted a serious disbalance will appear between the legislative and the executive. ... The Russian state-building... follows the principle of separation of powers and I think you know that it is precisely the fact that this principle has not been realised clearly and fully that is behind many acute problems and conflicts in the work of state bodies on various levels.
>
> Adoption of these amendments will mean a U-turn and a fall back on the way of Russian state-building. ...
>
> Let us not try to be too smart: if the amendments are adopted, the Supreme Soviet can become the sole ruler of Russia with all the consequences that follow from this.[18]

Curiously enough, rebuff took the form of an appeal to the US political practice:

> ... I would like to draw the attention of distinguished People's Deputies to the fact that the present law [*the law on the government passed by the Supreme Soviet*] does not contradict the Constitution of the United States of America. ... I would like to draw attention to the fact that in January President of the United States of America Clinton will appoint executive ministers, deputy ministers and ambassadors. And on the instructions of the committees and commissions the federal security agencies of the USA will examine these ministers carefully, beginning with income declarations, their family and private circumstances. The present law enables [us] to bring our Government under control precisely in this aspect (I think we must avail ourselves of this means [*eto nado vzyat' na vooruzhenie*]), and separation of powers, of which we persistently talk here, has nothing to do... [The speaker is interrupted by the Chair.][19]

Vladimir Shumeiko took the floor to protest against the proposed amendment to Article 109 of the Constitution that provided for the Supreme Soviet's control over structural reorganisations of the government. Shumeiko said the amendment contradicted Article 121[1]:

> ... Article 121[1] states that the President is head of the executive, the chief executive, that is he is to do all this himself.[20]

Nikolai Ryabov who presented the amendments to the assembly retorted that he saw no contradiction whatsoever between the two provisions.

On the whole, the bloc of amendments that dealt with the issues of government and of parliamentary control over its organisation, membership and activities consisted of seven amendments.[21] Of these, only three were eventually adopted. None of these stated in plain words that membership of the cabinet was subject to the Supreme Soviet's control. The four amendments that did fail to get the required two thirds of the vote were rejected. In each case missing were one to four votes.[22] Of the two closely related amendments that delineated the prerogatives of the President and the parliament concerning re-organisation of the administration one was rejected, the other adopted. The former provided that such re-organisations be subject to the Supreme Soviet's approval; the latter, that the President have right to make the respective proposals. In other words, the President was henceforth to be allowed, but not obliged, to turn to the parliament in case he wanted to change the structure of state administration.

The Congress discussed also the prospects for constitutional reform. The report was made by Oleg Rumyantsev, Executive Secretary of the Constitutional Commission.[23] As followed from Rumyantsev's speech, the Commission envisaged the reform to be a long process that included consultations with the "subjects" (members) of the Federation, a "round table" of the various political forces and an all-nation referendum on the basic constitutional principles. The Constitution would be presented to the next Congress to be convened after all these, probably in September 1993. The Supreme Soviet would then take up the issue of the election code and other legislative acts following from the new Basic Law.

The next days were spent on the numerous constitutional amendments not related to the "bloc on the government" until another, more serious, conflict broke out over the amendment to Article 121^6 of the Constitution. The article disallowed the President to dissolve the parliament and other legitimately elected bodies of power. The idea of the proposed amendment was to supplement the article with one more sentence to the effect that the President's powers were to terminate immediately in case he attempted to do it. Shumeiko protested again and the amendment was voted down with only 648 votes *pro* (against 183 *contra* and 54 abstentions).[24] Right after the vote Oleg Plotnikov of the *New Generation - New Politics* faction suggested the Congress reconsider the decision:

... this provision of the bill regulates the cases when the Congress or the Constitutional Court prove unable to administer restitution of the normal organisation of state, restitution of the fundamentals of law in accordance with established procedure. There is a procedure for the impeachment of the President in case he violates the law. It is carried out through the Supreme Soviet, through the Congress, through the Constitutional Court. There may be cases when it will not be able to activate this mechanism. For example, in case the President dissolves the Congress, or the Constitutional Court, or the Supreme Soviet, or changes arbitrarily the national/state system, his powers indeed end immediately because in such a case it is not possible to appeal against these actions in accordance with established procedure.

... The President solicits: please, remove the words that my powers end if I dissolve your Congress from the bill. Taking into account that I trust the President is not going to do this, I fail to understand this amendment of his.[25]

Shumeiko objected again:

... listen to what is written in the existing Constitution: "Powers of the President of the Russian Federation may not be used to change the national/state system..." and so on. I repeat: "may not be". And if we add "otherwise they terminate", we shall have porridge buttery and with butter added. The President has said many times that he is not going either to dissolve the Congress, or to do anything like that. And these words are absolutely superfluous here.[26]

Nevertheless the Congress voted once again. This time the amendment was supported by 690 deputies against 92: only four votes less than required for the motion to pass.

The next day, on 9 December, the Congress took up the issue of prime minister. Yeltsin nominated Gaidar, but the majority of the factions' spokesmen were highly critical of the candidate.[27] Pending vote by secret ballot the Congress returned to the constitutional amendments, and Plotnikov demanded for the third time the amendment to Article 121[6] be put to a new vote. To substantiate the demand he referred to "provocative calls in the press" and similar "calls by the President's circles" for the dissolution of the Congress.[28]

This time the amendment got 695 votes against 186 and was eventually adopted.[29] Shumeiko rejoined by drawing attention to an important defect in the amendment just ratified:

Article 121[10] specifies how and when the President is to be relieved of his post, whereas in accordance with Article 121[6] he is to be relieved "immediately", with [reference to] no order, no procedure. This is not to be allowed.

That is why, Ruslan Imranovich [*Khasbulatov*], as the President's representative I call [on you] insistently not to pass such a law as a whole. It is not a law, it cannot be a law when one article enumerates consummate order, and in another article you state "immediately", and that's all. It is not a law. [For goodness sake,] you are [supposed to be] law-makers.[30]

It is interesting to note that later, when all the amendments to the Constitution concerning interrelations between the branches of government were repealed by the Congress as part of the settlement between the parliament leaders and the President, Nikolai Ryabov would repeat Shumeiko's argument and admit that the amendment to Article 121[6], insofar as it provided for "no clear mechanism of realisation", was procedurally meaningless ("dead", as Ryabov would put it) and therefore useless.[31] In view of the role this article of the Constitution was to play in the September-October crisis of 1993[32] one is prompted to ask why it never occurred to the law-makers to try to make it procedurally meaningful and elaborate an appropriate "mechanism of realisation"? Could it be that, just as the relentless promoter of the amendment said it of himself, nobody in fact deemed the possibility real? Or was it that the bulk of the deputy corps had not learnt to think in terms of procedures after all? One more explanation is that any specification implied indicating the person who was to replace the president, and since the obvious answer was "vice-president", those who did not want Rutskoi were unlikely to support such specification.

On the same day the deputies cast ballot for the premier. The result was negative: Gaidar got 467 votes against 486.[33]

The next morning, 10 December, saw a new crisis. President Yeltsin appeared before the deputies and said:

The chain of actions is ready. Here it is.

First. Here, at the seventh Congress, to create intolerable conditions for the work of the Government and the President, in practice demoralise them.

Second. At any price to introduce amendments to the Constitution endowing the Supreme Soviet, that has become stronghold of the conservative forces and the reaction, with enormous powers and rights, but as before to guard it from responsibility. To take the rights, but shirk responsibility.

Third. To block the reform, to destroy all positive processes, not to let stabilise the situation.

And, finally, fourth. To hold in April 1993 the eighth Congress of People's Deputies, there to do away with the Government, and with the President, and with the reforms, and with democracy. And thus make a sharp turn back.[34]

Yeltsin condemned the ambition to re-establish the Congress's control over the executive as an attempt "to block the reform" and said:

> The Congress has made it evident how dangerous the dictatorship is not only of the executive, but also of the legislative.[35]

To judge from what happened after that, this statement, as well as Yeltsin's subsequent call on the deputies to secede from the Congress, came as a complete surprise to everyone, including Khasbulatov. The latter decided it was impossible for him to preside over the Congress any longer and transferred the chairmanship to Yuri Yarov. The registration showed that 715 deputies were present (they had been 886 at the beginning of the meeting), i.e. those who had left with the President must have numbered 171. Those who stayed expressed their discontent about the situation, blaming it on the President's coterie and denouncing the President's own behaviour as unconstitutional:

> Ignorant ambitious "grey cardinals" from the President's coterie push him into illegal actions again.[36]
> He [the President] suggests the reform be carried out essentially by efforts of one power alone: either the legislative or the executive. I think you understand this is in fact impossible, this really means dictatorship.[37]

However, a motion proposed by Alexander Utkin (of New Generation - New Politics) to promulgate Article 121[6] in its new version at once was rejected: it got only 191 votes against 468 with 81 abstentions.[38] Khasbulatov was called back and said:

> ... I rang the President up last night, told him of our decisions, told [him] also that we intended to pass the law on the government today and that if he wished to have Gaidar approved as Acting [Prime Minister], the Congress would not lay obstacles to it. He expressed his satisfaction with these decisions. We agreed on further cooperation. ... Unfortunately, however, this has not been the first time when we agree on something and then the next day absolutely different actions take place. I would like to give an example: on the eve of the Fifth Congress at 11 pm the President says that he will nominate one person as Premier tomorrow, and at 10 a.m. the next day he nominates himself. By the way, we overlooked it then and thus violated the Constitution, because the President has no right to assume the prime minister's duties. You know it perfectly well, but what happened happened.[39]

After a prolonged debate the Congress commissioned a group of deputies to draft an address to the people. It also appointed a delegation that was to negotiate with the President. The morning session ended with speeches by Vice-President Rutskoi and Ministers of Security (Barannikov), Interior (Yerin) and Defence (Grachev).[40] Barannikov and Yerin talked mainly of the present crime situation, but all the "power ministers" took the opportunity to pledge, albeit in general terms, their respective subordinates' non-interference in political matters.

In the afternoon the floor was taken by Zor'kin. The Chairman of the Constitutional Court suggested - to the applause of the audience - the Court mediate between the branches of government and help work out a compromise.[41] Pending the outcome of negotiations the Congress resumed the debate on crime.

Two days later, in the afternoon of 12 December, Zor'kin outlined the provisions of compromise:

(a) A nation-wide referendum was to be held on 11 April 1993 on the principles of the new Constitution. The text of the document to be submitted to the voters was to be authorised by the Supreme Soviet, but after consulting the President and the Constitutional Court. In case they disagreed about particular clauses, the voters were to be presented with alternative versions.

(b) The constitutional provisions that changed the existing balance between the branches of power, including the Supreme Soviet's right to suspend presidential decrees, the right of legislative initiative for the Council of Ministers and the immediate discharge of the President for dissolving legitimately elected bodies, were not to be applied pending the referendum. No new amendments of similar purport were to be considered, no new Constitutional Court judges appointed.

(c) The Congress was to hold a "soft" (popularity) vote for a number of candidates nominated by the President upon consultations with representatives of the subjects of Federation and of the factions; the President could then select one of the three favourites as his nominee for the chairmanship of the Council of Ministers and present him to the Congress for approval.

(d) Both parties were to revoke their appeals to the people.[42]

The agreement was put to vote without discussion and approved by 541 votes against 98 with 67 abstentions.[43] That was a simple majority, although the resolution "On Stabilisation of the Constitutional Order in the Russian Federation" implied revocation of a number of constitutional amendments and infringed upon the Supreme Soviet's constitutional prerogatives.[44]

On 14 December Yeltsin named his candidates for the premiership, as provided for by the settlement. They were five: Victor Chernomyrdin, Vice-Premier in Gaidar's cabinet responsible for the fuel and energy industrial complex (formerly Minister of Gas Industry in Ryzhkov's government); Yegor Gaidar himself; Vladimir Kadannikov, Director of the Volga Car Plant; Vladimir Shumeiko, First Vice-Premier in Gaidar's government; and Yuri Skokov, former First Deputy Chairman of the Council of Ministers (under Ivan Silayev), Secretary of the Security Council. Skokov came first with 637 votes, followed by Chernomyrdin (621). Gaidar was well behind with 400 votes, one vote more than Kadannikov.[45] Yeltsin chose Chernomyrdin, who was eventually approved as head of the government by 721 votes against 172 (with 48 abstentions).[46] Both the Sixth and the Seventh Congresses shed interesting light on the internal dynamics of interaction between the legislative and the executive in post-*perestroika* Russia. The separation of powers was basically understood by both parties to the conflict as "independent existence" rather than a system of mutual "checks and balances". Even when the idea of mutual control was stated explicitly, it remained something superficial, in fact nothing but declaration. No one seemed to worry about devising operative control mechanisms, as the story of Article 121[6] had revealed.

The relations between the branches of government followed the same general scenario. A cumbersome, ineffectual Congress, unable to attend properly to the practical matters of legislation, constitutional order and government, transfers most of its prerogatives (including even legislation) to the executive. The move is in full accord with the principles of *sobornost'*: legitimation of the regime is the representative body's sole political function. However, having endowed the executive with its own powers and seeing it fail, the Congress tries to regain control over the President and the government - to the obvious dislike of the latter. Their resentment takes dramatic forms, including an attempted, or rather declared, resignation of the Cabinet in April 1992 and an attempted dissolution (by means of secession) of the Congress in December.

The leaders of the parliament, the government and the President then enter negotiations. Conducted behind the scene, these result in some "unconstitutional" settlement that overrules the decisions just made to re-consolidate the congressional control over the executive. The Congress is unable to propose a viable alternative and acquiesces with a sort of grudging relief. A new round of confrontation ensues with the parliament's control of the situation growing ever weaker. We shall yet see the pattern reappear at the Ninth Congress.

The confrontation is obviously due to the mutual inability to work towards and reach a consensus about procedures of interaction. Every new compromise is not a step towards a procedural consensus, but an attempt to demarcate the spheres of responsibility, in other words to divide the world into different "ontological layers". If this is achieved, however, the political institutions that belong to different branches of government lose what might be called "common reality". The result is an ontological rupture: the parties to the institutional conflict cease to hear, least so understand, each other. Take, for example, the polemics at the Seventh Congress. The rhetoric is the same on both sides: "the reform", "the market", "the social security"; but the "worlds of operation" are ontologically different, with each party presuming to "know" better how the reforms are to be carried out. A political conflict is seen as a conflict of competing expertise: who is a better economist, Gaidar or Khasbulatov? Who has better advice? (It is precisely this question that brings about the cabinet's theatrical door-slamming at the Sixth Congress.)

There seems to be no ground for lasting agreements. Any arrangement is but a temporary truce to gain time and replenish resources. Each party seeks to impose its vision of the world, its "ontology" on the opponent. This can, indeed, be achieved in one way only: by eliminating the opponent - in the manner described in the first part of this book.

To sum up, the three years of the Second Republic saw no serious progress towards a "procedural consensus" in the society as a whole, although the need was felt - by individual politicians and even by some political forces.

3. The Spring Crisis

The Eighth Congress

The Seventh Congress re-structured the country's political agenda. With Chernomyrdin appointed Prime Minister, the issue of economic reform was pushed in the background. The irritating problem of an "Acting Premier" was also solved. Chernomyrdin's legitimacy was undisputable, and his reputation as a moderate let moderates in the parliament hope that the time for radicalism was over. Gaidar declined Chernomyrdin's offer to continue as vice-premier and quit the government.

The issue of constitution emerged as the pivotal issue of Russian politics. It soon became clear that the settlement reached at the Seventh Congress was in fact the President's victory. By giving his consent to the election of the premier, Yeltsin did nothing except what he had to do anyway, according to the Constitution. In exchange for this "concession", the parliament surrendered important constitutional prerogatives and put itself in an awkward situation. Dissatisfied with all this, the Supreme Soviet did nothing about the referendum scheduled, it will be recalled, for 11 April 1993.

The conflict between the branches of government was resumed. The deputies were actually in a trap: to adopt a new constitution meant new election. The "swamp" did not want it. These people had no illusions about being re-elected: they failed to build up support bases in their constituencies and could count on no support from political parties, for even the parties were on the decline. They were determined, at least, to drag out till the expiry of their term.

Having found itself in a difficult situation the leadership of the Supreme Soviet, weakened moreover by the growing conflict within the Presidium (after the Seventh Congress First Deputy Chairman Sergei Filatov quit his post to head the President's administration), decided to convene the next Congress of People's Deputies in March 1993, rather than in September as had been originally planned, to settle the issue of referendum.

In his opening address to the Congress Khasbulatov said:

> It seems that there is definite logic in the attempts to devalue the present Constitution, to destabilise the political situation, to work the contradictions on the federal level up to the limit. It seems to consist in the implication that the potential for carrying out ultraradical reforms by constitutional, democratic means has been exhausted.[47]

To judge from this passage, Khasbulatov must have realised that the scenario envisioning dissolution of the parliament by violent means was at least possible.

The Congress's agenda was limited to one point, viz. on the resolution "On Stabilisation of the Constitutional Order in the Russian Federation". The principal report was made by Nikolai Ryabov, Deputy Chairman of the Supreme Soviet.

Ryabov began with asserting that the resolution "On Stabilisation of the Constitutional Order", although it affected the constitutional prerogatives of the Supreme Soviet as a legislative assembly, had been adopted in fact by a simple majority, whereas constitutional decisions required a qualified (two-thirds) majority. Ryabov commented:

> Practice has shown, however, that even a slight deviation from the Constitution would not lead to an improvement in the general situation, to a mutual understanding between the powers, but would only aggravate the conflict between them, cause further de-stabilisation.[48]

The decisions made by the Fifth Congress, Ryabov alleged, had left the Supreme Soviet with only indirect levers of control over the executive: legislation, budget and the Central Bank. He suggested that the future referendum on the principles of the Constitution be considered as consultative. He insisted that the questions the voters would have to answer be discussed prior to the referendum, that the procedure for formulating the questions be stated clearly ("The absence of such a procedure has given rise to many a speculation here"[49]), that guarantees be worked out against discrimination in access to mass media for various political forces, and that the responsibility of both state bodies and individual officials for failing to fulfil the decisions of the referendum be defined.

This emphasis on procedures is an interesting phenomenon. Debates at the Eighth Congress show (as well as those of the previous one) that the members and leaders of the parliament did not underestimate the role of procedures both in the relations between the branches of power and in political life in general. Nevertheless, they were obviously tempted to use the very debate about procedures for political purposes, especially to prevent early parliamentary election.

The Congress possessed enough power and had ample opportunity to adopt a well-balanced Constitution - not those versions (proposed by the President's team or "the pro-presidential circles") that sought to deprive the parliament of sovereign powers and control over the executive. But rather than resign earlier, having assured appropriate constitutional prerogatives to their successors, the deputy corps opted for a longer term in a less favourable constitutional milieu.

The leaders of the Supreme Soviet were meanwhile fully aware of the potential dangers of the "stretched" interpretation of the President's executive powers as deriving from his "nation-wide mandate". Ryabov denounced unconstitutional settlements between the branches of power and the President's attempts to extend his powers by means of such settlements as inadmissible and said:

On the grounds of the results of the 1991 referendum on the approval for the presidency it is groundlessly asserted that the President has got a popular mandate for such actions. Meanwhile the fact is rejected outright (I would like to draw particular attention to that) that the institution of the presidency by us did not entail a change in the form of government. The law on the presidency passed by the Supreme Soviet stated that the President was the chief executive (head of the executive) accountable to the Congress.

Hence it is problematic to talk today of equal status of the Congress and the President.[50]

The speaker was late. Having embarked on the path of unconstitutional agreements with the President, the Congress created a precedent it was not easy to break. The practice discredited both the Constitution and the Congress: by voluntarily giving away the powers it was unable to realise because of its inadequate institutional structure and the anti-institutional political culture of its members the Congress was forfeiting its own political future.[51]

The Eighth Congress saw one more attempt to get back what had been lost. Ryabov proposed to invalidate the December agreement "On Stabilisation of the Constitutional Order" and proceed with the new constitution.

It was also suggested to hold simultaneous presidential and parliamentary elections ahead of schedule, in 1993, but the motion was voted down: it got only 480 votes instead of the required 517. The main arguments against early elections were the absence of the relevant legislation and the vagueness of the future constitutional system. This was a dead-end: it made little sense, indeed, to try to elect new deputies under provisions of the old Constitution, but the present deputy corps showed no signs of ever going to adopt a new one. In the long run, the Congress even decided against holding a referendum on the principles of the new constitution, in spite of the President's proposal to conduct it on 25 April (to hold it on 11 April, as scheduled initially, was too late anyway: the deadline established by the law on referenda for publishing the questions had been missed).

As to the constitutional amendments required to hold pre-schedule elections, the Congress made an obviously casuistic decision, viz. to commission the Supreme Soviet to consider the expediency of the changes in question. After the Supreme Soviet had failed to pass the long-awaited laws on elections and political parties, it was folly to expect so insipid a decision would prompt it to speed the matters up.

A formal reason given for proceeding slowly was the need to reach an understanding about the future constitution with the members of Federation. The idea looked dangerously like the Novo-Ogaryovo process of two years ago and threatened the very existence of the Federation. Negotiations with the constituent members could last as long as it pleased the participants and might well result in nothing.

In the meanwhile, the President's attitude was undergoing changes, too. The President suggested the referendum be held not on the principles of new constitution, but on "the principles of constitutional reform". The new wording raised the sensitive problem of who was to adopt the new constitution. The President's opinion was the job would have to be entrusted to a "Constituent Assembly representing all the multinational people". However, he did not specify on what conditions and by whom the assembly was to be convened. To be sure, neither the Constitution nor any other piece of legislation mentioned such a body, least so established procedures for its convocation. The very idea of a Constituent Assembly was but another example of politics "outside the constitutional field" (as a fashionable saying went) practised by the President since the times of the Fifth Congress.

The President's supporters at the Congress advocated the idea of a referendum of which the questions were to be defined by the President personally. Their arguments were decidedly populist in character:

Referendum is the will of the people. It is above our will, the will of those present here.[52]

The speaker's understanding of the proper pattern of interaction between the President and the parliament was peculiar, too:

Maybe, the President will not want to go to a referendum with our questions. Why do you [seek to] oblige him? The President is an independent power structure.[53]

The supporters of the President were growing ever more outspoken in their assertion that since the President had been elected at a general election ("by all the nation") he had a popular mandate to act as he pleased, even it were "outside the constitutional field". All he needed was popular support, and this he presumably had.

The Ninth Congress

From the President's standpoint, the results of the Eighth Congress were wholly unsatisfactory. The constitutional process was frozen for good. The Congress proved unwilling to do anything about it and obviously intended to continue till its term of office expired.

Under the circumstances, President Yeltsin made one more attempt to get rid of the Congress. On 20 March he appeared on TV and announced his intent to establish a "special regime of government" which implied stripping the Congress of its prerogative. Any legal acts that revoked presidential decrees or the government's orders were proclaimed null and void. The latter meant that the Supreme Soviet and the Constitutional Court were to be deprived of their powers, too. A referendum of confidence for the President was to be held on 25 April. The intention was not, of course, to have "confidence" in the President simply confirmed, but to get a *carte blanche* for the reform of political system to be carried out unilaterally, i.e. with no regard for the parliament.

On the night of 21 March Khasbulatov, Rutskoi and Zor'kin appeared on TV, too, to condemn the President's move, and on 26 March the Congress met again for its ninth - extraordinary - session. The decree "on special regime of government" the President had talked of in his TV address to the nation was never published; or rather, the text that was published made no mention of the most resolute anti-parliamentary measures announced by the President.

The relative strength of political trends represented at the Ninth Congress was made clear when the deputies set to making up the agenda. The formula proposed by the Presidium, viz. "On Urgent Measures to Secure the Constitutional Order of the Russian Federation", was supported by 670 deputies against 115 with 22 abstentions.[54] On the other hand, the defiant motion (by Nikolai Yegorov) to have members of the Supreme Soviet and judges of the Constitutional Court responsible for the convocation of an extraordinary Congress with so "pointless" an agenda pay the expenses incurred in this respect was rejected by 504 votes against 178 with 46 abstentions.[55] Those who supported Yegorov's motion and hence Yeltsin's address to the nation included members of the presidential administration: Sergei Filatov and Pyotr Filippov; chairmen of the "pro-presidential" committees of the Supreme Soviet: Evgeni Ambartsumov, Sergei Stepashin and Vyacheslav Bragin; prominent members of *Democratic Russia* and *Radical Democrats*: Vladimir Varov, Gleb

Yakunin, Lev Ponomaryov, Sergei Krasavchenko; renowned members of the intellectual and artistic elite: Yuri Afanasiev, Sergei Kovalyov, Oleg Basilashvili, Anatoli Shabad, Victor Sheinis; popular TV persons: Bella Kurkova, head of St.Petersburg TV, and Alexander Lyubimov, Vladimir Mukusev and Alexander Politkovski of the popular *Vzglyad* ("Look") programme.

It was thus evident that the coalition of the President's supporters consisted of the same political forces that had rallied around him at the time of his confrontation with the USSR leadership, viz. mass democratic movements (or rather what had remained of them), democratic intelligentsia, including democratic media, but with one notable extension: the "pro-presidential" power structures took a radical stand, too.

It would be interesting to compare the above list of presidential supporters with the list of those who supported the moderate motions to transform the Congress into a permanent bicameral legislature (the motion had been on the democratic agenda since the first days of the Russian parliament, it will be recalled, and had been repeated again and again) and abolish the Presidium of the Supreme Soviet, but voted against Yegorov's radical proposal. There were no front line politicians among these, but the group included co-ordinators of the "centrist" factions and a number of distinguished members of the academic establishment.

All the three motions were opposed by persons like Sergei Baburin and Victor Aksyuchits, as well as former radical democrats converted "patriots", such as Mikhail Chelnokov. The radical opposition was, moreover, dissatisfied with the "equivocal" wording of the agenda proposed by the Presidium. Many of the 243 deputies who voted against all the three motions just mentioned were former members of *Democratic Russia* and even *Radical Democrats*. The familiar but not so radical democratic proposal to eliminate the two-storey structure was supported by 332 deputies (against 364).

It was clear that neither the radical supporters of the President, nor "the moderates" were going to vote for the impeachment. The leaders of the Supreme Soviet seemed to realise that a move to impeach the President was doomed to fail. It must have been this understanding that had prompted them to propose a relatively "peaceful" version of the agenda.

A long debate followed participated, beside the deputies, by Chairman of the Constitutional Court Valeri Zor'kin, Prosecutor General Valentin Stepankov and the so called "power ministers": security, interior and defence.

The presidential party built their case on the following two assertions: the Constitution was "Brezhnevite"[56] and one did not have to abide by it; it had been rightful indeed for the President to ask for the people's opinion about his policies, and the decision of the people, once pronounced, had to be above the Congress and above the Constitution.[57]

The speakers also pointed out that the resolution of the Constitutional Court that had provided a formal basis for the impeachment was not free of procedural flaws itself:

> The Ninth Congress has been convoked on the basis of an unlawful resolution of the Constitutional Court that violated the procedure [envisaged] for discussing the President's address to the citizens of Russia. On the grounds of this unlawful resolution a hasty, undiscussed resolution has been passed by the Supreme Soviet that tramples on all laws, too, and makes use of the fact that the Congress is a supreme body [of power] today and may consider any question.[58]

This was a classical case of the "double standards" approach: the laws that seemed to be to the advantage of the President (e.g. the procedures of the Constitutional Court) were to be enforced; those to his disadvantage (the Constitution and the laws on the Constitutional Court in their entirety), ignored.

It was also suggested that the President's address to the nation on 20 March be considered not as "an action", but just as "a statement of opinion":

> The Chairman of the Constitutional Court has explained to us that the resolution [*of the Constitutional Court*] was passed not on the decree itself, but on the actions of the President that consisted in the public exposition of the contents of his decree. A very familiar Soviet juridical tradition (at any rate, the formula is well known to me): we try you not for your beliefs but for your actions. And what the actions consisted in - in the exposition of beliefs.[59]

The speaker obviously confused a rank-and-file citizen's right of free speech with the responsibility of a top civil servant.

On the whole, the arguments of the President's advocates did not sound particularly convincing. The interesting fact was that neither the President himself, nor his Prime Minister Victor Chernomyrdin mentioned any of these in their speeches at the Congress. Yeltsin would emphasise stability:

> We have found ourselves in a dead end. Therefore I had to use my right and appeal to the people. It is the responsibility of the President of the country to

guarantee the stability of the constitutional foundations under conditions of radical reforms.[60]

Chernomyrdin referred to the balance of powers:

> It is clear that surgical methods are not the best variant here. "To amputate" one the branches of power means to cripple Russia, if not outright kill it.[61]

The executive branch obviously seemed to have taken a far "milder" stand than a few days earlier when the President had made his TV address.

Another argument of the President's party, and one believed to appeal to a considerable part of the electorate, was the fact that Yeltsin owed his office to a general, "nation-wide" election. In the opinion of his most radical supporters that would place him above the parliament and the Constitution. Consciously or not, the argument invoked the traditional concept of Russian autocracy:[62]

> But we remember and shall propagandise everywhere that Yeltsin is a President of the all-nation choice. And if we want Russia to be respected, it would be a shame if we lambasted our President in the parliament, it will not make Russia any stronger.[63]

The arguments of the other party were juridical and political. The former cited violation of the Constitution in the President's address of 20 March and numerous other infringements of legislation (although not attested, as in the case of the recent TV address, by the Constitutional Court). Politically, Yeltsin was blamed for the breakdown of the Soviet Union, the failure of economic reforms and provocation of social conflicts:

> All your political biography of recent years has been nothing but a search for an enemy. Now the enemy is Gorbachev; now the enemy is Ligachev; now the enemy is the [Soviet] Union; now, the CPSU; now, as far as I remember, the six or the eight of the Russian parliament; now, the Russian parliament itself. ... In one document you say [of yourself] "guarantor of the Constitution"; in another (your speech[64]) you state that you have not sworn on this Constitution.[65]

> Article 121[6] states that the powers of the President of the Russian Federation may not be used to change the national/state system of the Russian Federation, to dissolve or suspend any legitimately elected bodies of power; otherwise they end immediately. We have thus every reason, distinguished colleagues, to confirm the termination of the President's powers by secret ballot and simple majority. ... By the way, I have calculated that in the course of his office the President has been violating the Constitution on the average not less than once a week.[66]

Deputies were highly critical of the President's coterie, too:

> Already here, in the Supreme Soviet, I have heard one of my former brothers-in-arms say: "The Supreme Soviet, the Constitutional Court have swallowed the bait". What kind of bait is it? It happens to be the President's address to the nation and that decree (I do not know whether it has been signed by that time or not) - but all that has been called "a bait".[67]

The attitude of the "high-rank" opposition, as represented by Ruslan Khasbulatov, Alexander Rutskoi and Valeri Zor'kin, was moderate enough. In his speech on 26 March Zor'kin suggested the Congress be abolished:

> At the same time the Congress might pass a law (a law on the constitutional level) that would let us dispense with the Congress of People's Deputies as an independent legislature and hold election to a bicameral parliament that would allow for the interests of both the Federation in general and all its subjects. ... It is urgent that laws be passed on elections, referendum, political parties and public associations, as well as on responsibility for failing to fulfil the decisions of the Constitutional Court.[68]

Khasbulatov said at once that he was ready to resign should the Congress decide personal conflicts were behind the crisis.[69] Rutskoi stated that

> ... a referendum on 25 April and probably elections in autumn are necessary to resolve the present problem in a civilised way, in order, God forbid, the society be not driven into clearing up the relations by force. I entreat you to take such a decision and follow this course.[70]

On 27 March Sergei Shakhrai articulated the President's official position as follows:

> The question "Do you have confidence in the President?" does not affect the Constitution nor presupposes any alterations in the Constitution. ... [If] the confidence is denied, the President resigns and new election is held in three months. [If] the Congress is denied confidence, elections are held for People's Deputies ahead of schedule; [if] confidence is denied to both, simultaneous elections are held for both the deputies and the President.[71]

The Congress then supported the motion to hold "a popular vote" by the majority of 621. The President proposed the formula "a popular vote" (rather than "a referendum") because that would allow to by-pass the law on referendum that defined the majority as fifty percent (plus one vote) of the total (registered) number of voters and pass the decision by the majority of fifty percent (plus one vote) of the actual turnout. Protests were heard at once; some deputies were also anxious lest the President dissolve the Congress after he got his vote of confidence.[72]

The Congress passed a resolution providing for compensation of private deposits that had been devalued by the recent inflation. The motion was clearly intended to impress the voters on the eve of the referendum. Yeltsin made another conciliatory statement, and the conflict looked like being about to be resolved. However, item 2 of the Congress's resolution that provided for "voluntary resignations of the President and Chairman of the Supreme Soviet" laid foundation for a new round.

On 28 March Khasbulatov opened the morning meeting with a proposal of a new compromise worked out by the leaders of the Supreme Soviet, the President, the Cabinet and the Constitutional Court. The agreement, modelled after the December settlement, annulled both the referendum and the presidential decree of 20 March and provided for simultaneous elections of the deputies and the President scheduled for spring 1994 at the latest. On the occasion of this new proposal Yeltsin took the floor again and promised to dispense with the popular vote of confidence.

Another settlement "behind the back of the Congress" suggested the practice was becoming a kind of new tradition; this time it turned everything upside down. The conflict was resumed with a renewed vigour. The factions' leaders were bringing new accusations against each other. Sharp criticism was levelled this time not only at the President, but at the Chairman of the Supreme Soviet, as well. It was motioned the latter be dismissed from his office for having entered into negotiations that had not been sanctioned by the Congress.[73] Khasbulatov retorted caustically that

> The Congress has met in order to discuss the question related to an attempted coup d'etat, but will end up by dismissing the Chairman of the Supreme Soviet.[74]

The resolution on the new compromise was rejected by 687 votes against 130. At the suggestion of Vladimir Isakov the Congress voted to add one more point to the agenda, viz. on impeachment of the President and dismissal of the Chairman of the Supreme Soviet. This sudden turn showed again that the Congress was in fact a disorderly institution, that the deputy corps was susceptible to abrupt changes of mood and, last but not least, that the deputies worried more about the Congress's continuation, i.e. about their own powers, than about their political or constitutional disagreements. After Khasbulatov's speech on 28 March the institutional nature of the conflict was made apparent. Secret ballot showed that Yeltsin's impeachment was supported by 617 deputies (the required majority being 689 votes) and opposed by 268.[75] 339 deputies voted to have Khasbulatov dismissed from chairmanship of the Supreme Soviet; 558 deputies voted against it (in this case the required majority was 517 votes).[76] The President's supporters rejoiced in what they believed to be their great victory.

In anticipation of the forthcoming referendum the Congress passed a resolution "On Discontinuance of Political Censorship on Television" and approved the list of questions for the vote. Despite lengthy debate on the exact wording of the questions, the one about confidence in the President was eventually approved as it had been proposed by the President himself. The deputies apparently failed to see the potential consequences of the formula, viz. activation of the President's "latent powers" on the basis of a "nation-wide" vote of confidence. The events of September-October 1993 might have never taken place, had the wording been more accurate, for example, "Do you trust (have confidence in) the President within his constitutional competence?" or something like that, i.e. making an explicit reference to the limits of the President's powers. (As mentioned above, some deputies had their doubts about the sagacity of it).

The Congress opted to "counterbalance" the expected outcome of the referendum in a different way, viz. by asking a question about the voters' attitude towards the socio-economic policies of the President. The deputies were confident the majority would answer in the negative, making up for the anticipated positive answer to the question about confidence in the President. But they underestimated the impact of mass media.

Two more questions were added: about early elections to the presidency and to the parliament. The Congress left the basic institutional conflict unsettled: the responsibility was shifted onto the voters.

The Referendum and the Ultimate Rupture

Preparation for the referendum was accompanied by a vigorous anti-parliamentary campaign waged by the mass media under executive control. The campaign's masterminds hit upon a catching formula "yes - yes - no - yes" which was reproduced in numerous variations on posters, in TV ads and pro-presidential newspapers. The idea was to provide a simple ideological link: if you supported the reform, you were to vote "yes - yes - no - yes", not trying to memorise what exactly that meant. With the voters' involvement and, in fact, the general interest in politics on the decline, the trick proved a great success. It would obviously be too much to expect an average voter to probe into the four questions in an attempt to understand why, for example, the parliament had to be re-elected while the President had not, although both had been elected in another country. The versified motto drummed in for a whole month by all possible means had done its bit. Although the proposal to have the parliament re-elected failed to get the required support (50 percent of the registered voters plus one vote) and, according to the law on referenda, the results were not legally binding, the majority of those who came to vote supported the re-election. Coupled with the impressive majority of those who pledged confidence in the President and rejected early presidential election and with the majority, albeit marginal, in favour of the President's economic policies, the outcome of the referendum was interpreted by the presidential party as entitling it to open anti-parliamentary actions.

Since May 1993 the executive behaved as if the parliament was no longer there. This defiant attitude culminated in Finance Minister Boris Fyodorov stating in summer that he was not going to abide by the budget the Supreme Soviet had approved. With no regard for the prerogatives of the Congress, the President convened a Constitutional Conference to work on the draft of the new constitution (June 1993) and clearly intended to have it adopted without the parliament. No election was held to the Constitutional Conference: its members were simply "invited" to participate.[77] The leaders of the Supreme Soviet were obviously uncomfortable. The Presidium was about to quarrel. The chairmen of most committees inclined towards dismissing Khasbulatov and replacing him by a person more acceptable to the President. It was hoped that this might ease the tension.

This *coup de parlement* seemed inevitable. However, it was prevented by a scandal that happened at the opening of the Constitutional Conference when Khasbulatov was rudely denied the floor. The members of the Presidium took the insult close to heart and refrained under the circumstances from further action against their Chairman in order not to show weakness.

Open confrontation was by now unavoidable. In July the Constitutional Conference presented a draft constitution that was based on the principle of separation of powers as understood by representatives of the executive. According to the draft, the role of parliament, that was henceforth to consist of two chambers, the State Duma and the Council of Federation, was to be restricted to passing laws; it was to be denied all powers of control. On the contrary, the sphere of the President's responsibility was envisaged as almost unlimited and he was to be proclaimed "the guarantor of the Constitution". Though the draft assumed that presidential decrees should not contradict the Constitution and federal laws and that in case they did the fact was to be attested by the Constitutional Court, it did not establish definite procedure to be followed in such a case. Nor did it indicate procedures to guarantee the rights and freedoms proclaimed; in this, however, the draft constitution did not deviate from the standard Soviet legislative practice that had always carefully avoided specifying procedures by means of which the Soviet citizens might have realised their celebrated rights (needless to say, the "rights" had thus been reduced to mere declarations).[78]

Unlike the version of the constitution that would later be submitted to the national referendum, the version of the Constitutional Conference provided for the Council of Federation to be elected, not "formed". However, strange as this may sound, no rules were stipulated for that election: the draft simply referred to a non-existent federal law.

Despite these and other flaws and in striking contrast to a similar occasion in 1988 (when the Soviet leadership had embarked on democratic reforms), no public discussion of the draft constitution was organised. This was all the more surprising, as the constitution was clearly meant to be adopted by a plebiscite, the parliament being all but expelled from the process. However, consent was sought from the members of Federation, and the process proved not an easy one. As was to be expected, the situation soon came to resemble the Novo-Ogaryovo process of the other days. Yeltsin turned to the Council of Federation, a non-constitutional body that united the heads of the provincial executive and legislative,[79] as a means to "push" the draft of the Constitutional Conference. The tactics were, however, hampered by the fact that the draft constitution provided for considerable restrictions on the powers of the "subjects" of Federation. To put it briefly, the same mechanism that had been used by Gorbachev in 1991, viz. to engage the support of republican leaders in an attempt to set off both conservatives and democrats in "the Centre", was activated again. In Gorbachev's time the tactics had resulted in the republican leaders perpetually increasing their demands up to the point when the very existence of the USSR had come under threat.

It is not inconceivable that it was that failure to negotiate with the provincial leaders and the memories of the Novo-Ogaryovo process in which Yeltsin himself had played the part of "the demolition man" that prompted the Russian President to embark on an entirely different course, one long advocated, indeed, by some of his close associates and resembling in a way the notorious August coup.

In September 1993 Yeltsin made advances to both radical democrats and the military. Yegor Gaidar was suddenly appointed Vice-Premier once again. The President himself paid a visit to the Dzerzhinski division where he had photos taken of him wearing camouflage uniform and a red beret.

4. The End of the Parliament

The "Step-by-Step Constitutional Reform"

On 21 September 1993 President Yeltsin appeared on the television to address the nation.[80] Having stated that the present deputy corps had "forfeited its right to be at the prime levers of state power"[81] and that the existing Constitution did not allow of "a decent way out of the crisis of statehood",[82] the President announced that he had "approved by his decree amendments and supplements to the existing Constitution of the Russian Federation".[83] According to the decree "On the Step-by-Step Constitutional Reform in the Russian Federation" (Decree No. 1,400) the parliament was to be suspended and election to a new legislature held. As to the existing Constitution, it remained valid insofar as it did not contradict the new decree.[84]

The structure of the new legislature, to be called the Federal Assembly, was established by a special statute "On the Federal Government Bodies in the Transitional Period". The Federal Assembly was to consist of two chambers. The lower house, the State Duma, was to be elected on a mixed proportional/majoritarian basis: 50 percent of members, from "electoral associations" ("party lists"); the other 50 percent, from single-seat territorial constituencies. In the upper house, the Council of Federation, each member ("subject") of Federation was to be represented by two persons, viz. the heads of the local executive and legislative. The election to the State Duma was to be held on 11-12 December 1993 according to rules specified in another special statute that was put in force by the same Decree No. 1,400. As to presidential election, the question was left to the discretion of the new Federal Assembly.

According to the Statute "On the Federal Government Bodies in the Transitional Period", the prerogatives of the Council of Federation were to include ratification of laws passed by the State Duma, ratification of presidential decrees imposing the state of emergency or martial law or providing for use of the Russian armed forces outside the country, appointment of elections to the presidency, appointment of the Prosecutor General.

The State Duma was to adopt federal laws, appoint the Chair of the government, hold votes of confidence for it, appoint and dismiss the commissioner for human rights (the Russian counterpart of an ombudsman, but with powers unspecified), declare amnesties.

The new parliament was to have no right of control over the government's activities.

The reaction of the legislative and the judiciary was prompt. At 10 pm an emergency meeting of the Presidium of the Supreme Soviet began in the White House. The Presidium resolved to consider the powers of President Yeltsin terminated since after signing Decree No. 1,400 and recognise Alexander Rutskoi as the Acting President of the Russian Federation since the same moment.

At 10.10 pm[85] the Constitutional Court met for an emergency conference that was attended by all the thirteen judges who had been elected by that time.[86] The status of the prospective ruling caused a debate. As far as it can be ascertained from the verbatim report (available in an abridged form[87]), the judges had no doubts about the unconstitutionality of the President's actions, including those of them who shared Yeltsin's appraisal of the political and constitutional situation in Russia and thought his actions were expedient. Properly speaking, the President himself did not deny his actions contradicted the Constitution. He just said that

> Security of Russia and its peoples is a higher value than the formal observance of self-contradicting norms created by the legislative that has ultimately discredited itself.[88]

The judges, or at least some of them, were in doubt as to what was required of the Constitutional Court in the situation. Impeachment of the President in accordance with the procedure provided for by Article 121[10] of the Constitution ("in case of violation of the Constitution of the Russian Federation") required a ruling by the Constitutional Court.[89] The same article, however, provided for the impeachment itself to be performed by the Congress of People's Deputies, the respective decision to be taken by the majority of two thirds of the total number of People's Deputies. Since the decree in question was meant to "halt" "the performance of the legislative, administrative and control functions by the Congress of People's Deputies",[90] activation of the mechanism established by Article 121[10] was assumed to be impossible. It had been in anticipation of this possibility, indeed, that the deputies had adopted the amendment to Article 121[6] of the Constitution providing for an "immediate" termination of the President's powers in case he dissolve or suspend a legitimately elected government body. According to the legislator's apparent intent and in the opinion of some judges of the Constitutional Court, that procedure did not require a ruling by the Constitutional Court. (Incidentally, Decree No. 1,400 "suggested", as the wording went, the Constitutional Court convene no meetings until the new Federal Assembly start its work).

Therefore, when Chairman of the Constitutional Court Valeri Zor'kin proposed a draft ruling that ascertained, apart from the unconstitutionality of the President's decree and his address to the citizens of Russia, the presence of grounds for his impeachment "in accordance with procedures established by Article 121[10] or 121[6] of the Constitution", protests were voiced. The draft proposed by Zor'kin was initially supported, by way of roll-call, by five judges (of whom one qualified his judgement almost at once); three judges (or probably four - the verbatim record allows of two different interpretations of one of the statements) objected to mentioning Article 121[6] (they were seconded by the one to have modified his opinion); four opposed the draft.[91] Since none of the decisions had got the support of the majority, the Chair was to put two proposals to have received most votes in their favour to a new vote. Zor'kin put only one of the two, and, one of the judges having corrected his position, it is not quite clear, indeed, whether it was to have precedence.[92] Nevertheless, when the new vote (by a show of hands) was held, nine members of the Constitutional Court out of thirteen supported Zor'kin's motion. The Court thus ruled that the decree and the address of the President contradicted the Constitution of the Russian Federation on eleven points and justified his impeachment or "activation of other special mechanisms of his responsibility in accordance with procedure established by Article 121[10] or 121[6] of the Constitution of the Russian Federation".[93] As far as it can be ascertained on the basis of the verbatim record, the reference to Article 121[6] was not discussed any more. This breach of procedure, however insignificant in itself, made up an excuse for the executive to ignore the decision of the Constitutional Court as not quite legitimate.

A similar lot awaited the decisions of the Supreme Soviet. The fateful role was played again by Article 121[6], or rather by its procedural "meaninglessness" (already discussed above[94]). The Supreme Soviet met for its seventh session at midnight of 22 September, and it took the deputies but a quarter of an hour to pass a resolution "On Termination of Powers of the President of the Russian Federation Yeltsin B.N.". The resolution was supported by 136 deputies with no *contra* and 3 abstentions.[95] Alexander Rutskoi was confirmed as Acting President of the Russian Federation by the majority of 130 votes against 3 with 3 abstentions.[96] The predominance of Yeltsin's opponents was due to the fact that those deputies who supported the President abided by his decree and did not turn up (respectively, 108 and 111 members of the Supreme Soviet did not vote). The decisions were thus taken by the simple majority of the Supreme Soviet members (at the time, 247 in two chambers). Since, however, no procedure (including provisions for quorum) was established for removing the president from power in the case envisaged by Article 121[6] and it was not even specified which body was to fulfil the act or attest the fact of removal, legal uncertainty remained. The presidential party insisted categorically that neither the Supreme Soviet, nor, moreover, its Presidium had the right to impeach the President; that might only be done by the Congress. Incidentally, the Supreme Soviet resolved to convene the Tenth Emergency (Extraordinary) Congress of People's Deputies immediately. The supporters of the parliament rallied around the White House.

On the other hand, representative of the parliamentary *Coalition in Support of Reform* called a press-conference and demanded Khasbulatov resign. The Joint Committee of Democratic Organisations of Russia[97] also called for resignation of the Chairman of the Supreme Soviet and resolved to file a complaint with the Prosecutor's Office against Khasbulatov for "an open call for the overthrow of the President of Russia legitimately elected by the people".[98]

The President's decree was discussed in numerous organisations, including local Soviets and provincial legislatures. The resolution passed by the Presidium of the Soviet of the Krasnopresnenski district of Moscow (on the territory of which the White House was situated) stated that, according to the Constitution, the President's powers had ended at 8.05 pm on 21 September and Vice-President Rutskoi had become Acting President of Russia. At night the Presidium of the Moscow City Council issued a statement to the effect that

> B.Yeltsin has made an attempt to dissolve the legitimately elected bodies of state power.[99]

Speaking at the session of the Supreme Soviet, the Prosecutor General, Valentin Stepankov, assured the Chairman and the deputies that his office would keep strictly within the bounds of the Constitution. The position of the "power structures" was naturally of primary importance in the situation that was. At Rutskoi's suggestion the Supreme Soviet dismissed two of the "power" ministers, Pavel Grachev (Defence) and Nikolai Golushko (Acting Security Minister), who were replaced, respectively, by Vladislav Achalov and Victor Barannikov. (Later Interior Minister Victor Yerin was sacked, too, Andrei Dunayev appointed in his stead). At the same session Chairman of the Constitutional Court Zor'kin announced the ruling of the Constitutional Court.

The executive retaliated by cutting off the government communication lines in the White House; long-distance telephones operated one way only: from the provinces to the White House.

In the morning of 22 September Defence Minister Pavel Grachev told reporters that neither he nor anyone else in the Russian Armed Forces took his dismissal and the appointment of a new minister seriously; according to Grachev, commanding generals of the military districts, fleets and armies pledged their obedience to the Minister of Defence (i.e. himself) and the President legitimately elected by the people (i.e. Yeltsin).[100]

The "removal" of the "power" ministers was, of course, a serious mistake. Grachev's initial reaction to the situation was reported to have been neutral enough: spokesmen of the Information and Press Department of the Ministry of Defence stated that no special orders were issued by the Minister in connection with the President's decree.[101] After August 1991 the army had been reluctant to interfere into politics; that attitude had been confirmed in March 1993, during Yeltsin's previous attempt to get rid of the parliament. However, this time the army leadership was all but pushed into confrontation with the legislative.

Supporters of the White House were forming their own armed units, mainly with the assistance of the Union of Officers led by Stanislav Terekhov. This semi-legal organisation was soon to play a very damaging role. Its attempt (on 23 September) to capture the headquarters of the

United Armed Forces of the CIS would provoke harsh measures against the White House. The atmosphere inside the latter was characterised by "the August syndrome". The deputies were waiting for volunteers and army units to put up an armed defence. However, all attempts to repeat Yeltsin's exploit of 1991, viz. to enlist the support of at least some army units, failed. The only "armed force" the White House managed to form was a special unit that consisted mainly of retired officers and members of some radical opposition groups and numbered a few hundred men. The pro-presidential mass media did not fail to mention the fact that the unit included, among others, members of the Russian National Unity, an extremist nationalist organisation headed by Alexander Barkashov, though, strictly speaking, it has remained unclear whether Barkashov's men (present, indeed, in the White House) were formally enlisted. The potential defenders that rallied round the White House were, for the most part, members of radical nationalist or communist organisations, too.

That encouragement of the radical "patriots" by the leaders of the White House served only to support the allegation that the parliament as a whole was "communist-fascist" in character, despite the obvious fact that communists and nationalists were by no means the only political trends represented in the "rebellious" legislature.

In the meantime, confrontation spread beyond the capital. To judge from the information that circulated in the Supreme Soviet, by 3 pm of 22 September 9 republican, 20 regional (*oblast'*) and 5 provincial (*krai*) Soviets of People's Deputies (i.e. legislatures of 34 out of the total 88 "subjects" of Federation) had condemned the President's decree and supported the Supreme Soviet. Deputy Chairman of the Supreme Soviet Veniamin Sokolov alleged that, according to his information, heads of local administrations divided roughly equally into supporters and opponents of the President's decree.[102]

On the other hand, head of the presidential administration Sergei Filatov (recently First Deputy Chairman of the Supreme Soviet himself) claimed that some 70 deputies offered their assistance in realising the decree.[103]

The situation in the provinces could be summarised as follows: the legislative tended to support the Supreme Soviet; the executive, the President.

It was somewhat different in the republics. In Bashkortostan (Bashkiria) the joint session of the Presidium of the Supreme Soviet and the

Council of Ministers condemned the President's decree as unconstitutional. The extraordinary session of the Karelian Supreme Soviet declared it invalid on the territory of the republic. The Supreme Soviet of Mordovia also ruled that the decree contradicted the Constitution of the Russian Federation.

The longer the confrontation, the more dangerous the situation. Torn between the branches of government, local authorities emphasised the need for simultaneous elections of both the President and the parliament. The issue soon emerged as the focal point of the entire conflict. The President's party argued simultaneous elections were impossible for the country could not be left "without authority". The argument was of little cogency, of course, for it went without saying that the President elect would only be sworn into office some weeks or, perhaps, even months after the election. Nevertheless, Yeltsin modified his previous decision about presidential election and announced that it would take place ahead of schedule, on 12 June 1994.[104]

By midnight of 23 September 480 deputies turned up at the Supreme Soviet; 689 were needed to open the Congress. At 10.33 a.m. on 23 September Khasbulatov opened the session of the Supreme Soviet by saying that the city telephones in the White House were also disconnected. To judge from the available information, some telephones in the Ministry of Defence were cut off, too, presumably in the offices of "unreliable" persons.[105] Khasbulatov also informed the deputies that sessions of regional Soviets had been held in 53 "subjects" of Federation and that

... the absolute majority of the Soviets, about 95-96 percent, resolutely denounce the anti-constitutional actions of the former President.[106]

On the other hand, at a meeting of the Council of Ministers Chernomyrdin told the participants that most heads of administrations supported the President's decree. The confrontation between the executive and the legislative throughout the country became a recognised fact.

On 23 September Nikolai Ryabov, one of the Deputy Chairmen of the Supreme Soviet, submitted his resignation. The Supreme Soviet accepted also the resignation of Sergei Stepashin, Chairman of the Supreme Soviet's Committee on Defence and Security. Both politicians joined the President.

Prosecutor General Stepankov, speaking at the same session, told the deputies that he was in no position to give a legal appraisal of Yeltsin's decree, such an appraisal lying outside the competence of his office. Stepankov protested, on behalf of his Office, from attempts to involve it in a political conflict. He also refused to bring legal action against Yeltsin quoting the latter's presidential immunity. According to the Prosecutor General, Article 121^6 treated of termination of the President's powers, not of his status (and hence of the immunity that went with it); the President might only be deprived of his "status" by the Congress of People's Deputies in accordance with the procedure established by Article 121^{10}. Since the impeachment implied by that article had not taken place, Yeltsin was still President and Rutskoi Vice-President. (Article 121^6 let the deputies down again). Khasbulatov retorted by suggesting a new Prosecutor General be nominated.

The Tenth Congress

On 23 September the Supreme Soviet amended the law on the status of People's Deputy. The amended version stated that "support by People's Deputies of the Russian Federation of a coup d'etat or other actions aimed at a forcible change of the constitutional order of the Russian Federation serves as the grounds for termination of the competence of People's Deputies of the country".[107] The decision allowed to lower the quorum required to open the Congress of People's Deputies. By 9.30 pm of 23 September 638 deputies were reported present, which was more than 67 percent of the total membership of the Congress, defined now as 941. The leaders of the Supreme Soviet decided the quorum was made up. However, the validity of the law that altered the status of People's Deputies, and with it the quorum of the Congress, was challenged at once by deputies from the President's party.

The Tenth Congress of People's Deputies of the Russian Federation opened at 10 pm on 23 September 1993. The only item on the agenda was "the coup d'etat". The report on the current political situation was made by Ruslan Khasbulatov. The Chairman of the Supreme Soviet characterised the actions of the President as a coup. Alexander Rutskoi, speaking after him, stated that the way out of the present predicament was simultaneous elections to the presidency and the parliament.[108] A resolution was drafted providing for simultaneous elections of the President and the Supreme Soviet on 11-12 December 1993.

In principle, the position taken by the Congress on this issue could be a basis for a compromise, for the main complaints against the parliament were its dubious legitimacy and its ungainly two-level structure. Both would be eliminated if the proposed resolution were enacted. The idea was meeting with growing support in the provinces. Their representatives met in St.Petersburg and tried to arbitrate between the parliament and the President, as a kind of "third force".[109] However, subsequent debate would show that not all deputies favoured new elections; some would argue the decision, if taken, would go against the results of the April referendum (Nikolai Pavlov), some would refuse to take it "under pressure" (Vladimir Isakov, Sergei Baburin).[110]

At night the Congress passed a resolution "On the Political Situation in the Russian Federation in Connection with the Coup d'Etat". President Yeltsin's actions were appraised as a "coup", and "all legal acts issued with B.Yeltsin's signature since 8 pm of 21 September 1993" were declared "legally invalid and not subject to execution on the entire territory of the Russian Federation". The Prosecutor General was ordered to take "all measures provided for by the law against the persons to have taken part in the preparation for and the execution of the coup d'état". The resolution declared it necessary to hold simultaneous early elections of the President of the Russian Federation and People's Deputies of the Russian Federation and endorsed "the actions taken by the Supreme Soviet of the Russian Federation and the Acting President of the Russian Federation, A.V.Rutskoi, to suppress the coup d'état".[111]

Earlier, the Congress had already "confirmed" the Supreme Soviet's resolutions on the termination of Yeltsin's competence and its transfer to Rutskoi. The deputies had voted by a show of hands,[112] the data on the outcome of the vote is not available. As far as it can be understood from the Chair's remarks preserved in the verbatim record, only two deputies had voted against the resolution concerning Yeltsin (with one abstention) and three against the resolution concerning Rutskoi (with four abstentions).[113] The exact number of those who had voted *pro* is not known. If we assume that all the participants of the Congress (as registered at the time it had opened) had been present and voted, though it might well not be the case, the resolution against Yeltsin must have been supported, allowing for the two votes *contra* and one abstention, by 635 deputies. That would have been 67 percent of the total number of competent deputies recognised at the moment by the Congress leadership (941), but only 61 percent of the total number of competent deputies who had attended the previous, Ninth, Congress (1,033). The procedure established by Article 121[10] for the impeachment of the President had not been used. The "night" resolution "On the Political Situation" did not impeach Yeltsin or appoint Rutskoi; it just took both facts for granted. The Congress also ratified the appointments to "power" ministries made earlier by the Supreme Soviet. The situation around the White House became tenser. The building was fenced with barbed wire and surrounded by the militia (since 25 September, by the Dzerzhinski Division). It could no longer be entered from the outside, though deputies would be allowed in and the exit remained open to everybody. On 25 September the government communication lines in the Constitutional Court building were disconnected, too.

The President and the government demanded that defenders of the White House disarm immediately. The presidential party alleged the latter were possessed of some 500 to 600 pieces of small arms. This issue of arms, along with that of simultaneous elections, was soon to be brought up as the crucial point in the negotiations between representatives of the two parties to the conflict.

In the meantime the "zero variant", proposed by Chairman of the Constitutional Court, Valeri Zor'kin, at the Congress meeting on 24 September[114] and endorsed by provincial leaders, was growing ever more popular around the country. The idea was to revoke both the President's decree No. 1,400 and the parliament's decisions impeaching President Yeltsin and appointing Rutskoi in his stead, in short to return to the situation as it had existed before 21 September, and to resolve the conflict by holding simultaneous elections to both branches of power in December (not in March as the Congress had voted earlier that day[115]). The proposal was supported by representatives of the *Civic Union* and some trade unions, but uncompromisingly renounced by *Democratic Russia*.

Yeltsin himself said in an interview given to the "News" (*"Novosti"*) TV programme on 27 September that he would make "no compromise with any bodies [of power]".[116] That very day the Chief Directorate for the Interior of Moscow issued a statement that it was "considering measures to prevent access to the White House". Since the White House had already been surrounded and access to it not allowed for some time, the "measures" in question must have implied suppression of demonstrations and rallies still going on around the White House outside the barrier of barbed wire. On 28 September Yeltsin's press secretary Vyacheslav Kostikov made a statement, on behalf of the President, that "no assault against the White House has been and is being planned".[117] On the same day President of Kalmykia, Kirsan Ilyumzhinov, and some other leaders of regional Soviets asked Valeri Zor'kin to allow them to hold a conference of leaders of the "subjects" of Federation on the Constitutional Court premises at 10 a.m. of

30 September as Zor'kin himself had suggested earlier. In the evening of 28 September the Congress of People's Deputies appealed to Patriarch Alexis II of Moscow and All Russia to intervene.[118]

When analysing these actions and statements, one should keep in mind the general political atmosphere. The Central Television was clearly biased towards the President. The information from the White House was carefully sorted. On 25 September the TV authorities refused to clear "The Red Square" [*Krasnyi kvadrat*[119]], a programme prepared by Dmitri Konchalovski and Alexander Lyubimov (the latter himself a People's Deputy). At the press-conference given on 28 September the incident was condemned as "a display of the grossest political censorship on TV".[120] St.Petersburg television, however, continued to broadcast a daily news programme "600 Seconds", the host, Alexander Nevzorov, known for his right-wing sympathies, reporting from the White House. The pressure on the White House increased: following the telephones, the electricity, water supply and sewerage were cut off, too. The attitude of the authorities gave Khasbulatov an opportunity to comment that

> The territory around the House of the Soviets [*the White House*] is the first political concentration camp, Yeltsin's democratic GULAG. The term "democratic dictatorship", invented by democrats, has got its visible expression.[121]

Attempts at Reconciliation

Nevertheless, on 29 September the pressure exerted by the "subjects" of Federation on the President and the government produced its first results. Deputy Chairman of the Supreme Soviet Veniamin Sokolov met with representatives of the other party to discuss the ways out of the crisis.

Later that day the Department of Foreign Relations of the Moscow Patriarchate issued the Patriarch's address:

> Russia is on the brink of a precipice. We are now facing a choice: either to stop the folly or to bury hopes for a peaceful future for Russia. ...
>
> Take no actions that might break the peace, fragile as can be! Do not try to solve political problems by force! ...
>
> No political goals can prevent the people in the White House from being supplied with medicines, food and water, medical care. It cannot be allowed that physical exhaustion provoked people into uncontrollable violent actions.

On behalf of the Church I call the opposing parties to dialogue and offer any form of required mediation at this fateful time.[122]

In the evening the Congress pleaded with the Patriarch again asking him to make efforts to prevent civil war in Russia.[123] At the same time a mass rally was held in front of Barrikadnaya Underground Station (the closest to the parliament building) in support of the White House. By the militia estimates, the rally was participated by some 5,000 people. The rally was blocked by riot police who forced the participants from the roadway.

On 30 September 54 representatives of the "subjects" of Federation met at the Constitutional Court building for a conference. They were joined by Veniamin Sokolov and Ramazan Abdulatipov delegated by the Congress. The conference was also attended by Archimandrite Theophanes representing the Patriarch. The latter informed the participants that the Patriarch proposed the parties meet at his residence, St.Daniel Monastery, to negotiate. The participants of the conference drew up a memorandum in which they undertook to do nothing that might damage the unity and integrity of the Russian Federation provided the following conditions were fulfilled: (1) the acts of the federal legislative and executive bodies passed after 8 pm 21 September be suspended and the constitutional situation that had existed prior to that moment restored; (2) simultaneous elections to the legislature and the presidency be held not later than February 1994; (3) the Constitutional Court present to the Council of Federation not later than 15 October draft bills defining the temporary structure of the federal government bodies; (4) the government of the Russian Federation act exclusively within its competence as defined by the Constitution and laws of the Russian Federation; (5) the executive revoke all acts that violated provisions of the Federal Treaty. The participants of the conference decided also to form a "Council of the Subjects of the Russian Federation".[124]

After that four delegates of the conference met with Victor Chernomyrdin to discuss lifting the blockade against the White House. The Prime Minister refused to discuss the problem until the arms distributed in the White House were surrendered.

On the same day President Yeltsin received in the Kremlin the leaders of the Joint Committee of Democratic Organisations of Russia. They all agreed that the "zero variant" of the Constitutional Court was absolutely unacceptable.

Throughout these days, starting with 21 September, political rhetoric was growing more and more confrontational. Alexander Rutskoi played the lead, but the other party was gradually taking the threatening tone, too.

On the night of 1 October representatives of the Supreme Soviet and the President met for negotiations. The parliament's party was represented by Abdulatipov and Sokolov; the President's party, by Filatov, Luzhkov and Soskovets. It was agreed that the electricity and heat supply to the White House would be resumed immediately and the "necessary" number of city telephones connected again. On the other hand, the arms distributed in the White House to persons not on the regular staff would be collected back and stored under mutual control; the outer guard of the White House was to be reduced both in personnel and in weapons. As the second stage of the settlement, both the outer cordons stationed around the White House and the guard units formed inside it were to be evacuated.

However, the agreed protocol was resolutely rejected by the White House's "Military Council" that consisted of the newly appointed "power" ministers: Achalov, Barannikov and Dunayev.[125] It was not clear, indeed, who was in control of the White House at the moment: the elected leaders of the Supreme Soviet or the parliament's "power" ministers. It must have been the position of the latter that prompted Khasbulatov and Rutskoi to disavow, in the course of the press-conference given in the besieged White House on 1 October, the agreement signed by Sokolov and Abdulatipov "by the consent of the Supreme Soviet leadership" (as Sokolov put it). Despite Sokolov's objections, the Congress denounced the protocol.

We may thus ascertain the presence of two parties in the White House: "the party of peace", that favoured "the zero variant", and "the party of war", that rejected it and staked on an "outright victory". The attitude of the latter was apparently due to the fact that Rutskoi and the new "power" ministers would lose their positions if the original situation were to be restored. At any rate, the subsequent developments seem to have depended largely on the relations and the rivalry between these two parties of which "the party of war" got eventually the upper hand. In this respect it seems noteworthy that already on 30 September, i.e. a day before the agreement in question was disavowed by the parliament's leaders, Sergei Kurginyan, a well-known conservative political analyst, had been expelled from the White House at gun point. Kurginyan had tried to persuade its leaders to accept "the zero variant" which, speaking objectively, seemed very much to the advantage of the Supreme Soviet: restoration of the situation that had existed prior to 21 September would have dealt a severe blow to the prestige of the President and could not help affecting the outcome of the future elections. After the incident, that had clearly pointed to some conflict inside the White House, Kurginyan had made a statement in which he had demanded the government lift the blockade against the White House in order

> ... to give a full chance for normalising the political process and securing its development along the lines of the Constitution and democracy.[126]

The subsequent events were as follows. In the morning of 1 October representatives of the parliament (headed now by First Deputy Chair of the Supreme Soviet Yuri Voronin), the President and the Constitutional Court met in the Patriarch's residence in his presence. By 2 October the parties agreed on the "Programme of measures to normalise the situation around the White House". The "Programme" provided for the protective barriers on both sides to be removed, a schedule for mutual reductions of weapons to be worked out, a common watch to be maintained on the places where collected arms would be stored, and rules for access of citizens to the White House to be set.[127] After that Prosecutor General Stepankov made a statement that, in his opinion, the negotiations in the St.Daniel Monastery eliminated the question of civilians being possessed of great number of weapons.

The events seemed to have swung to "the zero variant". President Yeltsin decided to hold a meeting of the Council of Federation on 9 October. It was also rumoured that a new presidential decree had been drafted - very much in the spirit of "the zero variant".

Dissolution by Shooting

However, hopes for a peaceful resolution of the conflict proved to have been illusory. Following the inexorable logic of a dualistic confrontation, matters drew to a tragic finale. Strained as it was, the situation made leaders on both sides encourage extremists. Amid active search for a compromise by politicians worried about the looming civil war, the parties to the conflict suspected each other of (and, probably, indeed engaged in) working out provocative pseudo-compromises meant to split the opponent and arouse mistrust in its ranks rather than find a mutually acceptable way out of the crisis. Leaving the President's camp aside, in what has been published of the verbatim records of the Congress, at least, curses addressed to the instigators of the coup alternate with mutual suspicions and accusations.

The situation had grown worse by 3 October. On the previous day the *Working Moscow* (*Trudovaya Moskva*) movement and the National Salvation Front had organised a rally in support of the Supreme Soviet on Smolenskaya Square (not far from the White House); the demonstrators had clashed with the riot militia, barricades had been set up. The next morning, speaking at a press-conference in the White House, Rutskoi attacked Yeltsin and said that "the zero variant" was unacceptable because it implied

> Boris Yeltsin and his accomplices will remain in power and one won't be able even to speak of a democratic election.[128]

3 October was a day off. A rally in support of the White House was scheduled to take place at 2 pm near the monument to Lenin on Oktyabr'skaya Square. The demonstrators, numbering several thousand, marched along Sadovoye Kol'tso towards the White House and, having forced their way through the thin lines of riot militia on Krymski Bridge, approached the parliament. At 3.25 pm the cordons still stationed around it, were broken through near Hotel *Mir*. Shots were made, several persons injured.

The mob that penetrated into the Square of Free Russia[129] was addressed by Rutskoi, speaking from the White House balcony. Rutskoi called on the demonstrators to go seize the Mayor's Office and the TV Centre in Ostankino. At 4.45 pm the Mayor's Office situated right across the square from the White House (in the former headquarters of the Council for Mutual Economic Aid) was taken by assault; after that General Makashov led some three thousand armed men to the TV Centre. The talks in St.Daniel Monastery were stopped; the Patriarch himself fell ill, infarction was suspected.

The subsequent events are shrouded in mystery. At 7.30 pm the First (Central), Third (Moscow) and Fourth Channels stopped broadcasting. People in the White House thought it was evidence that Makashov had seized the TV Centre. About 8 pm Yeltsin arrived in the Kremlin and signed a decree imposing the state of emergency in Moscow.

As far as the assault on Ostankino is concerned, the story was told differently by the opposing parties. According to the President's party, the mob led by General Makashov had tried to take the TV Centre by assault. The other party claimed the supporters of the Supreme Soviet had been met by internal troops lying in ambush in Ostankino and shot when holding a peaceful rally in front of the building entrance. As to the attempt (later to be reproduced in numerous TV programmes) to ram the entrance by a truck, the shots were said to picture the events that had taken place after the fire had already been opened.

The story is hard to believe: when Makashov and his men had been leaving for Ostankino, they had clearly intended to attack, not demonstrate. On the other hand, it is also clear that there was absolutely no need to stop broadcasting: whether the Ostankino Centre was threatened or not, broadcasting could be as well organised from other places. It was indeed resumed from a reserve studio, but later in the night. Yegor Gaidar called on Yeltsin's supporters to come in defence of democracy and assemble in front of the Moscow Council in Tverskaya Street. Some twelve thousand or so answered the summons; barricades were hurriedly set up, though it was difficult to say what they were meant to protect.

At 10.10 pm an airborne (Tul'skaya) and two armoured (Tamanskaya and Kantemirovskaya) divisions entered Moscow. What happened in the interval between that moment and the next morning, when the assault on the White House began, is not clear. Two rallies were held: by democrats, on the square in front of the Moscow Council; by parliament's supporters, in Krasnopresnenskaya Embankment. It is also not clear whether people on both sides were aware of the actual situation or not: Yeltsin's supporters, speaking on the reserve TV channel at night, talked of the chaos in the capital, the capture of some government buildings, the absence of militia in the streets, whereas the supporters of the Supreme Soviet seemed in fact to be doing nothing. As time went by, the number of demonstrators in front of the White House decreased significantly: people were leaving for their homes. As far as it can be judged from the available information, the supporters of the parliament had no real means to seize administrative buildings, as the most active of them had left for Ostankino where the President's party proved obviously the stronger of the two.

During the night representatives of the provinces made a series of attempts to prevent further aggravation of the conflict and resume the talks. Despite these, at 7.30 a.m. the assault on the White House began. Barricades were forced, and some two hours later units loyal to the President were reported to have forced the lower storeys.

A new round of negotiations followed, this time about surrender. People were leaving the White House. At 4.00 pm tanks stationed on the Novoarbatski Bridge over the Moskva River opened gun fire; the upper storeys of the building were set ablaze. About 5 pm the White House surrendered. The deputies were distributed between various police stations, the more radical of them escorted to the stadium in Luzhniki; by night they were all set free. Khasbulatov, Rutskoi and the "power" ministers of the parliament's party were arrested.

It still remains unclear what was going on inside the White House that day, what the casualties were and what happened to the majority of the White House defenders, including Barkashov's men. Sporadic shots were to be heard in the vicinity of the White House for one more day; the state of emergency in Moscow remained in force for about a fortnight.

An analysis of the last two days of confrontation suggests the following conclusions. "The parties of war" got the upper hand on both sides. What is surprising is Rutskoi and his "power" ministers' confidence that victory would be theirs. It did not take comprehensive research to understand that the balance of forces was not in favour of the Supreme Soviet and that in an open conflict its supporters would stand no chances to win. In the meantime, as mentioned earlier, a political settlement on the basis of "the zero variant" would have been very much to their advantage. There seems to be no explanation for the preponderance of "the party of war" on the parliamentary side but that the leaders of the Supreme Soviet mistook the events of 3 October for the beginning of a "popular uprising" against Yeltsin's regime and that they counted on mobilising multitudes of supporters as democrats had managed to do two years earlier.

However, this fallacious appraisal of the mass attitudes, especially in Moscow, had been characteristic of the "irreconcilable opposition" since the beginning of radical economic reform. Resentment against the President's policy had been growing indeed, but predominantly in the provinces, as the election to the Federal Assembly was soon to show: the pro-presidential *Choice of Russia* would get but half of the vote its leaders counted on and lag far behind the nationalistic Liberal Democratic Party of Vladimir Zhirinovski. It would have been far easier, indeed, to have that resentment realised by way of election than in the form of a "popular revolution". To have opted for an open confrontation and wrecked the talks proved a fatal mistake.

However, it is also noteworthy that radical democrats gained virtually nothing from the victory over the "communist-fascist" Supreme Soviet they had sought so much. For a few days after the 4 October they seemed to be in a state of euphoria expecting a radical land reform, an ultimate elimination of the communist opposition (on 4 October the political organisations that had "taken part in the mass disturbance" were, indeed, suspended[130] and a number of communist and nationalist newspapers temporarily banned[131]) and, first and foremost, a sweeping victory at the forthcoming parliamentary election. Their expectations were soon frustrated. Moreover, radical democrats themselves, having done their part and secured the executive's victory over the parliament, were no longer wanted. The conflict in Chechnya would prove it beyond doubt only a year later.

The leaders of radical democrats turned out to be as short-sighted as the radical patriots from the White House. By having assisted in eliminating the only political institution of unambiguous democratic potential, viz. a sovereign parliament, and supported authoritarian reformism, they discarded all levers of influence on the executive they might have had. The "*nomenklatura* revenge" had come, indeed, but not from where the radical democratic analysts of the "RF-Politics" had expected it to come: it was realised by the executive.

After the new constitution that deprived the parliament of virtually all means of control over the executive was adopted, radical democratic groups lost all prospects for political future.

Institutionally, Russia regressed to the situation that had existed prior to the constitutional reforms of the Gorbachev era. The principal democratic gains of *perestroika*, viz. *glasnost'* and relative freedom of political activity, were retained, but the institutional atmosphere was henceforth far less favourable for further progress of democracy.

Lessons of Another October

We can now attempt to answer some principal questions about Russian parliamentarianism in the period immediately preceding and immediately following the collapse of the Soviet Union.

The Russian parliament failed to operate as a fully developed representative institution, partly for formal (regular breach of procedures, etc.), but mainly for cultural reasons. *This parliament did not represent established political forces.* It was unable to take on the cardinal task of transforming the social and economic order, because the more immediate problem of the balance of power, crucial for any political regime, was left unsolved.

Under the circumstances the deputies tended to treat their views on concrete social, economic and political issues as secondary to the main job of asserting parliamentarianism as a constitutional principle and, indeed, as the basis of the political order.

On the one hand, the parliament was free enough from external pressures to put the issue of its own status above all other considerations. On the other hand, it was doomed to lose the ensuing struggle for power against the President (though it won the first round, against the Union authorities), as the absence of political parties made mobilisation of external mass support impossible.

(The alternative strategy of enlisting the support of provincial representative bodies proved self-defeating and served only to extend the conflict onto the regional and local levels. A combination of the popular ideal of "undisputed authority" and the local elites' obvious dislike for party politics, both rooted in the traditional culture of *sobornost'*, meant that mass mobilisation was no more possible in the provinces than it was in the capital. The stake was never to be won).

The fall of the Russian parliament, as well as political developments in other post-Soviet states, testify to the fact that no stable and effective parliamentary regime is possible in the absence of a developed system of political parties.

The prospects for Russian parliamentarianism depend, therefore, on Russia's ability to transform its traditional culture toward recognising and institutionalising divergent social and political interests that exist (or rather emerge) on its soil, as well as on the ability to maintain representative institutions as an arena on which a viable balance between these interests can be worked out.

If it fails to do this, a new authoritarianism will arise. Though it is often claimed that "enlightened" authoritarianism is Russia's only chance to accomplish the reforms,[132] we do not think that this way of transforming society is a solution to Russia's problems. While seeking to suppress the resistance of social forces keen on preserving some elements of the old social order, an authoritarian regime may well destroy whatever institutional mechanisms have been created to ensure public control over power-holders and democratic resolution of social conflicts. It was precisely the lack of these institutions that had impeded Russia's progress in the past and prompted the Soviet political elite to undertake the risky task of reforms.

The conflict that reached its climax in autumn 1993 was a typical institutional conflict. Its meaning and consequences, however, seem different for established and nascent democracies. At this transitory stage independent legitimation of the executive is likely to provoke a perpetual crisis of legitimacy which the new-born system may well fail to solve. This failure may paralyse and eventually undermine the reforms. But unlike situational crises, for which a strong presidency is often regarded to be a solution, this systemic crisis is born out of strong presidency and can only be solved by it at the expense of democracy itself.[133]

Notes

[1] As already mentioned, Boris Yeltsin won the 12 June 1991 election with 57.3 percent of the participants' vote. With the turnout above 50 percent, the election was quite legitimate. Nevertheless, in no electoral district participation exceeded 85 percent of the registered voters (about 65 percent in Moscow and St. Petersburg); in Tatarstan the election was boycotted. Although Yeltsin won in the first round already, he failed to get the support of more than 50 percent of registered voters.

[2] Cf. to Section 3 "Institutional Alternatives and Cultural Constraints" in Chapter 2.

[3] See Sub-sections on "The Political Structure of the Russian Parliament and the Problem of Factions' Identity" in Section 1 and "Internal Homogeneity of Factions" in Section 2, Chapter 7.

[4] On the distribution of the deputies' party preferences, see Biryukov *et al.* (forthcoming).

[5] *Seventh Congress RF* 1993, Vol. 1, p. 4.

[6] See I.Fedoseyev's proposal for the agenda (ibid., pp. 9-10).

[7] Ibid., pp. 46-65.

[8] Ibid., pp. 62-3.

[9] Ibid., pp. 74-93.

[10] Ibid., p. 90.

[11] Ibid., pp. 96-101.

[12] Ibid., pp. 117-35.

[13] Ibid., pp. 136-46.

[14] Ibid., p. 200.

[15] Ibid., p. 222.

[16] The old Slavic name of the letter A.

[17] *Seventh Congress RF* 1993, Vol. 1, p. 332.

[18] *Seventh Congress RF* 1993, Vol. 1, pp. 345-6.

[19] E.Tarasov's speech on 4 December (ibid., pp. 350-1).

[20] Ibid., p. 356.

[21] Ibid., pp. 354-60.

[22] Ibid., pp. 508-9.

[23] Ibid., pp. 368-73.

[24] Ibid., Vol. 2, p. 194.

[25] Ibid., p. 194.

[26] Ibid., pp. 195-6.

[27] Ibid., Vol. 3, pp. 11-34.

[28] Ibid., p. 65.

[29] Ibid.

[30] Ibid., p. 66.

[31] Ibid., Vol. 4, p. 200.

[32] See Sub-section on "The 'Step-by-Step Constitutional Reform'" in Section 4 of this Chapter.

[33] Ibid., Vol. 3, p. 124.

[34] Ibid., p. 127.

[35] Ibid., p. 129.

[36] I.Rybkin's speech on 10 December 1993 (ibid., p. 136).

[37] V.Isakov's speech on 10 December 1993 (ibid., p. 134).

[38] Ibid., p. 142.

[39] Ibid., p. 161.

[40] Ibid., pp. 165-90.

[41] Ibid., pp. 203-4.

[42] Ibid., Vol. 4, pp. 192-3.

[43] Ibid., p. 194.

[44] See ibid., pp. 301-3.

[45] Ibid., pp. 260-1.

[46] Ibid., p. 264.

[47] *Eighth Congress RF* 1993, Bulletin 1, p. 3.

[48] Ibid., p. 23.

[49] Ibid., p. 24.

[50] Ibid., p. 26.

[51] The institutional inadequacy of the two-level structure is discussed in Sergeyev and Biryukov 1993, pp. 163-7. See also Sub-section on "The Structure of the Russian Parliament" in Section 3, Chapter 4 of the this book.

[52] A.Surkov's speech *(Eighth Congress RF* 1993, Bulletin 7, p. 17).

[53] Ibid.

[54] *Ninth Congress RF* 1993, Bulletin 1, p. 9.

[55] Ibid. p. 6.

[56] See S.Veretennikov's speech on 26 March 1993 (ibid. Bulletin 2, p. 2):

> Otherwise [if a new constitution is not adopted - N.B. & V.S.] conflicts and confrontations are inevitable. They are rooted in the old Basic Law, a peculiar foundation of all the achievements of socialism.

[57] See V.Varov's speech on 27 March 1993 (ibid., Bulletin 3, p. 16):

> This is a question of power, and not just [any] power, but the power of the people.

[58] S.Veretennikov's speech on 26 March 1993 (ibid., Bulletin 2, p. 7).

[59] S.Kovalyov's speech on 27 March (ibid., Bulletin 3, p. 3).

[60] B.Yeltsin's speech on 26 March 1993 (ibid., Bulletin 1, p. 15).

[61] V.Chernomyrdin's speech on 27 March 1993 (ibid., Bulletin 3, p. 9).

[62] Compare to the official account of the "nation-wide" election of the Romanovs' dynasty in 1613 (*Chronograph* 1987, p. 354):

> Back hath come the spring of beneficent being, and streams of radiantly flowing life stretch around, for the light hath shone of our long-awaited hope, the great God. And, by His grace, from one end of the Russian land to her other end men of orthodoxy, humble and great, rich and beggars, young and old, enriched were with rich reason by Him who giveth life to all and illumed with the light of benevolent consent, and though of different places, spake with one mouth, and though in no agreement were, separated by great distances, were as of one council, in unity and equality. They willed by reason and chose by word and established by act, and their council was good. For it was not by human deliberation but by Divine provision that they prayed and solicited to have Czar Mikhail Feodorovich ascent the royal throne of the state of Muscovy.

[63] N.Vorontsov's speech on 27 March 1993 (*Ninth Congress RF* 1993, Bulletin 3, p. 13).

[64] The reference is to Yeltsin's TV address of 20 March.

[65] V.Shuikov's speech on 26 March (ibid., Bulletin 1, p. 19).

[66] M.Chelnokov's speech on 27 March (ibid., Bulletin 3, p. 12).

[67] M.Sorokina's speech on 26 March (ibid., Bulletin 1, p. 22). During the election Sorokina acted as Yeltsin's confidential agent; hence the reference to "former brothers-in-arms".

[68] Ibid., p. 11.

[69] Ibid., p. 3.

[70] A.Rutskoi's speech on 26 March (ibid., Bulletin 2, p. 15).

[71] Ibid., Bulletin 4, p. 4.

[72] See, for example, O.Smolin's speech on 27 March (ibid., p. 6).

[73] G.Smol'ski's (of *Industrial Union*) speech on 28 March (ibid., Bulletin 5, p. 15).

[74] Ibid.

[75] Ibid., Bulletin 6, p. 17.

[76] Ibid., p. 18.

[77] See Decree of the President of the Russian Federation "On Measures to Complete Elaboration of the New Constitution of the Russian Federation" of 12 May 1993 (*Constitutional Conference* 1993, pp. 6-7) and Decree "On Convocation of the Constitutional Conference and Completion of Elaboration of the Draft Constitution of the Russian Federation" of 20 May 1993 (ibid., pp. 7-8).

[78] This feature of the Soviet and post-Soviet legislation is analysed in detail in Chapter 9.

[79] Not to be confused with the upper chamber of the present Federal Assembly.

[80] For President Yeltsin's address to the citizens of Russia on 21 September 1993, see *Autumn-93* 1995, pp. I-VI.

[81] Ibid., p. III.

[82] Ibid., p. IV.

[83] Ibid.

[84] Decree of the President of the Russian Federation "On the Step-by-Step Constitutional Reform in the Russian Federation" (ibid., pp. VII-XIII).

[85] According to other sources, at 9.40.

[86] Article 165 of the Constitution provided for the Constitutional Court to consist of fifteen judges (see *Constitution RF* 1992, p. 4); however two seats were vacant. According to the December 1992 settlement between the parliament and the President no new members of the Constitutional Court were to be elected before a new Constitution was adopted (item 4 of the Seventh Congress's resolution "On Stabilisation of the Constitutional Order in the Russian Federation"; see *Seventh Congress RF* 1993, Vol. 4, p. 302; see also Section 2 "The Seventh Congress" in this Chapter).

[87] See *Autumn-93* 1995, pp. 11-7.

[88] President B.N.Yeltsin's address to citizens of Russia on 21 September 1993 (ibid., p. III).

[89] See *Constitution RF* 1992, p. 59.

[90] Decree "On the Step-by-Step Constitutional Reform in the Russian Federation" (ibid., p. IX).

[91] Ibid., pp. 16-7.

[92] At any rate, the Office of the Prosecutor General would allege later that Zor'kin "falsified" the outcome of the vote (ibid., p. 18).

[93] Ibid., p. 17.

[94] See Section 2 "The Seventh Congress" in this Chapter.

[95] See *Autumn-93* 1995, p. 24. Other sources give the outcome of that vote as slightly different, viz. 140 votes for the resolution against 3 with 3 abstentions (ibid, pp. 26-7); or 136 votes *pro* with 6 abstentions (*Chronicle* 1993, p. 10); 144 votes *pro*; 0, *contra*; 6 abstentions (ibid).

[96] See *Autumn-93* 1995, p. 25. By other sources: 137, *pro*; 5, *contra*; 3 abstentions (*Chronicle* 1993, p. 10).

[97] A somewhat mysterious organisation named differently by different sources and never heard of since.

[98] *Chronicle* 1993, p. 4.

[99] Ibid., p. 10.

[100] Ibid., p. 13.

[101] Ibid., p. 6.

[102] Ibid., p. 19.

[103] Ibid., p. 20.

[104] Decree of the President of the Russian Federation "On Early Election to the Presidency of the Russian Federation" (*Autumn-93* 1995, p. 76).

[105] *Chronicle* 1993, p. 50.

[106] *Autumn-93* 1995, p. 80.

[107] *Chronicle* 1993, p. 54.

[108] Ibid., p. 54-5.

[109] As will be shown in Chapter 7, "the third force", as different from both democrats and communists and represented mainly by provincial politicians, emerged long before the September crisis.

[110] *Autumn-93* 1995, pp. 134-5.

[111] *Chronicle* 1993, p. 69.

[112] The electronic system installed on the premises was not designed for the number of voters present.

[113] *Autumn-93* 1995, p. 105.

[114] Ibid.,. pp. 143-4.

[115] See Resolution of the Congress of People's Deputies of the Russian Federation "On the Early Elections of People's Deputies of the Russian Federation and the President of the Russian Federation" of 24 September 1993 (ibid., pp. 138-139).

[116] *Chronicle* 1993, p. 125.

[117] Ibid., p. 136.

[118] For the Appeal of the Tenth Emergency Congress of People's Deputies of the Russian Federation to Patriarch of Moscow and All Russia Alexis the Second, see *Autumn-93* 1995, pp. 231-2.

[119] Meaning the geometrical figure, not the open area in front of the Kremlin.

[120] *Chronicle* 1993, p. 135.

[121] Ibid., p. 137.

[122] Ibid., p. 157.

[123] See *Autumn-93* 1995, p. 252.

[124] *Chronicle* 1993, p. 169.

[125] For "The Record of Proceedings of the Meeting of the Military Defence Council of the House of Soviets of Russia for the Discussion of the Outcome of the Negotiations of the Delegation of the Congress of People's Deputies of the RF with Representatives of the Government of Chernomyrdin V.S.", see *Autumn-93* 1995, pp. 276-7.

[126] Ibid., p. 179.

[127] Ibid., p. 208.

[128] Ibid., p. 223.

[129] The square had got its name in August 1991.

[130] For the Decree of the President of the Russian Federation "On Urgent Measures to Secure the State of Emergency in the City of Moscow" of 4 October 1993, see *Autumn-93* 1995, pp. 441-2.

[131] For the relevant order of the Mayor of Moscow (Yuri Luzhkov), see ibid., p. 460. Banned were *Pravda, Sovetskaya Rossiya, Den', Rabochaya tribuna, "Glasnost'*.

[132] See, for example, Migranyan 1990, p. 7:

> The transition from an "ideal" totalitarian system to a democracy cannot be made in one big leap. As the first steps are made to loosen the totalitarian grip on the spiritual and, subsequently, the economic life of society, as various forms of non-state ownership are made legal, society tends to become increasingly complicated, giving rise to numerous conflicting interests. The latter's growing polarisation increases the possibility of chaos and the eventual collapse of the political system being restructured. It is therefore vital that while the complicated process of moulding and reinforcing civil society is going on in the economic and spiritual spheres, strong authoritarian rule should be maintained in the political sector, so as to impose certain restrictions on the present stage of democratic change.

[133] See also Section 2 "Presidentialism *versus* Parliamentarianism" and Section 3 "Institutional Alternatives and Cultural Constraints" in Chapter 2.

Parliamentary Behaviour at a Formative Stage

(Three Case Studies)

Who are these creatures?

What do they believe?

What do they pray for?

What do they receive?

Sana'i, "The Way of the Seeker".

7 Voting in the Russian Parliament: The Spectrum of Political Forces and the Conflict between the Executive and the Legislative

Two men on a horse scuffling, an excellent symbol of the constitution of state!

G.Ch.Lichtenberg, "Aphorisms".

In Part II of this volume we reviewed the principal events of Russia's parliamentary history in 1990-93 against the background of theoretical framework, viz. models of socio-cultural development as elaborated in Part I. Our pursuit in Part III is to substantiate the conclusions of macrosociological analysis by a minute analysis (involving statistical and mathematical models) of empirical data available to students of parliamentary behaviour. In other words, we intend to demonstrate that the Russian parliament of 1990-93 has been a good model for studying the Russian politics of this period in general - not just insofar as it was one of the main centres of political decision-making, but also because patterns of political behaviour exhibited by its members seem to have been representative of the society at large.

Three questions appear relevant to this:

(1) How did the political conflict about the need for and the ways of transforming the Russian society relate to the institutional conflict between the newly established bodies of powers?

(2) Are there any signs that the cultural atmosphere in Russia is becoming more favourable towards parliamentarianism than it has hitherto been or has, at least, the Russian parliamentary elite learnt something from the tragic experience of the last Soviet and the first Russian parliaments that

may help overcome the traditional anti-parliamentarian bias of both the masses and the establishment?
(3) What were the end results of the legislature's activities in the period in question and how they compared to those of the Soviet era?

To answer these questions inquiries have to be made into the three principal aspects of parliamentary activities, viz. voting, debates and legislation.[1]

1. Studying Group Voting Behaviour in Non-Party Settings

Changing Approaches to Changing Politics

One of the major problems of post-Soviet studies is, naturally, democratisation and, more specifically, political representation. Despite the fact that representative institutions formally existed under the Soviet regime (and had even been responsible for its very name), they were never regarded as genuine agencies of power. After new representative bodies were created by what might be called the first real elections in Soviet history, a difficult problem arose. The methods of inquiry perfected by the decades-long research of representative institutions of Western democracies appeared irrelevant, if only because the multiparty system, that Western scholars had always taken for granted, did not exist in the Soviet Union. A radical revision of these methods would be required, if they were to be applied to this new situation.

In that first stage of democratic development political culture seemed a decisive factor. The second stage (1990-93) was characterised by the growing importance of institutional issues. The parliament was busy asserting its status, first against its Union counterpart, then against its former head, who had been by that time elected President. Another important issue was formalisation of new political forces. It was believed that new political parties would soon fill the void created by the collapse of the Communist party and the emerging parliamentary factions were expected to take the lead in their formation.

An examination of voting behaviour in the Russian Parliament seems a viable approach to understanding these developments. In our opinion, it may provide answers to a number of vital questions about this period of Russia's contemporary political history. First and foremost among them are questions about the spectrum of political forces and the real balance between them and about the nature of the emerging political system. Voting in the Russian parliament has been the subject of research by both social and political scientists. Among recent publications one has to mention the works by Sobyanin[2] and the INDEM Centre.[3] They were the first to shed light on the situation in the Russian parliament, and any subsequent inquiry must reckon with their findings. However, both research teams pursued rather limited practical goals and tended to concentrate on a few salient figures. Besides, they had clear ideological and political commitments that could not help affecting the objectivity of their studies. Sobyanin's study, for instance, was consciously based on what was regarded an "ideal model" of "democratic behaviour". The model itself was construed by selecting issues, that were held to be of particular importance for democratic policy, and identifying "true democratic solutions" for them. "Deviations" from the attitudes thus prescribed were then used to assess the quality of voting behaviour of individual deputies and deputy groups.

The application of this model could (and did) demonstrate the existence of a bitter clash between Communists and Democrats at the earlier Congresses of People's Deputies. However, the weak point of the study was its arbitrary choice of criteria which was used as the basis for comparisons. This made it difficult to judge the objectivity of the results.

In 1991-92 a computer program was developed in the INDEM Centre (headed by Georgi Satarov) for the analysis of voting behaviour, intended mainly for the Parliament's Council of Factions. In this work the voting behaviour of various deputy groups was presented in the form of "clouds" on a two-dimensional plane. The method was supposed to characterise the political positions of individual deputies *vis-a-vis* the stand of the group or faction leadership. Though a convenient and convincing approach to understanding intragroup and intrafaction relations (doubtless a major point of parliamentary politics), these methods could not teach us much about the general evolution of the political spectrum inside the parliament, that is about the problem which at that time was the subject of the most heated discussion and which was to prove of crucial importance for political decision-making during the crisis of September-October 1993.

An alternative method of studying the evolution of political spectrum which is based on the analysis of voting behaviour is developed in this chapter. We believe its application will promote our understanding of both the recent political developments and the present political situation in Russia.

To our knowledge, no quantitative analysis of Russian parliamentary politics of 1990-93 has been attempted outside Russia yet. Recent publications in the *Journal of Democracy*[4] are quite conventional. An objective description of the situation in the recently dissolved Russian parliament, based on quantitative methods, seems therefore a timely and important task.

The Conflict of Powers: Political or Institutional?

The heated debates that preceded and followed the dissolution of the first Russian post-Communist parliament in September-October 1993 focused mainly on the political position of the parliament as a whole. The democratic press characterised that position as highly conservative and attributed the conflict between the parliament and the President to the political struggle between the pro-Communist deputy corps and the democratic Administration.[5]

An alternative hypothesis that pictured the growing controversy between the two branches of power as a typical institutional conflict, albeit aggravated by serious flaws in the Constitution and the obvious lack of conflict management skills on both sides, was far less influential.

The analysis of voting behaviour may prove crucial when choosing between these two hypotheses. But to provide a reliable answer, the study must first present a convincing picture of the spectrum of political forces that operated within the parliament, and then *compare the changes in this spectrum to the changes in political situation*.

The spectrum of political forces is usually understood as the latter's distribution along a one-dimensional axis. The model allows a natural and simple presentation of political differences, but fails to reflect the complexity of political positions, especially at transitory stages. There are no reasons to expect the political spectrum always to fit a bipolar scale. In this chapter we "map" the various political forces on a plane, rather than along a line. By this means we may also hope to present the evolution of political positions in a vivid and intelligible way.[6]

If individual "shots" characterise the relative "distances" between the various deputy groups at a particular period of time, a series of such "shots" can show how these "distances", and with them the overall pattern, changed. In this way we can assess the level of political accord within the parliament. We can then try to determine to what extent the political differences between its factions depended on the state of relations between the parliament and the President.

If political positions, especially those of the "centrist" groups, are found to reflect the level and character of relations between the executive and the legislative, this will indicate that the conflict is institutional, rather than political.

"Fluctuations" of the "Centre" could in principle be explained by the sequential nature of political objectives and the respective changes in priorities upon their partial attainment. The explanation would not stand for the Russian parliament of 1990-93, however, for its "Centre", despite its political heterogeneity, tended to "drift" in a surprisingly synchronous manner, which seems to point toward the original institutional hypothesis.

The Political Structure of the Russian Parliament and the Problem of Factions' Identity

The Russian parliament's deputy corps was originally divided into groups that united the members by occupation, territory, involvement in specific issues, and the like: military servicemen, medical workers, "Central Russia", the Urals deputy group, "Food and Health", etc.[7] Each deputy could in principle be and often was a member of any number of groups. The parliament, though politically polarised, was thus devoid of clear factional structure.

However, from the Fifth Congress onward factions were institutionalised that operated on a mutually exclusive basis. The minimum number of members that entitled the faction to an official status was set at fifty. The factions were mainly of importance at the Congresses, where political questions would normally be debated. As to the Supreme Soviet, its activities turned on committees rather than factions. Committees were, on the whole, more influential than factions, all the more so as they tended to behave in a uniform fashion when it came to political preferences. The latter depended largely on the political views of the chair. (As mentioned above, members of the committees had an official status within the Supreme Soviet, even if they were not its elected members and therefore were not entitled to vote on its deliberations. But they were its employees and had their offices on its premises. This, incidentally, increased the number of professional parliamentarians from 252 to about 450.)

Three periods are clearly distinguishable in the history of the first Russian parliament. The first one (from May 1990 to December 1991) is characterised by an institutional conflict with "the Centre" (the Soviet Union authorities) and a sharp ideological confrontation between communists and democrats; however, this did not prevent them from joining forces against "the Centre" and declaring the sovereignty of Russia. According to that Declaration, it will be recalled, Russian legislation took precedence over the legislation of the Soviet Union and was thus rendered free from the Centre's control. The initiative encouraged similar declarations in other republics and eventually led to the disintegration of the Soviet Union. (The formal decision abrogating the Union Treaty of 1922 was passed by the Supreme Soviet on 12 December 1991.)[8]

The second period (from December 1991 to July 1992) can be called the parliament's "star hour". It had gained and for some time maintained a kind of political supremacy. In doing so, it acquired certain features characteristic of a typical parliamentary institution, but entered an ever growing confrontation with the President. It was also a period of the factions' greatest influence, when their consultative body, the Council of Factions, became one of the key instruments in shaping the parliament's policies.

The third period (from July 1992 to the parliament's dissolution in September-October 1993) was marked by the ever growing confrontation with the President. Institutionally, the parliament was falling into decay. After committees were brought under the control of the Presidium, Khasbulatov's personal influence grew out of all proportion. This influence had no constitutional foundation and was entirely due to his ability to control the parliament's financial resources. It did not depend on the support of some faction or a group of factions, which fact made Khasbulatov the virtual leader of the "non-faction swamp" (a considerable number of deputies, including Khasbulatov himself, belonged to no factions). Numerous attempts to give the Council of Factions some official status failed, its influence was on the decline, as was that of the factions themselves.

It must be noted here that factions of the Russian parliament were not formed on the basis of political parties. Although various political parties were represented in the parliament, they were in fact established only after the election (with the obvious exception of the Communist Party). The borderlines between parties and factions were not identical: as mentioned above, members of the same party could belong to different factions, and vice versa.

The factions themselves were extraordinarily unstable. Deputies perpetually moved between factions.[9] The number of factions also changed, as factions whose membership fell below fifty lost official status (as was the case with *Civil Society* after the Seventh Congress). The fact that faction leaders were initially able to control considerable financial resources encouraged competition for leadership, and this competition caused large factions to split. As to the deputies, they were all elected on individual basis and had no obligations either to their parties or to their factions.

This situation poses a serious question as to the factions' identity. Can one actually analyse and compare the political positions of various factions if their memberships were constantly in shift, both in terms of individual composition and in terms of numbers?

One is also confronted with the problem of cohesion. Did the factions vote more or less alike, or was it the factions' nuclei alone which held clear political views, while most faction members had no firm beliefs and were, moreover, never really controlled by their leaderships?

It is to answer these questions that the following analysis of the Russian deputies' voting behaviour has been undertaken.

2. The Analysis of Voting and the Homogeneity of Factions

"Natural" Voting-Based Classification

Political homogeneity of factions is an important aspect of our analysis and one that affected the Russian parliament's entire political set-up. *A priori* one should not expect too high a homogeneity from factions that unite deputies belonging to different political parties.

To look closer into this problem, a computer database was created that compiled information on all roll calls for the Second to Ninth Congresses.[10]

The database provides easy access to the voting data both on particular issues or groups of issues and for individual deputies or groups of deputies. It has been supplied with special program tools with which to analyse and assess the concurrence of opinions within any arbitrarily chosen group of deputies as manifest in the voting.[11]

The easiest approach to the analysis of voting data is the "natural" classification of deputies by means of cluster analysis or multidimensional statistical analysis. This technique has been developed and tested in numerous studies of voting behaviour in the U.S. Congress,[12] the United Nations,[13] etc. It can be summarised as follows.

The voting of each individual is presented as a line consisting of four symbols: *"pro"*, *"contra"*, "abstained", "absent". These lines are then compared and a degree of solidarity established, which can be done in a number of different ways (for example, as a percentage of concurring positions). Methods of cluster analysis are then applied to identify groups within which the solidarity is above a certain level. Alternatively, factor analysis can be used to reduce the variety of initial data to a manifold of lesser dimension (usually between 3 and 5), and the results are then analysed as depending on these few factors.

Since natural classification (grouping) appeared more relevant, we opted for cluster analysis. However, applying cluster analysis to these particular voting data proved no easy job. This was due to the fact that the voting behaviour of Russian deputies was characterised by a number of peculiar features.

First, too many would be absent or abstain. Parliamentary discipline was generally low, and though the Congresses were usually attended by between 950 to 1,000 deputies, decisions would in fact be passed by assemblages hardly exceeding the quorum (about 625 on the average). This absenteeism, however, was not exclusively due to lack of discipline. Roll calls were carefully examined by both the parliament leadership and the administration, and deputies would be subject to considerable pressure from different quarters before any vote of importance. One of the consequences was that many deputies tended to evade voting on controversial issues in general. As to the factions, these were too weak to protect their members from outside pressure.

As a result, lines for almost all deputies were full of symbols *"absent"* or *"abstained"*. This made it difficult to define a reasonable degree of solidarity. The only feasible way was to strike out all the positions filled with these symbols. This would, however, leave us with lines too short and the remaining issues too trivial for the degree of solidarity, defined as a percentage of the concurring positions, to remain a meaningful characteristic.

Our second problem was that there were too many questions on which the deputies would vote all but unanimously, that is by a majority of 700 to

750 out of 800 to 900. This also made standard cluster analysis techniques difficult to apply, for using the degree of solidarity as a natural criterion for cluster formation would yield enormous clusters that allowed of no further diversification.

To overcome this difficulty, we tried to ignore all votes that proved "too unanimous", varying the exclusion threshold (between 70 to 80 percent) to determine how this change would affect the results, and cluster-analysing what was left.

In this case the results were as follows. If, upon the exclusion of the all-but-unanimous votes, high thresholds were used for cluster formation (above 50 percent), the deputies would scatter into a great number of very small groups (a few dozen groups of up to 2 to 3 persons). Lowering the threshold to about 40 percent resulted in re-appearance of a few mammoth clusters, whose political orientation it was impossible to define as they would include representatives of totally different political trends.

The obvious conclusion was that politically the parliament remained a rather amorphous structure: more often than not it would behave like a *Sobor*-type organism, whose sizeable "swamp" of deputies seemed to have no opinions of their own and voted under the influence of contingent political factors.

Internal Homogeneity of Factions

Finer methods of analysis were needed, therefore, to study the actual voting behaviour and the political attitudes of the various deputy groups (factions).

Our first task was to develop program tools that would allow us to obtain distribution functions for degrees of voting solidarity - for any chosen group of deputies and for any two such groups. The functions were obtained by the following procedure. In any group of deputies the degree of voting discordance was established for each pair of deputies as the percentage of the non-concurrent positions in their respective voting lines. (We found it more expedient to calculate the number of the non-concurrent, rather than the number of the concurring positions in order to prevent absenteeism from affecting the results too much.) The data were then presented in a diagram form with the degree of discordance shown on the category axis, and the number of pairs sharing that particular degree of discordance, on the value axis (see Figures 1-3). The intrafaction voting solidarity is thus shown as diminishing from left to right, that is with higher degrees of solidarity closer to the value axis.

These distribution functions served to characterise the degree of homogeneity both within any chosen group of deputies and between two such groups. In that latter case the distribution functions were obtained for pairs formed of representatives of two different groups. The diagrams were a vivid image of homogeneity: if that were high, the distribution function would have a sharp peak in the segment of low degrees of discordance (as in Figure 5); if homogeneity were low, the peak would either shift towards higher degrees of discordance (as in Figures 1-4) or the function would become altogether "blurred" (as in Figure 6). It was theoretically possible (and was, indeed, often the case) for two different sub-groups to exist within the given group: one highly correlated, the other displaying a low level of solidarity. (The sub-groups could intersect, of course.)

Our analysis of distribution functions for various factions and pairs of factions has revealed that no factions could properly be called homogeneous. The distribution function would typically reach its maximum for discordance degrees ranging between 30 to 60 percent. This means that most group members would vote in unison only on 4 to 7 issues out of 10. (It must be remembered that Figures 1-6 show discordance, not solidarity.) Even if peaks appeared in low discordance segments (less than 20 percent, indicating solidarity degree of more than 80 percent), their height was minor if compared to peaks in other segments. This means that only small groups within factions could indeed be considered truly homogeneous. (Neither have we observed a high degree of solidarity between factions.)

Figures 1-3 show the distribution functions for degrees of voting discordance of three factions, viz. *Communists of Russia, New Generation (New Politics)* and *Radical Democrats* (as exemplifying the two "extremes" and the "Centre" of the political spectrum) at the Sixth Congress.[14]

To get a comparative perspective, similar computations have also been fulfilled for a random selection of deputies[15], for factions of the German *Bundestag* and for what we have called *"Factions United"*, a group of 14 deputies selected to represent the 14 different factions of the Russian parliament.

The low intrafaction cohesion is best attested by the fact that no substantial differences exist between the distribution functions for the voting discordance between the three factions in question, on the one hand (see Figures 1-3), and in the group of deputies selected at random, on the other hand (see Figure 4).

On the contrary, the difference with the German parliament is striking, indeed. German Social Democrats appear to have voted uniformly on all occasions (see Figure 5). The voting solidarity in the other four factions of the *Bundestag* was even greater.[16]

However, low though the intrafaction voting solidarity was, one should not conclude that factions were altogether irrelevant: their discordance proved no match for that displayed by *"Factions United"* (see Figure 6).

The general conclusion derived from this analysis of distribution functions is that factions of the Russian parliament were in fact loose formations, with comparatively small "nuclei" of genuine political confreres and functioned like "deputy clubs" rather than as real political coalitions. The degree of control the faction leadership was usually able to exercise over its rank-and-file members was minimal, as was the leadership's influence on their voting behaviour. (It is worthwhile to mention here that factions had no formal heads, just "co-ordinators", and not one, but usually two or three). This is not to say that the factions played no significant role at all as far as votes were concerned. It is a known fact that in certain critical cases they proved, indeed, crucial, for example when Khasbulatov had to stand a vote of confidence as Chair of the Supreme Soviet at the Ninth Congress - the vote he eventually won.[17]

This general conclusion about the factions' homogeneity is also supported by our observations concerning the instability of their membership and their total number (which varied between seven and fourteen in the period of sixteen months between the Second Congress in December 1990 and the Sixth Congress in April 1992). We have calculated that out of 251 deputies who were voting members of the Supreme Soviet in January 1993 (i.e. after the Seventh and before the Eighth Congress) only 89 deputies (approximately one third) had never changed their factions: 77 had been members of just one faction and 12 did not participate in any faction. On the contrary, 162 deputies (almost two thirds) had participated in two or more factions or faction-type groups;[18] 67, in two; 48, in three; 35, in four; 11, in five; 1, in six factions. The average is 2.2 factions per deputy in the course of two and a half years (see Figures 7-8).[19] More "conversions" lay ahead.

This constant "migration" of deputies between factions and the frequent splits within the factions themselves make it necessary to look for finer methods of analysis than those conventionally used to study faction activities, if the actual pattern of political forces that were active in the Russian parliament in 1990-93 is to be understood.

3. The Conflict of Powers and the Evolution of Political Forces

Methods of Inquiry

The above analysis has shown that the techniques ordinarily used to identify natural groupings prove useless when applied to the voting in the Russian parliament. Although providing a general picture, namely the absence of sizeable politically cohesive groups within the deputy corps and the latter's *sobornost'*-type behaviour, cluster analysis yields no specific information about the relative positions of the various factions and deputy groups. In this section we propose a method of research that seems better adapted to the situation in question.

The conventional approach to the study of groups and factions in a representative assembly is to range them along some abstract axis that links two polar positions. The axis itself may be defined in different ways: between "radicalism" and "conservatism" or between "communism" and "anti-communism", for example. This one-dimensional perception has been inspired, in particular, by the way parliament members would sometimes seat in the assembly halls, forming a "right wing", a "left wing" and a "Centre".

Though this traditional perception of the political spectrum is, of course, metaphorical, it promotes our understanding of political realities, especially if the actual politics are reduced to the struggle between two major forces. More complex situations, however, render the model inadequate, as when the deputy corps is divided into a great number of small groups or when there are several divisive issues on the political agenda that allow of many different combinations.

Most political analysts, when dealing with the situation in the Russian parliament, sought to line up its deputy groups and factions along the axis ranging from "communists" to "democrats" with the totalitarian tendencies characteristic of the communist-oriented groups in mind. It was this model that would customarily be used to account for the major political clashes, including the parliament's struggle against the President, and notably the Autumn crisis of 1993. Our understanding of the conflict between the parliament and the President depends on whether this linear presentation of the political spectrum is indeed correct.

Our doubt in this respect rests on the fact that the Russian politics of 1990-93 pivoted on two major issues, not one. The first was transition from the old social order ("developed" socialism) to democracy and market economy; the second, federalism.[20]

These added dimensions make the "space" of political issues too complex for the positions of various political forces and the relations between them to be adequately presented on a one-dimensional model. We are thus faced with a challenging task of developing an analytical model that could reflect this multidimensional (at least, two-dimensional) character of the "space" of political problems.

This can be done on the basis of voting behaviour in the following way.

(1) The deputy corps is divided into several groups; the interrelations between these groups become the immediate object of analysis. The voting of each group is presented in a rectangular table showing group members (the lines) and the issues put to a vote (the columns).

(2) The table is then reduced to a line by reducing the columns to simple 1's and 0's as symbolising "yes" and "no". This line represents the group's political stand in a simpler and more vivid form. The group is taken to have supported a motion, if the majority of its members voted *pro*, or to have rejected it, if the majority of its members voted *contra*. (In the extremely rare cases of split decisions the ambiguity can be eliminated by identifying the group's position with that of its acknowledged leaders.) This procedure allows one to overcome problems posed by absenteeism or abstentionism.

(3) The relative "remoteness" of any two groups can then be expressed as the number of non-concurrent positions (each indicating a particular vote) in two such lines. It can be demonstrated that, mathematically speaking, this is a "good" distance - in the sense that it fits all the axioms of metric space.

(4) When these figures have been calculated for every pair of groups, their mutual positions can be presented as a symmetrical matrix of n^2 elements (where n is the number of groups) with 0's along the diagonal (see Table 1).

(5) Can the multidimensional space thus defined be reduced, with a sufficient degree of accuracy, to a two-dimensional space or, to put it otherwise, can this matrix be presented in the form of a chart, in which the "position" of each group were presented as a point on a two-dimensional plane and the metric distance between two points corresponded to the political "distance" between the respective groups? If that can be

accomplished, we shall obtain a vivid two-dimensional spectrum-map of political forces. In a sense, this mode of presentation would be a "metaphor" too, but of a kind that might enable us to "examine" and analyse changes in the mutual positions of deputy groups more complex than the ordinary shifts "from left to right" or "from right to left" along a one-dimensional axis. The "meanings" of these shifts could be derived from concrete analysis of the political positions of the groups in question and the general character of political developments.

The points' optimal arrangement on the plane, i.e. the one least distorted in comparison to the given matrix of "true distances", has been obtained by the following means. (1) The initial positions were assigned in a hit-or-miss fashion (although allowing for intuitive understanding of the overall pattern to avoid unnecessary computations). (2) To correct the unavoidable distortions each point was then treated as a particle in viscous liquid "drifting" under the impact of central forces. The forces' values were defined as differences between the metric distances between the points on the plane, on the one hand, and the respective matrix values (equal, in turn, to the number of the non-concurrent positions in the respective voting lines), on the other hand; the forces' directions, as signs of these differences. (3) The points' final positions were established by numerical solving of differential equations for mechanical movement in viscous liquid until the system reached equilibrium. (A special program was developed to undertake the computations involved.)

The residual values of forces, calculated for the equilibrium state, that represent the differences between the eventual "visible" distances (on the chart) and the "true" distances (as presented by the matrix elements), proved low. The relative average deviation, that is, the ratio between the average deviation and the average "distance", ranged between 0.01 for the Third Congress and 0.1 for the Fifth Congress (see Table 2).[21] These calculations show that the points were transferred onto plane with a high degree of accuracy.

We may legitimately claim therefore that the proposed model provides us with a good starting point in our analysis of political forces. It also enables us to scrutinise the evolution of their overall pattern by comparing the charts obtained for different Congresses and the changes in the groups' mutual positions. The political evolution of an individual group will appear as the "drift" of its position about the plane.

However, if the study is to include the temporal dimension, the data for the various Congresses have to be comparable. This takes us back to the problem of the factions' identity. We have approached it in the following way. The factions' memberships were fixed on the basis of membership lists as valid at the moment of the Sixth Congress of People's Deputies.

The choice of this particular Congress was based on the following considerations. The first five Congresses took place when the Russian parliament had not yet become the ruling representative body in the country. It was but a regional assembly with limited authority and limited responsibility. The political behaviour of its deputy corps was largely determined by the rivalry between the Russian and the Union parliaments. In their quest for power the Russian deputies often were, or believed themselves to be, compelled to vote contrary to their political beliefs and/or their better judgement.

As noted above, the period between December 1991 and July 1992 was the only one for which one may claim, with some confidence, that it saw the existence of a more or less normal parliamentary regime (with due allowance for the cultural constraints, of course). From mid-1992 onward, the ever growing confrontation between the parliament and the President was gradually destroying many of the parliament's structures. *Democratic Russia* split into two factions: the one preserving the original name and *Consensus for Progress*; *Civil Society* ceased to exist; the Council of Factions, having failed to get an official status, was losing ground.

We have therefore thought it expedient to "trace" the evolution of those deputy groups that existed at the moment of the greatest parliamentary freedom. In this connection by the word "faction" we shall henceforth in this chapter refer not to the actual factions as they existed by the time of the Congress in question (with the obvious exception of the Sixth Congress), but to the groups formed by ourselves on the basis of membership lists as valid at the time of the Sixth Congress, that is of those deputies who were members of the respective factions in spring 1993, but regardless of what factions they belonged to during other Congresses, especially as there would be many who belonged to no one at all. To avoid ambiguity we shall henceforward use quotation marks to distinguish these ideal "factions" from the actual factions as officially registered.

Discussion

The results obtained by this method attest to a considerable political diversity inside the Russian parliament. Its "factions" can be divided into three groups: pro-presidential (usually referred to as "democratic"), conservative (self-styled "patriotic") and the so called "centrist". The latter's political positions shifted substantially depending on the political situation and especially on the state of relations between the parliament and the President.

This classification supported by the results of our analysis of the relative political positions of the "factions" reveals, indeed, their attitude towards the constitutional principle of the balance of powers and to the person of the President.

Strictly speaking, the conservative ("patriotic") "factions" maintained stands that differed substantially on quite a number of important issues, which can easily be ascertained by looking through their platform planks and their leaders' public speeches. However, they all shared an opinion that what Russia needed was a parliamentary regime or, at best, a presidential republic with minimised presidential authority.

However strange it may seem, the "democratic" "factions", on the contrary, invariably advocated strong presidential authority.

As to the "centrist" "factions", their views underwent considerable changes in the course of this period. As far as this can be judged from their members' public statements, some "factions", such as *"Left Centre"* or *"Non-Party Deputies"* for instance, while supporting the presidential republic in principle, seemed to have grown cold to the idea of strong presidential authority after the conflict with the President broke out.

It appears advisable, before presenting our findings, to characterise the "factions" themselves. Their political "faces" will be discerned from Figures 17-28.[22] We shall therefore restrict ourselves to sketchy "social portraits" and brief comments.

"Agrarian Union" was originally registered as *Food and Health* group (May 1990); registered anew as *Agrarian Union* at the Fifth Congress (1991). Its members were mainly kolkhoz and sovkhoz ("collective" and "Soviet" farm) managers and former Communist Party functionaries with some relation to agriculture. Together with *"Fatherland"*, the "faction" was considered as *Communists of Russia*'s closest ally. Our findings confirm both these assumptions. As shown in Figure 17, the faction was close to *"Communists"* in the first period; "drifted" somewhat towards the "Centre", in the second period; and returned to an almost complete togetherness, in the final, third, period.

"Civil Society" was a faction of radical intellectuals who claimed to combine patriotism with democracy. It ceased to exist after the Seventh

Congress (the "positions" for the Eighth and the Ninth Congresses have been computed for the construed "faction" as defined above). The "faction", originally close to *"Democratic Russia"* (see Figures 9-11), crossed almost the entire span of the political spectrum-map to end up near the opposite focal point of *"Communists of Russia"* (Figure 18).

"Communists of Russia" were organised as a group at the First Congress (May 1990); registered as a faction at the first stage of the Fifth Congress (July 1991). They were mainly professional party workers, though some had only embarked on the career during Gorbachev reforms. However, the Russian Communist Party, which unlike other republican Party organisations was only established during *perestroika* (in 1990) and which the faction was considered to represent, was generally regarded as the stronghold of conservatives. In this study "the faction" is taken as one of the two reference points against which the political evolution of the other "factions" is viewed (see Figures 9-28).

"Democratic Russia" sprang up in the heat of the election campaign as a very broad political movement rallied around the candidates of democratic reputation. After the election was over, it continued as basically a club of Moscow and St. Petersburg intelligentsia. A deputy group of that name was registered at the First Congress in May 1990 and constituted as faction at the Third Congress (spring 1991). It considered itself and was generally believed by the public to be the focus of democratic forces in the Russian parliament. It was therefore originally taken as the second reference point for measuring the relative "distances" between the "factions" (see Figures 9-16). After the computations were completed, however, another "faction", *"Radical Democrats"*, turned out to be farther remote from the opposite end of the "axis" than *"Democratic Russia"* itself. As seen in this new perspective, the "faction", though never anywhere near *"Communists of Russia"*, shifted noticeably away from *"Radical Democrats"* in the last period (the Eighth and the Ninth Congresses, see Figure 19). Never failing in populist rhetoric,[23] the "faction" would occasionally become somewhat careless of formal parliamentary democracy.

"Fatherland" was organised in autumn 1990 (between the First and the Second Congresses) and united representatives of the military establishment. It was almost invariably close to *"Communists of Russia"* (see Figure 20).

"Free Russia" was formed at the Third Congress (April 1991) by Communist deputies who, led by Alexander Rutskoi, decided to break with

their conservative leadership and support Boris Yeltsin, then Chair of the Supreme Soviet, against his opponents. The "faction" was originally called *Communists for Democracy*. Its political attitudes were ambiguous, but on the whole the "faction" seems to have fit the definition of "post-Soviet social democracy" (as distinct from the more "westernised" versions thereof represented by *"New Generation"* or *"Left Centre"*). The "faction's" political evolution resembles closely that of *"Civil Society"*: originally part of the "democratic" wing, it "drifted" along the entire length of the reference "axis" towards *"Communists of Russia"* (Figure 21).

"Industrial Union" was registered at the Second Congress (December 1990) on the basis of a deputy group called *Organisers of National Economy*. The "faction" united mainly directors of industrial enterprises. A classical "centrist" "faction", *"Industrial Union"* "floated" around the middle of the political spectrum-map before "joining forces" with *"Communists of Russia"* at the last two Congresses (see Figure 22).

"Left Centre" was organised at the Second Congress (December 1992) by a group of deputies who saw themselves as liberal democrats. The "faction" was consistent enough in its support for parliamentary values and can be broadly viewed as favouring social democracy. Though mainly intellectuals, the "faction" had as its leader a former top-ranking officer of the Army's Political Department (Dmitri Volkogonov, who was also a well-known historian). The "faction" was close to *"Democratic Russia"* and evolved in a similar fashion (Figure 23).

"New Generation (New Politics)" was formed even before the opening of the First Congress and registered in May 1990. The "faction" united mainly young politicians aspiring to become the core of the future political elite. The "faction" members emphasised their adherence to Western democratic values. Their professed "centrism" had distinct social-democratic overtones. The "faction" was keen at conscientiously distancing itself from both extremes and was to be seen near the alternative "third" focal point in the second period (especially at the Seventh Congress, see Figure 14[24]). Having first moved to support Boris Yeltsin at the peak of his campaign against communists (the Third and the Fourth Congresses) and then Yeltsin's opponents during the institutional crisis (the Eighth and the Ninth Congresses), the "faction" apparently "travelled" longest around the political spectrum-map (Figure 24).

"Non-Party Deputies" were mainly non-elite intelligentsia, to a great extent provincial. The "faction", initially close to *"Democratic Russia"*, was gradually "drifting" toward the "Centre" (Figure 25).

"Radical Democrats" were constituted at the First Congress of People's Deputies (June 1990). The "faction" was among the staunchest proponents of market reforms. Paradoxically enough, its members also engaged in a typically populist style of political behaviour. While proclaiming itself "democratic", the "faction" was quite outspoken in its support of authoritarian presidency. It is interesting to note that, from the standpoint of their social background, the tone in the "faction" was set by the "military intelligentsia" (Vitali Urazhtsev, Sergei Yushenkov), and former law-enforcement officers (Vladimir Varov). There were many intellectuals as well (among the most prominent, Marina Sal'e), but these were largely concentrated in other "factions". As a result of the computations based on the above methods, the "faction" emerged as the farthest remote from *"Communists of Russia"*: the relative "distance" between the two "factions" proved invariably the longest of all.[25] It seemed logical therefore to substitute it for *"Democratic Russia"* as the second reference point for mapping the other "factions". It is in this capacity that the "faction" appears in all the figures that depict the evolution of political forces in the Russian parliament between the Second and the Ninth Congresses (Figures 17-28).

"Russia" emerged in autumn 1990, presumably as an alternative to both *Communists of Russia* and *Democratic Russia*. Socially, it was a rather heterogeneous group, uniting anti-Communist "patriots", the so called *derzhavniki*.[26] Their initial anti-communism quickly faded, as the empire they were so anxious to preserve collapsed before their eyes. Having sided with *"Communists of Russia"* in their attack against Yeltsin at the Third Congress (the first period), the "faction" distanced itself from them again in the second period - to eventually come to an all but complete fusion with *"Communists of Russia"* and *"Fatherland"* by the Ninth Congress (see Figure 26).

"Sovereignty and Equality" was a coalition of the Soviet "national" *nomenklatura*, i.e. the Party and state officials from the various national autonomous regions. With problems of regional government naturally at the top of its agenda, the "faction" was instrumental in rendering Russian politics multidimensional and emerged as the alternative "third" focal point when the entire pattern grew triangular in shape (see Figures 12-14 and 27). The pattern changed abruptly when the parliament came into conflict with the President (Figures 15-16), and the "faction" joined the amalgam of political forces rallied around *"Communists of Russia"* (Figure 27).

"Workers' Union" was formed at the First Congress (May 1990), originally as *Workers' and Peasants' Union*, and renamed *Workers' Union* -

Reform without Shock at the Second Congress (December 1990). Uniting working class deputies and "new" trade-union activists, the "faction" saw itself as moderately democratic and from April 1992 on was part of the bloc called *Constructive Forces* (together with *New Generation* and *Industrial Union*). The "faction" was moving ever closer to *"Radical Democrats"* throughout the first period, then away from them in the second period. It allied itself with the anti-presidential bloc that sprang up at the Eighth Congress, but was never properly in it (see Figures 15 and 28).

We have omitted factions that were formed after the Sixth Congress, such as *Motherland* and *Consensus for Progress*. It must also be noted that most factions had originally functioned as "deputy groups". There were many People's deputies who were suspicious of the very word "faction".[27] After the Sixth Congress the role of factions diminished again. The foreground was taken by blocs, which were rather amorphous alliances with intricate interrelations both between themselves and between their constitutive factions. The three blocs were *Constructive Forces* (formed by *Industrial Union, New Generation* and *Workers' Union*), *Democratic Centre* (*Free Russia, Left Centre, Non-Party Deputies* and *Sovereignty and Equality*) and *Russian Unity* (*Agrarian Union, Civil Society, Communists of Russia, Fatherland* and *Russia*). *Democratic Russia* and *Radical Democrats* joined none of these, but formed an alliance called *Coalition in Support of Reform* on the basis of non-exclusive individual membership.

The formal analysis of political positions (by the methods described above) seems to confirm our earlier classification of "factions" that was based on political statements and platform planks. Figures 9-16 show the evolution of political spectrum between the Second and the Ninth Congresses. (The reference "axis" is flanked by *"Communists of Russia"*, on the one end, and *"Democratic Russia"*, on the other, i.e. the two principal rivals at the opening of the parliament.) Figures 17-28 depict the evolution of individual "factions". (The reference "axis" is flanked by *"Communists of Russia"* and *"Radical Democrats"*, that eventually emerged as the two most "remote" of all the "factions".)

Conclusions

Judging from these figures, the history of the Russian parliament of 1990-93 can be divided into three periods roughly corresponding to the periods described above.[28]

The first four Congresses demonstrated confrontational politics that best approximated to the classical "linear" model of the political spectrum (see Figures 9-11). Most striking is the Third Congress (March-April 1991, Figure 10): two focal points are distinctly visible, the borderline is clear-cut, with only one "faction", *"Industrial Union"*, more or less equally removed from the two extremes.

The second period (from the Fifth to the Seventh Congress, Figures 12-14) saw the "factions" "drift" away from the two extremes. The old "poles" were left in relative isolation and, with the issue of federalism coming to the foreground, a third focal point emerged, occupied by *"Sovereignty and Equality"*. The entire pattern became triangular in shape. *"Sovereignty and Equality"*, together with *"New Generation (New Politics)"*, constituted the core of the alternative "third force". The rest of the "factions" spread around the centre of the "triangle".

The third period (the Eighth and the Ninth Congresses,[29] Figures 15-16) was marked by a new confrontation, this time with the President. *"Radical Democrats"* were in obvious isolation. It is this almost complete estrangement of the most "pro-presidential" of all the "factions" that enables us to assert that the conflict between the parliament and the President was institutional rather than ideological. Almost all other "factions" (including those that would normally support the President's policies, "democratic", as well as "centrist") seemed to consolidate around the anti-presidential focus as represented by *"Communists of Russia"* (most visibly, at the Eighth Congress; see Figure 15).

Summing up, one may say that the first period was characterised by an institutional conflict with the Union authorities and a sharp ideological confrontation between communists and democrats. Politics of the second period (after the election of the first Russian President and before an open break with him) revolved around the issues of economic reform and federalism and approached closest to the classic model of parliamentary politics. Throughout the third period the parliament was busy fighting the President; in this it managed to achieve, despite obvious ideological divisions, relative political consolidation born out of mutual desire for institutional survival. This summary is also confirmed by the evolution of individual "factions" (see Figures 17-28).

The misfortune of the Russian parliament was that this institutional conflict unfolded in a dualistic atmosphere of an acute cultural crisis. Moreover, despite the fact that the logic of its leaders' behaviour was determined largely by institutional, as distinct from ideological, considerations (as the above analysis indicates), the parliament readily allowed itself to get involved in an ideological confrontation and embark on a kind of holy crusade. It proved able to win the first campaign, against its Union counterpart, because it had on its side all the advantages of mass resentment against the old regime. It was far less fortunate when it came to challenging its own former chairman become President. With most democratic prejudice in its favour, the parliament might stand a fair chance of winning a purely institutional conflict even if it were initially denied, as in fact it was, the means of mobilisation available to political parties. But to wage its institutional war in the spirit of dualism would amount to discarding its main trump, the type of social integration it embodied and promised.

Notes

[1] The following analysis (Chapters 7-8) summarises some of the results of the research project fulfilled in 1993-94 in collaboration between the Department of Politics, the University of Leeds, and the Centre for Analysis of Scientific and Industrial Policies, the Russian Academy of Sciences, with the support of the Social and Economic Research Council, Great Britain (ESRC Award Reference No. R000234454, "Political Culture and Social Innovation: The Russian Supreme Soviet"). The results, both preliminary and final, have been published in (1) N.Biryukov, J.Gleisner and V.Sergeyev, "The Crisis of *Sobornost'*: Parliamentary Discourse in Present-Day Russia", *Discourse and Society*, vol. 6, No. 2; (2) V.Sergeyev, A.Belyaev, N.Biryukov, Ya.Dranyov and J.Gleisner, "Voting in the Russian Parliament (1990-93): The Spectrum of Political Forces and the Conflict between the Executive and the Legislative", *Journal of Behavioral and Social Sciences*, No. 2 (special issue on "Parliamentary System and Presidential System in Crisis); (3) N.Biryukov, L.Byzov, J.Gleisner and V.Sergeyev, "Emergence of a New System of Political Forces and a New State Order in Russia, 1990-93", *Journal of Contemporary History* (forthcoming); (4) V.Sergeyev, A.Belyaev, N.Biryukov, Ya.Dranyov and J.Gleisner, "Group Voting Behaviour and the Evolution of Political Spectrum: The Russian Parliament in 1990-93", *CENSIS* (forthcoming). They have been presented at the International Symposium on "Presidential System and Parliamentary System in Crisis" (Tokai University Pacific Center, Honolulu, Hawaii, 3-6 November 1994; N.Biryukov).

[2] See Sobyanin and Yuriev 1991.

[3] To our knowledge, the results have not been published and circulated only within the Supreme Soviet.

[4] See McFaul *et al.* 1994.

[5] The reasons behind this approach are analysed in "Introduction".

[6] See Sub-section on "Methods of Inquiry" in Section 3 of this chapter, for a detailed description of the method.

[7] By the end of May 1990 25 such groups were registered by the Secretariat of the First Congress (see *First Congress RSFSR* 1992, Vol. 2, pp. 266-7 and 407).

[8] For the text of the resolution, see Koval' (ed.) 1993, p. 71.

[9] See Sub-section on "Internal Homogeneity of Factions" in Section 2 of this chapter for details.

[10] No computerised roll call information is available for the First Congress, as the necessary equipment had not been installed; and for the Tenth Congress, for obvious reasons (see Note 112 to Chapter 6).

[11] See Sub-section on "Methods of Inquiry" in Section 3 of this chapter for the detailed description of the techniques involved.

[12] See, for example, Hammond and Fraser 1983; Satarov and Stankevich 1983.

[13] See Alker and Russett 1965.

[14] See Sub-section on "Methods of Inquiry" in Section 3 of this chapter for comments on the political spectrum and the salience of the Sixth Congress. For similar figures relating to some of the other Congresses, viz. the Third and the Eighth (as representative of, respectively, the earlier and the later periods of the parliament's history), see Sergeyev *et al.* 1995. No significant differences will however be observed.

[15] All deputies whose names began with "A".

[16] The deviations from the "faction line" seem not to exceed the permissible limit of operator mistakes. (Roll calls are rare occasions in the Bundestag, and the computations were fulfilled on data spanning several years; the data had to be entered into the computer manually).

[17] See Sub-section on "The Ninth Congress" in Section 3, Chapter 6.

[18] This did not necessarily imply leaving one faction and joining another. Unlike registered factions, many deputy groups did not require exclusive membership. However, from our computations we have excluded groups that were based on principles other than political affinity: occupational and territorial affiliations or problem-centred groups (such as *Military Servicemen, Medical Workers, Moscow Deputy Group, Army Reform, Chernobyl, Glasnost', Soviets and Local Government, The North*, ethics group, etc.). We have also reduced the total number of groups by identifying groups that, although changing names, tended to "inherit" membership, e.g. *Communists for Democracy* and *Free Russia*.

[19] The calculations are based on the data published in Barsenkov et al. 1993b.

[20] When seen in the historic perspective, this two-dimensional pattern seems to be a regular feature of revolutionary politics: France witnessed the basic issue of eliminating the *ancien regime* overburdened with the problem of centralism, the United States and Argentina had to deal with the issue of federalism while fighting their wars of independence. (See Jaures 1969-72, T. 5, ch. 9; Hamilton *et. al.* 1961; Gandia 1940).

[21] The Fifth Congress proved, indeed, a rare exception in this respect in that it also accounted for the highest relative individual deviation of 16.2 against the initial distance of 26 (between *New Generation* and *Sovereignty and Equality*). A similar, though lower, distortion was observed for these factions' relative positions at the Sixth Congress. Otherwise, comparatively high relative deviations affected very close "factions" only. To judge from the relative average deviations, even these distortions failed to upset the general disposition, and the overall pictures can be considered as reasonably authentic. At any rate, in most cases deviations were far less significant than that.

[22] Noteworthy, however, is the surprising fact that the "factions'" spokesmen were not particularly eager to enlarge upon the subject.

[23] See Section 2 "Semantic Correlates of *Sobornost'*: Populist Rhetoric at the Ninth Congress of People's Deputies" in Chapter 8.

[24] See Note 21 to this Chapter.

[25] Measured as the number of non-concurrent positions in the voting lines, these "distances" were for Congresses from Second to Ninth, respectively 58 (54), 181 (180), 102 (97), 38 (32), 257 (227), 132 (126), 58 (58), 49 (49). Figures in brackets are the next highest. With one

exception only, these happen to be the "distances" between *"Radical Democrats"* (again) and *"Fatherland"*. (The exception was the Fifth Congress, when the second, but still the second, greatest "distance" proved to be that between *"Democratic Russia"* and *"Communists of Russia"*.)

[26] See Note 15 to Chapter 4.

[27] For the anti-factional bias of the Russian political culture, see Sub-section on *"Sobornost'* as a Model of Political Representation" in Section 1, Chapter 3 and Sergeyev and Biryukov 1993, pp. 147-51.

[28] See Sub-section on "The Political Structure of the Russian Parliament and the Problem of Factions' Identity" in Section 1 of this chapter.

[29] The Tenth Congress would obviously fall within this period, but no roll calls seem to have been made at it (the electronic system, at least, was not used; see Note 112 to Chapter 6); at any rate, the data, if exist, are not available for analysis.

8   The People and the Legislative: Populist Trends in Contemporary Parliamentary Discourse

... it must be admitted that they share the birthright of all speakers, that of speaking unclearly and untruly.
                                                          J.Austin, "Other Minds".

1. The Problem of Political Agency: Methodological Considerations

Throughout this book we have had many occasions to comment on the anti-parliamentarianism of the Russian political culture. We have examined the three troubled years of the first Russian post-communist parliament and observed its eventual defeat at the hands of the executive. The latter did not hesitate to take advantage of the antiparliamentarian attitudes of the Russian political elite and the bulk of the populace in order to enhance its chances in that institutional conflict. The executive's victory was furthermore facilitated by the apparent flaws in the performance of the parliament itself. The crucial question is whether the Russian parliamentary elite has acquired any features and skills that promise to make their activities more effective. In our opinion, the future of Russian democracy depends on the answer to this question.

Our approach in this chapter is to inquire into basic cognitive structures behind the Russian parliamentary discourse and to ascertain whether records of recent parliamentary debates contain any signs of transition from the traditional (organismic) to the modern (procedural) understanding of politics and promise corresponding changes in the type of social integration. Or, to be more specific, whether the traditional understanding of the people as a single whole (characteristic of the culture of sobornost') and the main, if not only, history-maker (characteristic of the populist version thereof and explicitly asserted by the less sophisticated versions of Marxist theory of historical materialism) is undergoing any meaningful change as compared to the previous stage of Russia's parliamentary development?

Our theoretical assumptions can be summarised as follows. Formally speaking, predicates of actions can be referred to subjects of different kinds. Some of these stand for agencies that are capable of purposeful actions, i.e. can think in terms of ends and means, describe and evaluate situations in rational (or, at least, coherent) ways and plan series of steps meant to lead to designated goals.

An individual person obviously fits the description. The qualification can also be extended to include organisations, provided they have the proper deliberating and decision-making structures. A political party of the classic West European type would be a good example of such an organisation. A still better example is provided by parliaments.

A different category is formed by agencies that can be said to perform actions, but only of the kind that are neither purposeful nor planned. Typical examples, though hardly of importance in political discourse, are natural elements: a snowstorm can damage communication lines, but does not do it intentionally. These need not concern us here: our interest is with "pseudo-agencies" of the sort that stand for collective human actions. Most important or, at least, most common among them are entities like "the people", "the nation" or a "social group".

Whereas the procedural understanding of politics is based on the assumption that "biography is about chaps" and politics is the game of those who are capable of purposeful actions, in the discourse of *sobornost'* actions are typically attributed to pseudo-agencies. In certain contexts this makes little or no sense. A statement like "The nation is reviewing the consequences of the defeat" sounds bizarre, though it would appear appropriate if applied to individual politicians or political parties. The trick is that though we have no reason to deny that anyone can deliberate on "the consequences of a defeat", it would be hard to expect different individual contemplations to yield a coherent result, unless some special coordinating organs have seen to that. It is logically possible, of course, to assume such coherency to be a spontaneous product of social interaction or, better still, of identical dispositions. But taking these for granted would constitute the mode of thinking defined earlier as *sobornost'*.

Sometimes such expressions are mere metaphors (cf. a contemporary Russian philosopher's[1] alleged reaction to the results of December 1993 election: "Russia, you have gone mad!"). However, even statements like this become substantial in the framework of *sobornost'*: for whether they are intended as metaphors or not, they need not be recognised as such and can well be accepted as plain statements of fact. This is a good example, indeed, of the anti-procedural mode of thinking (characteristic of the culture of *sobornost'*) which makes no special distinction between actions that are purposeful and planned and those spontaneous reactions that are motivated by "the immediate grasping of the situation".

One of the more important by-products of this mode of thinking is the inability to see the fundamental difference between a political party and a political movement, and hence the inability to form political parties that would function like their western prototypes. Unlike political parties, political movements usually dispense with centralised coordinating and decision-making organs and basically rely on what spontaneous coordination arises out of the participants' similar views and aspirations. This spontaneous "coordination" can sometimes be effective at "negative" stages of political conflicts (while fighting *against*), but proves futile when it comes to doing something constructive.

It is worthwhile noting here that in the Soviet political discourse the "Party", presumably the key factor in the amazing Soviet achievements, would regularly be depicted not so much as a political institution (with organs and procedures cleverly designed to secure this outstanding performance), but rather as some semi-mystic union of people who directly communicate with "the spirit of history" (or, in a more "materialistic" interpretation, are endowed with the capacity to "grasp" the objective tendency of the historic process) and are, therefore, infallible.

Since it is not the culture of *sobornost'* as such that is the subject of this study, but its crisis (and possible disintegration), we need operational criteria that would allow us to establish the fact and evaluate the extent of the changes. Analyses of texts that relate to the Soviet period have revealed the predominance of pseudo-agencies (such as "the peace-loving peoples of the world", "the reactionary forces", "the imperialist circles", etc.), at least in the official political discourse; it was precisely this overflow of pseudo-agencies that made those texts sound so incomparably meaningless.[2] However, Soviet political discourse was also capable of accommodating authentic political agencies when it came to matters of genuine concern to the key decision-makers, as a study of the 1963 tripartite negotiations on the limited nuclear test-ban indicates.[3]

For that study a special technique of text structure representation was developed, based on the cognitive maps method and intended to identify types of political discourse.[4] The idea was to use the notion of "process" to distinguish authentic political agencies from pseudo-agencies.

In Soviet political discourse political situations were ordinarily presented as clusters of interacting processes. Each process would be characterised by a certain degree of intensity, and changes in political situations would be attributed to changes in the intensity of one (or some) of the constituent processes. Typical examples are statements like "the might of the Socialist camp has increased" or "the peace movement is growing increasingly active".

This ontological pattern determines the structure of activity. In contrast to the causal sequence typical for texts that deal with authentic agencies, a "process" presupposes no purpose (for a process's end-point is not, strictly speaking, an objective) and, consequently, no action planning. When it comes to interpreting the outcome, therefore, it is the intensity of effort that is to be assessed rather than the quality of planning. The idea behind this attitude is that since a "process" is something organic and indivisible, "improvement" can only mean "acceleration" and the only means to accelerate a "process" is to intensify efforts that contribute to it. Characteristic in this respect are metaphors commonly used in the Soviet political discourse to express this attitude. One most striking was Gorbachev's slogan of *"uskorenie"* ("acceleration").

Contrasting "processes" with "procedures" and authentic "agencies" with "pseudo-agencies" seems a handy operationalisation of differences between polar political cultures, viz. the western procedure-oriented culture and the process-oriented culture of *sobornost'*. If this is true, changes in this respect could be used to identify potential cultural transformations.

Cultures do not change overnight. It is therefore reasonable to expect different modes of thinking to alternate with each other, and a particular pattern of alternation can be quite symptomatic.

The hypothesis underlying this study is that explanatory techniques used in political discourse range along a certain scale of accessibility and that whereas in stable cultural situations the difference is basically that of greater or lesser sophistication, in situations of cultural transformation (i.e. a transition from one type of political culture to another) alternative socio-ontological models are usually involved. Cultural changes begin with values. This is because values are salient. On the other hand, they are cultures' most superficial elements. (Besides, first to be adopted are most likely to be what are called "facade values".) New values can coexist with old beliefs stored at deeper levels of consciousness. "Deeper" does not necessarily mean "less accessible". New modes of thinking require deliberate effort and are usually practised in situations of relative emotional ease. On the contrary, in crisis situations, when cognitive horizons shrink under the strain of circumstance, tested familiar stereotypes are much more likely to be invoked.

But familiarity of explanatory techniques alone does not guarantee plausibility of particular explanations. Even routine explanations must at least seem to fit the situation. However, pseudo-agencies and crises prove agreeable: if reference to a pseudo-agency does have a shade of plausibility, this is, indeed, in a crisis situation, i.e. a situation in which a collective entity like "the people" can be said to live in conditions that are more or less the same for all the persons involved.

But even a general crisis is a manifold setting and does not necessarily have to affect everyone in the same way. The present economic situation in Russia, for instance, cannot convey the same meaning for the 5 to 10 percent of the population who have become or expect to become very rich, on the one hand, and those 40 to 50 percent who have been or are likely to be driven to the verge of poverty. For such a situation to fit the pattern of *sobornost'*, it must be "re-defined" so as to appear to preserve a universal meaning. This is basically a rhetorical (or propagandistic) problem that is usually solved by concentrating on a selected aspect of the situation and insistently presenting it as the only really important one.

Russian radical democrats have once succeeded in portraying the present plight as a struggle between the communist elite and the democratic masses. Elsewhere we have already argued that the Soviet political culture was, indeed, an elitist version of the traditional culture, which also allowed of a populist interpretation. The collapse of the Soviet political system has brought about differentiation of the populist (typical of the late 19th century) and elitist (Marxist or, rather, Leninist) elements of the syncretism created by the October revolution. "The people" regained that mysterious quality of being always right and always in tune with the ultimate reality it once had to cede to Bolsheviks, the self-professed midwives of the historic progress.[5]

The practical methodological problem is how to distinguish between references to "the people" that suggest the mentality of *sobornost'* and the conventional democratic rhetoric. Cognitive maps provide the answer.

As a rule, it is not difficult to identify formal political agencies in the conventional western political discourse pivoted on institutions and procedures. Nor is it difficult to determine the agencies' character traits, goals and values as viewed and presented by the speaker (author). Simple syntax analysis usually allows specification of (a) the circumstances in which the agency operates, (b) its actions and (c) the consequences of these actions. On this basis a standard causal explanation can then be constructed that would normally include: (i) the antecedent in which the agency's name is the subject and values, goals, character traits and/or circumstances are the predicate(s); (ii) the operator of implication; and (iii) the consequent in which the action(s) is (are) the subject and the outcome is the predicate.

This explanatory pattern is scarcely possible if one deals with a pseudo-agency. A subject of this kind is not easily predicated. Circumstances are not likely to be the same for "the whole people": exceptions (such as a state of war) are feasible, but rare, while apart from them generalisations make little sense. Common "mental predicates" are even harder to pinpoint: shared values are usually not specific enough to account for concrete actions and it is not realistic to expect a goal to be shared by "all the people" unanimously unless in an exceptional situation. Thus, exceptionability emerges as a *conditio sine qua non* of a causal explanation that involves a pseudo-agency (hence the persistent recurrence of exceptional circumstances in the Soviet political discourse) and can serve as a convenient marker.

Situational and mental predicates excluded, the only viable alternative is reference to a character predicate, i.e. the agency's intrinsic and, therefore, inalienable attribute. Here enters the "process": a continuous cause must have a perpetual effect. By this way a description of a concrete time-related situation is supplanted by a description of a never-ending sequence, a flow of events only varying in intensity. This would in turn presuppose the agency's spontaneous (i.e. mindless) activity as a logically indispensable parameter of the situation. "Process" can therefore be used as another semantic marker of pseudo-agency.

2. Semantic Correlates of *Sobornost'*:
Populist Rhetoric at the Ninth Congress of People's Deputies

Methods of Inquiry

To verify this hypothesis, we have undertaken a comprehensive study of the verbatim records of the Congresses of People's Deputies of the Russian Federation (1990-3). By means of semantic analysis of the use of a number of selected notions we have hoped to detect potential changes in patterns of political thinking.

In this chapter we present the findings that relate to the Ninth Congress (26-29 March 1993). There are three reasons that determine this choice. On the one hand, this was one of the shortest Congresses in the three-year history of the institution: convened but a few days after the previous Eighth Congress was over and immediately after President Yeltsin's TV address in which he had expressed his intention to introduce a "special regime of government" and the Constitutional Court's nightly session denouncing the President's move, the Congress had extraordinary status and lasted for four days.[6] This has enabled us to meet two requirements that are hardly compatible under most circumstances, viz. to make the study both short and exhaustive. On the other hand, the situation of crisis the Congress had to deal with proved instrumental in pushing aside the newly acquired habits of thought and exposing the latent ontological attitudes of the Russian political elite (as envisaged by the cognitive model).[7] The Congress, it will be recalled, failed to impeach the President, as was initially suggested (although the President's was a pyrrhic victory), and agreed to hold a national vote of confidence for both the President and itself scheduled for 25 April 1993.[8] The last, but not the least of our considerations has been that the Ninth Congress is the latest one for which complete verbatim records are available and may therefore be reasonably assumed to represent the final stage in the cultural development in question.

Our conclusions are based on the use of the term "the people" (or its functional substitutes, like "the nation", "Russia", etc.) by members of the Congress. The choice of the notion has been motivated by the role that terms representing "pseudo-agencies" play in Russian political discourse. We have registered all of the occasions "the people" (or its synonyms) appear in the records. (Our concern was naturally with nouns, but one exception appeared necessary. That was the expression "the President of the all-nation choice", adverbial in Russian, but obviously conveying the meaning of a collective entity's unanimous, *sobornost'*-style action.) We realise, of course, that using the term does not necessarily imply it stands for a political agency. We have, therefore, sought to separate the latter interpretation, using the semantic methods described in the previous section.

It has also been our assumption that conclusions of significance can only be made on a comparative basis. For this reason we have been more concerned with the notion's relative frequency than with the absolute number of instances in which it occurs in the texts. For that reason the texts have been measured and the relative frequencies calculated by dividing the number of cases the relevant words appear in the speeches by the speeches' lengths, expressed in arbitrary units (see Tables 3-5 for details). The frequencies themselves are given in relative units, "1" being the average for the particular selection of texts (with the exception of Figure 35, where for reasons of scale the average is given as "10").

After the data were compiled in a master table (arranged by the sittings), they were processed in various ways. The master table itself is naturally too large to fit in a book of reasonable volume; its summary will be found in the Appendix (Figures 29 and 30, Table 3). Since the distribution of pseudo-agencies has proved far from even, we have deemed it expedient to deal with smaller units than the sittings and have summarised the data by the parts thereof (using the officially announced breaks to demarcate the parts).

Moreover, as even within these parts of the sittings the use of pseudo-agencies was by no means uniform and the relevant terms tended to occur in clusters of speeches closely following one another, we have chosen one of the sub-sittings (the second part of the fifth sitting) for a comprehensive presentation to demonstrate this "infection" pattern (Figures 31 and 32).

Our next step has been to re-arrange the data by factions (Figures 33 and 34, Table 4). These have then been ranged in the reverse order of frequencies to provide a comparative review of the Russian political elite's mental patterns (Figure 35, Table 5). Since our conclusions are based primarily on the interpretation of this scale and as the relative frequency, and hence the faction's position on the scale, depend on the texts' length, as well as on the occurrence of pseudo-agencies, these appear in Figure 35 as the background columns for reference and possible corrections.

Discussion

Our findings reveal significant differences in the use of pseudo-agencies, both between sittings and between factions. Of the 14 sub-sittings of the Ninth Congress four stand out as particularly abundant in pseudo-agencies. These are the second part of the first sitting, the second sitting, the first part of the third sitting (the record occurrence of 41 instances and the record frequency of 2.5 points) and the second part of the fifth sitting (see Figures 29 and 30, Table 3). On the other hand, three sub-sittings heard no mention of pseudo-agencies: the first part of the fifth sitting, the second and the third parts of the sixth sitting. Though they were all very short (the total length of texts 52, 56 and 46, respectively, i.e. about one tenth of the average) and can safely be ignored, we still have at least six sub-sittings of normal duration with the occurrence of pseudo-agencies well below the record.

Such a marked difference calls for an explanation. Contextual analysis demonstrates that the use (or disuse) of pseudo-agencies depends on the character of debates: they disappear almost entirely when the deputies are engaged in routine parliamentary work (working out and editing their decisions) and promptly appear again when real or imaginary crises provoke confrontation.

The Congress started by setting the agenda. The twofold character of the issue, both procedural and political, is reflected in the moderate use of pseudo-agencies (occurrence 6, relative frequency 0.5). This increased sharply when the general discussion of the situation began after the introductory speeches by the Chairman of the Constitutional Court before and by the President immediately after the break (occurrence 13, relative frequency 1.5). This was continued at the second sitting and the first part of the third sitting (occurrence 34 and 41, relative frequency 2.2 and 2.5, respectively).

After the break the Congress voted to end the discussion, making exception for a couple of selected deputies. One of the speeches that followed, containing a characteristic "processual" (also confrontational) statement "The general crisis is growing deeper",[9] accounts for the only reappearance of a pseudo-agency at the sub-sitting. Otherwise, this comparatively short session was confined to an exchange of opinions between the Chairman of the Supreme Soviet (Ruslan Khasbulatov) and the

Chairman of the Order Group (Grigori Dorofeyev) about the priority of steps *apropos* the future resolution (occurrence 1, relative frequency 0.2).

At their fourth sitting the deputies considered the proposals concerning the referendum and proceeded to work on the resolution about "urgent measures to secure the constitutional order". Since both issues had political (highly confrontational) as well as procedural aspects, the sitting was characterised by a comparatively moderate use of pseudo-agencies (occurrence 8, relative frequency 0.6).

The fifth sitting opened with Khasbulatov's short speech in which the Chairman of the Supreme Soviet outlined the compromise decision worked out by a number of key actors the night before. The proposal was strongly condemned by leaders of the "irreconcilable opposition". The discussion that followed yielded a high number of pseudo-agencies (occurrence 31, relative frequency 1.6), though mainly concentrated over a comparatively short period of time. (We shall come back to this topic after we have completed the general review of the Congress.)

During the first part of the sixth sitting the deputies were preoccupied with the text of the resolution on the state-owned mass media. This routine work produced the lowest use of pseudo-agencies for a sub-sitting of normal duration (occurrence 2, relative frequency 0.2). Both of the other parts of the sixth sitting were very short and can be omitted from the analysis.

The last three sub-sittings were basically of the same character: laborious and rather monotonous work on the numerous amendments to the two principal resolutions, on securing the constitutional order and on the referendum (occurrence 7, 4, 8, relative frequency 0.5, 0.4, 0.4).

To come back to the fifth session, the discourse of pseudo-agencies seems to follow a rather peculiar pattern of distribution. Of the 31 instances in which the pseudo-agencies appear in the debate, 26 are found in only five speeches that practically follow each other (Figures 31 and 32, entries 19, 20, 22, 24, 26). Though only two factions, *Radical Democrats* and *Democratic Russia*, account for 21 of these, they do not stand alone and, what is more important, they do not always demonstrate the same uniformity. (We shall deal with the factions somewhat later.) So this is not a matter of factions temporarily monopolising the rostrum - or, at least, not this alone, - especially as the next two sequences, albeit far less impressive, involve members of other factions (entries 32, 33 and 39, 40).

However, if our hypothesis about levels of accessibility is correct, this overconcentration was to be expected. It is simply a by-product of a situation-triggered relapse into traditional patterns of thinking. The relapse becomes "infectious", because its very presence serves to increase the tension that has first produced it.

The first speaker (Gennadi Benov, *Fatherland*) just mentions "our long-suffering Russia".[10] The next one (Vitali Urazhtsev, *Radical Democrats*, but speaking on behalf of the deputy group "Army Reform") begins with a statement that "the people are agitated"[11] and then proceeds to talk of them being maltreated:

> Why did these men [members of the military establishment] steal the people's property and why are they not going to give it back to the people?[12]

The third speaker (Vladimir Varov, *Radical Democrats*) gets very emotional:

> But I am afraid of something even more terrible. I am afraid of treachery - treachery of the people, and again by all branches of power.[13]

The fourth one (Alexei Surkov, *Democratic Russia*) is already burning with indignation:

> ... we must consider who has come here and why. If they have come here to help Russia out of [this] economic situation and political dead end, this is one thing... But this is in case we want something to originate here, beside the purpose for which maybe half have come here of those who have long cherished a purpose... [sic!] What purpose? To drive Russia to a kind of instability that will make Bosnia and Herzegovina [appear], as the saying goes, a normal phenomenon. And then to prove: here, the people, you have got rid of the Communist ideology, here, the people, you have elected this President, now look, where we have come, gentlemen.
>
> We must think after all, and first of all of our morality. Russia is standing behind us. If not behind you, then behind us Russia is standing, and we must therefore think of how this Russia is going to sow now, how this Russia is going to harvest. How this Russia will really create the business class, create the farmer class. You don't need it. You have long since forgotten about it. You need power. You have no other wish but power.[14]

Then, after a speech totally devoid of pseudo-agencies (Umar Temirov, *Sovereignty and Equality*), there gradually comes an appeasement (Georgi Smol'ski, *Industrial Union*):

The people have given us rights and hence they must be used.
Can the people set us a deadline like that? I think not.[15]

Let us now turn to the most significant and, perhaps, the most sensational of our findings, those relating to the factions (Figures 33, 34 and 35, Tables 4 and 5).

Factions differ sharply as to the use of pseudo-agencies, both in occurrence, from 22 (*Democratic Russia*) to 2 (*Sovereignty and Equality*), and in frequency, from 3.4 (*Motherland*) to 0.3 (*Communists of Russia*).

Most revealing, however, is the scale made up by ranging the factions in the reverse order of frequencies (Figure 35). It is, perhaps, not too surprising that (but for a few casual exceptions easy to explain away) the scale correlates with the general political spectrum.[16] On the one end we have *Communists of Russia* (occurrence 4, relative frequency 0.3), neighbouring on *Sovereignty and Equality* (occurrence 2, relative frequency 0.4); on the other end (leaving aside *Motherland*, a faction with a somewhat indistinct political complexion, whose outstanding record may simply be due the lowest participation, and *Industrial Union*, the second-least participant, see Figure 33, Table 5) one finds the two principal democratic factions, viz. *Democratic Russia* (occurrence 22, relative frequency 3.0) and *Radical Democrats* (occurrence 14, relative frequency 2.0) closely followed by *Consensus for Progress* (occurrence 10, relative frequency 1.8) and *Left Centre - Cooperation* (occurrence 8, relative frequency 1.7). The central sector is occupied by the "patriotic" (*Fatherland, Russia, Agrarian Union*) and "centrist", or rather, "drifting" factions (*New Generation - New Politics* and *Workers' Union - Reforms without Shock*), all bordering on the average. *Free Russia*, also a complicated blend of politicians, would have been among the latter, but for the outstanding participation (especially at the last two sittings) owed basically to Nikolai Ryabov, spokesman for the Editorial Commission. (The record participation of the no-faction group was mainly due to Ruslan Khasbulatov's chairing most of the sittings, as *Communists of Russia* owed much of theirs to the similar status of Yuri Voronin. It must also be noted that *Fatherland* was likely to be farther up the scale, had not Ravkat Chebotarevski swelled its participation by talking shop on behalf of the Counting Commission of which he was the Chairman. The record-holding *Motherland* would also look more natural if accommodated somewhere close-by.)

Taking correlation with the political spectrum for granted, what remains surprising is the scale's vector - the opposite to what might be expected.

Conclusions

This reversal may well point to significant changes in the mentality of the Russian political elite. For, strange as it may sound, the political forces that advocate radical reforms (involving substantial institutional transformations) still can and do resort to the traditional anti-institutional rhetoric of *sobornost'*. The possibility is also available to the "*derzhavniki*" whose primary concern is restoration of the empire (the former Soviet Union),[17] though their record, with the exception of *Motherland*, was not particularly impressive.

On the contrary, the communists, once so dexterous in the rhetoric of *sobornost'*,[18] have now found themselves in a situation where they can no longer exercise their renowned skills. The explanation is, indeed, very simple. This party claims to be concerned, first and foremost, with the grave economic situation. Since the present economic situation stratifies rather than consolidates the society, appeal to "the people" as a whole becomes irrelevant. This is all the more so as the primary beneficiaries of the Gaidar/Chubais-style privatisation (and, consequently, the communists' principal target) are bureaucrats, old as well as new, i.e. a social group that certainly can be contrasted with "the people" but, unlike the bourgeoisie, cannot be "annihilated". The result is that the present-day communists cannot follow the example of their Bolshevik predecessors and invoke the traditional Russian political utopia of *sobornost'* by combining the Marxist theory of class struggle with the no-less-Marxist myth of a future classless society. This explains why references to "the people" have almost disappeared from the Communist discourse, though they are still prominent in the rhetoric of radical democrats and non-communist "patriots" (factions like *Motherland* or the former *Civil Society*[19]). Unlike the latter, *Sovereignty and Equality*, which basically represents the establishment of the national autonomous units, combines a communist background with a genuine mistrust of overcentralisation. The rhetoric of *sobornost'* is naturally not welcome in this political niche, although militant nationalists, their primary rivals at the local level, might well find an adequate native substitute.

Thus the new political or, rather, socio-economic situation affects a major component of the political culture, at least as far the communist segment of the political spectrum is concerned. These changes seem to correlate with the communists' sudden turn towards political pluralism and their surprising concern for parliamentary procedures, as amply demonstrated by Ivan Rybkin, one of their former leaders and later their successful nominee for the chairmanship of the State Duma.[20]

Here is a fundamental paradox: bureaucratic quasi-reforms promoted by radical democrats have forced communists from their traditional cultural stronghold and encouraged them to acquire new political skills. The result is that we now have, on the one hand, a democratic President who owes his position to the election campaigns of 1989-91 conducted very much in the spirit of *sobornost'* and to *sobornost'*-minded voters, a President whose primary support in the period of question came from factions most avid for the rhetoric of *sobornost'*, and, on the other hand, a post-communist parliament about to get engaged (if its leaders are to be believed) to classical social democracy.

This last transformation seems to have begun at the Sixth Congress (April 1992) and passed a turning point after the September-October crisis and the election of 12 December 1993. By "privatizing" *sobornost'* radical democrats, perhaps unknowingly to themselves, have enlisted support for the procedure-oriented political culture of the likely winners of the next political round. We have already witnessed similar developments, first in Lithuania (where nationalistic populism served as a native functional analogue of *sobornost'*) and then in Hungary and Poland.

It is true, Russia has already seen communists espouse the cause of democracy and is only too familiar with the kind of democracy they brought it. But it is also a fact that the present-day descendants of the Bolsheviks can no longer use their old tricks to win mass support. Conceptually this is, perhaps, our most important point: political culture, as embodied in operational experience, is likely to prove of greater significance in the long run than declared political goals. Russians have often been reproached for favouring authoritarianism, but who would suspect democrats of becoming its most eloquent defenders? We have already heard champions of human rights and popular freedoms praise

Pinochet. Shall we see former worshippers of Lenin seek the friendship of European socialists?

Notes

[1] Yuri Karyakin.

[2] See Sergeyev 1991.

[3] See Bohnam *et al.* (forthcoming).

[4] See Sergeyev 1987, Parshin and Sergeyev 1990.

[5] See Sergeyev and Biryukov 1993, pp. 145-6.

[6] See Note 28 to Chapter 4.

[7] This consideration made us prefer the Ninth to the Fourth and the Eighth Congresses that also lasted for four days, but seemed, on the whole, less dramatic. It might have been more rewarding, from this standpoint, to turn to the Tenth Congress, convened after President Yeltsin's decree on "the step-by-step constitutional reform". However, some of the factions did not attend (which could not help distorting the overall picture) and, anyway, the Congress's records are not available.

[8] See Sub-section on "The Ninth Congress" in Section 3, Chapter 6.

[9] A.Tuleyev's (*Fatherland*) speech, *Ninth Congress* 1993, Bulletin 3, p. 20.

[10] Ibid., Bulletin 5, p. 11.

[11] Ibid..

[12] Ibid., p. 12.

[13] Ibid.

[14] Ibid., p. 13.

[15] Ibid., p. 14.

[16] For a detailed discussion of the political spectrum of the Congress of People's Deputies, see Section 3 "The Conflict of Powers and the Evolution of Political Forces" in Chapter 7.

[17] See Note 15 to Chapter 4.

[18] On a typical example of this rhetoric as used by a communist politician, see V.Mesyats's undelivered address at the First Congress of People's Deputies of the USSR (*First Congress USSR* 1989, Vol. 5, pp. 316-17) and our analysis thereof in Biryukov and Sergeyev 1993 and, somewhat more detailed, in Sergeyev and Biryukov 1993, pp. 136-40. Mesyats was First Secretary of the Moscow Regional Party Committee.

[19] By the time of the Ninth Congress *Civil Society* was disbanded.

[20] In 1993 Rybkin ran for the State Duma on the Agrarian Party list.

9 Legislation of the Second Republic: Democratic Values and Democratic Procedures in the Juridical Context of *Sobornost'*

Surprised I am that the Sons of Earth do not care for the meaning of words of the Law and the essence of their being.

"Zohar".

1. Processual Thinking and Framing Legislation: Methods of Analysis

We now turn to the analysis of the legislative's main, or, at least, name-giving function, law-making. If the parliament is to become the principal agent in transforming the nation's political culture, instrumental in ensuring a new type of social integration, it seems appropriate to enquire whether its members have, indeed, developed a new vision of society and, especially, whether their professional output does, indeed, contribute to spreading the model of procedural consensus (as a *conditio sine qua non* of parliamentary politics) onto the society at large?

In slightly more than three years of its existence the parliament issued a great number of legislative acts; a still greater number were drafted but remained unpassed. It employed many legal experts and advisers. The key question to be asked about this aspect of the parliament's activities is *whether the legislation it adopted was different in character from the legislation of the Soviet era?*

For this we must consider briefly the Soviet legislation. What did a law promulgated by the USSR Supreme Soviet look like? In essence, it was a "framing" law. This means that the law would typically define the general sphere of its application, the principal goals or directions of the changes it was intended to bring about, and institutions responsible for its administration (if necessary, new institutions would be established). Direct rules were rare birds on the pages of Soviet law texts. The majority of real rules regulating the application of laws would be contained in "instructions", "directives" or similar secondary legislative acts drafted and issued by the relevant ministries and departments. The latter would thus have every possibility to *change* the meaning of a law (right up to the opposite) by "clarifying" and "interpreting" its basic concepts, by "adding" any number of provisions that, unlike the law itself, would be directly applicable.

The result was that adopting a law meant virtually nothing until the so called "mechanisms of realisation" (a hierarchy of secondary acts and "instructions") were devised. These would be subject to approval by a considerable number of ministries and departments. For an instruction of this kind to come into effect, it would have to be sanctioned ("visaed") by all the departments involved. It was as if the bureaucracy enjoyed the "collective right of veto" as far as legislation was concerned. A department that was not satisfied with some provisions of a draft "instruction" could withhold its "visa" and thus prevent the already enacted law from coming into force as long as it pleased, unless, at least, pressure were brought to bear on it from the highest levels.

It would be interesting to review the activities of the "democratic" Russian parliament from this standpoint. Despite the fact, natural as it was, that the share of direct rules in the laws adopted by the Russian parliament increased if compared to the Soviet times, the routine of putting them in force remained essentially the same. It became even more complicated, in a way, than it had used to be - due to the increase in the number of agencies whose consent was to be solicited. For example, committees of the Supreme Soviet were entitled to provide their "clarifications" for the texts of legislative acts; in this respect, therefore, they operated as a kind of substitute ministries or, at least, enjoyed powers that had formerly belonged to the latter. "Framing" provisions remained the legislation's typical feature. To give but one example, the Law on Military Conscription and Military Service, passed in February 1993, provided for "alternative service"[1] but failed to enumerate in its 65 articles occupying 31 pages (least so institute) the agencies where conscripts might serve and even specify the conditions that would entitle those, who found service with the troops unacceptable for some reason, to seek and be allowed alternative service. It is not surprising under the circumstances that courts have found it difficult to try cases falling under so vague a law.

This pattern of legislation is related to a fundamental feature of the Soviet political culture, of which we have already had a chance to write on these pages, viz. the characteristic tendency to present political situations as clusters of interrelated natural processes characterised by varying degrees of intensity.[2]

The comparison of the political behaviour of two deputy corps, that of the USSR[3] and that of the Russian Federation,[4] reveals the growing understanding of the role of parliamentary procedures in ensuring normal operation of representative institutions by members of the latter. Nevertheless, the congenial understanding that a procedural consensus was also essential for the society at large to ensure its integration under conditions of modernity was still lacking. The latter would imply changing the very character of bills of law, viz. an increased share of directly applicable rules in the text of the law itself and its adoption together with a packet of secondary acts that regulate its coming into force and subsequent administration. However, nothing of the kind happened while the first Russian post-communist parliament was in power and even after it was dissolved in 1993. The present Russian Constitution, repeatedly proclaimed to be a law of direct effect, has not changed the situation. Otherwise former Chairman of the Council of Federation (the upper house of the Federal Assembly) Vladimir Shumeiko would have no reason to complain, when interviewed by a TV reporter on the Chechen crisis, that laws in Russia are ineffective in general; nor could the Constitutional Court comment, when required to pass a judgement on the constitutionality of the President's decree ordering "restoration of the constitutional order" in Chechnya, that the federal law on the state of emergency was passed in a form that made it largely irrelevant and that important body of relevant legislation was simply lacking.[5] The entire constitutional situation about Chechnya provides a good illustration of the quality of legislation enacted by the Russian parliament.

Another stunning example (already cited before) is Article 121[6] of the Russian Constitution valid on the day Yeltsin's decree No. 1,400 was signed. Despite the explicit provision that the President was to be removed from power at once should he try to dissolve or suspend the parliament, neither the Constitution itself nor any other act of law specified the procedure for that removal. That gave Yeltsin a chance to ignore the decisions of both the Supreme Soviet (on the pretext that impeachment of the President was not its prerogative) and of the Congress of People's Deputies (as lacking a quorum required by another article of that Constitution) and even the ruling, allowing of no appeal, of the Constitutional Court (for, strictly speaking, the Court was only to decide whether the President's actions provided grounds for his impeachment). It is hard to believe that the deputies had consciously sought to create this procedural ambiguity when they had voted for that provision. This only shows that the deputy corps failed to understand clearly what serious consequences procedural lacunae in so important legislative texts as the Constitution might have.

Another important feature of the Second Republic's legislative practice was the ambiguous status of presidential decrees. The 1 November 1991 resolution of the Fifth Congress that invested the President with "additional powers" created a singular juridical situation: certain presidential decrees ought to have precedence over legislative acts of the Russian Federation unless revoked by the Supreme Soviet in the course of a week. Paradoxically enough, the same provision that stripped the Supreme Soviet of its constitutional status as the nation's main legislating institution amplified the role of the Chairman and the Presidium, for it could only be through them that a presidential decree might come to be considered by the Supreme Soviet. The Chairman had only to "keep" a decree in his office for a few days for it to come into effect automatically. It was precisely this trick that sealed the fate of privatisation when the law passed by the Supreme Soviet was superseded by the presidential decree on the same subject even though the latter contradicted the former's basic provisions.

After the resolution on the "additional powers" had been passed, therefore, two powerful centres of personified legislative activity emerged: the President and the Chairman of the Supreme Soviet. The arrangement could not help provoking a major institutional conflict involving the President, on the one hand, and the parliament, on the other (to say nothing about personal rivalry). In fact, by having granted legislative powers to the President, the parliament created a situation in which it could not take them back: throughout 1992 and 1993, as we have seen, any attempt to divest the President of those, by definition provisional, powers would be countered by a series of presidential decrees that either ignored the legislation that issued from the Supreme Soviet or challenged the very legitimacy of the Supreme Soviet and the Congress of People's Deputies as legislative institutions. After all, Decree No. 1,400 could be seen (as the President's party did not fail to point out) as precisely realisation of the "additional" powers granted to the President by none other than the parliament itself.

If we now turn to the semantic structure of presidential decrees, we would find their texts even more (in fact, much more) "frame-like" than the bills of law enacted by the Supreme Soviet. Decrees granting privileges, for example, would typically stipulate that the implementation was to take place upon "elaboration of the rules of application by the appropriate ministries". It goes without saying that with the date of implementation not specified in the decree itself, the relevant departments, in case they did not want the decree to be implemented, could go on "elaborating the rules of application" *ad infinitum*. Characteristically enough, the practice persists: although certain export privileges had been abolished by a presidential decree signed in March 1995, *Gazprom* (a state gas company) was still enjoying them half a year later.

The same is true of the legislation of the parliament proper. To give but one example, on the twelve pages of the draft Law on Science (the Council of Federation's version) prepared in 1994 we have come across two (sic!) direct rules: one, providing for the establishment of regional Academies of Sciences; the other, fixing extras on the "regional" academicians' salaries. Otherwise, the draft was a collection of "framing" clauses.

To sum up. Though the legislation adopted by the Russian parliament was undoubtedly superior in quality to the legislation of the Soviet period - mainly due to better procedural arrangements (preliminary discussions in standing committees, successive hearings, etc.) - the accustomed practice of enacting bills unaccompanied by packets of secondary legislative acts depreciated even what would have otherwise been "sound" laws because it failed to exclude the possibility of their arbitrary interpretations. The important consequence was that the official, and much celebrated, goal of curbing the all-powerful bureaucracy and ensuring "the rule of law" (or, rather, establishing "a law-based state")[6] was not attained.

The greatest damage was done by the practice of parallel legislation. Not only were legislative acts issued by the presidential structures inferior, on the whole, to those of the parliament for the simple reason that they would be usually prepared in greater haste and with less professional deliberation. Of even more fateful consequence was the fact that the President's legislative powers devalued the respective activities of the parliament because they encouraged nihilistic attitude (supported, to be sure, by the conscientious propaganda) towards the parliament's legislation in the lower levels of bureaucracy: one could never be sure that a bill of law enacted by the Supreme Soviet would not be "overruled" by a contradicting presidential decree which the Supreme Soviet would fail to rescind in due time.

The Russian parliament was thus all but transformed from an authoritative legislature into a kind of "workshop for the study of the principles of legislative activities". Although the latter might well prove to be a good school of parliamentarianism for the Russian political elite, the transformation could hardly be hoped to boost the prestige of the institution and improve prospects for representative democracy in Russia in general.

In order that framing structures in texts of laws may be identified, methods of text analysis are required that would enable one to distinguish between rules allowing of direct and indirect application. For this purpose formal methods of meaning representation known as cognitive maps (and already exercised in this study) can be used again. The idea of cognitive maps is to identify formal causal relations implied by the text in question after the following pattern: situation A causes, i.e contributes to (+) or prevents (-) situation B. The irrelevant aspects left aside, the entire text can thus be divided into causally related fragments.[7]

For the purpose of this study it is worth mentioning once again that this method of representation, described here as *procedural*, must be distinguished from an alternative method of representing social situations, viz. *processual*, as based on radically different ontological assumptions. The processual mode of thinking assumes that the world is a tangle of interrelated processes, of which each is a self-sufficient sequence of causally related events, independent in essence from external influence and characterised by varying degrees of intensity.

If this is the way the legislator's mind operates, rules of direct effect are unlikely, generally speaking, to appear in the texts he drafts, for such a rule would imply a situation in which an action taken by a person or some other agency entails a response action by another person or agency, e.g. police, courts of law, etc. Rules of direct effect are thus defined with a view to deeds, not processes. The framing legislation characteristic of the Soviet legal thinking and practice however presents situations after the "processual" pattern, with actions of the relevant agencies affecting processes rather than other agencies.

Take, for example, a phrase typical for the Russian political/legal discourse: "Law enforcement agencies ought to intensify their struggle against criminality" (see Figure 36). The sentence makes no sense from the standpoint of law seen as a collection of direct rules. The obvious implication being that "the law enforcement agencies" do not enforce law as they (normally) should, the sentence is open to three interrelated interpretations. It may be seen as a statement of fact (albeit in an unconventional syntactical form); or it may be an appraisal of a situation (presumably negative); or a command or, perhaps, an emotive-type invocation (presumably to improve).

Let us consider these interpretations in the reverse order. If this is a command (as the imperative "ought" clearly indicates), it obviously misses the point. The law enforcement agencies are solicited to act not against criminals, but against a "situation" or, rather, a "phenomenon" of "criminality". The solicitation implies that the phenomenon be described and explained. The latter is apparently an academic, rather than a police-force undertaking. If a clause of law assumes that police officers are to consult scholars before taking legal actions, it is anything but a "direct legal rule".

If this is an appraisal of the situation, it implies a command to change it - as a logical inference from the presumably negative character of the appraisal (no legal actions would apparently be necessary, if the appraisal were positive). But if it implies a command, the inference is not to contradict the appraisal. For either "the law enforcement agencies" are themselves responsible for the situation as it is or not. If they are responsible, they cannot be reasonably expected to improve the situation - not unless delinquents are named and action is taken against them. This would in turn require that a clear-cut distinction be drawn between the part of the personnel that is to take on the task of improving the situation and the part of it that is to be the principal target of this effort. There are no signs of these in the text, however. If, on the other hand, the failure is due to some causes outside human control, the command is pointless, for an "objective situation" cannot be ordered to improve. Thus the "processual" vision renders the clause meaningless.

Finally, as a statement of fact the message can be either right or wrong. If it is right, it is either relevant or not. If it is relevant, it implies an appraisal and presumably a command, but not a rule (enter the arguments of the preceding paragraphs). If it is irrelevant, it implies nothing whatsoever. But if it is wrong, it can only mean one thing, viz. that the law enforcement agencies must investigate and punish more crimes than have been committed, which is, of course, sheer nonsense.

Insofar as they fail to indicate either the "object" or the "subject" of the action prescribed (or both) in a meaningful form, none of the three interpretations of the sentence in question entitles one to read it as establishing a rule, least so a direct rule.

2. Semantic Correlates of *Sobornost'*: Naming and Omitting Legitimate Agents in Russian Constitutional Texts

The Soviet Constitution

Perhaps, the most illuminating examples of this frame of mind and this kind of legal arrangements are to be found in the Russian constitutional texts. The prize belongs undoubtedly to the Soviet Constitution of 1977. Its Article 50, for instance, proclaimed the conventional democratic rights: of assembly, of a free press, of free speech, etc. According to the Constitution,

> Exercise of these political freedoms is ensured by putting public buildings, streets and squares at the disposal of the working people and their organisations, by broad dissemination of information, and by the opportunity to use the press, television and radio.[8]

We shall leave without comments the obvious discrepancy between the article's two clauses: although the "rights" are said to belong to "citizens", the means required to exercise them may presumably be sought only by "the working people" (*trudyashchiesya*). More relevant to this analysis is the failure to indicate any agency, be it a person or an institution, that was directly responsible for providing the promised "public buildings, streets and squares" or securing access to "information", "press, television and radio" and specify the conditions that entitle "workers" or "their organisations" to claim them. The same stands true of the entire Chapter 7 that treated of "the basic rights, freedoms and duties of citizens of the USSR".

Article 51 stated that

> In accordance with the aims of building communism, citizens of the USSR have the right to associate in public organisations that promote their political activity and initiative and satisfaction of their various interests.[9]

For all that we know, there existed no Soviet legal text that would specify the conditions for and/or procedures of establishing and registering a "public organisation". (The only exception was resolution of the All-

Union Central Executive Committee[10] and the Council of People's Commissars[11] "On Religious Associations" of 8 April 1929, but even that was not available to the general reader[12].) That did not mean, however, as one accustomed to the Anglo-Saxon common law practice might erroneously assume, that such organisations might be established by anyone willing to do so and might function unregistered. In the Soviet circumstances the absence of procedures for establishing "public organisations" meant that no such organisation might be established, except by political agencies that were above the law, in which case no registration would, of course, be necessary. The clause implied therefore something different from what was explicitly stated. Needless to say, this duplicity of meaning was in full accord with the separation of the overt (profane) and covert (sacred) spheres characteristic of the politics of *sobornost'*. Under the circumstances, the legislator was safe to promise that

> Public organisations are guaranteed conditions for successfully performing the functions defined in their rules[13]

for that implied no obligations on any side. Still, persons or institutions responsible for ensuring the above "conditions" were not named again.

Articles 49 and 58 were meant to regulate intercourse between private citizens and state officials. The latter were

> obliged, within established time-limits, to examine citizens' proposals and requests, to reply to them, and to take appropriate action,[14]

though the text failed to specify who exactly was "to reply" and "to take action" and how soon. The same was true of citizens' complaints:

> Complaints shall be examined according to the procedure and within the time-limit established by law,[15]

and legal claims:

> Citizens of the USSR have the right to compensation for damage resulting from unlawful actions by state organisations and public organisations, or by officials in the performance of their duties.[16]

The right to claim damages is a standard provision of civil law. The above clause, therefore, was either superfluous, if the legislator had no special procedures in mind for damage done by state organisations or state officials, or grossly insufficient, if he had.

The celebrated "right to housing" was to be ensured in a similar fashion by the development and upkeep of state and socially-owned housing, by assistance for co-operative and individual house building; by fair distribution, under public control, of the housing that becomes available through fulfilment of the programme of building well-appointed dwellings, and by low rents and low charges for utility services.[17]

The above text might embellish a propaganda leaflet, were the wording less laboured, but was not becoming to a legal document. Not only could "fair distribution, under public control" ensure nothing unless it was ensured itself (by something the legislator did not care to mention), but it was, moreover, conditioned by "fulfilment" of an unspecified "programme". The entire phrase reminded strongly, indeed, of one of the laws of materialist dialectics, viz. the law of transition of quantity to quality: the "law" promised new quality but contained no formula by which one could ascertain what particular quality was to be expected and when.

The Constitutional Legislation of the Second Republic

Although amended by the Sixth Congress of People's Deputies in 1992, Article 58 of the Russian Constitution of 1978 that treated the "right to housing" remained a literal replica of the respective article of the old Soviet Constitution (except that "the citizens of the Russian Federation" were substituted for "the citizens of the USSR").[18] The "Rumyantsev's draft constitution", approved in general by the same Sixth Congress, was less "dialectical", but hardly more specific:

(1) Everyone has a right to a well-appointed dwelling. No one may be arbitrarily deprived of his dwelling. ...

(2) The state and the local government encourage house building, create other conditions for realisation of the right to housing.

(3) Needy persons are to be provided with a well-appointed dwelling free or at reasonable rent from the state or municipal [housing] resources in accordance with rules established by law.[19]

By combining a declaration (part 1) with a statement of fact or, if one would prefer to put it this way, a wish (part 2) and a framing provision with a reference to the would-be regulations (part 3), the article can serve as a text-book example of the Russian legislators' mental attitudes.

Characteristically enough, Article 40 of the present Russian Constitution has reproduced the above provisions almost word for word.[20] The Sixth Congress amended, in fact, the entire Chapter 5 of the 1978 Constitution - presumably to accommodate the international standards of human rights and civil liberties.[21] The new version of Article 32 signified a major departure from the old Soviet tradition of treating the whole issue of human rights as an interference in internal affairs of a sovereign state:[22]

> Universally recognised international rules that relate to human rights have precedence over laws of the Russian Federation and directly generate rights and duties of the citizens of the Russian Federation.[23]

The legislator's good will can hardly be doubted; however, the fact that he preferred the non-committal "universally recognised" to a positive reference to specific legal documents, despite the fact that the former were supposed to "directly generate" something of importance, is also noteworthy. One might argue, of course, that the intent was to leave room for future provisions, but this is precisely our point: like their Soviet predecessors, the Russian legislators seem to be unduly concerned about always "having room" for afterthoughts, as if they did not want to commit themselves. Perhaps, the reason why all Soviet constitutions were also called "Basic Laws" was that they were meant to be continuously detailed and adjusted. None of them explicitly claimed to be an act of law with direct effect.

Well, "Rumyantsev's draft constitution" did:

> The Constitution of the Russian Federation shall have direct effect and be applied on the entire territory of the Russian Federation. Laws and other legal acts that contradict the Constitution of the Russian Federation shall not be legally valid.[24]

Nevertheless, Chapter III alone contained in its fourteen articles nine unspecified reservations about "civil and political rights and liberties" (the chapter's subject matter) plus three more references to unspecified "federal" and other laws.[25]

Whereas the old Soviet Constitution claimed that freedom of the press was ensured by "the opportunity to use the press, television and radio", the 1992 draft contained no reference to so abstract a guarantee. But neither did it name any specific guarantor, being presumably satisfied with a participle without an object:

Freedom of mass media is guaranteed. Censorship is not allowed.[26]

Pseudo-agencies of the kind analysed in the preceding chapter misbecome a legal text, of course (though are occasionally encountered[27]). This does not mean, however, that the processual mode of thinking of which they are a manifestation must remain unexpressed. Its impact on the Russian constitutional texts is attested by the characteristic tendency to omit agents that are to perform the functions and actions in question. However inappropriate for legal matters, this mode of thinking was, nevertheless, no mere deficiency, but should rather be seen as a cultural trait. If the absence or anonymity of agents one would expect to be indicated with utmost precision was, indeed, due to misunderstanding or negligence, that was a useful misunderstanding and a well calculated negligence.

Let us compare, for instance, Parts 2 and 3 of Article 121[8] of the Russian Constitution. (The entire Chapter 13[1], it will be recalled, was a supplement adopted by the Fourth Congress of People's Deputies in May 1991[28]; Article 121[8] was, moreover, further amended by the Sixth Congress a year later[29]. It was certainly not among the Constitution's "overlooked" portions.) Its final version ran as follows:

> Decrees of the President of the Russian Federation may not contradict the Constitution and laws of the Russian Federation. In case an act of the President contradicts the Constitution, a law of the Russian Federation, valid is the rule of the Constitution, the law of the Russian Federation.

> The President of the Russian Federation has a right to suspend acts of Presidents of the republics and of Councils of Ministers (Cabinets of Ministers) of the republics of the Russian Federation, as well as annul acts of provincial (*kraevoi*), regional (*oblastnoi*), municipal (*gorodskoi*) administrations, of administrations of the autonomous region, autonomous districts in case they contradict the legislation of the Russian Federation.[30]

Although both parts dealt with almost identical situations, viz. the President's (Part 2) and other executives' acts that contradicted the Constitution (Part 3), the two cases were treated differently. The agent that was to suspend or annul the acts of the latter was explicitly named: that was the President; but no agent was indicated in the former case. Part 3 was thus a rule of direct; Part 2, of indirect effect. While the problem of regional and local administrations' violating the law was juridically clear and could be promptly solved by interference of the central executive, the status of the President's decrees was left ambiguous. They might have been revoked by the Constitutional Court, of course, just as any other legislative act that contradicted the Constitution, but how about the meantime? Imagine an official having received a presidential decree the constitutionality of which he had reasons to doubt. What was he supposed to do: obey it immediately, as assumed by Part 1 of the same Article 121[8] ("Decrees of the President of the Russian Federation are mandatory on the entire territory of the Russian Federation"[31]), or wait until its constitutionality was confirmed or repudiated? The Constitution suggesting no definite answer, it is hard to imagine the collision would not be solved in favour of the unequivocal demand of Part 1. After all, orders, if authoritative, must be carried out. This is a kind of legality, of course, but it is legality of a kind that is more appropriate for a military organisation than for a "law-based society".

The Present Russian Constitution

The present Russian Constitution does not differ in this respect from the one it replaced. (Insofar as it was adopted by the 12 December 1993 referendum, it is admittedly beyond the time limits of this study, but the transgression seems justified on two points. In the first place, the 1993 Constitution is an immediate outcome of the conflict that has been our main concern in this volume - it was meant to secure the fruits of the executive's victory. In the second place, our aspiration in this chapter is to highlight the cultural background to the legislative activity, rather than inquire about particular legislative documents; it seems appropriate therefore to probe into the immediate future in order to ascertain whether the conclusions to be drawn from the recent experience are still valid).

To come back to the subject of presidential decrees, Part 1 of Article 90 of the present Russian Constitution has no reservations about the scope of the President's decretal competence. The article states simply that

The President of the Russian Federation issues decrees and orders.[32]

Unlike this final version, the draft constitution approved by the Constitutional Conference on 12 July 1993 (presumably, the present Constitution's principal source) set limits on the presidential authority in this respect:

The President of the Russian Federation issues decrees and orders in accordance with powers conferred on him by the Constitution of the Russian Federation and federal laws.[33]

Comparison of the two versions shows that the legislator's eventual intention was to let the President issue decrees and orders about anything he deems necessary. From this standpoint, the competence of the President appears to be as unlimited as the onetime mocked all-embracing competence of the dissolved Congress of People's Deputies.

Parts 2 and 3 of Article 90 reproduce the collision described in the preceding section. On the one hand,

Decrees and orders of the President of the Russian Federation are mandatory on the entire territory of Russian Federation.[34]

On the other hand,

Decrees and orders of the President of the Russian Federation may not contradict the Constitution of the Russian Federation and federal laws.[35]

Officials must wonder again, whether they are bound by Part 2 in cases implied by Part 3. It is true, the new Constitution, unlike the previous one, enumerates the agencies authorised to initiate the proceedings in the Constitutional Court. These include (apart from the President, the two chambers of the Federal Assembly, the Government, the Supreme Court and the Supreme Court of Arbitration) one fifth of the Council of Federation, one fifth of the State Duma and the legislative and executive bodies of the members of Federation.[36] There may be other plaintiffs, in case citizens' constitutional rights and liberties are affected.[37] However, the Constitutional Court itself is characteristically omitted: it may no longer act on its own initiative - another echo of the 1993 conflict[38].

Still, the procedure is not described in full. The Constitution says nothing about the legal status of acts that are subject to the Court proceedings until the decision is taken (perhaps, a minor point if the Court decides quickly) and is somewhat vague about their legal consequences after that (a major point). They are said to "become invalid" (*utrachivayut silu*).[39] The expression is, by the way, an exemplary manifestation of the processual mode of thinking, as if the acts became this or that all by themselves; "are revoked" would be more appropriate, provided the participle be accompanied by an object indicating the agent: revoked by whom? The Constitution, however, fails to specify from what time they are to be considered invalid: since the very beginning or only after the

Constitutional Court has passed its judgement? Assuming the matter is left to the discretion of the Court and will be decided in its ruling, what about the actions already taken on the revoked decree? What is the procedure in this case: is the President supposed to issue a counter-decree rescinding the previous one that would also disavow the actions taken on the latter? What if he does not? Granted, there are provisions for such situations in other bodies of law and one may, in principle, proceed by analogy, but would that not denigrate the Constitution as a law of direct effect?

A similar collision may arise with respect to international treaties that do not conform to the Constitution. According to Part 6 of Article 125 they are not to be "put in force and applied".[40] Presumably, the failure to conform has to be ascertained by the Constitutional Court. However, according to item "d" of Part 2, Article 125, not all international treaties lay within its competence, but only those that "have not come into force".[41] What about treaties that have already "come into force"? There is no mention in the Constitution about international treaties coming into effect to be conditional on a preliminary positive verdict by the Constitutional Court. In fact, the Constitution does not prescribe any procedure for international treaties at all. Since the Constitutional Court cannot be expected to, and indeed may not, proceed on its own initiative, it is quite conceivable that a treaty that does not conform to the Constitution comes into force (and thus escapes the competence of the Constitutional Court) before some authorised agency brings the issue to it.

Moreover, Part 4 of Article 15, belonging, incidentally, to the most authoritative of all chapters, Chapter 1 - "Foundations of the Constitutional Order",[42] states plainly that

> Universally recognised principles and rules of international law and international treaties of the Russian Federation are a constituent part of its legal system. If an international treaty of the Russian Federation establishes rules different from those provided for by the law, the rules of an international treaty are to be applied.[43]

An international treaty cannot therefore contradict a law, for if there is a contradiction, the presumption is it is the law that contradicts the international treaty, though, of course, it should not ("the Rumyantsev's draft constitution specified: "a *ratified* international treaty"[44]). A treaty can, however, contradict the Constitution, but may it? It certainly may not if it "entails restrictions on human rights and civil liberties" and affects "the foundations of the constitutional order" (Article 79), but otherwise? One might infer, by omission and from the just quoted Article 15 (assuming that "the law" it refers to includes constitutional provisions other than those of Chapter 1), that they may - in principle; but they may not, it will be recalled, be "put in force and applied" (Part 6, Article 125). To sum up, treaties that do not conform to the Constitution may not be put in force, but if, despite this, they have come into force, they become "a constituent part" of the legal system and are to have priority over other laws. Why not employ a couple of logicians before setting out to draft a new constitution?

Finally, according to Article 106, federal laws that ratify or denounce international treaties are subject to "mandatory consideration" by the Council of Federation.[45] But what government body is supposed to ratify or denounce them in the first place? Presumably, the State Duma, if ratification and denunciation are a matter of federal legislation, as Article 106 seems to imply; however, the Constitution does not state explicitly they are. A sad omission, but minor if compared to the issue of federal laws in general.

Part 1 of Article 105 states that

Federal laws are adopted by the State Duma.[46]

However, Article 103 that enumerates, presumably in the form of an "exhaustive" list, the Duma's prerogatives makes no mention of passing laws (to say nothing about considering, least so rescinding, presidential decrees).[47] On the other hand, the list is not explicitly stated to be exhaustive. Article 105 implies it is not, and if it is not, the Duma may attend to other matters, as well. Moreover, if this list is not exhaustive, neither are other similar lists, for example, the list of agencies authorised to enquire about the constitutionality of normative acts and internal or international treaties (Part 2, Article 125). By analogy, the list of the President's prerogatives is also "open", even though it already seems wide enough to include almost everything.[48] (Curiously enough the previous Constitution asserted this quite explicitly:

[The President of the Russian Federation] has *other* powers bestowed on him by the Constitution of the RSFSR and by laws of the RSFSR.)[49]

It seems inconceivable that the legislator, while remaining within the limits of the Russian legal tradition, might have intended to have all such lists in the Constitution "open" without stating this in an explicit form; for the tradition does not support the assumption that anything not explicitly forbidden is allowed, but rather that anything that is not explicitly allowed is forbidden. (To this one may add, after our analysis in the preceding section, that the predominantly framing character of Russian legislation renders even much of what has been explicitly allowed actually impossible.) Since, however, the Constitution makes no distinction between the various lists in this respect and since some of the lists are clearly assumed not to be exhaustive, it would be logical to apply the same rule to all of them and infer they are all "open".

Yet is it a matter of logic? Is it not a matter of the type of logic, in other words - of the mode of thinking? Standard logic is, after all, the logic of procedural thinking; processual thinking (that has generated this particular document) seems to follow the patterns of "dialectical logic". Granted there exists a "dialectical logic", but there are, to our knowledge, no "dialectical logicians". So the constitution-makers were probably right to do without logicians in the long run!

A few more illustrations to press the point. Part 2 of Article 80 calls the President guarantor of the Constitution, of human rights and civil liberties. In this capacity

> In accordance with the procedure established by the Constitution of the Russian Federation he takes measures to protect the sovereignty of the Russian Federation, its independence and state integrity, ensures coordinated functioning and interaction of the state government bodies.[50]

The Constitution makes another reference to itself. To what part? Where exactly is the appropriate procedure indicated?

The situations in question are dealt with in Articles 85 (inadequate coordination and cooperation, potential threat to rights and liberties), 87 (external threat to sovereignty, independence and integrity) and 88 (internal threat). Part 1 of Article 85 mentions unspecified "conciliatory procedures" and, in case these prove of no avail, "respective [whatever that means - N.B. & V.S.] court of law".[51] Part 2 is quite specific about the President and somewhat evasive about the courts: the President is empowered to suspend acts of the local executive in case they violate human rights and civic liberties and contradict the law until a "respective court of law" passes its judgement.[52] Article 87 is again unequivocal as far as the President is concerned (he imposes martial law), but calls for further elucidation with respect to the Council of Federation and the State Duma (these are to be notified of the fact "without delay").[53] The role of the former is specified in Article 102 (Part 1, item "b"): the Council of Federation is to approve or, presumably, disapprove of the respective presidential decree.[54] What the

State Duma is supposed to do about the martial law, remains unclear. Article 88 (perhaps, the most sensitive of all) is, characteristically, another example of framing legislation: rather than establish a procedure for the imposition of a state of emergency, as assumed by Article 80, it makes a further reference to a "federal constitutional law".[55] Otherwise, it operates like Article 87: the two houses are to be immediately notified; the Council of Federation then proceeds to decide whether it approves of the decree or not (item "c", Part 1, Article 102); the State Duma, presumably, holds debates.

Here we come across a peculiar lacuna. Article 102 (Part 1, item "b") appears to imply that imposition of martial law is a precondition for committing armed forces to action. But unlike, sending troops abroad,[56] the Constitution does not state explicitly their use inside the country requires the parliament's consent and, indeed, even martial law. In fact, the Constitution does not mention any condition for imposing martial law except aggression or an immediate threat of aggression.[57]

Let us consider the case of Chechnya from the standpoint of the present Russian Constitution. Constitutionally, Chechnya is a part of Russia (Article 65, Part 1)[58]. Hence it follows that the revolt in Chechnya cannot be called an aggression and does not require, nor would justify imposition of martial law (Article 87, Part 1). Since martial law is not imposed and troops sent to Chechnya do not cross the Russian border, they may be sent there without the consent of the parliament (Article 102, Part 1, items "b" and "d"). If, therefore, the President, in his capacity as Commander-in-Chief of the Russian Armed Forces (Article 87, Part 1)[59] and guarantor of the Constitution (Article 80, Part 2), orders the army to Chechnya, he is in his full right, and the parliament cannot object. Or, rather, it can - on the strength of the freedom of thought and speech (Article 29, Part 1),[60] but *can do nothing* about it. Neither can the Constitutional Court, except to rule that the Constitution has not been violated. As, indeed, it has not, though no one is to be congratulated.

Thus, the framing character of the Constitution results in the executive invariably having the last word, or if not the last word, then, at least, a free hand!

The most striking of all the clauses are unquestionably those that treat of the Federal Assembly. We have already referred to the curious way the Constitution defines the prerogatives of its two chambers. But one would, at least, expect the Constitution to establish the procedures for their elections. It does not. Part 2 of Article 96 states that *even this* is subject to special federal laws.[61] This recurring unwillingness to make definite rules has threatened lately to wreck the election to the State Duma (December 1995), when a number of salient actors demanded the law be amended already after the run-up had begun.

But even this incongruity pales before the absurd regulation (or, rather, the absurd lack of regulation) relating to the Council of Federation. The Constitution states explicitly that the State Duma, at least, is to be elected. The Council of Federation is to be "formed", whatever that means. The only definite provision is that each member ("subject") of the Federation is to be represented by two persons: one, for the legislative (representative); the other, for the executive branch of regional government.

The provision is open to a number of different interpretations. Let us consider first members of the Council of Federation representing the legislative. They cannot be elected directly by the populace, because in that case they would no more represent the regional legislative than any other resident of the respective territory (unless, perhaps, heads of the legislative are elected directly - certainly, an unconventional arrangement), though they would, of course, represent the "subject" of Federation. This leaves us with two alternatives: the respective delegate to the Council of Federation may be specially elected by the regional legislature or else hold the seat *ex officio*, by virtue of being elected, say, to its chairmanship.

As to those who represent the regional executive, the situation is much more complicated. The recent practice has been for heads of, at least, some regional administrations to be appointed by the President (the respective powers were grant him by the Fifth Congress's resolution "On Organisation of the Executive in the Period of Radical Economic Reform"[62]). The present Constitution does not mention such a right, but the President may appoint his "plenipotentiaries"[63] (whose status is, incidentally, not specified). Article 77 of the present Constitution provides for the system of regional government to be subject to regulation by members of Federation, but they must abide by

> the foundations of the constitutional order of the Russian Federation and general principles of organisation of representative and executive government bodies established by federal laws.[64]

However,

> Within the jurisdiction of the Russian Federation and the powers of the Russian Federation concerning matters under joint jurisdiction of the Russian Federation and the subjects of the Russian Federation the federal executive

bodies and the executive bodies of the subjects of the Russian Federation *form a united system of executive power* in the Russian Federation.[65]

And further on:

In order to exercise their authority federal executive bodies may institute their territorial bodies and appoint the respective officials.[66]

This is, in fact, a pearl of framing legislation. What are the "general principles of organisation of representative and executive government bodies" or by what "federal laws" are they "established"? And, first and foremost, what is the executive of a member of Federation: a part of the "united system of executive power" or the executive branch of the system of regional government? To be more specific and to return to the issue of "forming" the Council of Federation, is the delegate of a member of Federation's executive to represent the former or the latter, or both?

The scope of alternatives here is much wider than in the case of the legislative, but most of them are either undemocratic or impractical or illogical. The first question is whether the member of Federation is to be represented by the first person in the regional executive hierarchy or by some other deputy? The latter raises the maddening problem of choosing such a deputy. Is he to be appointed by the first person or elected, say, by a conference of regional civil servants or by the regional legislature? The former would hardly qualify for a democratic procedure; the latter, for a representation of the executive; the third alternative is simply ridiculous.

The only viable choice is, therefore, for the seat to go to the head of the regional executive. But here we are faced with three more alternatives: the person may be appointed to the office from above (presumably, by the President) or elected either by the populace or by the legislature. The former would again be undemocratic; the latter, illogical. The inference is he has to be elected by the populace.

However, that would mean that the "subjects" of Federation cannot, in fact, decide on the system of their government "independently", as Article 77 stipulates. Direct election of the chief executive implies the incumbent is independent of the regional representative assembly (as, indeed, of the central executive). It would be more logical to state this in plain words and provide for the appropriate system of checks and balances, rather than leave the matter in obscurity, as if Russia had no constitution at all. There are, of course, other legislative acts, but considering the powers of the Council of Federation and the intricate issues of both national and local politics involved, is this not something for the Constitution to settle - if not finally, then at least definitively?

The constitutional text is not always that evasive. Some procedures are specified carefully enough, especially when it comes to exercising the executive authority. It is quite specific, for example, about the President's right to cancel resolutions and orders of the government, in case they contradict the Constitution, federal laws or presidential decrees,[67] or suspend executives acts of the members of Federation, in case they contradict the Constitution, federal laws or international obligations of Russia or infringe on human rights and civil liberties.[68] In both cases the grounds are defined and all relevant agencies named. It is true, the body that decides whether the Constitution or laws have been indeed violated is not indicated explicitly, but this is hardly necessary for the cancellation to become effective: any matter can always be presented as contradicting a presidential decree, for even if it is not, all the President has to do is to issue an appropriate decree, and whether that is violated or not is obviously for the President to decide (at least, this is not among the Constitutional Court's prerogatives). As to suspension, this is effective *ex vi termini*, for the President's decision is assumed to precede the final judgement by "the respective Court".

On the contrary, when the annulment is the prerogative of the legislative, the procedure is deplorably lacking. Moreover, careful comparison of a number of constitutional documents reveals the curious fact that different elements of the procedure are usually omitted.

According to the old federal Constitution, for example, the right to cancel resolutions and orders of the government in case they contradicted the Constitution or federal laws belonged to the Supreme Soviet.[69] The fact had to be ascertained by the Constitutional Court,[70] but the initiator of the action was not indicated. Of two procedures, viz. the cancellation and the ascertainment of unconstitutionality, the former was described in full; the latter, only in part: one of the agents involved was omitted. With the present Constitution the situation is *vice versa*: the procedure for establishing unconstitutionality is defined (there is a list of authorised initiators); the procedure for cancelling, is not (decrees are said to "become invalid"). The draft of the Constitutional Conference failed to indicate both, the initiator and the canceller, thus making rescindment of presidential decrees practically impossible, although it stated plainly that they might not contradict the Constitution[71] and provided for the Constitutional Court to decide whether they did.[72]

The above analysis suggests that the legislator must have been fully aware of the omissions; otherwise they would hardly alternate from one his issue to another, yet never fail to be present in the long run. The implication about the sincerity of the legislator's commitment to the cause of constitutionalism, or at least to clear-cut separation of powers, is not particularly inspiring.

All this does not mean that a sound constitutional text may omit nothing.

As Walter Murphy correctly argues,

An effective text cannot be a prolix code regulating all details of public or private life, not only because no one can offer a credible, detailed prediction of the future but also because such a code would lose much of its worth as a teacher of the civic virtues of constitutional democracy.[73]

Still, for the operational integration of a body politic to be ensured, the constitution must, at least, establish *definite procedures for resolving potential disputes between branches and institutions of government.* Such rules must have direct effect, i.e. indicate all the agents involved in all the three stages of a prospective legal settlement, viz. initiation (bringing the action), resolution (making the judgement) and execution (taking the corrective measures). If even one is omitted, the rule cannot be applied without supplementary provisions. Semantic deficiency indicates procedural imperfection.

Notes

[1] Part 2 of Article 1 of Law of the Russian Federation "On Military Conscription and Military Service" of 11 February 1993 (see *VSNDiVR* 1993, No. 9, p. 499).

[2] See Section 1 "The Problem of Political Agency: Methodological Considerations" in Chapter 8.

[3] See Biryukov and Sergeyev 1993, pp. 63-6.

[4] See Biryukov *et al.* 1995, p. 153.

[5] See *SZRF*, 1995, No. 33, pp. 6293-303. For the Law of the Russian Soviet Federal Socialist Republic "On the State of Emergency" of 17 May 1991, see *VSNDiVS*, 1991, No. 22, pp. 863-71.

[6] For the discussion of the difference between the notions of "the rule of law" (as understood within the Anglo-Saxon legal tradition) and "the

law-based state" (the translation for the German *Rechtsstaat*), see Sakwa 1993, pp. 83-4.

[7] The techniques of cognitive maps are described in detail in Axelrod (ed.) 1976, and Joensson 1982.

[8] *Constitution USSR* 1985, p. 33.

[9] Ibid., pp. 33-4.

[10] The analogue of the future Presidium of the Supreme Soviet.

[11] The government.

[12] See *Legislation* 1971, pp. 83-97. The book was published strictly "for official use" and was only to be received by special permission.

[13] *Constitution USSR* 1985, p. 34.

[14] Ibid., p. 33.

[15] Part 1 of Article 58 (ibid., p. 35).

[16] Part 3 of Article 58 (ibid.).

[17] Article 44 (ibid., p. 31).

[18] *Constitution RF* 1992, p. 16.

[19] Article 40 (see *Draft Constitution* 1992, p. 33).

[20] *Constitution RF* 1993, p. 16.

[21] See Law of the Russian Federation "On Amendments and Supplements to the Constitution (Fundamental Law) of the Russian Soviet Federal Socialist Republic" (*Sixth Congress RF* 1992, vol. 5, pp. 456-64).

[22] In the 1970s controversy over the "basic principles" of the Helsinki Concluding Document Soviet delegations would invariably refer to the principle of sovereignty to counterbalance the principle of human rights. Demands to bring national law and national legal practice into full conformity with the international regulation of human rights would be routinely declined as an infringement of national sovereignty.

[23] *Constitution RF* 1992, pp. 10-11.

[24] Part 2 of Article 3 (*Draft Constitution* 1992, p. 23).

[25] See *Draft Constitution* 1992, pp. 28-31.

[26] Article 73 (ibid., p. 41).

[27] See, for example, the preamble to the 1977 Soviet Constitution (*Constitution USSR* 1985, pp. 9-14). It may be objected that almost every democratic constitution contains phrases like "We the People of the United States..." However, the implication is that of a representative assembly speaking on behalf of the electorate ("... do ordain and establish this Constitution") or, as in the case of the present Russian Constitution that was adopted by a referendum, of the electorate itself. It is thus something different from a passage like this (*Constitution USSR* 1985, p. 9):

> The Great October Socialist Revolution, made by *the workers and peasants of Russia* under the leadership of the Communist Party headed by Lenin, overthrew *capitalist and landowner* rule, broke the fetters of oppression, established the dictatorship of the *proletariat*, and created the Soviet state... *Humanity* thereby began the epoch-making turn from capitalism to socialism. [Italics added]

or (ibid., p. 10):

> Continuing their creative endeavours, *the working people of the Soviet Union* have ensured rapid, all-round development of the country and steady improvement of the socialist system. [Italics added]

We count six pseudo-agencies in these two excerpts. (Mark also the use of characteristically "processual" verbs and verbal nouns: "continuing... endeavours", "ensured... development", "improvement of the... system"). It is noteworthy that, apart from sentences implying the electorate ("We, the multinational people of the Russian Federation, ... adopt the CONSTITUTION of the RUSSIAN FEDERATION"), the preamble of the present Russian Constitution alludes also to (*Constitution RF* 1993, p. 3):

> the memory of *forefathers* who have passed on to us [their] love and respect for the Fatherland, [their] belief in good and justice... [Italics added]

[28] See *Fourth Congress RSFSR* 1991, Vol. 3, pp. 135-8.

[29] See Law of the Russian Federation "On Amendments and Supplements to the Constitution (Fundamental Law) of the Russian Soviet Federal Socialist Republic" of 21 April 1992 (*Sixth Congress RF* 1992, Vol. 5, pp. 482-483).

[30] *Constitution RF* 1992, p. 59.

[31] Ibid., p. 58.

[32] See *Constitution RF* 1993, p. 38.

[33] Part 1 of Article 90 of the Constitutional Conference's draft constitution (see *Draft Constitution* 1993, p. 129).

[34] Part 2 of Article 90 (see *Constitution RF* 1993, p. 38).

[35] Part 3 of Article 90 (ibid.).

[36] Part 2 of Article 125 (ibid., p. 53).

[37] Part 4 of Article 125 (ibid., p. 54).

[38] The previous Constitution did not restrict the Constitutional Court in this respect; see Article 165[1] (*Constitution RF* 1992, pp. 74-5).

[39] Part 6 of Article 125 (*Constitution RF* 1993, p. 54).

[40] Ibid.

[41] Ibid.

[42] Article 16 (ibid., p. 9):

> 1. Provisions of the present chapter of the Constitution [Chapter 1] constitute the foundations of the constitutional order of the Russian Federation...

> 2. No other provisions of the present Constitution may contradict the foundations of the constitutional order of the Russian Federation.

[43] Ibid., p. 9.

[44] Part 4 of Article 3 (see *Draft Constitution* 1992, p. 23). [Italics added]

[45] *Constitution RF* 1993, pp. 45-6.

[46] *Constitution RF* 1993, p. 45. The clause is followed by another self-reference (Part 2; ibid.):

> Federal laws are passed by a majority of the total number of deputies of the State Duma, unless otherwise stipulated by the Constitution of the Russian Federation.

Direct reference to the respective articles would be more appropriate.

[47] Ibid., pp. 42-3.

[48] See Articles 80, 83-90 (ibid., pp. 33, 34-8).

[49] Item 11 of the law on constitutional amendments of 24 May 1991 (see *Fourth Congress RSFSR* 1991, Vol. 3, p. 137). [Italics added] See *Constitution RF* 1992, p. 58 for the amended version of Item 16 of Article 121[5].

[50] Ibid., p. 33.

[51] Ibid., p. 36.

[52] Ibid.

[53] Ibid., p. 37.

[54] Ibid., p. 43.

[55] Ibid., p. 37. Cf. to the Constitutional Court's ruling on the constitutionality of the President's decree about Chechnya (see p. 323 in Section 1 of this chapter).

[56] Article 102, Part 1, item "d" (ibid., p. 43).

[57] Part 2, Article 87 (ibid., p. 37).

[58] Ibid., p. 24.

[59] Ibid., p. 37.

[60] Ibid., p. 12.

[61] Ibid., p. 40.

[62] See *VSNDiVS* 1991, No. 44, p. 1722.

[63] Item "j" of Article 83 (*Constitution RF* 1993, p. 35).

[64] Ibid., p. 32.

[65] Part 2 of Article 77 (ibid.). [Italics added]

[66] Part 1 of Article 78 (ibid.). [Italics added]

[67] Part 3, Article 115 (ibid., p. 50).

[68] Part 2, Article 85 (ibid., pp. 36-7).

[69] Item 20, Part 1, Article 109 (*Constitution RF* 1992, p. 47).

[70] Article 165[1] (ibid., p. 74).

[71] Part 3 of Article 90 (*Draft Constitution* 1993, p. 130).

[72] Part 1 of Article 125 (ibid., p. 138).

[73] Murphy 1991, pp. 178-9. For a discussion of the relevant issue of interpreting incomplete or not fully compatible constitutional texts, see Murphy 1993.

Conclusion: Transition to Democracy: Political Shock Therapy or a Conflict of Legitimacies

This world is extremely obscure and extremely important - the danger is out of proportion to the reactions it causes; it is the reactions that are really dangerous.

P. Valéry.

The above analysis of political developments in Russia in the post-*perestroika* period is a good occasion to formulate a number of questions that appear to be of general interest to historical sociology, viz. about the ways in which regimes of representative rule come to supplant those of authoritarian power. Comparison of the great European revolutions of the last four centuries reveals a repeated pattern of development, at least in the institutional domain.

A decrepit authoritarian regime, in an attempt to carry out some pressing social reforms and enlist the necessary support of the society at large, establishes representative institutions, - initially with limited authority and under its own close control.

However, the very character of the new institutions and the imminent penetration of them by people of "new mentality" and sufficiently broad social connections combine to endow the representative institutions with a kind of legitimacy the discredited *ancien regime* has long since lost. (Were it not discredited and lacking legitimacy, the old regime would have no use for representative institutions at all.)

During the English revolution the growing influence of the parliament, whose functions had been essentially limited to providing financial support for the government's policies, was mainly due to the government's complete failure in that particular (financial) field: the extravagance of the Court and the corruption of the aristocracy. A similar situation existed in France on

287

288 Russian Politics in Transition

the eve of the Great Revolution, except that the *Etats Généraux*, formally recognised as an institution of state government, had not been convened for already 175 years. This last circumstance must have contributed substantially to their rapid radicalisation.

On the whole, the situation in the Soviet Union on the eve of and during *perestroika* was essentially the same. It is noteworthy that the institutional transformations did not begin until the regime's financial fiasco (brought about by the ineffectiveness of state-governed economy and quickened by a new round of arms race and the war in Afghanistan) had become apparent.

Convocation of a representative assembly precipitates an institutional conflict between the executive organs of the old regime and the newly established (or newly legitimated) representative body. Of importance here is the balance of power and legitimacy: a political institution would naturally seek the amount of power that "matches" its legitimacy.[1]

The representative body is bound to win the first round of this conflict for its struggle against the old regime is supported by the society at large. In this it acts in fact as *an independent political force* with its own political programme. In other words, *when in a conflict with the old regime, a representative institution appears to be something notably different from a parliament operating in a normal democratic society* (whether the government of the latter be parliamentary or presidentialist), viz. an arena on which various political forces meet to negotiate a national consensus. By becoming politicised, i.e. acting as an independent political force, the parliament enjoys an ever growing support of the society at large that is essentially populist in character, for it wages its war in a classic populist manner - as a struggle *against*, not *for*. However justified historically, morally or politically, its activities in this period remain purely destructive from the institutional standpoint. So long as the principal task is mobilisation of the nation against the *ancien régime*, persons with a distinctly populist frame of mind tend to become leaders of the parliamentary party.

After the victory over the old regime is achieved (ensured indeed by the latter's senility), the parliament suddenly finds itself in a situation in which it lacks clear political perspective: having eliminated its political enemy, the parliament has accomplished its political programme and has "exhausted" with this its *raison d'être*. However, this does not mean that the grievances that undermined the legitimacy of the old regime and brought about its collapse have been settled, too: elimination of a regime is not equivalent to solution of its problems. The latter would require positive programmes and constructive actions, in short a "Reform".

In the meantime, there turns out to be no consensus about the character of this "Reform" in the triumphant parliament, for it has hitherto had neither a stimulus, nor a particular desire to work on it, having acquiesced in the kind of consensus that arose spontaneously out of its opposition to the old regime. Under the circumstances the populist-minded group of parliamentary leaders that wielded the greatest influence at the previous stage of the conflict with the old authorities seeks to monopolise the right to supervise the "Reform". In the absence of a clear programme of the reform carrying out a series of poorly coordinated socio-economic measures serves only to aggravate the crisis that has ruined the old regime.

After the victory the parliament naturally becomes the principal recruitment base for the new executive. The institutional conflict resumes, but the position of the legislative turns out to be far less favourable now than it was. On the one hand, the new executive has been made up, partially at least, of its own members (and the most distinguished and "progressive" of them at that) and hence has absorbed a substantial share of the legitimacy that was concentrated in the parliament when the latter was fighting the old regime. On the other hand, what has remained of the deputy corps is basically an amalgamation of the opponents of the reforms and the "swamp" (modifying the historical slang, a *"rump"*): by its very representative character, the parliament could not help having supporters of the old regime among its members, but in the ensuing institutional game the presence of these "old-regime" factions is another trump-card in the executive's hand.

Having assumed responsibility for the "Reform", the executive of the new regime faces the unpleasant task of explaining to the people why their grievances, instead of being redressed, appear to have redoubled. As time goes by, it becomes more and more difficult (or, at least, less and less convincing) to blame everything on the old authorities. One has to look for new scapegoats. The candidates are obvious: "the agents" of the old regime that managed to squeeze in the new government structures. These people sabotage the "Reform" and must in all justice bear the guilt for its negative effects.

The institutional confrontation enters its second round, in which the parliament, weakened by the "desertion" of its "best people" to the executive and no longer enjoying the kind of mass support it could count on in its struggle against the old regime, falls easy prey to the new executive. It is either "purged" of representatives of the old regime (as was the case in England after the parliament's victory over the king and during the Reign of Terror in France) or simply turned out.

In the meantime, the new regime happens to reproduce some of the worst features of the old one in an exaggerated, or at least less "graceful" and "civilised", form. The ideals of representative democracy, as a form of balance between the various political forces of the society, remain unrealised; representatives of the old regime are defranchised (in various ways); coercive methods employed in this result in the bounds of law being constantly transgressed and give rise to the peculiar phenomenon of "revolutionary justice". The farther the process unfolds, the deeper the new authorities' involvement in the hopeless struggle against "the enemies" becomes. They soon realise they have been trapped and must make the uninspiring choice between holding new election - with every chance to lose it - and relapsing into the authoritarian practices of old.

The result is that the principal task the society faces, viz. to transform the regime and create a network of effectively functioning modern political institutions is not fulfilled. The "vicious cycle" of abortive institutional transformations is repeated. Russia has already passed through it twice in the course of this century: for the first time, when its first post-revolutionary parliament, the Constituent Assembly, was dissolved by the Bolsheviks in 1918; for the second time, when the same fate befell its first post-communist parliament, the Congress of People's Deputies, in 1993 (to say nothing about the end of the Soviet Union and its representative institutions in 1991).

The comparison of the historic examples suggests that societies seeking transition from authoritarianism to democracy must try to avoid the self-destroying cycle of these institutional conflicts. This means that the constitutional reform is better carried out not in a piecemeal fashion, with the representative institutions established or reanimated while the old executive bodies are still in control, but at one stroke, i.e. accompanied by the simultaneous transformation of the executive.

For this the election to the representative assembly must be held in the conditions of political pluralism that has already been ensured constitutionally. At the initial stage of the revolution political pluralism appears to be realised by the very presence of two opposing parties:

advocates of the old regime and proponents of reforms. However, in an attempt to augment its chances for survival, the old regime usually seeks to hold the election while this pluralism is still outside "the constitutional field".

Such an election usually results in the opposing political forces being represented in the parliament in a ratio that does not correspond to their real weight in the society. A two-party parliament representative of the society at large is thus not created and the subsequent polarisation of the executive and the legislative, that come to operate as substitute political parties, is consequently not prevented.

In other words, what a society at this transitional stage requires is a "shock" reform of its system of political institutions implying preservation of the existing political forces and new constitutional arrangements as a form of a nation-wide consensus between them, instead of preservation (or slow transformation) of the old institutions and forcible elimination of one of the political forces.

"Shock therapy" must thus be employed in the political, not in the economic sphere. It seems that such shock therapy in the political field, based on a preliminary consensus about procedures of politics, is the society's only chance to avoid the institutional traps described above and forestall the competition of legitimacies and the ensuing superimposition of the institutional and political conflicts, i.e. a situation fraught with the downfall of new democratic institutions and restoration of authoritarianism (albeit in a novel, "revolutionary", disguise).

If institutional transformations are carried out in a "shock" manner, the disbalance of legitimacies (of which the dynamics have been described above) does not occur, for all the institutions are established at once and their very system embodies the consensus achieved in the field of *operational experience.*

It is this absence of a conflict of legitimacies that seems to account for the successful, i.e. comparatively "painless", cases of democratisation (that, unfortunately, happen to be an exception rather than a rule): the institution of a democratic regime in the United States in the late 18th century or Spain's democratic revival in the 1970s. In both cases the executive and the legislative were renovated *simultaneously* which facilitated a nation-wide consensus about the proper balance between them and helped keep the political process within the framework of this balance. The two nations could safely proceed with the necessary "adjustments" of the separated powers then and develop a viable system of mutual checks and balances, a task that would appear almost hopeless should a political conflict assume the form of an institutional one.

In less remote circumstances (in time, as well as in space) comparatively successful transformations of this kind have been fulfilled in a number of East European countries, e.g. Poland and Hungary, where the appropriate strategic consensus has been reached at the "nation-wide" "round-tables" prior to the constitutional reforms. The nations that saw their old regimes collapse before such a consensus was worked out (Czechoslovakia, the Soviet Union, Yugoslavia) had to pay the heavy price of disintegration for this absence of a "shock" constitutional reform.

The situation in the former Soviet Union (in Russia, as well as in most other states that have emerged on its ruins) has been further aggravated by establishing presidentialist governments which, in the absence of a procedural consensus, seems to leave but one alternative to the futile confrontation of institutions, viz. a complete submission of the legislative to the executive.

Notes

[1] For the analysis of the social and juridical issues involved, see Beetham 1991.

Bibliography

Aberbach, J., R.Putnam and B.Rockman (1981), *Bureaucrats and Politicians in Western Democracies*, Cambridge, Mass.: Harvard University Press.

Afanasiev, Yu. (ed.) (1988), *Inogo ne dano* [No Other Is Given; in Russian], Moscow: Progress.

Agger, R., D.Goldrich and B.Swanson (1972), *The Rulers and the Ruled*, Belmont: Duxbury Press.

Alker, H. and B.Russett (1965), *World Politics in the General Assembly*, New Haven: Yale University Press.

Aslund, A. (1994), *Shokovaya terapiya v Vostochnoi Evrope i Rossii* [Shock Therapy in Eastern Europe and Russia; a revised Russian edition], Moscow: Respublika.

Autumn-93 (1995), *Moskva. Osen'-93: Khronika protivostoyaniya* [Moscow. Autumn-93: A Chronicle of Confrontation; in Russian], Moscow: Respublika.

Averintsev, S. (1982), "The 'Roman Idea' and the Medieval Reality" [in Russian], in T.Parnicki, *Serebryanye orly* [Silver Eagles], Moscow: Progress, pp. 424-9.

Axelrod, R. (ed.) (1976), *Structure of Decision: The Cognitive Maps of Political Elites*, Princeton: Princeton University Press.

Balzer, H. (ed.) (1991), *Five Years That Shook the World: Gorbachev's Unfinished Revolution*, Boulder et al.: Westview Press.

Barsenkov, A., V.Koretski and A.Ostapenko (1993a), *Politicheskaya Rossiya segodnya: Ispolnitel'naya vlast', Konstitutsionnyi sud, lidery partii i dvizhenii. Spravochnik* [Political Russia Today: The Executive Authority, the Constitutional Court, Leaders of Parties and Movements. A Reference Book; in Russian], Moscow: Moskovski Rabochi.

Barsenkov, A., V.Koretski and A.Ostapenko (1993b), *Politicheskaya Rossiya segodnya: Vysshaya predstavitel'naya vlast'. Spravochnik* [Political Russia Today: The Top Representative Authority. A Reference Book; in Russian], Moscow: Moskovski Rabochi.

Beetham, D. (1991), *The Legitimation of Power*, Houndsmills, Basingstoke, Hampshire - London: Macmillan.

Beetham, D. (1994), "Key Principles and Indices for a Democratic Audit", in D.Beetham (ed.), *Defining and Measuring Democracy* , London - Thousand Oaks, California - New Delhi: SAGE Publications, pp. 25-43.

Berdyaev, N. (1939), *Spirit and Reality*, London: Geoffrey Bles.

Berdyaev, N. (1944), *Slavery and Freedom*, New York: Charles Scribner's Sons.

Berdyaev, N. (1947a), *The Russian Idea*, London: Geoffrey Bles.

293

Berdyaev, N. (1947b), *Solitude and Society*, London: Geoffrey Bles.

Berdyaev, N. (1951; L, 1953), *Tsarstvo Dukha i tsarstvo Kesarya* [The Kingdom of Spirit and the Kingdom of Caesar;{tc ", 1953), *Tsarstvo Dukha i tsarstvo Kesarya* [The Kingdom of Spirit and the Kingdom of Caesar;" \f y} in Russian], Paris: YMCA-Press.

Biryukov, N., L.Byzov, J.Gleisner and V.Sergeyev (forthcoming). "Emergence of a New System of Political Forces and a New State Order in Russia, 1990-93", *Journal of Contemporary History*.

Biryukov, N., J.Gleisner and V.Sergeyev (1995), "The Crisis of *Sobornost'*: Parliamentary Discourse in Present-Day Russia", *Discourse and Society*, vol. 6, No. 2, pp. 149-75.

Biryukov, N. and V.Sergeyev (1992), "Die Buerde der Tradition", in M.Harms and P.Linke (eds.), *Ueberall Klippen: Inner- und Aussenpolitische Gegebenheiten Russlands*, Berlin: Verlag Volk und Welt, pp. 81-103.

Biryukov, N. and V.Sergeyev (1993), "Parliamentarianism and *Sobornost'*: Two Models of Representative Institutions in Russian Political Culture", *Discourse and Society*, Vol. 4, No. 1, pp. 57-74.

Biryukov, N. and V.Sergeyev (1994), "The Idea of Democracy in the West and in the East", in D.Beetham (ed.), *Defining and Measuring Democracy*, London - Thousand Oaks, California - New Delhi: SAGE, pp. 182-98.

Biryukov, N. and V.Sergeyev (1995), "Democracy and *Sobornost'*: The Crisis of the Traditional Political Culture and the Prospects for Russian Democracy (Summary)" [in Russian and English], in L.Repina, V.Sogrin and D.Model (eds.), *Politicheskaya istoriya na poroge XXI veka: Traditsii i novatsii / Political History on the Eve of the XXI Century: Traditions and Innovations*, Moscow: Institute of Universal History, Russian Academy of Sciences, pp. 150-159.

Blair, B.G. (1985), *Strategic Command and Control: Redefining the Nuclear Threat*, Washington, D.C.: The Brookings Institution.

Blais, A. and S.Dion (1990), "Electoral Systems and the Consolidation of New Democracies", in D.Ethier (ed.), *Democratic Transition and Consolidation in Southern Europe, Latin America and Southeast Asia*, London: Macmillan, pp. 250-65.

Bohnam, G.M., P.Parshin and V.Sergeyev (forthcoming), "Comparative Analysis of Styles of Political Reasoning: Kennedy, Khrushchev and the Limited Test-Ban Negotiations", *International Studies Quarterly*.

Bulgakov, S. (1971), *Svet nevechernii: Sozertsaniia i umozreniia* [The Light Which Does Not Fade: Contemplations and Speculations; in Russian], Westmead, Farnborough, Hampshire: Gregg International Publishers [reprint of the 1917 Moscow edition].

Burlatski, F. (1988), "On Soviet Parliamentarianism" (in Russian), *Literaturnaya gazeta*, 26 (16 June).

Carter, A., J.Steinbruner and Ch.Zraket (eds.) (1987), *Managing Nuclear Operations*, Washington, D.C.: The Brookings Institution.

Cherepnin, L. (1978), *Zemskie sobory Russkogo gosudarstva v XVI-XVII vv.* [The Zemskie Sobors of the Russian State in the 16th-17th centuries; in Russian], Moscow: Nauka.

Chronicle (1993), *Khronika tekushchikh sobytii: Moskva, Oktyabr'-93* [A Chronicle of Current Events: Moscow, October-93; in Russian], in *Vek XX i mir* (*XX Century and Peace*; a special issue of the magazine), Moscow.

Chronograph (1987), From "The 1617 Chronograph" [in medieval Russian and Russian], in *Pamyatniki literatury Drevnei Rusi: Konets XVI - nachalo XVII vekov* [Literary Monuments of Early Russia: Late 16th - early 17th century], Moscow: Khudozhestvennaya literatura, pp. 318-57.

Constitutional Conference (1993), *Konstitutsionnoe soveshchanie: Informatsionnyi byulleten'* [Constitutional Conference: Information Bulletin; in Russian], No. 1, Moscow: Izdanie Administratsii Prezidenta Rossiiskoi Federatsii.

Constitution RF (1992), *Konstitutsiya (Osnovnoi zakon) Rossiiskoi Federatsii - Rossii.* [Constitution (Fundamental Law) of the Russian Federation - Russia. Adopted at the Extraordinary Session of the Supreme Soviet of the RSFSR of the Ninth Convocation, on 12 April 1978, with Amendments and Supplements Introduced by the Laws of the RSFSR of 17 October 1989, of 31 May, 16 June and 15 December 1990, of 24 May and 1 November 1991 and the Law of the Russian Federation of 21 April 1992; in Russian], Moscow: Izvestiya.

Constitution RF (1993), *Konstitutsiya Rossiiskoi Federatsii.* [Constitution of the Russian Federation. Adopted by the Nation-Wide Vote on 12 December 1993; in Russian], Moscow: Yuridicheskaya literatura.

Constitution RSFSR (1973), Constitution (Fundamental Law) of the Russian Soviet Federal Socialist Republic [Adopted on 21 January 1937; in Russian], in *Obrazovanie i razvitie Soyuza Sovetskikh Sotsialisticheskikh Respublik: Sbornik dokumentov* [Formation and Development of the Union of Soviet Socialist Republics: A Collection of Documents], Moscow: Yuridicheskaya literatura, pp. 469-87.

Constitution USSR (1947), *Constitution (Fundamental Law) of the Union of Soviet Socialist Republics* (As amended by the Supreme Soviet of the U.S.S.R., on February 25, 1947, on the recommendations of the Drafting Commission), Moscow: Foreign Languages Publishing House.

Constitution USSR (1985), *Constitution (Fundamental Law) of the Union of Soviet Socialist Republics.* (Adopted at the Seventh (Special) Session of the Supreme Soviet of the USSR, Ninth Convocation, on 7 October 1977), Moscow: Novosti Press Agency.

Constitution USSR (1988), *Konstitutsiya (Osnovnoi zakon) Soyuza Sovetskikh Sotsialisticheskikh Respublik.* [Constitution (Fundamental Law) of the Union of the Soviet Socialist Republics. With Amendments and Supplements introduced by the Law of the USSR of 1 December 1988 at the Extraordinary Twelfth

Session of the USSR Supreme Soviet of the Eleventh Convocation; in Russian], Moscow: Izvestiya.

Cotler, J. (1995), "Crisis politica, outsiders y democraduras: El "fujimorismo", in *Partidos y clase politica en America Latina en los 90 /* Compilado por C.Perelli, S.Picado y D.Zovatto. San Jose, Costa Rica: IIDH - Capel, pp. 117-41.

Dahl, R.A. (1971), *Polyarchy: Participation and Opposition*, New Haven, Connecticut - London: Yale University Press.

Davydov, A. (1990), "The First Stage is Coming to an End: More Mandates than Aspirants" [in Russian], in *Proryv v demokratiyu* [Breakthrough to Democracy], Moscow: Izvestiya.

Draft Constitution (1992), *Proekt Konstitutsii Rossiiskoi Federatsii: Sbornik materialov* [Draft Constitution of the Russian Federation: A Collection of Material; in Russian], Moscow: Respublika.

Draft Constitution (1993), Constitution of the Russian Federation: A Draft [in Russian], in *Konstitutsionnoe soveshchanie: Informatsionnyi byulleten'* [Constitutional Conference: Information Bulletin], No. 1, Moscow: Izdanie Administratsii Prezidenta Rossiiskoi Federatsii, pp. 109-55.

Duroselle, J.-B. (1981), *Tout empire perira*, Paris: Publications de la Sorbonne.

Eighth Congress RF (1993), *Vos'moi S'ezd narodnykh deputatov Rossiiskoi Federatsii* [The Eighth Congress of People's Deputies of the Russian Federation; in Russian], 7 bulletins, [Moscow:] Izdanie Verkhovnogo Soveta Rossiiskoi Federatsii.

Fennel, J.L.I. (ed.) (1955), *The Correspondence between Prince A.M.Kurbsky and Tsar Ivan IV of Russia. 1564-1579.* Cambridge: The Cambridge University Press.

Fifth Congress RSFSR (1993), *Pyatyi (vneocherednoi) S'ezd narodnykh deputatov RSFSR* [The Fifth (Extraordinary) Congress of People's Deputies of the RSFSR; in Russian], 23 bulletins, [Moscow:] Izdanie Verkhovnogo Soveta RSFSR.

First Congress RSFSR (1992), *Pervyi S'ezd narodnykh deputatov RSFSR: Stenograficheski Otchyot* [The First Congress of People's Deputies of the RSFSR: The Verbatim Record; in Russian], 6 vols, Moscow: Respublika.

First Congress USSR (1989), *Pervyi S'ezd narodnykh deputatov SSSR: Stenograficheski Otchyot* [The First Congress of People's Deputies of the USSR: The Verbatim Record; in Russian], 6 vols, Moscow: Izdatel'stvo Verkhovnogo Soveta SSSR.

Fourth Congress RSFSR (1991), *Chetvyortyi (vneocherednoi) S'ezd narodnykh deputatov RSFSR: Stenograficheski Otchyot* [The Fourth (Extraordinary) Congress of People's Deputies of the RSFSR: The Verbatim Record; in Russian], 4 vols, Moscow: Izdatel'stvo Verkhovnogo Soveta RSFSR.

Fourth Congress USSR (1991), *Chetvyortyi S'ezd narodnykh deputatov SSSR: Stenograficheski otchyot* [The Fourth Congress of People's Deputies of the

USSR: The Verbatim Record; in Russian], 4 vols, Moscow: Izdatel'stvo Verkhovnogo Soveta SSSR.

Frank, S. (1926), *Die russische Weltanschauung*, Charlottenburg: Pan-Verlag Rolf Heise.

Frank, S. (1930), *Dukhovny'a osnovy obshchestva: Vvedenie v sotsial'nuyu filosofiyu* [The Spiritual Foundations of Society: Introduction into Social Philosophy; in Russian], Paris: YMCA-Press.

Friedman, M. (1963), *Capitalism and Freedom*, Chicago: The University of Chicago Press.

Gandia, E. de (1940), *Historia de la Republica Argentina en el siglio XIX*, Buenos Aires: Anjel Estrada.

Griboyedov, A. [no date], *The Mischief of Being Clever (Gore ot uma)*, [London:] School of Slavonic Studies, the University of London.

Grushin, B. (1993), "Russia, '93 - New Myths, New Realities: Have We Denounced the Old World?" [in Russian], *Nezavisimaya gazeta*, 15 June.

Gulyga, A. (1995), *Russkaya ideya i eyo tvortsy* [The Russia Idea and Its Creators; in Russian], Moscow: Soratnik.

Hadenius, A. (1994), "The Duration of Democracy: Institutional vs Socioeconomic Factors", in D.Beetham (ed.), *Defining and Measuring Democracy*, London - Thousand Oaks, California - New Delhi: SAGE, pp. 63-88.

Hamilton, A., J.Madison and J.Jay (1961), *The Federalist Papers*, New York: Mentor Book.

Hammond, Th.H. and J.M.Fraser (1983), "Baselines for Evaluating Explanations of Coalition Behaviour in Congress", *Journal of Politics*, Vol. 45, No. 3, pp. 635-56.

Hayek, F.A. (1978), *New Studies in Philosophy, Politics, Economics and the History of Ideas*, Chicago: The University of Chicago Press.

Hayek, F.A. (1989), *The Fatal Conceit: The Errors of Socialism*, Chicago: The University of Chicago Press [Vol. 1 of *The Collected Works* of F.A.Hayek].

Hegel, G. (1966), *The Science of Logic*, 2 vols, London: George Allen and Unwin - New York: Humanities Press.

Hildebert (1969), Hildeberti Cenomannes Episcopi *Carmina Minora*, Leipzig: BSB B.G. Teubner Verlagsgesellschaft.

Hoffmann, E.P. (1994), "Challenges to Viable Constitutionalism in Post-Soviet Russia", *The Harriman Review*, Vol. 7, No. 10-12, pp. 19-56.

Horowitz, D.L. (1990), "Comparing Democratic Systems", *Journal of Democracy*, Vol. 1, No. 4, pp. 73-9.

Hume, D. [no year], "Of the First Principles of Government", in *Essays Literary, Moral, and Political*, London: Ward, Lock, and Tyler, Warwick House, pp. 23-5.

Ioann [Snychev] (1994-95), "Rus' of *Sobornost'*: Outlines of Christian Statehood" [in Russian], *Nash sovremennik*, 1994, No. 8, pp. 3-12; No. 9, pp. 3-12;

298 Russian Politics in Transition

No. 10, pp. 22-35; Nos. 11-12, pp. 7-16; 1995, No. 2, pp. 13-24; No. 4, pp. 100-6; No. 7, pp. 77-83.

Jaures, J. (1969-72), *Histoire socialiste de la Révolution française*, 6 vols, Paris: Editions Sociales.

Joensson, Ch. (1982), *Cognitive Dynamics and International Politics*, London: Frances Pinter.

Koval', B. (ed.) (1993), *Rossiya segodnya: Politicheski portret v dokumentakh. Vyp. 2. 1991-1992. Stanovlenie gosudarstvennosti. Armiya i politika. Novye partii. Tserkov' i obshchestvo* [Russia Today: A Political Portrait in Documents, Issue 2. 1991-92. Statehood Formation. Army and Politics. New Parties. Church and Society; in Russian], Moscow: Mezhdunarodnye otnosheniya.

Kryshtanovkaya, O. (1995), "Transformation of the Old *Nomenklatura* into the New Russian Elite" [in Russian], *Obshchestvennye nauki i sovremennost'*, No. 1, pp. 51-65.

Lapidus, G.W. (ed.) (1995), *The New Russia: Troubled Transformation* (Boulder - San Francisco - Oxford: Westview Press).

Law on Elections (1989), *Zakon Rossiiskoi Sovetskoi Federativnoi Sotsialisticheskoi Respubliki o vyborakh narodnykh deputatov RSFSR* [Law of the Russian Soviet Federal Socialist Republic on Elections of People's Deputies of the RSFSR; in Russian], Moscow: Sovetskaya Rossiya.

Legislation (1971), *Zakonodatel'stvo o religioznykh kul'takh: Sbornik materialov i dokumentov* [Legislation on Religious Worship: A Collection of Material and Documents; in Russian], Moscow: Yuridicheskaya literatura.

Lenin, V. (1961), *What Is to Be Done? Burning Questions of Our Movement*, in *Collected Works*, Vol. 5, Moscow: Foreign Languages Publishing House, pp. 347-529.

Lenin, V. (1964), *Imperialism, the Highest Stage of Capitalism: A Popular Outline*, in *Collected Works*, Vol. 22, Moscow: Foreign Languages Publishing House, pp. 185-304.

Lijphart, A. (1977), *Democracy in Plural Societies: A Comparative Exploration*, New Haven, Connecticut: Yale University Press.

Lijphart, A. (1984), *Democracies: Patterns of Majoritarian and Consensus Government in Twenty-One Countries*, New Haven, Connecticut - London: Yale University Press.

Lijphart, A. (1990), "The Power-Sharing Approach" in J.V.Montville (ed.), *Conflict and Peacemaking in Multiethnic Societies*, Lexington, Massachusetts: Lexington Books, pp. 491-509.

Lijphart, A. (1994, preprint), "The Puzzle of Indian Democracy: A Re-interpretation", University of California (San Diego).

Linz, J.J. (1990a), "The Perils of Presidentialism", *Journal of Democracy*, Vol. 1, No. 1, pp. 51-69.

Linz, J.J. (1990b), "The Virtues of Parliamentarianism", *Journal of Democracy*, Vol. 1, No. 4, pp. 84-94.

Lipset, S.M. (1990), "The Centrality of Political Culture", *Journal of Democracy*, Vol. 1, No. 4, pp. 80-3.

Livy (1965), *The Early History of Rome*, Harmondsworth, Middlesex: Penguin Books.

Lossky, N. (1953), *Dostoevski i ego khristianskoe miroponimanie* [Dostoevsky and His Christian World Concept; in Russian], New York: Izdatel'stvo imeni Chekhova [Chekhov Publishing House].

Lossky, N. (1994), *Bog i mirovoye zlo* [God and Universal Evil; in Russian], Moscow: Respublika. [First published in 1941]

Machiavelli, N. (1979), *The Prince*, in *The Portable Machiavelli*, New York et al. Penguin Books, pp. 77-166.

Mandel, D. (1992), "Post-*Perestroika*: Revolution from Above v. Revolution from Below", in S.White, A.Pravda and Z.Gitelman (eds.), *Developments in Soviet and Post-Soviet Politics*, Houndmills, Basingstoke, Hampshire - London: Macmillan. pp. 278-99.

McFaul, M. (1995), "Why Russia's Politics Matter", *Foreign Affairs*, Vol. 74, No. 1, pp. 87-99.

McFaul, M., V.Lysenko, P.Reddaway, A.Tsipko, S.Sestanovitch, J.Dunlop, V.Mau and Ch.Fairbanks Jr. (1994), "Is Russian Democracy Doomed?", *Journal of Democracy*, Vol. 5, No. 2, p. 3-42.

Migranyan, A. (1990), *Perestroika as Seen by a Political Scientist*, Moscow: Novosti.

Murphy, W.F. (1991), "Comments on the Draft of the Russian Constitution", in *Comments and Recommendations on the Draft Constitution of the Russian Federation*, Washington, D.C.: United States Institute of Peace.

Murphy, W.F. (1993), "Constitutions, Constitutionalism and Democracy", in D.Greenberg, D.N.Katz, M.B.Oliviero and S.V.Wheatley (eds.), *Constitutionalism and Democracy: Transitions in the Contemporary World*, New York - Oxford: Oxford University Press.

Neumann, J. von and O.Morgenstern (1947), *Theory of Games and Economic Behavior*, Princeton: Princeton University Press.

Ninth Congress RF (1993), *Devyatyi (vneocherednoi) S'ezd narodnykh deputatov Rossiiskoi Federatsii* [The Ninth (Extraordinary) Congress of People's Deputies of the Russian Federation; in Russian], 8 bulletins, [Moscow:] Izdanie Verkhovnogo Soveta Rossiiskoi Federatsii.

Parfyonov Ph. (1991), "Hardening Authoritarianism is the Best Variant, as Well as a Harsh Reality" [in Russian], in *Nezavisimaya gazeta*, 28 November.

Parshin, P. and V.Sergeyev (1990), "Conceptual Reconstruction and Conflict Resolution: Further Reflections on the Caribbean Crisis": (A paper presented to the 1990 ISA Annual Convention in Washington, D.C.)

Party Worker (1991), *Spravochnik partiinogo rabotnika. 1990* [A Party Worker's Reference Book. 1990; in Russian], Vol. 30, Moscow: Politizdat.

Pipes, R. (1974), *Russia under the Old Regime*, Harmondsworth, Miiddlesex et al.: Penguin Books.

Riggs, F.W. (1994), "Conceptual Homogenization of a Heterogeneous Field", in M.Dogan and A.Kazancigil (eds.), *Comparing Nations: Concepts, Strategies, Substance*, Oxford, UK - Cambridge, USA: Blackwell, 1994, pp. 72-152.

Riggs, F.W. (1994, preprint), "Ethnonationalism, Industrialism and the Modern State", University of Hawaii.

Sakwa, R. (1993), *Russian Politics and Society*, London - New York: Routledge.

Satarov, G.A. and S.B.Stankevich (1983), "Voting in the U.S. Congress: An Essay in Multidimensional Analysis" (in Russian), *Sotsiologicheskie issledovaniya*, No. 1, pp. 156—65.

Second Congress RSFSR (1992), *Vtoroi (vneocherednoi) S'ezd narodnykh deputatov RSFSR: Stenograficheski Otchyot* [The Second (Extraordinary) Congress of People's Deputies of the RSFSR: The Verbatim Record; in Russian], 6 vols, Moscow: Respublika.

Sergeyev, V. (1987), "Patterns of Understanding of Political Development" [in Russian], in *Uchyonye zapiski Tartusskogo gosudarstvennogo universiteta* [Transactions of the Tartu State University], 751.

Sergeyev, V. (1988), "Tiger in a Swamp: M.Robespierre's Political Portrait" [in Russian], *Znanie - sila*, No. 7.

Sergeyev, V. (1989a), "Despotism of Freedom: Rhetoric of the French Revolution" [in Russian], *Inostrannaya literatura*, No. 7.

Sergeyev, V. (1989b), "Text Structure and Analysis of Argumentation in Kurbsky's *First Epistle*" [in Russian] in *Metody izucheniya istochnikov po istorii russkoi obshchestvennoi mysli perioda feodalizma* [Methods of Studying Sources for the History of Russian Social Thought in the Feudal Period], Moscow: Institute of History of the USSR.

Sergeyev, V. (1991), "Precedent Logic and Building of International Order: Using the Past to Construct the Future (Exemplification and Models of Pre-Understanding)" (A paper presented to the 1991 ISA Annual Convention in Vancouver.)

Sergeyev V., A.Belyaev, N.Biryukov, Ya.Dranyov and J.Gleisner (1995), "Voting in the Russian Parliament (1990-93): The Spectrum of Political Forces and the Conflict between the Executive and the Legislative", *Journal of Behavioral and Social Sciences*, No. 2 (special issue on "Parliamentary System and Presidential System in Crisis), pp. 66-108.

Sergeyev V., A.Belyaev, N.Biryukov, Ya.Dranyov and J.Gleisner (forthcoming), "Group Voting Behaviour and the Evolution of Political Spectrum: The Russian Parliament in 1990-93", *CENSIS*.

Sergeyev, V. and N.Biryukov (1993), *Russia's Road to Democracy: Parliament, Communism and Traditional Culture*. Aldershot, Hampshire: Edward Elgar Publishing Ltd.

Seventh Congress RF (1993), *Sed'moi S'ezd narodnykh deputatov Rossiiskoi Federatsii: Stenograficheski Otchyot* [The Seventh Congress of People's Deputies of the Russian Federation: The Verbatim Record; in Russian], 4 vols, Moscow: Respublika.

Sixsmith, M. (1991), *Moscow Coup: The Death of the Soviet System*, London: Simon & Schuster.

Sixth Congress RF (1992), *Shestoi S'ezd narodnykh deputatov Rossiiskoi Federatsii: Stenograficheski Otchyot* [The Sixth Congress of People's Deputies of the Russian Federation: The Verbatim Record; in Russian], 5 vols, Moscow: Respublika.

Sobyanin, A. and D.Yuriev (1991), *S'ezd narodnykh deputatov RSFSR v zerkale poimyonnykh golosovanii: Rasstanovka sil i dinamika razvitiya politicheskogo protivostoyaniya* [The Congress of People's Deputies of the RSFSR as Mirrored in Roll Calls: The Pattern of Forces and the Dynamics of Development of Political Confrontation; in Russian], Moscow [no publisher indicated].

Third Congress RSFSR (1991), *Tretii (vneocherednoi) S'ezd narodnykh deputatov RSFSR* [The Third (Extraordinary) Congress of People's Deputies of the RSFSR; in Russian], 17 bulletins, [Moscow:] Izdanie Verkhovnogo Soveta RSFSR.

Third Congress USSR (1990), *Vneocherednoi Tretii S'ezd narodnykh deputatov SSSR: Stenograficheski otchyot* [The Extraordinary Third Congress of the USSR People's Deputies: The Verbatim Record; in Russian], 3 vols., Moscow: Izdatel'stvo Verkhovnogo Soveta SSSR.

Titarenko, A. (1974), *Struktury nravstvennogo soznaniya: Opyt etiko-filosofskogo issledovaniya* [The Structures of Moral Consciousness: An Essay in Ethico-Philosophical Research; in Russian], Moscow: Mysl'.

Tucker, R. (1987), *Political Culture and Leadership in Soviet Russia: From Lenin to Gorbachev*, New York, London: W.W.Norton & Co.

Vanneman, P. (1977), *Politics and the Legislative Process in the Soviet Political System*, Durham, North Carolina: Duke University Press.

Vasilyev, V. (1994), "What We Need Is Not the Duma, but a Legislative Assembly" [in Russian], *Nezavisimaya gazeta*, 10 June.

Vishnevskaya Yu. (1993), "An Epistle on Despotism to a Friend in St. Petersburg" [in Russian], *Nezavisimaya gazeta*, 19 June.

Vycheslavzeff, B. (1955), *Vechnoe v russkoi filosofii* [The Permanent in Russian Philosophy; in Russian], New York: Izdatel'stvo imeni Chekhova [Chekhov Publishing House].

White, S. (1979), *Political Culture and Soviet Politics*, London - Basingstoke: Macmillan.

White, S. (1992), "Towards a Post-Soviet Politics", in S.White, A.Pravda and Z.Gitelman (eds.), *Developments in Soviet and Post-Soviet Politics*, Houndmills, Basingstoke, Hampshire - London: Macmillan. pp. 2-21.

Abbreviations

SZRF - *Sobranie zakonodatel'stva Rossiiskoi Federatsii* [Collected Legislation of the Russian Federation], Moscow: Izdanie Administratsii Prezidenta Rossiiskoi Federatsii.

VSNDiVS - *Vedomosti S'ezda narodnykh deputatov RSFSR i Verkhovnogo Soveta RSFSR* (since 1992, No. 6 - *Vedomosti S'ezda narodnykh deputatov Rossiiskoi Federatsii i Verkhovnogo Soveta Rossiiskoi Federatsii*) [Register of the Congress of People's Deputies of the RSFSR and the Supreme Soviet of the RSFSR (since 1992, No. 6 - Register of the Congress of People's Deputies of the Russian Federation and the Supreme Soviet of the Russian Federation); in Russian], Moscow: Izdanie Verkhovnogo Soveta RSFSR (Rossiiskoi Federatsii).

Appendix

Figure 1. Intrafaction voting discordance: Distribution function (Communists of Russia, the Sixth Congress).

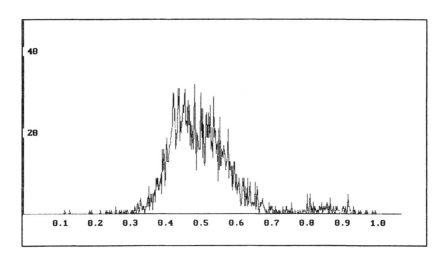

Figure 2. Intrafaction voting discordance: Distribution function (New Generation (New Politics), the Sixth Congress).

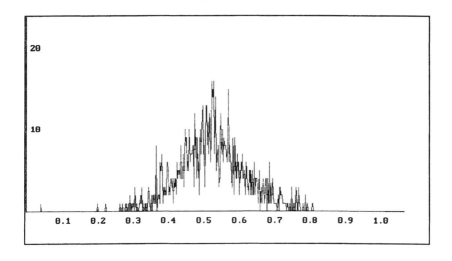

Figure 3. Intrafaction voting discordance: Distribution function (Radical Democrats, the Sixth Congress).

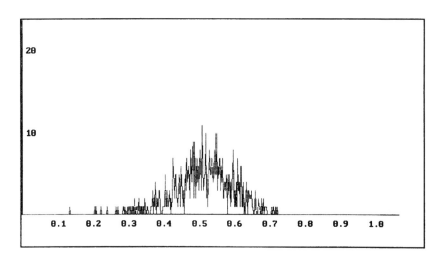

Figure 4. Voting discordance: Distribution function (A Random Selection of Deputies,[1] the Sixth Congress).

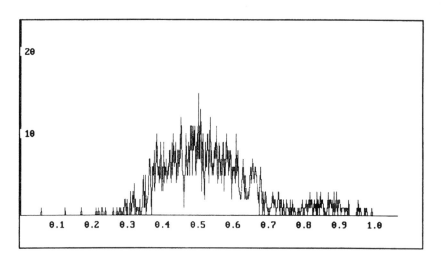

---

[1] A group of deputies whose names begin with "A".

**Figure 5. Intrafaction voting discordance: in the German *Bundestag:*
Distribution function (Social Democratic Party, 1983-87).**

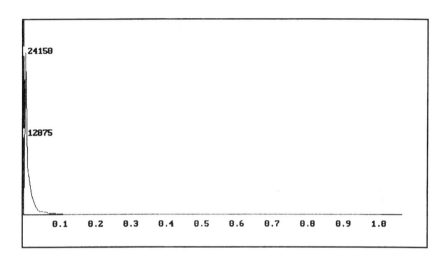

**Figure 6. Voting discordance: Distribution function ("Factions United",[1]
the Sixth Congress).**

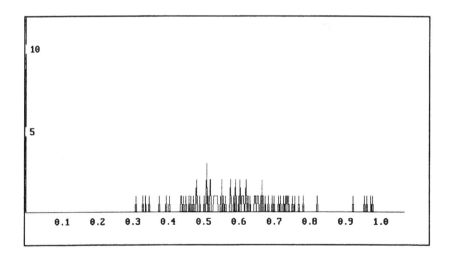

---

[1] A group of 14 deputies, each representing one of the 14 factions.

Figure 7. Participation of factions by members of the Supreme Soviet (by January 1993).

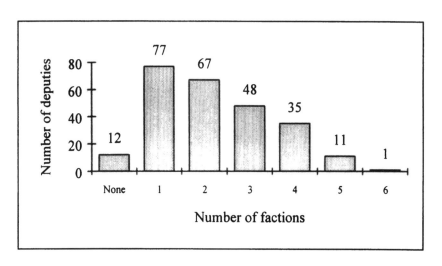

Figure 8. Participation of factions by members of the Supreme Soviet (by January 1993).

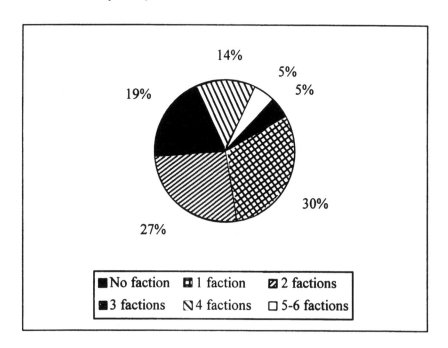

Figure 9. Political spectrum-map:
   The Second Congress of People's Deputies.

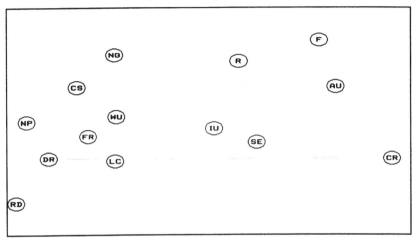

Figure 10. Political spectrum-map:
   The Third Congress of People's Deputies.

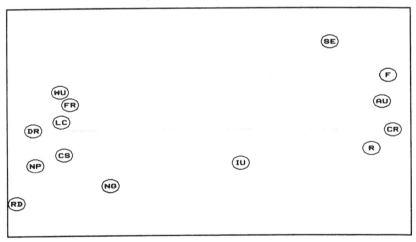

AU	Agrarian Union	LC	Left Centre
CR	Communists of Russia	NG	New Generation (New Politics)
CS	Civil Society	NP	Non-Party Deputies
DR	Democratic Russia	R	Russia
F	Fatherland	RD	Radical Democrats
FR	Free Russia	SE	Sovereignty and Equality
IU	Industrial Union	WU	Workers' Union

Figure 11. Political spectrum-map:
The Fourth Congress of People's Deputies.

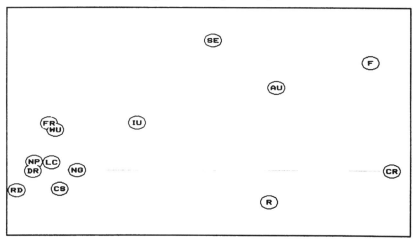

Figure 12. Political spectrum-map:
The Fifth Congress of People's Deputies.

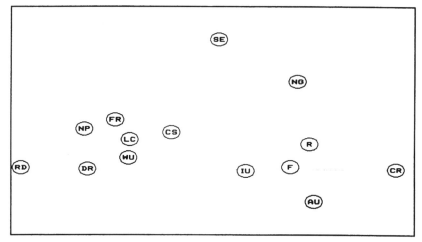

AU	Agrarian Union	LC	Left Centre
CR	Communists of Russia	NG	New Generation (New Politics)
CS	Civil Society	NP	Non-Party Deputies
DR	Democratic Russia	R	Russia
F	Fatherland	RD	Radical Democrats
FR	Free Russia	SE	Sovereignty and Equality
IU	Industrial Union	WU	Workers' Union

Figure 13. Political spectrum-map:
   The Sixth Congress of People's Deputies.

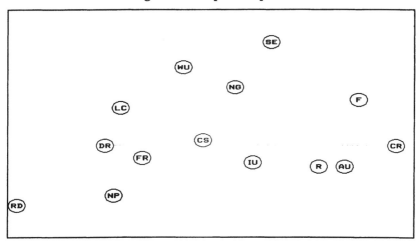

Figure 14. Political spectrum-map:
   The Seventh Congress of People's Deputies.

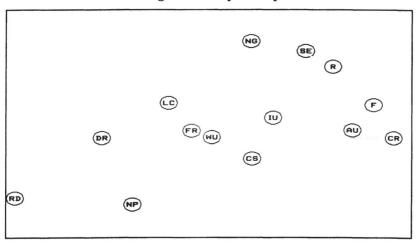

AU	Agrarian Union	LC	Left Centre
CR	Communists of Russia	NG	New Generation (New Politics)
CS	Civil Society	NP	Non-Party Deputies
DR	Democratic Russia	R	Russia
F	Fatherland	RD	Radical Democrats
FR	Free Russia	SE	Sovereignty and Equality
IU	Industrial Union	WU	Workers' Union

Figure 15. Political spectrum-map:
The Eighth Congress of People's Deputies.

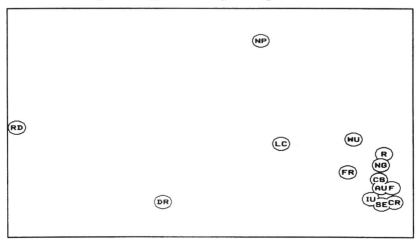

Figure 16. Political spectrum-map:
The Ninth Congress of People's Deputies.

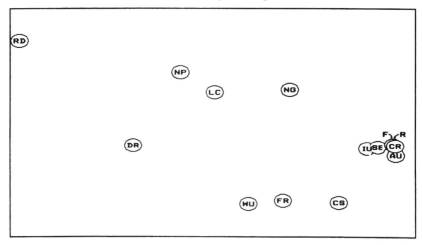

AU	Agrarian Union		LC	Left Centre
CR	Communists of Russia		NG	New Generation (New Politics)
CS	Civil Society		NP	Non-Party Deputies
DR	Democratic Russia		R	Russia
F	Fatherland		RD	Radical Democrats
FR	Free Russia	SE	Sovereignty and Equality
IU	Industrial Union		WU	Workers' Union

Figure 17. Political evolution: Agrarian Union.

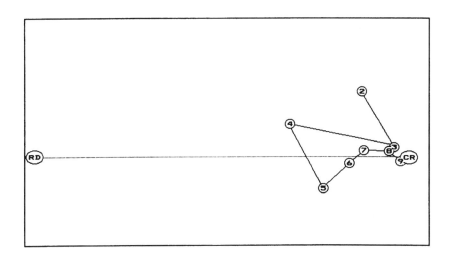

Figure 18. Political evolution: Civil Society.

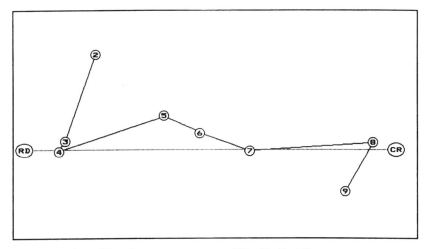

CR Communists of Russia   RD Radical Democrats

Figure 19. Political evolution: Democratic Russia.

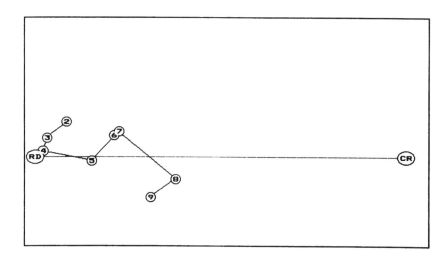

Figure 20. Political evolution: Fatherland.

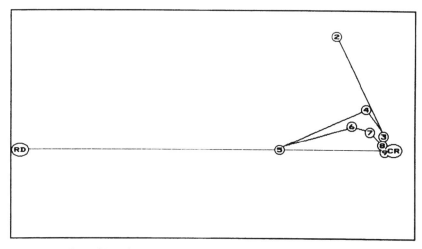

CR   Communists of Russia   RD   Radical Democrats

Figure 21. Political evolution: Free Russia.

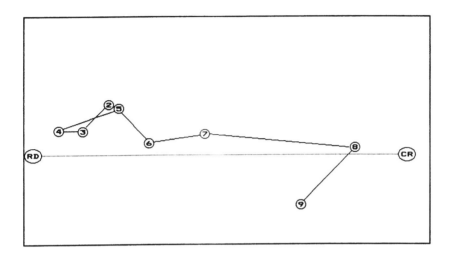

Figure 22. Political evolution: Industrial Union.

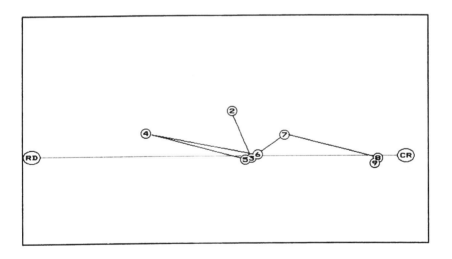

CR   Communists of Russia   RD   Radical Democrats

Figure 23. Political evolution: Left Centre.

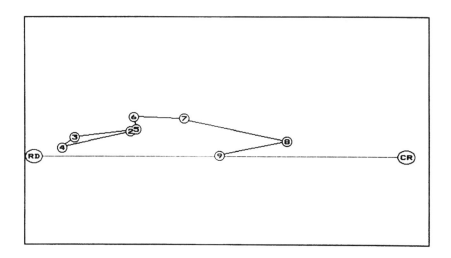

Figure 24. Political evolution: New Generation (New Politics).

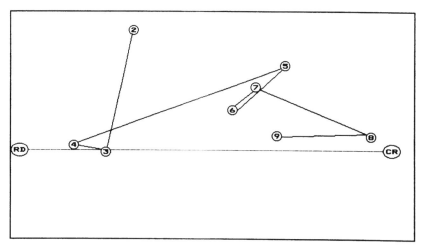

CR   Communists of Russia   RD   Radical Democrats

Figure 25. Political evolution: Non-Party Deputies.

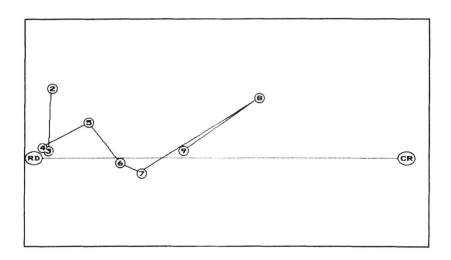

Figure 26. Political evolution: Russia.

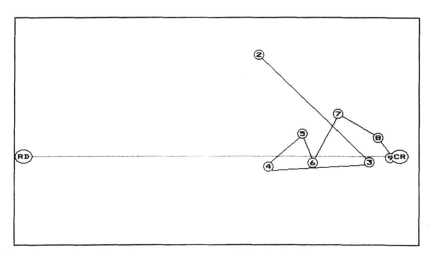

CR   Communists of Russia   RD   Radical Democrats

Figure 27. Political evolution: Sovereignty and Equality.

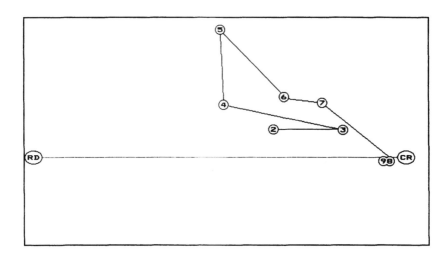

Figure 28. Political evolution: Workers' Union.

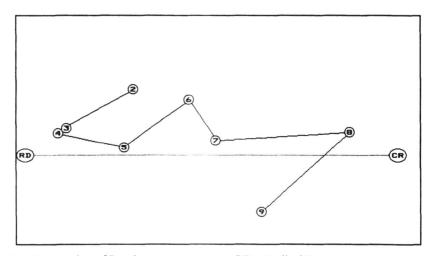

CR   Communists of Russia   RD   Radical Democrats

Figure 29. Semantic correlates of *sobornost'*:
Occurrence of pseudo-agencies (sittings).

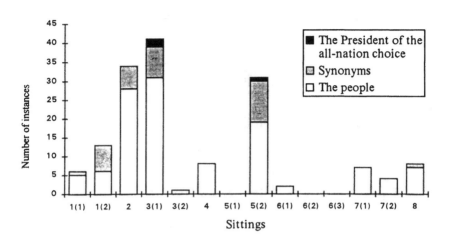

Figure 30. Semantic correlates of *sobornost'*:
Relative frequency of pseudo-agencies (sittings).

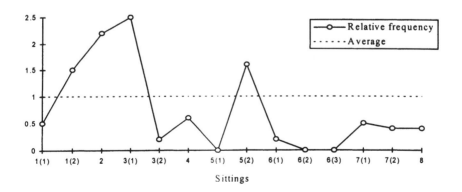

**Figure 31. Uneven distribution of pseudo-agencies:
Occurrence (The 2nd part of the fifth sitting).**

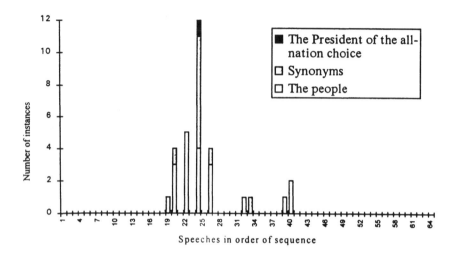

**Figure 32. Uneven distribution of pseudo-agencies:
Frequency (The 2nd part of the fifth sitting).**

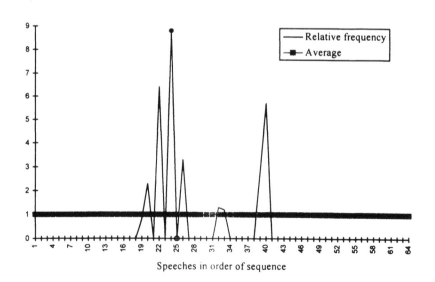

Figure 33. Semantic correlates of *sobornost'*:
Occurrence of pseudo-agencies (factions).

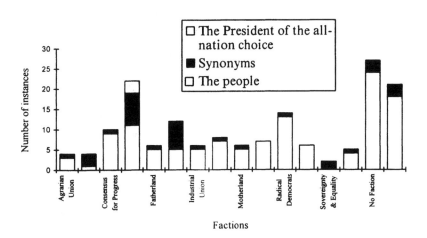

Figure 34. Semantic correlates of *sobornost'*:
Relative frequency of pseudo-agencies (factions).

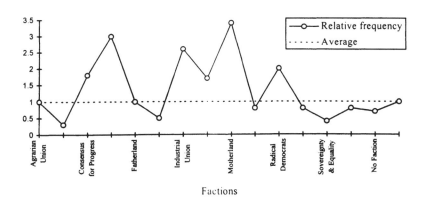

Figure 35. Review of factions: Participation and rhetoric (in reverse order of relative frequency).

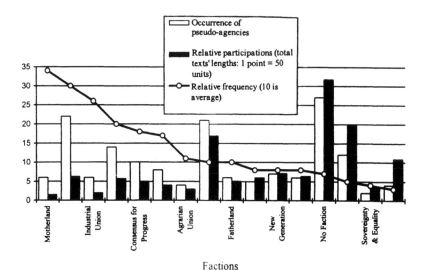

Factions

Figure 36. Logical Decomposition of a Processual Imperative.

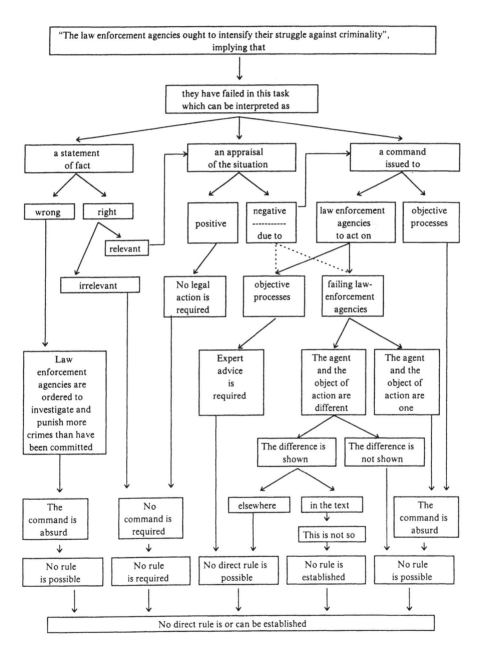

Table 1. Political "Distances" between "Factions": The Sixth Congress of People's Deputies.[1]

Matrix of "true" distances (the numbers of non-concurrent positions in the respective voting lines).

0	113	158	137	158	75	31	222	77	37	69	37	98	149
113	0	71	54	69	72	98	131	56	140	62	120	33	58
158	71	0	37	30	117	143	68	91	191	101	163	72	37
137	54	37	0	31	98	122	93	76	172	78	146	53	30
158	69	30	31	0	117	143	70	91	193	99	167	68	29
75	72	117	98	117	0	60	179	62	102	42	74	69	106
31	98	143	122	143	60	0	207	70	54	54	46	83	134
222	131	68	93	70	179	207	0	157	257	159	227	136	85
77	56	91	76	91	62	70	157	0	108	52	94	47	84
37	140	191	172	193	102	54	257	108	0	100	34	131	180
69	62	101	78	99	42	54	159	52	100	0	74	51	86
37	120	163	146	167	74	46	227	94	34	74	0	107	156
98	33	72	53	68	69	83	136	47	131	51	107	0	63
149	58	37	30	29	106	134	85	84	180	86	156	63	0

Matrix of "visible" distances (as seen on the chart upon the numerical solving of the differential equations; approximated to round numbers).

0	118	157	137	162	76	18	223	82	35	62	32	97	153
118	0	76	51	64	60	102	130	36	147	64	118	37	46
157	76	0	26	24	127	139	66	96	191	95	170	65	41
137	51	26	0	25	102	119	88	71	170	75	148	41	27
162	64	24	25	0	121	144	66	91	195	100	171	65	20
76	60	127	102	121	0	65	188	32	96	56	64	65	105
18	102	139	119	144	65	0	205	67	52	44	41	79	136
223	130	66	88	66	188	205	0	157	257	161	236	129	84
82	36	96	71	91	32	67	157	0	111	36	83	33	77
35	147	191	170	195	96	52	257	111	0	96	33	130	185
62	64	95	75	100	56	44	161	36	96	0	76	36	92
32	118	170	148	171	64	41	236	83	33	76	0	107	159
97	37	65	41	65	65	79	129	33	130	36	107	0	56
153	46	41	27	20	105	136	84	77	185	92	159	56	0

---

[1] The factions are given (both in lines and in columns) in the following order: (1) Agrarian Union; (2) Workers' Union; (3) Non-Party Deputies; (4) Free Russia; (5) Democratic Russia; (6) Sovereignty and Equality; (7) Russia; (8) Radical Democrats; (9) New Generation (New Politics); (10) Communists of Russia; (11) Industrial Union; (12) Fatherland; (13) Civil Society; (14) Left Centre.

Table 2. The Degree of Accuracy of the Two-dimensional Approximation.

Congress	Number of roll calls	Maximum "distance" between "factions"[1]	Average "distance" between "factions"[2]	Average deviation[3]	Relative average deviation[4]
II	166	58	26.6	2.0	0.0763
III	285	181	86.3	1.0	0.0120
IV	250	102	41.8	1.0	0.0245
V	127	38	16.4	1.7	0.1045
VI	593	257	98.7	5.3	0.0539
VII	249	132	49.6	2.1	0.0425
VIII	77	58	17.5	0.6	0.0360
IX	74	49	18.0	0.5	0.0274

---

[1] The maximum element of the original matrix of "true distances".

[2] The average value of the original matrix element.

[3] The difference between the "true" and the "visible" distances.

[4] Column (4) divided by column (3).

Table 3. Semantic Correlates of *Sobornost'*: Populist Rhetoric at the Ninth Congress of People's Deputies (Summary of Sittings).

Congress/ Sitting (Part)[1]	Date	Total length of texts[2]	People as agency[3] The People	President Synonyms		Total	Relative frequency[4]
IX-1 (1)	26.03.93	494	5	1	0	6	0.5
IX-1 (2)	26.03.93	355	6	7	0	13	1.5
IX-2	26.03.93	639	28	6	0	34	2.2
IX-3 (1)	27.03.93	673	31	8	2	41	2.5
IX-3 (2)	27.03.93	273	1	0	0	1	0.2
IX-4	27.03.93	595	8	0	0	8	0.6
IX-5 (1)	28.03.93	52	0	0	0	0	0
IX-5 (2)	28.03.93	794	19	11	1	31	1.6
IX-6 (1)	28.03.93	528	2	0	0	2	0.2
IX-6 (2)	28.03.93	56	0	0	0	0	0
IX-6 (3)	28.03.93	46	0	0	0	0	0
IX-7 (1)	29.03.93	601	7	0	(1)	7	0.5
IX-7 (2)	29.03.93	454	4+(3)	0	0	4	0.4
IX-8	29.03.93	811	7+(2)	1	0	8	0.4
Undelivered speeches		303	5+(1)	0	0	5	0.7
Total		6674	123+(6)	34	3+(1)	160	1

---

[1] Sittings are divided into parts according to the number of officially announced breaks.

[2] In arbitrary units: 1 = 1 cm of the text column in *Ninth Congress RF* 1993.

[3] Column (4) shows the number of instances in which the term "the people" occurs in the records; column (5), its synonyms ("Russia" and the like); column (6), the expression "the President of the all-nation choice" ("*vsenarodno izbranny Prezident*"); parentheses refer to indirect speech: quotations, paraphrases, allusions to someone else's words; these are not included in the final figure shown in column (7).

[4] Column (7) divided by column (3), the average (calculated from the last row entries "Total") taken as 1.

Table 4. Semantic Correlates of *Sobornost'*: Populist Rhetoric at the Ninth Congress of People's Deputies (Summary of Factions, in Alphabetic Order).

Faction	Total length of texts[1]	People as agency[2]		President	Total	Relative frequency[3]
		The People	Synonyms			
Agrarian Union	148	3	1	0	4	1.1
Communists of Russia	544	1	3	0	4	0.3
Consensus for Progress	233	9	1	0	10	1.8
Democratic Russia	311	11	8	3	22	3.0
Fatherland	252	5	1	0	6	1.0
Free Russia	987	5	7	0	12	0.5
Industrial Union	98	5	1	0	6	2.6
Left Centre - Cooperation	200	7	1	0	8	1.7
Motherland	74	5	1	0	6	3.4
New Generation (New Policy)	357	7	0	0	7	0.8
Radical Democrats	285	13	1	0	14	2.0
Russia	319	6+(3)	0	(1)	6	0.8
Sovereignty and Equality	183	0	2	0	2	0.4
Workers' Union - Reforms without Shock	248	4+(1)	1	0	5	0.8
Non-Parliament officials	847	18	3	0	21	1.0
Deputies outside factions	1588	24+(2)	3	0	27	0.7

[1] In arbitrary units: 1 = 1 cm of the text column in *Ninth Congress RF* 1993.

[2] Column (3) shows the number of instances in which the term "the people" occurs in the records; column (4), its synonyms ("Russia" and the like); column (5), the expression "the President of the all-nation choice" ("*vsenarodno izbranny Prezident*"); parentheses refer to indirect speech: quotations, paraphrases, allusions to someone else's words; these are not included in the final figure shown in column (6).

[3] Column (6) divided by column (2), the average (calculated from the last row entries "Total") taken as 1.

Table 5. Semantic Correlates of *Sobornost'*: Populist Rhetoric at the Ninth Congress of People's Deputies (Summary of Factions, in Order of Relative Frequency).

Faction	Total length of texts[1]	The People (Synonyms)		President	Total	Relative frequency[3]
Motherland	74	5	1	0	6	3.4
Democratic Russia	311	11	8	3	22	3.0
Industrial Union	98	5	1	0	6	2.6
Radical Democrats	285	13	1	0	14	2.0
Consensus for Progress	233	9	1	0	10	1.8
Left Centre - Cooperation	200	7	1	0	8	1.7
Agrarian Union	148	3	1	0	4	1.1
Non-Parliament officials	847	18	3	0	21	1.0
Fatherland	252	5	1	0	6	1.0
Workers' Union - Reforms without Shock	248	4+(1)	1	0	5	0.8
New Generation (New Policy)	357	7	0	0	7	0.8
Russia	319	6+(3)	0	(1)	6	0.8
Deputies outside factions	1588 [MK1]	24+(2)	3	0	27	0.7
Free Russia	987	5	7	0	12	0.5
Sovereignty and Equality	183	0	2	0	2	0.4
Communists of Russia	544	1	3	0	4	0.3
Total	6674	123+(6)	34	3+(1)	160	1

[1] In arbitrary units: 1 = 1 cm of the text column in *Ninth Congress RF* 1993.

[2] Column (3) shows the number of instances in which the term "the people" occurs in the records; column (4), its synonyms ("Russia" and the like); column (5), the expression "the President of the all-nation choice" ("*vsenarodno izbranny Prezident*"); parentheses refer to indirect speech: quotations, paraphrases, allusions to someone else's words; these are not included in the final figure shown in column (6).

[3] Column (6) divided by column (2), the average (calculated from the last row entries "Total") taken as 1.

About the Authors

Nikolai Ivanovich Biryukov (born 1949) holds a PhD (Candidate of Science by Russian nomination) in philosophy (1983) and is currently Associate Professor, Department of Philosophy, Moscow State Institute of International Relations (University). A Member of the Russian Philosophical Society, his main research interests are the theory of political leadership, comparative analysis of political cultures, and political philosophy.

Victor Mikhailovich Sergeyev (born 1945) holds a PhD (Candidate of Science by Russian nomination) in physics and mathematics (1974) and a Second Doctorate Degree (Doctor of Science) in history (1994) and is currently Deputy Director of the Analytic Centre for Scientific and Industrial Policies, Russian Academy of Sciences. He is also a Corresponding Member of the Russian Academy of Natural Sciences (1994) and a member of the Editorial Board of *International Studies Quarterly*, and of the International Advisory Board for the *Journal of Conflict Resolution*. His main research interests are artificial intelligence, semiotics, comparative analysis of political cultures and analysis of political texts.

Victor Sergeyev and Nikolai Biryukov are co-authors of **Russia's Road to Democracy: Parliament, Communism and Traditional Culture**, Aldershot, Hampshire: Edward Elgar Publishing Ltd., 1993.

329